Author Judith H. McQuown Provides Tips Even Your Lawyer and Accountant Don't Know.

Did you know that:

- **Y**ou can take money and assets out of your corporation without **p**aying taxes on them?
- **Y**ou can borrow from your pension fund to buy personal real **e**state?
- **Y**ou can spend up to $10,000 a year, tax-free, on art and **a**ntiques for the office?
- **Y**ou can invest corporate profits to earn dividends that are **9**5.5% tax-free?
- **Y**ou can pay taxes of only 15 percent on a net income of $75,000?
- **T**here's a good reason *not* to begin your corporate checkbook **w**ith check #101?

Both a complete guide and strategy planner, with a unique state-by-state tax workbook, *Use Your Own Corporation to Get Rich* is *the* book for anyone starting or running a business in the '90s!

"**T**o win at the game of business you must first know the winning strategies. Trial and error is far too costly a path. Judith H. **Mc**Quown has put all of the winning strategies for making your **ow**n corporation make you money in one accurate, hard-hitting **bo**ok."

—Charles J. Givens,
author of *Wealth Without Risk*

An Alternate Selection of the Executive Book Club
An Alternate Selection of the Writer's Digest Book Club

USE·YOUR·OWN CORPORATION TO GET RICH

How to *Start*
Your Own Business
and Achieve
Maximum Profits!

How to *Build*
Your Existing Business
and Increase
Your Profits!

Judith H. McQuown

POCKET BOOKS
New York   London   Toronto   Sydney   Tokyo   Singapore

This publication is intended to provide accurate information with regard to the subject matter covered. The reader, however, is cautioned that this book is sold with the understanding that the Publisher is *not* engaged in rendering legal, accounting or other professional service. Readers are urged to consult their individual legal or tax advisor for advice regarding their own personal needs and problems.

POCKET BOOKS, a division of Simon & Schuster Inc.
1230 Avenue of the Americas, New York, NY 10020

McQuown, Judith H.
    Use your own corporation to get rich/Judith H. McQuown.
      p.   cm.
    Includes index.
    ISBN: 0-671-70308-0 : $10.00
1. Corporations—Handbooks, manuals, etc. 2. One-man companies—
Handbooks, manuals, etc. 3. Corporation law—United States—
Popular works. I. Title.
HD2741.M39   1991
658.4′01—dc20   90-47665
                                                          CIP

First Pocket Books trade paperback printing March 1992

10 9 8 7 6 5 4 3 2 1

Printed in the U.S.A.

*For all
who are inspired
by the American Dream*

ACKNOWLEDGMENTS

This book owes much to the help of many experts, for whose time and enthusiasm I am most grateful.

Special thanks go to "the Wolosoff team" at a certain Big Six accounting firm: Todd J. Wolosoff, Esq., CPA; Ranan J. Wichler, Esq., CPA; and especially Stephen A. Baxley, Esq., CPA, who sat patiently for many hours of interviews and helped with some of the charts and sample tax returns.

I also wish to thank Diana Benzaia, president of Wordcrafters Unlimited; Michael Sonnenberg, CFP, CLU, ChFC, president of Dollar Concepts, Inc.; Robert G. Hahn, president of Red Bank Pension Services, Inc.; Leonard B. Stern, president of Leonard B. Stern & Co., Inc.; Bennett H. Pearl, senior pension consultant, National Life Insurance Company of Vermont; Harold Glassberg, CPA, senior partner, Glassberg, Holden & Mermer; and Kenneth R. Greenhut, CPA, senior partner, Kaufman, Greenhut, Lebowitz & Forman.

At Pocket Books, I am grateful for the enthusiastic help of Leslie Wells, my editor.

I am especially grateful to Dominick Abel, my agent.

And, most of all, my deepest thanks to Harrison Roth, consummate strategist in all things.

CONTENTS

ix

1

How to Make "Interesting Times" Pay Off

May you live in interesting times.

—Old Chinese proverb

Have you been dreaming of owning your own company or going into independent professional practice? Welcome aboard—it's the American dream!

Owning a business or professional practice is the way that most American millionaires and billionaires got that way. Just look at two of the wealthiest men in America: Sam Walton, founder of Wal-Mart Stores, and Bill Gates, electronics wizard since adolescence and founder of Microsoft. Liz Claiborne's company, an over-the-counter growth stock for many years, is one of the few publicly owned companies with a woman CEO. On Wall Street, twenty-two years ago, Muriel Siebert made history as the first woman to buy a seat on the New York Stock Exchange and formed her own successful company, Muriel Siebert and Company.

But you don't have to want to be a millionaire or take your company public to become an entrepreneur and set up your own corporation. You may want to become an entrepreneur for the joy of creating something that is all your own, to earn a comfortable living, to set your own hours (although you may work 60-hour weeks!), to experience the pleasure of being your own boss rather than a middle manager or executive in a vast uncontrollable corporate hierarchy.

1

Entrepreneurism is so popular that in 1989—the most recent year for which there are complete records—Americans started *1.3 million* new enterprises and set up more than 677,000 new corporations.

Some of the resurgence of entrepreneurism is due to the soft economy. Wall Street layoffs have reached 50,000 and more are in sight. Large-corporation mergers, which totaled more than 6,000 in 1988 and 1989, have led to firings by the thousands. Even the giant accounting "Big Eight" have merged into the "Big Six."

The junk-bond debacle has created a waterfall of bankruptcy filings as companies that cannot meet their debt payments self-destruct and throw thousands more out of work. The multibillion-dollar collapse of the savings-and-loan industry and its domino effect on the banking and insurance industries will cause mass firings of thousands more.

So will those euphemistic terms "corporate restructuring" and "downsizing." Faced by increased global competition and declining profits, corporations throughout the United States are closing plants and divisions and laying off hundreds of thousands of talented, experienced workers. Even such "lifetime employers" as IBM and AT&T have persuaded tens of thousands of management employees to accept juicy early-retirement packages in order to slash their labor costs.

And what are many of these talented people doing? They are utilizing their corporate experience in these interesting, exciting times to become successful entrepreneurs. The Chinese ideograph for *opportunity* combines the characters for *risk* and *unknown,* and these former corporate employees are taking the leap into opportunity and potential success. According to the Small Business Administration, more than 1 million Americans started up their own small businesses every year in the 1980s, and those figures increased by nearly 30 percent by the last year of the decade. Entrepreneurism is expected to increase even more dramatically in the 1990s.

Marvin Mills of Washington State lost his production-manager job when the Japanese-owned factory where he worked closed. Within months he set up the See First Video Company and began making industrial videos. His business is now going strong. Because he uses part of his home as his office and his television set for editing, his overhead is minimal and he can afford to charge only $250 per minute of completed taping. His closest competitor, who has substantial overhead, charges $1,000 per minute. Marvin is one example of a manager who turned his layoff into a window of opportunity.

Many entrepreneurs are women and minorities, because, as corporate employees, they have bumped up against the "glass ceiling" which limited their upward rise. Women are starting small businesses at twice the rate of men. Women-owned businesses comprise 30 percent of the 14.5 million small businesses in the United States! And members of minorities own 800,000 small businesses.

The heady winds of entrepreneurism have reached even the traditional bastions of the Establishment. A survey taken at the fifth reunion of the Harvard Business School MBA Class of 1983 found that 52 percent of the class considered themselves to be entrepreneurs. And, according to James Challenger, president of the Chicago management-consulting and outplacement firm of Challenger, Gray and Christmas, a record 20 percent of executives and managers fired in 1989 and the first quarter of 1990 have decided to go into business for themselves rather than face the possibility of being let go again.

If you "Inc.'d. Yourself" during the Roaring Eighties, you're part of a growing trend. Just look at these numbers:

1981	581,661 new corporations formed
1982	556,942 new corporations formed
1983	600,400 new corporations formed
1984	634,991 new corporations formed
1985	662,047 new corporations formed
1986	702,738 new corporations formed
1987	685,572 new corporations formed
1988	685,095 new corporations formed
1989	677,397 new corporations formed
1990	<u>695,500</u> (estimated) new corporations formed
	6,482,343

There is another more powerful, longer-term reason that more and more people are incorporating. If you're a baby boomer—one of 56 million strong, aged 30 to 44—you are part of an enormous number of well-educated professionals who are competing against each other for a limited number of executive-suite jobs. Impatient with waiting for the present generation of management (now in their early 50s and 60s) to retire, you may be unwilling to wait 10 or 15 years for the remote possibility of a company presidency. Instead, you head for the entrepreneurial frontiers of personal services, high technology, niche businesses, and instant presidency of your own corporation.

As a means of breaking into entrepreneurial life, you may be moonlighting at one or even two extra jobs. One in fifteen Americans—6.2 percent—moonlights now, and the number, which is at its highest level in 30 years, is rising and is expected to continue to rise through the 1990s. As the cost of living increases, people who want to maintain their standard of living have to earn more money to maintain it. It's a bit like the Red Queen's Race in *Through the Looking-Glass*, running as hard as you can just to stay in the same place.

Much of that moonlighting leads to successful full-time entrepreneurism and incorporation.

The advantages of incorporation are myriad. Among them are:

The ease of doing business—Potential clients, suppliers, and bankers usually prefer to deal with corporations than with sole proprietorships. Discounts for corporate employees are common and generally apply even to employees of one-person corporations.

Lower taxes—By using income-splitting strategies shown in this book, you can earn as much as $75,000 a year and *still be taxed at 15 percent, a savings of over $10,000 a year in federal income taxes.*

Limited liability—Incorporating can protect your personal assets in the event of business bankruptcy or lawsuits.

Tax-free dividends—Dividends paid to your corporation on the domestic preferred and common stock it owns in its portfolio are 70 percent tax-free. *Your overall corporate tax rate on those dividends is only 4.5 percent!*

Better pension benefits—You can use your pension fund like your own private bank and borrow from it on very favorable terms.

Better medical and insurance fringe benefits—When your corporation pays your family's medical bills, it is not subject to the 7½ percent deduction, which can cost you thousands of dollars. *Every penny of your medical expenses can be written off—this book will show you how to do it easily and legally.*

Deferred compensation—You can lower your taxes by having your corporation defer your salary or bonus.

And then there's the incalculable psychic gratification of being your own boss.

Whatever *your* reasons for incorporating, *Use Your Own Corporation to Get Rich* will show you how to maximize your corporate advantage in many areas through its unique interactive system, where *you* provide the data. Some of those areas are:

• How to pay minimum taxes no matter where you and your corporation are located
• How and when to shift in and out of a Subchapter S corporation
• How and when to juggle your fiscal year
• How to profit from a net operating loss
• How to avoid IRS tax traps
• How to evaluate the advantages and disadvantages of leasing
• How to purchase and depreciate your assets

and how to take advantage of the many other strategies used by sophisticated, expensive financial planners.

Use Your Own Corporation to Get Rich is the next step after *Inc. Yourself.* Setting up your new corporation is just the beginning. Running your own corporation for fun and profit lasts for many years.

May you live in interesting times!

May you prosper!

2

How to Choose Between a General Business Corporation and a Subchapter S Corporation

You probably have already heard about S corporations and Subchapter S corporations—the terms are interchangeable—and may be wondering whether to choose an S corporation or a C (general business) corporation. This chapter will give you all the information you need to help you decide. It will help you work through your own individual numbers so that you can compare the relative advantages and disadvantages of each form of corporation in terms of *your own needs.*

Deciding whether your corporation should be a general business corporation ("C" corporation) or a Subchapter S corporation ("S" corporation) is probably the most important business decision you will ever make. *A general business corporation is taxed like a separate business entity:* the corporation pays you a salary, and *it* pays tax on the profits that you retain in the corporation. *A Subchapter S corporation is taxed like a partnership: its profits and losses are not taxed.* Instead, corporate income or losses are credited or debited to the shareholders in proportion to their shareholding, and *the shareholders pay the income tax.*

5

THE THEORY

The Tax Reform Act of 1986 suddenly made Subchapter S election very desirable because, for the first time in U.S. tax history, the maximum corporate income-tax rate is now only 1 percent higher than the nominal maximum individual rate. (When the maximum individual tax rate was 50 percent, the corporate rate had a much greater advantage.) If you can flow earnings through your corporation and have them taxed at a slightly lower rate, you're getting immediate use of the money while enjoying the limited-liability protection of a corporation.

In contrast, if you were to let your corporate profits build up in a general business corporation for liquidation at some future date, you are taking a chance on what the tax rules will be when you liquidate your corporation.

As you'll see on p. 12, people whose corporations offer "services in the field of law, health, engineering, architecture, accounting, actuarial science, performing arts, and consulting" are put between Scylla and Charybdis. If they choose a C corporation, its income will be taxed at a flat 34 percent, rather than having the first $50,000 taxed at 15 percent and the next $25,000 taxed at 25 percent.

Or they can choose an S corporation, which is taxed like a sole proprietorship or partnership: at higher rates than a C corporation for the first $75,000 of corporate income.

AND SOME EXAMPLES

What if you're not a member of the "perilous professions" referred to above? Then you can choose whether to form an S corporation or a C corporation based on their advantages, as described in detail in this chapter. For now, though, here are examples of the ideal S corporation owner and the ideal C corporation owner.

Henry, a caterer in Atlanta, is 27 years old and single. He has virtually no medical expenses and is not interested in retaining money in his corporation to invest for tax-free dividends. He wants all the income now. Therefore Henry chooses an S corporation, in order to have the liability protection that does not exist in a sole proprietorship, and pulls all the money out of his corporation every year.

Kate, who is 38 years old, owns a one-person public-relations agency in Chicago. She has heavy medical expenses that are bound to escalate over the years, and she is interested in using her corporation to lower her taxes through the income-splitting strategies described later in this chapter. She likes the idea of having her corporation receive dividends that are 70 percent tax-free, and of borrowing from her pension fund to buy a condominium. Therefore Kate chooses a C corporation.

GROUND RULES FOR A SUBCHAPTER S CORPORATION

- no more than 35 shareholders—a husband and wife are treated as a single shareholder
- all shareholders must be U.S. citizens
- only one class of stock
- shares cannot be owned by another corporation or a partnership

NOTE: Some trusts qualify as owners; you'll need legal advice.

TO ELECT SUBCHAPTER S STATUS

File IRS Form 2553 with the District Director of the IRS before the fifteenth day of the third month of your corporation's *taxable year.* (For a calendar-year corporation, the deadline is March 15.)

NOTE: It's a good idea to hold a special meeting of your corporation to declare that you have made a Subchapter S election. *You can use the sample minutes on the following page.*

MINUTES OF A SPECIAL MEETING OF THE MAID IN HEAVEN CORPORATION

MINUTES of a special meeting of the MAID IN HEAVEN CORPORATION, held at the corporate offices at 123 Easy Street, New York, New York, at 9:00 in the morning on Wednesday, January 2, 1991.

The meeting was duly called to order by the President and sole stockholder, who stated the object of the meeting.

On motion duly made, seconded, and unanimously carried, the following resolution was adopted:

WHEREAS, the corporation's accountants have recommended election of Subchapter S status for the corporation, it is

RESOLVED, that the corporation will elect Subchapter S status as quickly as possible by filing IRS Form 2553 with the District Director of the Internal Revenue Service.

There being no further business, the meeting was adjourned.

Dated the second day of January, 1991.

James Vandaleur
Secretary

James Vandaleur
President

JUDITH H. McQUOWN

ELECTION BY SMALL BUSINESS CORPORATION (FORM)

Form **2553** (Rev. April 1988) Department of the Treasury Internal Revenue Service	**Election by a Small Business Corporation** (Under section 1362 of the Internal Revenue Code) ▶ **For Paperwork Reduction Act Notice, see page 1 of instructions.** ▶ **See separate instructions.**	OMB No. 1545-0146 Expires 2-28-91

Note: *This election, to be treated as an "S corporation," can be approved only if all the tests in Instruction B are met.*

Part I   **Election Information**

Name of corporation (see instructions)	**A** Employer identification number (see instructions)	**B** Principal business activity and principal product or service (see instructions)
Number and street	**C** Name and telephone number of corporate officer or legal representative that may be called for information	
City or town, state, and ZIP code	**D** Election is to be effective for tax year beginning (month, day, year)	**E** Date of incorporation

F   Is the corporation the outgrowth or continuation of any form of predecessor?   ☐ Yes   ☐ No   **G** Place of incorporation

If "Yes," state name of predecessor, type of organization, and period of its existence ▶ ....

H   If this election takes effect for the first tax year the corporation exists, enter the earliest of the following: (1) date the corporation first had shareholders, (2) date the corporation first had assets, or (3) date the corporation began doing business (month, date, year). ▶

I   Selected tax year: Annual return will be filed for tax year ending (month and day) ▶ ....
See instructions before entering your tax year. If the tax year ends any date other than December 31, except for an automatic 52–53-week tax year ending with reference to the month of December, you must complete Part II on the back. If the date you enter in I is the ending date of an automatic 52–53-week tax year, write "52–53-week year" to the right of the date. See instructions.

J Name of each shareholder, person having a community property interest in the corporation's stock, and each tenant in common, joint tenant, and tenant by the entirety. (A husband and wife (and their estates) are counted as one shareholder in determining the number of shareholders without regard to the manner in which the stock is owned.)	**K** Shareholders' Consent Statement. We, the undersigned shareholders, consent to the corporation's election to be treated as an "S corporation" under section 1362(a). (Shareholders sign and date below.)*	**L** Stock owned		**M** Social security number or employer identification number (see instructions)	**N** Shareholder's tax year ends (month and day)
		Number of shares	Dates acquired		

*For this election to be valid, the consent of each shareholder, person having a community property interest in the corporation's stock, and each tenant in common, joint tenant, and tenant by the entirety must either appear above or be attached to this form. (See instructions for Column K, if continuation sheet or a separate consent statement is needed.)

Under penalties of perjury, I declare that I have examined this election, including accompanying schedules and statements, and to the best of my knowledge and belief, it is true, correct, and complete.

Signature and
Title of Officer ▶

Date ▶

See Parts II and III on back.

[¶ 1100]   Form **2553** (Rev. 4-88)

Form 2553 (Rev. 4-88)   Page **2**

Part II   Selection of Tax Year (See Instructions for required attachments and other details.)

O   Check the applicable box below to indicate whether the corporation is:

☐ Adopting the tax year entered in item I, Part I.

☐ Retaining the tax year entered in item I, Part I.

☐ Changing to the tax year entered in item I, Part I.

P   Check the applicable box below to indicate the representation statement the corporation is making as required under section 4 of Revenue Procedure 87-32, 1987-2 C.B. 396.

☐ Under penalties of perjury, I represent that shareholders holding more than half of the shares of the stock (as of the first day of the tax year to which the request relates) of the corporation have the same tax year or are concurrently changing to the tax year that the corporation adopts, retains, or changes to per item I, Part I. I also represent that the corporation is not described in section 3.01(2) of Revenue Procedure 87-32.

☐ Under penalties of perjury, I represent that the corporation is retaining or changing to a tax year that coincides with its natural business year as defined in section 4.01(1) of Revenue Procedure 87-32 and as verified by its satisfaction of the requirements of section 4.02(1) of Revenue Procedure 87-32. In addition, if the corporation is changing to a natural business year as defined in section 4.01(1), I further represent that such tax year results in less deferral of income to the owners than the corporation's present tax year. I also represent that the corporation is not described in section 3.01(2) of Revenue Procedure 87-32. (See instructions for Part II for attachments required by section 4.03(3) of Revenue Procedure 87-32.)

Note: *If you do not use item P and the corporation wants a fiscal tax year, then complete either item Q or R. Item Q is used to request a fiscal tax year based on business purpose and to make a back-up section 444 election. Item R is used to make a regular section 444 election. See cautionary statement in instructions regarding back-up calendar year election.*

Q   Check the applicable box(es):

Check here ☐ if the fiscal year entered in item I, Part I, is requested under the provisions of section 6.03 of Revenue Procedure 87-32. Attach to Form 2553 a statement and other necessary information pursuant to the ruling request requirements of Revenue Procedure 88-1, 1988-1 I.R.B. 7. The statement must include the business purpose for the desired fiscal year. Check here ☐ to show the corporation intends to make a back-up section 444 election in the event the corporation's business purpose request is not approved by the IRS.

Check here ☐ to show that the corporation agrees to adopt or change to a tax year ending December 31 if necessary for the IRS to accept this election for S corporation status in the event: (1) the corporation's business purpose request is not approved and the corporation makes a back-up section 444 election, but is ultimately not qualified to make a section 444 election, or (2) the corporation's business purpose request is not approved and the corporation did not make a back-up section 444 election.

R   Check the applicable box(es):

Check here ☐ to show the corporation will make, if qualified, a section 444 election to have the fiscal tax year shown in Part I, item I. The corporation makes the election by completing **Form 8716**, Election To Have a Tax Year Other Than a Required Tax Year, and either attaching it to Form 2553 or filing it in accordance with the instructions for Form 8716.

Check here ☐ to show that the corporation agrees to adopt or change to a tax year ending December 31 if necessary for the IRS to accept this election for S corporation status in the event the corporation is ultimately not qualified to make a section 444 election.

Part III   Qualified Subchapter S Trust (QSST) Election Under Section 1361(d)(2)**

Income beneficiary's name and address	Taxpayer identification number
Trust's name and address	Taxpayer identification number

Date on which stock of the corporation was transferred to the trust (month, date, year) ▶

In order for the trust named above to be a QSST and thus a qualifying shareholder of the S corporation for which this Form 2553 is filed, I hereby make the election under section 1361(d)(2). Under penalties of perjury, I certify that the trust meets the definition requirements of section 1361(d)(3) and that all other information provided in Part III is true, correct, and complete.

_____   Date
Signature of income beneficiary or signature and title of legal representative or other qualified person making the election

**The use of Part III to make the QSST election can be made only if stock of the corporation has been transferred to the trust on or before the date on which the corporation makes its election to be an S corporation, and if the QSST election and the Form 2553 election have the same effective date. The QSST election can also be made and filed separately as specified in Regulations section 1.1361-1A(i)(3). The QSST election has to be made separately as specified in Regulations section 1.1361-1A(i)(3) if the stock transfer and S election have not been made as stated above.

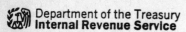

**Department of the Treasury
Internal Revenue Service**

Instructions for Form 2553
(Revised April 1988)

Election by a Small Business Corporation

(Section references are to the Internal Revenue Code unless otherwise specified.)

Paperwork Reduction Act Notice.—We ask for this information to carry out the Internal Revenue laws of the United States. We need it to insure that you are complying with these laws and to allow us to figure and collect the right amount of tax. You are required to give us this information.

Changes You Should Note

• **User Fee.—**Certain electing corporations must pay a user fee. See General Instruction G for details.

• **Revised Part II.—**Item Q of Part II was revised and new item R was added to provide for new section 444 provisions. Section 444 allows certain S corporations to elect to have a tax year other than a required tax year ending December 31. The section 444 election is made by filing **Form 8716**, Election To Have a Tax Year Other Than a Required Tax Year. See the instructions for Part II.

• **New Part III.—**Part III was added to allow beneficiaries of certain Qualified Subchapter S Trusts (QSSTs) to make a section 1361(d)(2) QSST election when filing Form 2553. See the instructions for Part III.

A. Purpose.—To elect to be treated as an "S Corporation," a corporation must file Form 2553. The election permits the income of the S corporation to be taxed to the shareholders of the corporation except as provided in Subchapter S of the code. Part III of Form 1120S may be used by beneficiaries of certain Qualified Subchapter S Trusts (QSSTs) to make the QSST election required by section 1361(d)(2).

B. Who May Elect.—Your corporation may make the election to be treated as an S corporation only if it meets the following tests:

1. It is a domestic corporation.
2. It has no more than 35 shareholders. A husband and wife (and their estates) are treated as one shareholder for this requirement. All other persons are treated as separate shareholders.
3. It has only individuals, estates, or certain trusts as shareholders. See instruction for Part III regarding qualified subchapter S trusts.
4. It has no nonresident alien shareholders.
5. It has only one class of stock. See sections 1361(c)(4) and (5) for additional details.
6. It is not an ineligible corporation as defined in section 1361(b)(2).
7. It has a permitted tax year as required by section 1378 or makes a section 444 election to have a tax year other than a permitted tax year. Section 1378 defines a permitted tax year as a tax year ending December 31, or any other tax year for which the corporation

establishes a business purpose to the satisfaction of the I.R.S. See the instructions for Part II for details on making a section 444 election.

8. Each shareholder consents as explained in the instructions for Column K.

See sections 1361, 1362, and 1378 for additional information on the above tests.

C. Where To File.—File this election with the Internal Revenue Service Center where the corporation will file **Form 1120S**, U.S. Income Tax Return for an S Corporation. See the Instructions for Form 1120S for Service Center addresses.

D. When to Make the Election.— Complete Form 2553 and file it either: (1) at any time during that portion of the first tax year the election is to take effect which occurs before the 16th day of the third month of that tax year (or at any time during that year, if that year does not extend beyond the period described above), or (2) in the tax year before the first tax year it is to take effect. An election made by a small business corporation after the 15th day of the third month but before the end of the tax year is treated as made for the next year. For example, if a calendar tax year corporation makes the election in April 1987, it is effective for the corporation's 1988 calendar tax year.

E. Acceptance or Non-Acceptance of Election.—The Service Center will notify you if your election is accepted and when it will take effect. You should generally receive a determination on your election within 60 days after you have filed Form 2553. If the 1st box in Part II, Item Q, is checked on page 2, the corporation will receive a ruling letter from IRS in Washington, D.C., which approves or denies the selected tax year. When Item Q is checked, it will generally take an additional 90 days for the Form 2553 to be accepted.

Do not file Form 1120S until you are notified that your election is accepted. If you are now required to file **Form 1120**, U.S. Corporation Income Tax Return, or any other applicable tax return, continue filing it until your election takes effect.

You will also be notified if your election is not accepted.

Care should be exercised to ensure the election is received by the Internal Revenue Service. If you are not notified of acceptance or nonacceptance of your election within 3 months of date of filing (date mailed), or within 6 months if Part II, Item Q, is checked, you should take follow-up action by corresponding with the Service Center where the election was filed. If filing of Form 2553 is questioned, an acceptable

proof of filing is: (1) certified receipt (timely filed); (2) Form 2553 with accepted stamp; (3) Form 2553 with stamped IRS received date; or (4) IRS letter stating that Form 2553 had been accepted.

F. End of Election.—Once the election is made, it stays in effect for all years until it is terminated. During the 5 years after the election has been terminated under section 1362(d), the corporation can make another election on Form 2553 only if the Commissioner consents. See section 1362(g) and Revenue Ruling 86-141, 1986-2 C.B. 151, for more information. See sections 1362(d), (e), and (f) for rules regarding termination of election.

G. User Fee.—Corporations filing Form 2553 and requesting a fiscal year under section 6.03 of Revenue Procedure 87-32, 1987-2 C.B. 396, must pay a new $150 user fee. Payment of the fee (check or money order) should not be made with or attached to Form 2553 when it is filed at the Service Center. The Service Center sends Form 2553 to the I.R.S. in Washington, D.C. and it notifies the taxpayer that the fee is due. See Revenue Procedure 88-13, 1988-7 I.R.B. 7, for additional information.

Specific Instructions

Part I.—Part I must be completed by all corporations.

Name and Address of Corporation.—If the corporation's mailing address is the same as someone else's, such as a shareholder's, please enter this person's name below the corporation's name.

A. Employer Identification Number.—If you have applied for an employer identification number (EIN) but have not received it, enter "applied for." If the corporation does not have an EIN, you should apply for one on **Form SS-4**, Application for Employer Identification Number, available from most IRS or Social Security Administration offices. Send Form SS-4 to the IRS Service Center where Form 1120S will be filed.

B. Principal Business Activity and Principal Product or Service.—Use the Codes for Principal Business Activity contained in the Instructions for Form 1120S. Your principal business activity is the one that accounts for the largest percentage of total receipts. Total receipts are gross receipts plus all other income.

Also state the principal product or service. For example, if the principal business activity is "grain mill products," the principal product or service may be "cereal preparation."

C. Name and Telephone Number.—Enter the name and telephone number (area code and seven digit number) of a corporate officer or legal representative of the corporation that I.R.S. may contact to resolve questions (or obtain additional information) that may arise when the corporation's Form 2553 is reviewed.

D. Effective Date of Election.—Enter the beginning effective date (month, day, year) of the tax year that you have requested for the S corporation. Generally, this will be the beginning effective date of the tax year for which the ending effective date is shown in item I, Part I. For a new corporation (1st year the corporation exists) it will generally be the date shown in item H, Part I. The tax year of a new corporation starts when it has shareholders, acquires assets, or begins doing business, whichever happens first. If the effective date for item D for a newly formed corporation is later than the date in item H, the corporation should file Form 1120, or Form 1120A, for the tax period between these dates.

I. Selected Tax Year.—If a corporation selects a tax year ending other than December 31 (but excluding a 52-53-week tax year with reference to the month of December), the corporation must complete Part II in addition to Part I.

Temporary Regulations section 1.441-2T(e)(3) grants automatic approval to the S corporation to use a 52-53-week tax year with reference to the month of December.

Column K—Shareholders' Consent Statement.—Each shareholder who owns (or is deemed to own) stock at the time the election is made must consent to the election. If the election is made during the corporation's first tax year for which it is effective, any person who held stock at any time during the portion of that year which occurs before the time the election is made, must consent to the election although the person may have sold or transferred his or her stock before the election is made. Each shareholder consents by signing and dating in column K or signing and dating a separate consent statement described below. If stock is owned by a trust that is a qualified shareholder, the deemed owner of the trust must consent. See section 1361(c)(2) for details regarding qualified trusts that may be shareholders and rules on determining who is the deemed owner of the trust.

An election made during the first 2½ months of the tax year is considered made for the following tax year if one or more of the persons who held stock in the corporation during such tax year and before the election was made did not consent to the election. See section 1362(b)(2).

If a husband and wife have a community interest in the stock or in the income from it, both must consent. Each tenant in common, joint tenant, and tenant by the entirety also must consent.

A minor's consent is made by the minor or the legal guardian.

Continuation Sheet or Separate Consent Statement.—If you need a continuation sheet or use a separate consent statement, attach it to Form 2553. The separate consent statement must contain the name, address, and employer identification number of the corporation and the shareholder information requested in columns J through N of Part I.

If you wish, you may combine all the shareholders' consents in one statement.

Column L.—Enter the number of shares of stock each shareholder owns and the dates the stock was acquired. If the election is made during the corporation's first tax year for which it is effective, do not list the shares of stock for those shareholders who sold or transferred all of their stock before the election was made but who still must consent to the election for it to be effective for the tax year.

Column M.—Enter the social security number for shareholders that are individuals. Enter the employer

identification number for estates. Enter the social security number or employer identification number for shareholders that are qualified trusts. The deemed owners of qualified trusts make the consent in column K. Enter the social security number or employer identification number of the deemed owner of the trust in column M.

Column N.—Enter the month and day that each shareholder's tax year ends. If a shareholder is changing his or her tax year, enter the tax year the shareholder is changing to. If the election is made during the corporation's first tax year for which it is effective, you do not have to enter the tax year of shareholders who sold or transferred all of their stock before the election was made but who still must consent to the election for it to be effective for the tax year.

Signature.—Form 2553 must be signed by the president, treasurer, assistant treasurer, chief accounting officer, or other corporate officer (such as tax officer) authorized to sign.

Part II

Item O.—Item O is completed by all corporations completing Part II.

Item P.—Item P is completed by a corporation that selects a fiscal year, and that qualifies under section 4.01(1) or 4.01(2) of Revenue Procedure 87-32, 1987-2 C.B. 396. In addition, if the corporation selects a fiscal year that qualifies under section 4.01(1), then it must attach a statement to Form 2553, showing the amount of gross receipts for the most recent 47 months (show each month separately) as required by section 4.03(3)(b) of the revenue procedure. Sections 4.01(1) and 4.01(2) provide for expeditious approval of certain corporations' requests to adopt, retain, or change to a fiscal year. The representation statements in Part II of Form 2553 highlight the requests provided for in section 4 of the revenue procedure. A corporation adopting, retaining, or changing its accounting period under the procedure must comply with all applicable conditions of the procedure.

Form 1128, Application for Change in Accounting Period, should not be used to request a tax year for or during the 1st year the corporation elects to be an S corporation.

Item Q.—Item Q is completed as follows:

(1) The corporation checks the 1st box to make a request as specified in section 6.03 of Revenue Procedure 87-32. Section 6.03 provides that if a corporation wants to adopt, retain, or change to a fiscal year described in section 4 or 5 of the procedure, it should attach a statement to Form 2553 pursuant to the ruling request requirements of Revenue Procedure 88-1, I.R.B. 1988-1, page 7. (Changes to this revenue procedure are usually incorporated annually into a new revenue procedure as the first revenue procedure of the year.) The statement must show the business purpose for the desired tax year. See Revenue Ruling 87-57, 1987-2 C.B. 117, for examples of business purpose.

(2) The corporation checks the 2nd box in item Q to show its intention to make a back-up section 444 election. The back-up section 444 election is made in addition to the request for a fiscal year based on business purpose. The back-up election applies in the event the IRS does not approve the corporation's request for a tax year based on business purpose. **Note:** *Under certain circumstances, the tax year requested under the section 444 back-up election may be different than the tax year requested under business purpose. See the instructions for Form 8716 for details on making a back-up section 444 election.*

(3) The corporation checks the 3rd box in item Q to make a calendar year back-up election. The calendar year back-up election applies if: (a) the corporation's business purpose request is denied or (b) the business purpose request was denied and the section 444 back-up election was made but later the corporation was not eligible to make the election. In certain cases, the corporation will not be eligible to make the section 444 election when it becomes a member of a tiered structure. **Caution: If the back-up calendar year election is not made and a fiscal tax year is not allowed under the other provisions of item Q, the corporation's election to be an S corporation is invalidated.**

Item R.—Item R is completed as follows:

(1) The corporation checks the 1st box in item R to show that it is making or intends to make the section 444 election. The corporation makes the election when filing Form 2553 by completing Form 8716 and attaching it to Form 2553. Form 8716 can also be completed and filed after Form 2553 is filed. See the instructions for Form 8716 for details on filing Form 8716.

(2) The corporation checks the 2nd box in item R to make a back-up calendar year election. **Caution: If the back-up calendar year election is not made and the corporation is not allowed to make a section 444 election or is allowed to make the section 444 election but does not make it, the corporation's election to be an S corporation is invalidated.**

If the corporation is not qualified to make the section 444 election after making the item Q section 444 back-up election or indicating its intention to make the election in item R, and therefore it later files a calendar year return, it should write "Section 444 Election Not Made" in the top left corner of the 1st calendar year Form 1120S it files.

Part III.—Certain Qualified Subchapter S Trusts (QSSTs) may make the QSST election required by section 1361(d)(2) in Part III of Form 2553. Part III may be used to make the QSST election only if: (a) corporate stock has been transferred to the trust on or before the date on which the corporation makes its election to be an S corporation, and (b) the QSST election and the Form 2553 election have the same effective date.

The deemed owner of the QSST must also consent to the S corporation election, column K, page 1, of Form 2553. See section 1361(c)(2).

WHEN SUBCHAPTER S IS THE OBVIOUS CHOICE

If the principal function of your corporation is "services in the field of

- law
- health
- engineering
- architecture
- accounting
- actuarial science
- performing arts
- consulting"

the Revenue Act of 1987 raised your corporate taxes to *a flat 34 percent from as little as 15 percent*. This move forced most people in these professions into choosing Subchapter S as their corporate form in order to save as much as 19 percent in taxes.

EXAMPLES

Old corporate profit	$25,000	$50,000	$75,000
New corporate tax (34%)	8,500	17,000	25,800
Old corporate tax	3,750	7,500	16,000
Increased tax if Subchapter S corporation is not elected	4,750	9,500	9,800

YOUR ESTIMATE

Old corporate profit	$ _____
New corporate tax (34%)	_____
Old corporate tax	_____
Increased tax if Subchapter S corporation is not elected	_____

NOTE: If you use a great deal of expensive equipment in your professional practice, a C corporation may still be the better choice for you because it offers more advantageous write-offs. Get some expert tax advice.

You may wish to adopt the following strategy which I designed for a computer consultant who felt he couldn't redefine his job description to escape the title "consultant," but who had heavy annual expenses for equipment that suggested he choose a C corporation. In this strategy, I have maximized my client's expenses quite legitimately so that, although his C corporation is in the 34 percent federal income-tax bracket, it is paying taxes on minimal profits.

$70,000	estimated corporate income
$10,000	computer equipment purchase—expensed currently
1,500	medical insurance
5,000	rent (paid to himself)
36,000	salary
9,000	pension-fund contribution
4,000	overhead
2,500	employer's Social Security contribution
$68,000	total expenses
$ 2,000	corporate profit
x 34%	
$ 680	federal corporate income tax

EXCEPTIONS

Many service corporations do not fall into the above group, which, fortunately, is quite clear-cut. Here are some exceptions:

- authors
- artists
- agents
- sales representatives
- personal and business service providers

NOTE: *Consultants* who are clever enough to create another job description for their services may be able to escape this new corporate trap.

THE INCOME-SPLITTING ADVANTAGE

As stated in the first paragraph of this chapter, the key difference between a general business corporation and a Subchapter S corporation is that a general business corporation allows you to split your corporate income between yourself and your corporation and a Subchapter S corporation's profits (and losses) flow through to you and are taxed directly to you. An S corporation puts the profit in your pocket; a C corporation lets you invest the profit on a tax-deferred basis.

Let's look at how income of $40,000 under these two corporate forms might be taxed to a shareholder who is single:

	C corporation	S corporation
Income	$40,000	$40,000
Less salary	− 20,000	− 0
Net income	$20,000	$40,000
Taxed at corporate rate	× 15%	—
Corporate tax	$ 3,000	$ 0
Salary	$20,000	$40,000
Less exemptions	− 2,000	− 2,000
	$18,000	$38,000
Less standard deduction	− 3,000	− 3,000
Net taxable income	$15,000	$35,000
Income tax	$ 2,254	$ 7,396
Corporate tax	3,000	0
Total taxes	$ 5,254	$ 7,396
Amount saved with C corporation	$ 2,142	
Percentage saved	29%	

Married shareholders, where only the stockholder works, save somewhat less.

Now let's look at the maximum tax savings available through the income-splitting feature of a C corporation:

	C corporation	S corporation
Income	$75,000	$75,000
Less salary	− 25,000	− 0
Net income	$50,000	$75,000
Taxed at corporate rate	× 15%	—
Corporate tax	$ 7,500	$ 0
Salary	$25,000	$75,000
Less exemptions	− 2,000	− 2,000
	$23,000	$73,000
Less standard deduction	− 3,000	− 3,000
Net taxable income	$20,000	$70,000
Income tax	$ 3,196	$18,444
Corporate tax	7,500	0
Total taxes	$10,696	$18,444
Amount saved with C corporation	$7,748	
Percentage saved	42%	

NOTE: *As you see, by using a C corporation, you can earn $75,000 and still pay no more than 15% in taxes!*
NOW TRY IT YOURSELF!

YOUR ESTIMATE

	C corporation	S corporation
Income	$ _____	$ _____
Less salary	− _____	− ___0___
Net income	$ _____	$ _____
Taxed at corporate rate (15% for $0–$50,000 + 25% for $50,000–$75,000 + 34% for remainder over $75,000)	x _____ %	—
Corporate tax	$ _____	$ 0
Salary	$ _____	$ _____
Less exemptions	− _____	− _____
	$ _____	$ _____
Less either standard deduction or estimated itemized deduction	− _____	− _____
Net taxable income	$ _____	$ _____
Income tax	$ _____	$ _____
Corporate tax	_____	___0___
Total taxes	$ _____	$ _____
Amount saved with C corporation	$ _____	
Percentage saved	_____ %	

ON A SCALE OF 1 (LOWEST) TO 10 (HIGHEST), HOW IMPORTANT IS THE INCOME-SPLITTING FEATURE OF THE C CORPORATION TO YOU?

If you think you can save $8,000–$10,000 a year in taxes, rate this feature 9–10 points. If you plan to take a maximum salary, or think you'll save less than $3,000 a year in taxes, rate this feature 1–3 points. If you find yourself somewhere in the middle, rate this feature 4–8 points, according to how important you think it will be to you in future years.

_____ points

MEDICAL BENEFITS

Increased medical benefits are another major reason for owner-employees to choose a C corporation rather than an S corporation. Like owners of unincorporated businesses, S corporation owners can deduct 25 percent of their medical premiums. All other medical expenses are subject to the 7.5 percent deduction based on adjusted gross income which wipes out thousands of dollars' worth of medical deductions every year. If your family's adjusted gross income is $60,000, you lose the first $4,500 of medical expenses.

But owner-employees of a C corporation who have adopted a simple medical reimbursement plan, such as the one shown on pp. 18–19, can have their corporations pay for the medical expenses of themselves and their families. Better yet, medical expenses are paid out of *pretax income,* so that *every dollar of deductions counts.*

Before showing you the thousands of dollars in medical deductions that are available to entrepreneurs who choose C corporations, I want to point out two red flags that may apply to a few people:

- these medical benefits are available to owner-*employees,* not to absentee corporate owners;
- the medical-benefit plan cannot discriminate between *owner*-employees and other full-time employees (those who work more than 20 hours per week)

Most entrepreneurs and professionals set up one-person or husband-and-wife corporations with no other employees, so these red flags don't apply to them. They can take immediate advantage of large medical deductions.

Here are some medical deductions some colleagues came up with in a brainstorming session. Some of them may look high, but medical expenses are the most rapidly rising sector of the economy. And now eyeglass frames can cost $175–$250! Use these categories and figures as a guide to estimate your medical expenses next year.

Now let's calculate the real out-of-pocket cost of those medical deductions. First we'll subtract 7.5 percent of adjusted gross income, then multiply by the marginal tax bracket. *Remember: If you are in the 28 percent bracket, you actually pay 72 percent of your medical expenses.*

If your medical expenses run at least $5,000 per year, you should probably consider electing C corporate status.

ON A SCALE OF 1 (LOWEST) to 10 (HIGHEST), HOW IMPORTANT IS THE INCREASED-MEDICAL-BENEFITS FEATURE OF THE C CORPORATION TO YOU?

——————— points

	Metropolitan-Area Costs		Your Estimate
	Single	Family of 4	
Health/hospital insurance	$1,200	$ 2,500	$ _____
Medical bills unreimbursed by insurance (e.g., elective or plastic surgery*)	1,000	1,500	_____
Dental	300	800	_____
Orthodontia	0	1,200	_____
Prescription drugs unreimbursed by insurance	150	400	_____
Eyeglasses or contact lenses (est. 2 pair for you, 1 pair each for other members)	300	750	_____
Health club membership (doctor's note needed: bad back, weight control, stress reduction*, etc.)	$1,200	$ 2,000	_____
Physiotherapy/massage (doctor's note needed*)	1,000	2,000	_____
Counseling/therapy	3,000	5,000	_____
Other medical expenses (list)			
_____			_____
_____			_____
_____			_____
	$8,150	$16,150	$ _____

*Among permitted deductions in this category are such cosmetic expenditures as hair transplants, facelifts, cellulite operations, collagen injections (wrinkle removal), and electrolysis.

*According to a recent IRS ruling, the treatment must "cure a specific ailment or disease," rather than the looser IRS Regulations definition of "prevention or alleviation of a physical or mental defect or illness." Therefore ask your doctor to word his/her note in terms of treatment of high blood pressure, rather than obesity or weight control, or back pain, rather than stress reduction.

	Single	Family of 4	Your Estimate
Total medical expenses	$8,150	$16,150	$ _____
Less 7.5% of adjusted gross income (estimated at $40,000 single, $60,000 family)	−3,000	−4,500	− _____
	$5,150	11,650	
Multiplied by marginal rate	×28%	×28%	× _____ %
Dollar value of medical deduction	$1,442	$ 3,262	$ _____
Actual cost of medical deduction (medical deduction less dollar value of medical deduction)	$6,708	$12,888	$ _____

Here's a sample medical reimbursement plan you can use, along with the minutes of a special meeting at which the plan was adopted:

(NAME OF YOUR CORPORATION)
MEDICAL REIMBURSEMENT PLAN

ARTICLE I—Benefits
The Corporation shall reimburse all eligible employees for expenses incurred by themselves and their dependents, as defined in IRC §152, as amended, for medical care, as defined in IRC §213(d), as amended, subject to the conditions and limitations as hereinafter set forth. It is the intention of the Corporation that the benefits payable to eligible employees hereunder shall be excluded from their gross income pursuant to IRC §105, as amended.

ARTICLE II—Eligibility
All corporate officers employed on a full-time basis at the date of inception of this Plan, including those who may be absent due to illness or injury on said date, are eligible employees under the Plan. A corporate officer shall be considered employed on a full-time basis if said officer customarily works at least seven months in each year and twenty hours in each week. Any person hereafter becoming an officer of the Corporation, employed on a full-time basis, shall be eligible under this Plan.

ARTICLE III—Limitations
(a) The Corporation shall reimburse any eligible employee (without limitation) (no more than $_____) in any fiscal year for medical care expenses.
(b) Reimbursement or payment provided under this Plan shall be made by the Corporation only in the event and to the extent that such reimbursement or payment is not provided under any insurance policy(ies), whether owned by the Corporation or the employee, or under any other health and accident or wage-continuation plan. In the event that there is such an insurance policy or plan in effect, providing for reimbursement in whole or in part, then to the extent of the coverage under such policy or plan, the Corporation shall be relieved of any and all liability hereunder.

ARTICLE IV—Submission of Proof
Any eligible employee applying for reimbursement under this Plan shall submit to the Corporation, at least quarterly, all bills for medical care, including premium notices for accident or health insurance, for verification by the Corporation prior to payment. Failure to comply herewith may, at the discretion of the Corporation, terminate such eligible employee's right to said reimbursement.

ARTICLE V—Discontinuation
This Plan shall be subject to termination at any time by vote of the board of directors of the Corporation; provided, however, that medical care expenses incurred prior to such termination shall be reimbursed or paid in accordance with the terms of this Plan.

ARTICLE VI—Determination

The president shall determine all questions arising from the administration and interpretation of the Plan except where reimbursement is claimed by the president. In such case, determination shall be made by the board of directors.

MINUTES OF SPECIAL MEETING OF DIRECTORS
OF
(NAME OF YOUR CORPORATION)

A special meeting of the board of directors of (name of your corporation) was held on (date) at (time) at (address where meeting was held).

All of the directors being present, the meeting was called to order by the chairman. The chairman advised that the meeting was called to approve and adopt a medical care expense reimbursement plan. A copy of the plan was presented to those present and upon motion duly made, seconded, and unanimously carried, it was

RESOLVED, that the "Medical Care Reimbursement Plan" presented to the meeting is hereby approved and adopted, that a copy of the Plan shall be appended to these minutes, and that the proper officers of the corporation are hereby authorized to take whatever action is necessary to implement the Plan, and it is further

RESOLVED, that the signing of these minutes by the directors shall constitute full ratification thereof and waiver of notice of the meeting by the signatories.

There being no further business to come before the meeting, upon motion duly made, seconded, and unanimously carried, the meeting was adjourned.

_____
Secretary

_____ _____
Chairman Director

_____ _____
Director Director

TAX-FREE DIVIDENDS

For many entrepreneurs, the prospect of dividends that are 70 percent free of federal income taxes is the deciding vote that convinces them to choose a C corporation. *Only a C corporation can split income between your salary and its retained corporate income,* and it is this retained corporate income that will be invested in high-yield stocks.

With contributions of only $7,500 a year, your corporate portfolio can grow to nearly $200,000 in just ten years! During that time, dividends on the stocks in your portfolio can total almost $70,000—nearly equaling the ten-year contribution. And, during that time, taxes on those dividends, assuming a continuation of present tax rates, will be less than $4,700! (You may have to pay more tax when you liquidate your portfolio, but meanwhile you can just enjoy letting your corporate investments grow on a tax-deferred basis.)

ON A SCALE OF 1 (LOWEST) TO 10 (HIGHEST), HOW IMPORTANT IS THE TAX-FREE DIVIDENDS FEATURE TO YOU?

If the prospect of this legal tax shelter excites you, and your corporation can afford as little as $5,000 a year for investments, turn immediately to pp. 119–21 for a detailed description of how you can profit substantially from small annual corporate investments.

_____ points

OTHER FRINGE BENEFITS

These C corporation fringe benefits are minor, so I haven't included them in the point system. Take advantage of them if you choose a C corporation, but don't make that choice solely in order to receive them.

$5,000 death benefit—Your corporation can make a tax-free death-benefit payment to your estate or beneficiaries.

"Free" $50,000 group term life-insurance policy—I call this insurance "free" because premiums are fully deductible by your corporation, but the IRS does not treat them as income to you. Sometimes referred to as §79 insurance, this "free" life insurance consists of one-year renewable term policies of up to $50,000 face value as group insurance in groups of ten people or more. However, even a "group" of one—you—can obtain a similar renewable term policy that will be recognized by the IRS. If your corporation has employees, you can legally discriminate on a class basis in selecting the face value of the insurance policy. Many small corporations choose $50,000 for their officer/employees and $10,000 for their other employees.

Pension-fund loans—You may borrow from your corporate pension fund to buy a home or provide a child's college or postgraduate education. This strategy is especially profitable if you have a defined-contribution pension plan (see pp. 90–92) because there is no limit to the funds which can accumulate in it.

Let's assume that you borrow $50,000 from your pension fund for the down payment on your home. Mortgage rates range from 8 percent to 9½ percent. You are free to charge any reasonable rate of interest, so you choose 10 percent simple interest for a loan you plan to repay in two years. (You can pay your pension fund a slightly higher rate of interest—especially if it's simple interest. But keep in mind that the IRS frowns on loan-sharking—even between yourself and your pension fund.)

What do you get out of this transaction? Each year you can pay your pension fund $5,000 over and above your corporation's contribution to it, so that your pension fund can grow more quickly, *and* you can deduct the $5,000 interest on your mortgage loan on your personal income-tax return. You get to put more money into your pension fund and to take a personal tax deduction that can be worth thousands of dollars a year.

ADDING IT UP

In the three major categories of C corporation fringe benefits—income splitting, increased medical deductions, and tax-free dividends—you have chosen how important each C corporation fringe benefit is to you on a scale from 1 to 10.

Now add up your ratings. If your score is below 10, these advantages of a C corporation aren't very important to you. You have said that you don't plan to use them to a considerable extent. Therefore, you'll probably do better with an S corporation. If your score is between 11 and 20, subtract your score for the tax-free dividends benefit which you calculated on p. 20; it's the "swing vote." Then, if your score is over 14, you'll probably do better with a C corporation. If your score is between 20 and 30, you'll almost certainly do better by choosing a C corporation.

STATES' RITES

Now you're almost finished. Although you should make your S corporation/C corporation election based on the federal tax code, and most states recognize Subchapter S, a few maverick states and cities do not recognize Subchapter S corporations. If your S corporation is domiciled in those states or cities, it will have to file federal tax returns as an S corporation and local tax returns as a C corporation.

This mixed status has powerful implications, none of them pleasant or easy to deal with. Your corporation has to pay a state tax on its income because it is treated like a C corporation. However, *you* will still be required to pay tax on your individual state income-tax return, based on your receipt of your S corporation's flow-through of earnings.

Following is a list of states and municipalities that do and don't recognize Subchapter S status. If you are planning to incorporate as an S corporation in a state that does not recognize Subchapter S status, you may wish to get professional advice from a tax lawyer or an accountant.

Recognizes Federal Subchapter S Status

ALASKA

ARIZONA

FLORIDA—except to the extent that S corporation is liable for federal income tax. However, Florida law defines taxable income according to a revenue code prior to the Subchapter S Revision Act of 1986

HAWAII—only if all shareholders are Hawaii residents

IDAHO

ILLINOIS—with complex modifications. Consult your tax adviser.

IOWA

KENTUCKY

MARYLAND—but corporation will be taxed on Maryland income attributable to each nonresident shareholder

MASSACHUSETTS—with complex modifications. Consult your tax adviser.

MINNESOTA

MISSOURI

MONTANA

NEW MEXICO

NORTH DAKOTA—but an S corporation may elect to be taxed as a C corporation

PENNSYLVANIA

SOUTH CAROLINA

SOUTH DAKOTA—except for financial institutions

UTAH

VERMONT

WEST VIRGINIA

WISCONSIN—with a few minor modifications

Recognizes Federal Subchapter S Status, But Nonresident Shareholders Are Taxed on Their Income from State Sources

ALABAMA

ARKANSAS

CALIFORNIA

COLORADO—but state Court of Appeals has held that distributions of S corporation income to nonresident shareholders are not taxable

DELAWARE—with a few minor modifications

GEORGIA

INDIANA

KANSAS

MAINE

MISSISSIPPI

NEBRASKA

NEW YORK—New York City is listed below

OHIO—but nonresident shareholders may be entitled to claim the nonresident tax credit

OKLAHOMA

OREGON

RHODE ISLAND—corporation is subject to franchise tax

VIRGINIA

Does Not Recognize Subchapter S Status

CONNECTICUT—S corporations must pay state business (income) tax

DISTRICT OF COLUMBIA—S corporation is treated as an unincorporated business. Please check with your tax adviser.

LOUISIANA

MICHIGAN—S corporations must pay single business tax, but there is a special exemption and tax credit. Consult your tax adviser.

NEW HAMPSHIRE—S corporations must pay state business profits tax

NEW JERSEY—S corporations are subject to the corporate business tax

NEW YORK CITY—S corporations are taxed as though they were C corporations

NORTH CAROLINA—S corporations are taxed as though they were C corporations

TENNESSEE—S corporations are subject to the Tennessee excise (income) tax

TEXAS—S corporations are subject to the Texas franchise tax

WASHINGTON—S corporations are subject to the franchise and gross receipts taxes

WYOMING—S corporations are subject to the corporation franchise tax

No Taxes Are Imposed

NEVADA

YOU CAN CHOOSE MORE THAN ONCE

Many entrepreneurs with income from other sources find that it pays for them to start as a Subchapter S corporation if they are expecting corporate losses for the first year or two. That way they can benefit immediately by using these losses on their personal income-tax returns to offset personal income. (With a C corporation, they would have to carry the losses forward to years in which their corporation had profits; fortunately, there's a fifteen-year carry-forward.)

When their corporation becomes profitable, they terminate Subchapter S status so that they can benefit from the profitable income-splitting strategies, increased medical benefits, and corporate investments whose dividends are 70 percent tax-free, as discussed earlier in this chapter.

Finally, as the corporation becomes increasingly profitable and starts to earn six figures annually, savvy entrepreneurs often reelect Subchapter S status so that their corporation doesn't face the twin perils of the accumulated earnings trap (see p. 120) or the double taxation of corporate income; once as corporate earnings, and once as income the owner-shareholders receive from their corporation.

It's easy to elect and to terminate Subchapter S status, but difficult to return to it without undergoing a five-year waiting period, or obtaining approval from your IRS District Director, who may make you pay Uncle Sam for the privilege. Because of the potential difficulty and expense of reelecting Subchapter S status before your five years' wait is up, you may want to consult your tax adviser about Subchapter S election. Most one-person service corporations will find Subchapter S status desirable at some point in their corporate lives and should therefore examine its election and/or termination every year.

Now that you've made the most important business decision of your corporate life, it's time to fill those corporate coffers. The next chapter, "How to Land the Project and What to Charge for It," will help you increase your corporate income.

3

How to Land the Project and What to Charge for It

Congratulations! You're in business for yourself! It's an infinite upside or downside, and you'll probably find that you're doing more selling than ever before. No matter what business or profession you are in, you'll be selling yourself and your talents. And that's what this chapter is about: It's a cornucopia of sales and marketing advice from experts in many fields.

Even if you started your corporate venture just last week, it's important to look established and prosperous. Everyone knows about the dress-for-success philosophy, and most people realize that an elegant three-figure leather briefcase or attaché case is part of a successful image and that a plastic case can destroy it. (Happily, your briefcase is a tax-deductible expense.)

However, many people don't realize that their stationery, business cards, and even checks are equally important in creating a successful corporate image. These pieces of paper are often seen before a personal contact is made and can create a powerful positive or negative effect.

YOUR STATIONERY AND BUSINESS CARDS

Take some time to design your stationery and business cards. They are advertisements for you and your services. People in creative fields have a great deal of freedom in designing their stationery and business

25

cards. My friend Richard Greenfield, who writes horror novels and screenplays, has a four-color business card emblazoned with a werewolf. Expensive? Perhaps, but potential clients remember him and his card, and he's gotten many assignments because of it.

Business cards can be more dramatic than stationery. Many of your contacts collect hundreds of business cards every year. If they can't find something memorable about yours, they may relegate it to a file with hundreds of others. Even worse, they may toss it out. Your business card is a statement in itself. In contrast, the *content* of the letter or proposal on your stationery is the important statement. You don't want a fussy or overly dramatic letterhead detracting from your message.

Good stationery design uses a uniform paper color and texture and ink color on letterheads and business cards to create a well-thought-out corporate image. Different colors of paper and ink create a haphazard, careless image, which reflects poorly on you and can lose business for you.

It's worth spending a little extra money for a heavyweight textured rag-content paper because that kind of stationery makes your company look prosperous. Many companies also benefit from choosing a paper color other than dead white and an ink color other than black. Ivory, cream, and pale gray can be effective paper colors; your letters will stand out in a sheaf of white correspondence. In inks, a rich wine or dark blue is elegant and dramatic. For my stationery, I chose textured ivory paper and wine ink that matched Cartier's "Les Must" wine leathers. I can't prove it, but maybe the prospective clients who receive my proposals and brochures printed in that wine ink will think subliminally of Cartier's elegance and success, and that will influence their impression of me.

Typeface is a very personal choice. Legibility should be your primary concern; some typefaces are simply more legible than others. Then see whether there are two or three typefaces that "call out" to you. Why two or three? When your printer designs your letterhead with your name and address, you'll probably discover that the arrangement of letters and numerals in your own name and address looks much better in one typeface than in the others.

Practical advice: If possible, obtain estimates and delivery dates from two or three local printers and choose the printer with the best combination of price and delivery date. Sign off on both the layout and the mechanical; your extra time now will prevent horrendous errors later.

Why a local printer? On a recent order for new stationery, I had to go to the printer five times in two weeks: (1) to choose four typefaces to see how the letterhead would look; (2) to pick up those layouts, choose three kinds of paper, and an ink color; (3) to return the layout of the typeface chosen—with corrections—so that a mechanical could be made; (4) to approve the mechanical and place my order; (5) to pick up the finished stationery.

Good-quality stationery printed in colored ink should cost less than $250 for 500 letterheads, 500 second sheets, 500 envelopes, and 500 business cards, including all mechanicals.

YOUR CHECKS

Usually your clients have no reason to see your checks. However, if you are coordinating a project and laying out money to be reimbursed, your clients might need to see copies of your checks. For this reason, I suggest choosing your check design to further your corporate image. Forgo the pretty patterns in favor of the plainest design—or one with a simple monogram—unless you are convinced that the check patterns say something about your work or profession—e.g., checks with breeds of hunting dogs or purebred cats for a veterinarian or breeder, checks with teddy bears or dolls for a toy store or antique dealer, checks with flowers for a florist.

Strategy: When you open your corporate checking account, ask your bank to start numbering your checks with a random number like #351 or #576, rather than the customary #101 or #1001. That way no one to whom you write a check will be able to guess how new your company is.

PROMOTION PIECES

Many small service corporations send out prospecting letters and some kind of brochure, or follow up sales calls with covering letters and brochures. Most of these brochures function as client/experience lists: "Here's what we do, here's what we can do for you, here's what we've done, these are some of our clients, these are our professional memberships, honors, awards." They are designed to convert prospects to clients.

The focus is different from that of a résumé or *curriculum vitae,* which is used generally to ask for a full-time job and which emphasizes education and year-by-year job experience. In fact, if you wear two very different hats, you may want to have two different professional brochures—e.g., as graphic artist and as interior designer.

My professional brochure, which is shown on the following pages, may give you some ideas. It is printed on ivory card stock in the same shade of wine ink as my letterhead, and is scored so that it can be folded in half and placed inside a standard business envelope, along with a covering letter. Together these mailing pieces form a unified, well-designed package which has gotten me a great deal of work.

The front cover is a summary of who I am and what I do; the back cover simply repeats my name, address, and telephone number. The inside of the brochure is a listing and description of some of my best work and my professional memberships and honors. Note that I have updated the brochure in two places—in wine ink, naturally. I'm in favor of updating a professional brochure as long as it can be done neatly. After three or four updated items, though, it's probably time to get your brochure reprinted.

JUDITH H. McQUOWN
Journalist & Publicist

PROFESSIONAL SERVICES

Major Writing Assignments
Product Introductions
Annual Reports
Speeches
Media Tours

Contact:

Judith H. McQuown
Judith H. McQuown & Co., Inc.
444 East 44th Street
New York, NY 102230

(212) 737-6480

TYPICAL ASSIGNMENTS

MAJOR MEDIA PLACEMENTS

Pan Am Clipper

Cover stories on cashmere, London clubs, stately homes.

Financial World

Contributing Editor, FW Personal Planner. More than 25 investment-related articles, including many profiles of investment experts.

Boardroom Reports

Contributing Editor, Bottom Line/Personal magazine. Since 1978, over 100 articles about travel, investments, antiques, including many profiles & interviews with experts.

New York Business Speaks

Profile of J. Peter Grace.

Physician's Guide to Money Management and Physician's Assets

Since 1984, many investment-related features, including profiles of investment experts.

Fact: The Money Management Magazine

Contributing Editor. Over 20 cover stories and features.

PR/ADVERTISING PROJECTS

Architectural Digest

Advertorial for Crum & Forster Insurance on collecting and protecting antiques.

Drexel Burnham Lambert Incorporated

Articles and reports on options and interest rate options.

Brielle Galleries

Catalog copy.

*American Express OPTIMA TIMES
Center-spread article on cruises.*

BOOKS AND MAJOR WRITING

Seven books on investments, travel and fashion, one of which — *Inc. Yourself: How to Profit by Setting Up Your Own Corporation* — has sold over 250,000 copies since 1977 and was taken by five book clubs. Sixth edition ~~will be~~ published by Macmillan in November 1988 *chosen by Fortune Book Club + The Executive Program.*

Contributing Editor and sole author of *TRIPS*, an 8-page semimonthly travel newsletter published by a subsidiary of Marshall Field.

Publisher and writer of *McQuown's Designer Markdowns*, weekly fashion newsletter.

HONORS/MEMBERSHIPS/ EDUCATION

Who's Who in the East
Who's Who of American Women
World Who's Who of Women
Contemporary Authors

American Society of Journalists & Authors

Hunter College — Dean's List
New York Institute of Finance

SPECIAL SERVICES

Spokeswoman — TV and radio
Speechwriting
Media tours

PORTFOLIO & SAMPLES UPON REQUEST

SALES CALLS

Many entrepreneurs and service providers already have sizable client lists when they "INC." themselves. For them, the act of incorporation is an excellent excuse to make a sales call: "Hello, I'm calling to tell you that I've just set up a corporation called Great Designs, Inc., and now I'll be able to give you even better service than before. Is there anything I can do for you now? What are you looking for?"

> Friday mornings are good times for these sales calls. Clients are usually mellow on Friday, and it's easier to get them to say yes.

Delivering work is another chance to pick up a new assignment. I don't know why so many entrepreneurs miss out on this opportunity. Let's say that you'll be delivering the Smith project tomorrow, hopefully a day ahead of your deadline. Call your client today: "Hello, John. I'm delivering the Smith project tomorrow, a day ahead of schedule. Do you have another project we can work on?"

Note that you've scored points by your early delivery and by notifying the client when you were going to deliver the project. At the same time, you are planting in his mind the idea of giving you his next project, *and* of pulling it together to give you tomorrow, a move which will also get it off his desk. At least seven times out of ten, the next day, when you deliver the Smith project, you'll leave John's office with the Jones project.

For making sales calls, I find a stack of lined 3″ × 5″ index cards very useful. I write the name, address, phone number of a client and name and phone number of my contact on the front (lined) side. The names of spouse, kids, pets, and hobbies go on the front, too. I'll also jot down in pencil, so that I can erase and update easily, the date of my last call and what was happening in my client's life—e.g., "Remodeling house." "Going on vacation in October." "Daughter applying to college." On the back of the card, I'll note the dates and descriptions of projects I did for the client and how much I billed for them. In this format, I can keep cards alphabetically, but also pull out the ones I want for specific sales calls. The cards are the right size and shape for tucking away in a purse or briefcase when I'm out of my office. When I telephone and ask about the paint job or wiring, or the vacation, or at which schools Susie was accepted, my clients know I've been thinking about them, and they are more likely to give me their next project.

Make sales calls on a regular basis, even if your schedule is completely booked. You can always line up work for the future. It takes less than a minute to make a "touching-base" phone call, and your clients will appreciate hearing from you often and briefly.

Similarly, depending on the kind of services you perform, you may be able to make quick sales calls by mail simply by sending your clients newspaper and magazine articles with a brief note on your business card: "Thought you'd be interested in this."

It can take months or even years to land a client. And, like catching fish, the larger the client, the longer it takes to land. Perseverance will pay off. Executives at American Express OPTIMA Card read about me in May 1988 and called me to discuss a project. I finally got the assignment in August 1988, after having made dozens of calls to the people at American Express and their advertising agency. My first contact with Virgin Atlantic airways was in August 1988. I called Virgin's PR director and spoke generally of my talents and capabilities. Because she traveled a lot, we finally had a breakfast meeting in October. She asked me for some samples, and I sent them. I followed up with phone calls about every two weeks. Finally, after about a dozen sales calls, where we chatted about her projects and I asked for work, I received an assignment in March 1989.

Does it pay to spend so much time courting clients? Yes, with reservations. Your largest, most profitable clients may take as long as a year to land. You'll need to develop a strong client base to provide current income while you woo the larger prospects. Then, if your sales strategies are successful, you can benefit from Pareto's Law: 20 percent of your clients will provide 80 percent of your business.

THE PROSPECTS ARE PLEASING

Once they have "INC.'d" themselves, many entrepreneurs and professionals want to build their client lists quickly. Networking is one of the fastest routes. Join professional organizations, attend as many meetings as you can, and *circulate*. Volunteer for committees and be willing to be a spokesperson. *Get yourself known*.

David W. Kennedy, former president of the American Society of Journalists and Authors, is an expert in insurance and real estate. For him, teaching adult-education classes has led to consulting assignments. He can call himself a consultant because he has not incorporated. He advises professionals and entrepreneurs: "Even when you are socializing, you have the opportunity to do business. Always carry your business cards with you—don't leave home without them. At a party, when you chat with people about what you do, they may ask for your card."

Follow-through is important, says Kennedy. "I ask my clients for referrals, and I always send my clients thank-you notes."

Another author who is an expert in her field is interviewed fairly often, especially for new magazines. She asks her interviewers for information about the new magazines and then calls the magazines' editors or publishers for story assignments, using her own interview in the magazine as an introduction.

LOOKING FOR LEADS IN ALL THE RIGHT PLACES

Successful entrepreneurs read voraciously (as much as possible) and omnivorously (as many sources as possible). I cheerfully admit to scavenging my co-op floor's compactor room for magazines and newsletters that my neighbors—professionals in other fields—discard. This habit has gotten me contacts and assignments from sources that otherwise I would not have known about.

My favorite broker brings me current copies of *Registered Representative,* possibly the finest and certainly the most popular magazine for stockbrokers. As stockbrokers do telephone selling every day, I expect to pick up valuable hints about calling clients and leads, even though I sell different products and services.

Case in point: The September 1989 issue had two excellent articles. One wrote up a day of "combat calling," in which ten New Jersey brokers participated in a 16½-hour blitz. The group made more than 5,000 calls, spoke to 2,100 contacts, identified 140 good prospects, and made 60 appointments. To add to the team spirit, they wore combat fatigues and empty ammo clips and had a toy plane buzz them periodically.

What did I get out of this article? The desire to spend one Friday morning in the near future making at least 30 cold calls to executives whose companies might require my services if they knew about them. I also learned that to be most effective, I'll have to arrange my calls in advance, make lists, prepare a script, and do follow-up work. For all this effort, I should pick up at least three or four new clients. And, to keep up my spirits, I'll wear my favorite perfume and put some flowers on my desk.

In the second article, five million-dollar brokers shared their secrets. Four out of five had advice I could implement—not a bad batting average.

Evan Katz of Shearson Lehman Hutton's Short Hills, New Jersey, office, emphasizes the presentation of why his product (a particular investment) looks attractive: "Learn the nuances of the job and learn what's right for the client."

Robert Bonwell of Prudential-Bache in Charleston, West Virginia, uses seminars as his sole prospecting tool. Although he looks for small towns where his talk would be the event of the week, a strategy which I would find impractical and unprofitable, I learn from his experience and resolve to increase my seminars from three or four per year to at least one every month.

Jerry Bott of Kidder Peabody in Jacksonville, Florida, teaches me the importance of referrals: "All clients are asked at their annual review if they know of someone who could benefit from the firm's services." He also believes in cultivating "centers of influence" like attorneys and accountants.

Steuart Evans of Robinson-Humphrey in Huntsville, Alabama, offers an excellent telephone strategy: "Find reasons to call your clients with news connected to something they're working on."

Remember: You are not wasting your time if you do a lot of reading outside your field—especially in fields that emphasize telephone sales, since most of your contacts probably will be by telephone. One good idea from this reading can be worth thousands of dollars to you.

LANDING THE PROJECT

All your prospecting has paid off. Potential clients are asking you for proposals or bids. Proposals and bids vary greatly in different industries and professions, but here are some ground rules that are common to all:

(1) Make sure you know what the client wants done. Review the client's needs with him or her before you begin your formal proposal.

(2) Make your *presentation* orally, if the client prefers it, but put the *proposal* in writing so that there are no misunderstandings.

(3) Begin by identifying or reiterating the client's needs. Then state what you will do to satisfy those needs. Depending on the project, you can state your price now or in a contract or letter agreement sometime later.

(4) Appearances count, especially if you are a small, new company. After you have drafted and reviewed your proposal, have it typed and proofread carefully to make sure that there are no errors or omissions, and keep the original immaculate. Paper folders in rich burgundy, navy, or silver will protect your proposal and enhance its appearance.

To give you some ideas on how to create a proposal for a service, following is a proposal I wrote for British Airways:

SCOTTISH SHOPPING SPREE

BACKGROUND: Since January 1985, the pound has risen from $1.05 to approximately $1.70—an increase of more than 60 percent.

PROBLEM: American leisure travelers' perception that Britain is too expensive to visit.

SOLUTION: Provide an upscale, value-packed shoppers' tour on which participants can save $500–$1,000, and even more!

For example:

- "Designer X," whose exciting cashmere designs for men and women are sold by Saks Fifth Avenue, Gucci, Nina Ricci, and boutiques all over the world. Cashmere separates usually selling for $600+ in the US, sell for £30–£70 at our secret source.

  SAVINGS: Approximately $500 per item, including VAT rebate.
- Ballantyne solid-color cashmere sweater, selling for $500 in the US, sold for £50 at our secret source.

  SAVINGS: $425, including VAT rebate.
- Ballantyne hand-intarsia flower-patterned cashmere sweater, selling for $700 in the US, sold for £70 at our secret source.

  SAVINGS: $600, including VAT rebate.

CONCLUSION:

With savings like these, fluctuations in the rate of exchange become virtually meaningless. The SCOTTISH SHOPPING SPREE not only pays for itself, but also for a stay in London afterward!

BENEFITS TO
BRITISH AIRWAYS:

British Airways can profit from the SCOTTISH SHOPPING SPREE package in many ways:

1. The package fills seats to Edinburgh, as well as to London. This generates additional revenue.
2. The package is designed for marginal leisure travelers, who need an "excuse" to take a(nother) short trip to Britain, and thus should generate additional revenue.
3. The package can be designed for shoulder and low-season travel periods, to fill empty seats, which will generate additional revenue.
4. As the land package will be exclusive to British Airways and cannot be purchased separately, people who love to shop will have to fly British Airways, rather than one of its competitors. This will increase market share and generate additional revenue.

TENTATIVE
ITINERARY

Sunday evening.   Fly to London Heathrow.

Monday morning.   Shuttle to Edinburgh. Transfer to hotel.

Monday afternoon.   Visit a Scottish cashmere designer who sells to Barneys, Mark Cross, and many other boutiques.

Tuesday.   After breakfast, visit Ballantyne factory outlet and factory shops and studios in the

	Borders, including "Designer X," and a crystal factory outlet. Lunch in Hawick.
Wednesday.	After breakfast, visit factory shops and studios northeast of Edinburgh. Lunch in St. Andrews.
Thursday.	After breakfast, tour Edinburgh and/or return to London and U.S. at will.

NOTE: If desired, I can combine the above with an English shopping tour Thursday, Friday (and Saturday) that would let travelers return Saturday or Sunday.

PROFESSIONAL BROCHURE ENCLOSED (This is the brochure on pp. 28–29.)

Note how many times, in the "benefits to client" section of the proposal, I use the words "this should/will generate additional revenue." Show your prospects how your work will benefit them, and you'll turn them into clients.

GETTING THE CONTRACT

Now you're ready to negotiate your contract.

STOP! There's a better way. A letter agreement is just as binding as a contract, but clients perceive it as being far less threatening.

Here is a simple letter agreement whose format you can use. Make two copies on your letterhead. Sign both copies and send them to your client. Ask him/her to sign and date one copy and return it to you. Your signed and dated letter agreement has the force and effect of a contract, with no threatening "whereases" and confusing or ambiguous clauses.

Mr. John Smith
Megalops Insurance Company
350 Fifth Avenue
New York, New York 10001

Dear Mr. Smith:
    Pursuant to our conversation this morning, I am sending you this letter to serve as an agreement between us for a 5,000-word manuscript for a brochure on pension plans for the one-person corporation (detailed description of the work to be done), to be delivered on or before March 15, 1991 (delivery date).
    You will provide me with background material and a list of contacts and telephone numbers for potential interviews.
    The fee for this manuscript is $5,000, based on ten days' work at a per diem rate of $500 per 7-hour day. Megalops will pay all expenses, such as messenger, long-distance phone bills, and fax service. Any rewrites will be charged at the same per

diem rate of $500; and if Megalops changes its mind on this assignment, it will still be responsible for time and expense charges incurred to date.

Megalops will pay one-half the fee ($2,500) upon signing of this letter agreement and the remaining half ($2,500), plus expenses within 30 days of its receipt of the manuscript (on or before April 15, 1991).

If these terms meet with your approval, please sign and date one copy of this letter agreement and return it to me with Megalops' check for $2,500.

I look forward to working with you on this exciting project.

_____
Elizabeth Bennett

_____
Title

Entrepreneurial Visions Corp.

_____
Date

_____
John Smith

_____
Title

Megalops Insurance Company

_____
Date

WHAT TO CHARGE FOR THE PROJECT

It's a sad fact that most entrepreneurs charge too little for their time and work. This situation arises because they forget to include overhead and the cost of fringe benefits in calculating their per diem rates. They think, "If I'm worth $50,000 a year, I should bill $1,000 a week or $200 per diem." Actually, if they were employed full time by another company, their cost to the company in salary, fringes, and overhead would exceed $75,000. And, allowing for vacation and holidays that reduce working days per year from 260 (52 weeks × 5 days) to 235, the per diem rate should be $350, not $200.

In the following table, veteran medical author and communications expert Diana Benzaia, whose firm, Wordcrafters Unlimited, has as its clients hospitals, national health organizations, and pharmaceutical companies, shows you how to calculate your per diem rates, based on three expertise and salary levels. Her advice, while couched in terms of writers, is applicable to all service businesses and professions, because it emphasizes the true value of your time.

HOW TO CALCULATE YOUR PER DIEM—Examples for 3 levels of expertise

What would be your salaried value at a full-time job?	$25,000	$50,000	75,000
Add ⅓ for fringe benefits paid to employees	8,250	16,500	24,750
Add cost of your overhead as a freelance—usually about $5 per $25 earned	5,000	10,000	15,000
Add a profit for the risk taken as an entrepreneur 10%	2,500	5,000	7,500
TOTAL	$40,750	$81,500	$122,250
Calculate # days per year person of your caliber works			
WEEKS VACATION	2	3	4
Weekdays left	250	245	240
Minus holidays	10	10	10
DAYS WORKED	240	235	230
DIVIDE $ TOTAL BY DAYS WORKED	$170	$345	$531
Assess market/set per diem	$175–200	$350	$500–550

For monthly retainer (at least 3 days/month, 1-yr contract) cut by $50.

Benzaia adds her comments: "Most freelancers set their fees too low because they think only of the first line of the chart: salary. They forget that as independent business people there are many other components to the fee structure. When it comes to fringe benefits, include the fact that you have to provide your own health, life, and disability insurance, plus other perks normally given to executives of your caliber.

"In calculating the cost of your overhead, check Schedule C of your tax return for your total actual overhead. If you are in a business that uses expensive supplies, your total may be much higher than $5 per $25 earned. Your profit should be at least 10 percent. In certain markets and businesses, it may be 15 percent.

"When you assess your market, include such factors as whether you have a specialty, and is it one that tends to generate lower (e.g., travel or food writing) or higher (e.g., medical or business writing) fees. Consider the availability of services such as yours in your community, and fees others are charging if services such as yours are widely available.

"Written contracts to purchase at least three days of your services per month for one year should be the minimum for your giving a break on your price. The benefit to you is the security of a regular monthly check without the hassels of dunning.

"Try never to work for a flat fee. Even if you are good at estimating time, the project can turn into a loser. If the material you are working on is to be reviewed by a committee, with multiple revisions requested, you can wind up on the short end of the stick. Write into your contract the agreed-upon estimate of time and costs and add a sentence or two noting that the final fee will be determined by your actual time spent on the project and that, at any time, if it appears that the project will exceed the estimate by more than 10 percent, the client will be notified immediately."

Our time and talents are our only merchandise: let's not shortchange ourselves.

4

How to Get Maximum Savings and Tax Savings from Your Corporate Assets

One major—but little-realized and little-used—corporate asset was discussed in the previous chapter. This small object can generate thousands of dollars in savings for your corporation every year. It's your business card.

> Scene in a major hotel or car-rental agency:
> *Clerk:* Do you qualify for our corporate discount?
> *You:* I don't know—what does it require?
> *Clerk:* Just your business card.

The corporate discount applies to one-person corporations as well as to corporate giants, and usually ranges from 10 percent to 20 percent. It's worth lots of money—especially if you do a lot of business traveling. And even such elegant stores as Tiffany's offer corporate discounts.

> *Strategy:* If the clerk doesn't mention a corporate discount, ask whether there is one.

The remaining savings discussed in this chapter relate to more tangible assets. As your corporation grows and prospers, you'll probably need new hardware: a computer, fax machine, a company car, and so on. Maximizing tax savings through buying this equipment can mean thousands of dollars a year in write-offs for your corporation. And, when you sell these assets, if favorable capital-gains legislation has been passed, the law will be skewed once again for long-term capital gains and short-term ordinary losses. You'll win both ways.

DEPRECIATION UPDATE

Depreciation rules, liberalized by the Economic Recovery Tax Act of 1981, which created the Accelerated Cost Recovery System (ACRS) for tangible assets placed in service, trade, or business in the United States, have been tightened considerably by the Tax Reform Act of 1986. This legislation repealed the investment tax credit and replaced ACRS with the Modified Accelerated Cost Recovery System (MACRS), which stretches out depreciation periods so that it takes more time to write off an asset.

The recovery period of an asset depends upon its class of property, based on its useful life.

Class	Useful Life
3 years	Less than or equal to 4 years
5 years	Between 4 and 10 years*
7 years	Between 10 and 16 years
10 years	Between 16 and 20 years
15 years	Between 20 and 25 years
20 years	25 years and over

*Includes all cars and light trucks regardless of useful life

The recovery period is determined by its class; a 7-year asset has a recovery period of 7 years even though its useful life is between 10 and 16 years.

Here are the property-class schedules for commonly used business property. Close to 90 percent of your property will probably be 3- to 5-year property; at least 8 percent will probably be 7-year property.

3-Year Property (§179 Property)
Tractor units for use over-the-road
Special tools and devices

5-Year Property (§179 Property)
Computers and peripheral equipment
Typewriters, calculators, copiers

Airplanes (except those used in commercial or contract
    carrying of passengers or freight) and helicopters
Automobiles and taxis
Buses and trucks
Trailers and trailer-mounted containers
Equipment used to drill oil and gas wells
Equipment used in timber cutting
Equipment used in the wholesale and retail trades
Equipment used in the provision of personal and professional
    services (e.g., laundry, beauty, and barbershop assets, and
    assets used by doctors, attorneys, and accountants)
Assets used in connection with research and experimentation

7-Year Property (§179 Property)

Office furniture, fixtures, and equipment
Equipment used in agriculture and animal husbandry
Single-purpose agricultural or horticultural structures
Equipment used in providing recreation and entertainment
    services on payment of a fee or admission charge, such as
    bowling alleys or movie theaters (but excluding theme or
    amusement parks, golf courses, ski slopes, racetracks)

Real estate has its own rules. Please refer to the applicable section later in this chapter.

Under the new depreciation rules, generally referred to as §179 rules, you may still deduct $10,000 as first-year depreciation for one asset or a group of assets, subject to the following limitations:

(1) The assets must be §179 property: they must be
    (a) tangible, depreciable personal property with a useful life of three
        years or more;
    (b) used in active conduct of your trade or business;
    (c) purchased—*i.e.*, a taxable acquisition from an unrelated party.

(2) You may also take first-year depreciation, as computed below, *but* the depreciable base must first be reduced by the amount of the §179 deduction.

Example: Your corporation buys a computer for $20,000. If you choose to deduct $10,000 during the first year, in order to reduce your net taxable income by $10,000, you must reduce your computer's depreciable base from $20,000 to $10,000.

(3) If more than $200,000 worth of property eligible for §179 depreciation is placed in service during one year, the amount of the deduction is reduced by the excess over $200,000.

Example: Your phenomenally successful corporation puts $204,000 worth of gizmos into service in 1991. Because this figure exceeds the

$200,000 limitation by $4,000, you will have to reduce the $10,000 first-year deduction by $4,000. You will be able to take a first-year deduction of $6,000 (and to depreciate $198,000).

(4) The §179 deduction cannot produce a loss; your corporate deduction is limited to the income from your trade or business (operating income). However, the excess deduction can be carried over.

Example: You have a corporate profit of $8,500. You may deduct only $8,500 of your §179 first-year deduction this year and can carry over the remaining $1,500 deduction to next year.

HOW MACRS WORKS

MACRS, which replaced ACRS on January 1, 1987, must be used for all tangible property placed in service after January 1, 1987, except

(1) property which you elect to exclude and to use alternate depreciation (see below);
(2) films, videos, and recordings.

Here is the basic formula for calculating MACRS:

Amount of depreciation deduction = applicable method X recovery period
    (subject to convention limitations—see "Making the Most of the Midyear Convention" below)

The applicable method—a mathematical formula—assumes that the salvage value of your asset is always $0, and uses the 200 percent declining-balance figures:

If the Recovery Year is:	3-year	5-year	7-year	10-year	15-year	20-year
		the Depreciation Rate is:				
1	33.33	20.00	14.29	10.00	5.00	3.750
2	44.45	32.00	24.49	18.00	9.50	7.219
3	14.81	19.20	17.49	14.40	8.55	6.677
4	7.41	11.52	12.49	11.52	7.70	6.177
5		11.52	8.93	9.22	6.93	5.713
6		5.76	8.92	7.37	6.23	5.285
7			8.93	6.55	5.90	4.888
8			4.46	6.55	5.90	4.522
9				6.56	5.91	4.462
10				6.55	5.90	4.461
11				3.28	5.91	4.462
12					5.90	4.461
13					5.91	4.462
14					5.90	4.461
15					5.91	4.462
16					2.95	4.461
17						4.462
18						4.461

and the Recovery Period is:

If the Recovery Year is:	3-year	and the Recovery Period is:		10-year	15-year	20-year
		5-year	7-year			
		the Depreciation Rate is:				
19						4.462
20						4.461
21						2.231

Source: Internal Revenue Service

There are several notable exceptions. The 150 percent declining-balance figures are used for 15- or 20-year property (see below) and for property where you elect to use these figures, on a class-of-property basis. If you make this election, it applies to the whole class of assets.

MAKING THE MOST OF THE MIDYEAR CONVENTION

Before we can look at some examples, you have to understand the midyear convention in accounting. As a general rule, the IRS assumes that every piece of property gets put into service on June 30 regardless of the actual date you have put it in service. Thus, during the first and last year that you can depreciate an asset, you cannot deduct more than one-half year's worth of depreciation. That is why a three-year asset is depreciated over four years, a five-year asset is depreciated over six years, and so on. If you buy an asset on January 1, 1991, you will still be able to take only one-half year's worth of depreciation.

Well, then, what about putting the asset into service on December 31 and claiming the half-year's worth of depreciation? Sorry, the IRS has anticipated this ploy. If 40 percent of the value of what you put into service in any year is put in in the last quarter, you are assumed to have put all of your property into service in the middle of the last quarter, and thus can deduct only 12½ percent of the first year's depreciation. For example, if your company buys a car in October, you will be able to claim only 1½ month's worth of depreciation, as though you had placed the car in service on November 15.

Note: This rule covers *all your asset purchases.* If you bought $10,000 worth of equipment in 1991, with $5,900 purchased in January and $4,100 purchased in December, the entire $10,000 of equipment would be treated as though it had been put into service as of November 15.

> *Optimum Strategy:* If you want to maximize your depreciation deduction, the optimum time to place an asset in service is September 30. By doing so, you pick up three months' worth of extra depreciation in the first year.

Now let's look at several examples. You'll be able to calculate your depreciation quickly by using the chart below. It bases all the percentage figures on your original depreciable base, rather than on bases which are adjusted every year for depreciation already taken.

You buy a color copier and fax machine for $20,000. They are classed as five-year property.

Cost			$20,000
1991 first-year §179 deduction			−10,000
Depreciable base			$10,000
1991 depreciation	(20.00%)		2,000
1992	"	(32.00%)	3,200
1993	"	(19.20%)	1,920
1994	"	(11.52%)	1,152
1995	"	(11.52%)	1,152
1996	"	(5.76%)	576

Your corporation writes off $10,000 as a §179 deduction and $2,000 for depreciation on IRS Form 4562, as shown on the following page, and carries the total over to page 1 of IRS Form 1120 or 1120A (the short form used by most small corporations). The depreciation deductions are the same kind of business deductions as rent, utilities, or repairs.

In the second year, your corporation can write off $3,200 for depreciation even though it hasn't spent any money in that year. That's why depreciation is often called a "noncash deduction." From 1993 through 1996 your corporation can deduct a total of $4,800 for depreciation without spending another penny.

Or you buy office furniture for $30,000. It is classed as seven-year property. You already have used your first-year deduction on your copier and fax machine.

Cost = depreciable base			$30,000
1991 depreciation	(14.29%)		4,287
1992	"	(24.49%)	7,347
1993	"	(17.49%)	5,247
1994	"	(12.49%)	3,747
1995	"	(8.93%)	2,679
1996	"	(8.92%)	2,676
1997	"	(8.93%)	2,679
1998	"	(4.46%)	1,338

Form **4562**	**Depreciation and Amortization**	OMB No. 1545-0172
Department of the Treasury Internal Revenue Service	▶ See separate instructions. ▶ Attach this form to your return.	**1989** Attachment Sequence No. **67**

Name(s) as shown on return	Identifying number
GREAT DESIGNS, INC.	13-0000000

Business or activity to which this form relates

GRAPHIC DESIGN

Part I   **Depreciation** *(Use Part III for automobiles, certain other vehicles, computers, and property used for entertainment, recreation, or amusement.)*

Section A.—Election To Expense Depreciable Assets (Section 179)

1 Maximum dollar limitation	**1**	$10,000
2 Total cost of section 179 property placed in service during the tax year (see instructions)	**2**	20,000
3 Threshold cost of section 179 property before reduction in limitation	**3**	$200,000
4 Reduction in limitation (Subtract line 3 from line 2, but do not enter less than -0-.)	**4**	
5 Dollar limitation for tax year (Subtract line 4 from line 1, but do not enter less than -0-.)	**5**	$ 10,000

(a) Description of property	(b) Date placed in service	(c) Cost	(d) Elected cost
6 COLOR COPIER + FAX MACHINE	1/1/89	$20,000	10,000

7 Listed property—Enter amount from line 28	**7**	
8 Tentative deduction (Enter the lesser of: (a) line 6 plus line 7; or (b) line 5.)	**8**	10,000
9 Taxable income limitation (Enter the lesser of :(a) Taxable income; or (b) line 5) **(see instructions)**	**9**	10,000
10 Carryover of disallowed deduction from 1988 (see instructions)	**10**	
11 Section 179 expense deduction (Enter the lesser of: (a) line 8 plus line 10; or (b) line 9.)	**11**	10,000
12 Carryover of disallowed deduction to 1990 (Add lines 8 and 10, less line 11.) ▶	**12**	

Section B.—MACRS Depreciation

(a) Classification of property	(b) Date placed in service	(c) Basis for depreciation (Business use only—see instructions)	(d) Recovery period	(e) Convention	(f) Method	(g) Depreciation deduction
13 General Depreciation System (GDS) (see instructions): *For assets placed in service ONLY during tax year beginning in 1989*						
a 3-year property						
b 5-year property		$10,000	5 YRS.		MACRS	$2,000
c 7-year property						
d 10-year property						
e 15-year property						
f 20-year property						
g Residential rental property			27.5 yrs.	MM	S/L	
			27.5 yrs.	MM	S/L	
h Nonresidential real property			31.5 yrs.	MM	S/L	
			31.5 yrs.	MM	S/L	
14 Alternative Depreciation System (ADS) (see instructions): *For assets placed in service ONLY during tax year beginning in 1989*						
a Class life					S/L	
b 12-year			12 yrs.		S/L	
c 40-year			40 yrs.	MM	S/L	

15 Listed property—Enter amount from line 27	**15**	
16 GDS and ADS deductions for assets placed in service before 1989 (see instructions)	**16**	

Section C.—ACRS and/or Other Depreciation

17 Property subject to section 168(f)(1) election (see instructions)	**17**	
18 ACRS and/or other depreciation (see instructions)	**18**	

Section D.—Summary

19 Total (Add deductions on line 11 and lines 13 through 18.) Enter here and on the appropriate line of your return (Partnerships and S corporations—see instructions)	**19**	12,000
20 For assets shown above and placed in service during the current year, enter the portion of the basis attributable to section 263A costs (see instructions)	**20**	

For Paperwork Reduction Act Notice, see page 1 of the separate instructions.   Form **4562** (1989)

Your deductions and depreciation for this year total $16,287. If your corporation is in the 15 percent bracket, they are worth $2,443 in actual dollars. If your corporation is in the 25 percent bracket, they are worth $4,072 in actual dollars. And if your corporation is in the 34 percent bracket, they are worth $5,538 in actual dollars.

Would your corporation receive a larger write-off by taking the first-year $10,000 deduction on the furniture rather than on the office equipment? Let's try it.

Office equipment	
cost = depreciable base	$20,000
1991 depreciation (20.00%)	4,000
1992 depreciation (32.00%)	6,400
1993 " (19.20%)	3,840
1994 " (11.52%)	2,304
1995 " (11.52%)	2,304
1996 " (5.76%)	1,152
Office furniture cost	$30,000
1991 first-year §179 deduction	− 10,000
Depreciable base	$20,000
1991 depreciation (14.29%)	2,858
1992 " (24.49%)	4,898
1993 " (17.49%)	3,498
1994 " (12.49%)	2,498
1995 " (8.93%)	1,786
1996 " (8.92%)	1,784
1997 " (8.93%)	1,786
1998 " (4.46%)	1,338

Yes! Your deductions and depreciation for this year total $16,858. And next year the differences are even greater: $11,298 vs. $10,547.

Strategy: When you are placing assets that cost varying amounts of money into service, calculate which asset will give you the greatest tax benefit by using the $10,000 first-year deduction for it.

EXCEPTIONS TO THE MIDYEAR CONVENTION

There are a few exceptions to the midyear convention. The most common is the mid-*month* convention, which assumes that property is acquired or disposed of at the midmonth of its actual acquisition or disposal, and which *must be used for real estate.*

OTHER FORMS OF DEPRECIATION

There are two more forms of depreciation. *Alternative depreciation* must be used for property outside the United States and for property used to produce tax-exempt income. Alternative depreciation may be used if elected for personal property. The election will then apply to all property in that class placed in service in the year of election. The alternative method may also be used for real estate, where the election may be made on a property-by-property basis.

The straight-line method of depreciation is used, and the depreciation periods are extremely long. The recovery period for real estate is 40 years, which means that 2½ percent of the cost can be depreciated every year for 40 years. Personal property without a class life takes a 12-year recovery period. Personal property with a class life uses that class life as its recovery period.

Why would anyone want to use a depreciation system which results in lower depreciation deductions over a far longer time period? In a few rare cases, it might be useful for someone who needs depreciation deductions over a long number of years. For most small corporations, however, alternative depreciation is not a good deal.

Regular depreciation still exists, but, on a practical level, it is available only to intangibles (copyrights, patents, etc.) and films, records, tapes, and videos.

For these forms of depreciation, it may be wise to consult an accountant.

The following tables contrast MACRS and straight-line depreciation:

3-YEAR PROPERTY

	MACRS	Straight-Line
Year 1	33.33%	16.67%
Year 2	44.45	33.33
Year 3	14.81	33.33
Year 4	7.41	16.67

Note that in the first two years you can depreciate 78 percent of the property's value under MACRS, but only 50 percent with the straight line method.

5-YEAR PROPERTY

	MACRS	Straight-Line
Year 1	20.00%	10.00%
Year 2	32.00	20.00
Year 3	19.20	20.00
Year 4	11.52	20.00
Year 5	11.52	20.00
Year 6	5.76	10.00

Note that in the first two years you can depreciate 52 percent of the property's value under MACRS, but only 30 percent with the straight-line method.

7-YEAR PROPERTY

	MACRS	Straight-Line
Year 1	14.29%	7.16%
Year 2	24.49	14.48
Year 3	17.49	14.28
Year 4	12.49	14.28
Year 5	8.93	14.28
Year 6	8.92	14.28
Year 7	8.93	14.28
Year 8	4.46	14.28

Note that in the first two years you can depreciate 39 percent of the property's value under MACRS, but only 21 percent with the straight-line method.

UNCLASSIFIED PERSONAL PROPERTY

12 years under straight-line method

Year 1	4.19%
Years 2–12	8.33
Year 13	4.18

"Assuming that you have the choice," says a California accountant and tax attorney, "the key question is whether you want your corporation's deductions front-loaded or back-loaded. Ninety percent of the rational world wants its deductions front-loaded and only ten percent wants them back-loaded. But remember that if corporate tax rates rise, you'd get more bang for your buck if you back-loaded your deductions."

YOUR CORPORATE CAR

Cars owned by your corporation and used exclusively for business have their own rules and their own depreciation schedules. They apply to both new and used cars.

At first glance, it would seem that the rules governing company cars are ludicrous, to put it kindly. What could you call regulations which define a luxury car as one that cost $16,000 or more new in 1984, but only $12,800 or more new in 1989?*

The depreciation rules for cars apply to both new and used autos.

Stringent limitations on depreciation apply only to "luxury passenger automobiles": those with four wheels, with a gross vehicle weight of 6,000 pounds or less, designed primarily for road use, and whose cost in 1989 exceeded $12,800. Trucks or vans, vehicles with more than four wheels, off-the-road vehicles, and vehicles used directly in the business of transporting people and property are exempt.

For luxury automobiles placed in service in 1990, here are the maximum depreciation deductions:

Recovery Period	Maximum Depreciation Deduction
Year 1	$2,660
Year 2	4,200
Year 3	2,550
Year 4 and subsequent	1,475

At this rate, you can see that it might take 14 years to depreciate a $25,000 car!

Furthermore, these rules are for 100 percent business use of your car. If your car is used for business between 51 percent and 99 percent of all use, you will have to prorate its business depreciation and take your personal use as a taxable perk. And if its business use is 50 percent or less of all use, you must use alternative depreciation.

Fortunately, there are several strategies for finessing the luxury-car rule.

*The 1990 definition was published after press time, in November 1990.

1. The simplest is to have your corporation buy a new or used car for $12,800 or less. Then your corporation can take a deduction of $2,660 in the first year and $4,200 in the second year, regardless of the car's cost. It's a flat amount—not a percentage. If you have managed to find your $6,000 dream car at a police or IRS auction, you'll be able to write it off in two years.

2. Or your corporation can buy a heavyweight vehicle, or one with more than four wheels. Then your corporation can treat it as five-year property. Look at the difference between how a $40,000 luxury truck and a $40,000 BMW or Mercedes-Benz are depreciated:

	Truck			Car		Difference
Year 1	(20.00%)	$ 8,000	Year 1	$ 2,660		$ 5,340
Year 2	(32.00%)	12,800	Year 2	4,200		8,600
Year 3	(19.20%)	7,680	Year 3	2,550		5,130
Year 4	(11.52%)	4,608	Year 4	1,475		2,133
Year 5	(11.52%)	4,608	Year 5	1,475		2,133
Year 6	(5.76%)	2,304	Year 6	1,475		829
		$40,000		$13,835		

Remainder to depreciate $26,165
Number of years at $1,475 = 18
Total years = 24

If you lease your corporate car, remember that deductions for leased autos are limited to the same low amounts as depreciation deductions for purchased cars. The lease payments will be capitalized and broken down into interest, a payment for the use of the car, and a figure for depreciation. If the fair market value of the car at the inception of the lease exceeds $12,800, the depreciation component will be restricted to its stated maximum. When you examine a lease, you have to say, "Break this payment down into its components for me so that I can see what I am permitted to deduct," in order to find out what the lease's tax benefits are and its true cost to your corporation. Your corporation may also have to take into its income a portion of the annual lease payments it pays for a "luxury car." If you are considering leasing a car whose fair market value exceeds $12,800, it's a good idea to consult an accountant.

Whatever type of car your company purchases or leases, it can also deduct such operating expenses as car insurance, license fees, maintenance, repairs, parking fees, tolls, gas, and oil. These deductions and proof of your business use of the company car are subject to strict recordkeeping requirements. You may wish to use the format of the log on the following page.

Car Mileage & Operating Expenses

Date	Destination—Purpose of Trip—Contact	Odometer		Mileage Breakdown			Expenses			
		Begin	End	Busi-ness	Invest-ment	Per-sonal	Gas, Oil, Lube	Parking —Tolls	Other	Describe

Post on Monthly Basis to Car Recap

Note: Retain receipts for all lodging. Retain receipts for transportation and single expenditures of $25 or more.

Business use of a car is a complicated topic, with many rules and even more exceptions. You may find IRS Publication 917, "Business Use of a Car," which is revised every November to help with that year's tax returns, useful reading.

A final word of advice about your corporate car: Never make any decision solely for tax purposes. For some entrepreneurs, it's smart business to have a BMW or a Maserati, even though it will take forever to depreciate it. For some people, it's the right decision to have a car that they use 60 percent for business and 40 percent for personal matters.

CORPORATE REAL ESTATE

Once real estate could be depreciated on a ten-year straight-line basis. Those golden days are gone. Now residential real estate placed into service after January 1, 1987 is depreciated on a 27½-year straight-line basis, and commercial real estate is depreciated on a 31½-year straight-line basis—or about 3½ percent and 3 percent per year, respectively.

As mentioned earlier, real estate uses the mid-*month* convention, rather than the midyear convention. Property placed into service anytime during the month is held to have been placed in service on the fifteenth of that month. Whether your corporation places a piece of real estate in service on January 1 or 31, it will be held to have been placed in service on January 15. (However, with only approximately 0.25 percent of the property depreciable every month, placing the property in service on the last day of the month rather than on the first day still confers only a minuscule tax saving.)

STATES' RITES

States have their own depreciation systems. Most states use the federal system; a few do not. If your state uses a different depreciation system, it may be wise to consult an accountant.

States Which Use the Federal Depreciation System

Alabama	Iowa	New York
Alaska	Kansas	North Carolina
Arizona	Louisiana	North Dakota*
Arkansas	Maine	Ohio*
Colorado	Maryland	Oklahoma
Connecticut*	Massachusetts	Oregon
Delaware	Michigan*	Pennsylvania
District of Columbia	Minnesota	South Carolina
Florida	Mississippi	Tennessee
Georgia	Missouri	Utah
Hawaii	Montana	Vermont
Idaho	Nebraska	Virginia*
Illinois	New Hampshire	West Virginia
Indiana	New Mexico	Wisconsin

*With modifications

States Which Use Different Depreciation Systems

California—except in enterprise zones
Kentucky
New Jersey

States Which Have No Corporate Income Tax

Nevada
South Dakota
Texas
Washington
Wyoming

ANTIQUES AND OTHER LUXURIES AS CORPORATE FURNISHINGS

There is a great deal of controversy about using art and antiques as corporate furnishings. The IRS has notified many doctors that they may not deduct the cost of art in their waiting rooms. The doctors claim that the artwork helps them attract patients, and that their patients have come to expect art in the waiting rooms. (It goes without saying that the artwork may help the doctors justify high fees.) But the IRS has taken the position that the art is just a frill and is not in the same category as couches and coffee tables.

Well, then, what about a Georgian mahogany desk for your office instead of either a modern designer desk or an unfinished door topping a pair of file cabinets? The IRS would surely prefer that your corporation paid only $100 for the file-cabinet-and-door arrangement. But, unless you try to furnish your office with an original Adam or Sheraton museum-quality desk for $50,000, you are fairly safe, as long as you follow the suggestions in this section.

If you decide that you'd like an antique desk, for example, try to keep it's cost under $10,000, so that your corporation can expense it during the first year you have it by listing it on IRS Form 4562 as "office desk."

Be aware that, if the IRS should ever question this part of your tax return—an unlikely occurrence—you will have to prove that, although the desk *is* an antique, it still has a useful life under §179 rules, and therefore is a depreciable asset. The courts have pointed out that taxpayers will have to prove these points:

1. You will have to show that the desk will exhaust its value or suffer wear and tear from use over a period of time. It will be helpful to obtain an expert witness's evaluation of the desk's useful life and wear and tear over time.

2. You should establish that desks you have had in the past have actually suffered significant damage and wear and tear and have had to be replaced.

3. You should establish your intent to replace the desk after a reasonably definite, fixed period. If you are going to keep the desk forever and use it forever, the IRS is probably going to say, "No useful life." And if you are planning to keep the desk as an investment, the IRS is probably going

to say, "No useful life." You have to show that you bought this desk for use, that you don't take good care of things, and that after seven or eight years you're going to scratch the heck out of it and it's probably going to be trashed. The desk won't be worth anything near what you paid for it.

If you can prove all this, should the IRS question you, the IRS would probably say, "Yes, your desk does have a useful life of seven years." What's in your favor: an antique desk is not a piece of artwork. It has a function, and it gets *used*.

Luxury office touches are deductible if you can prove that they are "ordinary and necessary in carrying on a trade or business," according to the IRS. "Ordinary" and "necessary" are really two components of the same requirement. "Ordinary" means that your luxury office touches are used by others in your profession; "necessary" means that they are helpful to the establishment, development, and maintenance of your profession or business, and that they are appropriate and reasonable under the circumstances.

To the extent that you show that you are dealing with wealthy clients, luxury business touches are clearly ordinary and necessary. After all, you can't take notes with a Bic pen at a client conference, or serve coffee in a Styrofoam cup—not when other law firms are using Spode china. If other professionals use china, you can and should, too—if only to demonstrate your professional credibility and success.

Similarly, you could probably write off a Georgian silver coffee or tea set, for serving clients, as long as it wasn't made by Paul Storr or Paul de Lamerie.

Fresh flowers for your office? They are another acceptable expense, but keep it on the low side. And a Mont Blanc pen? Why not, but don't try to write one off every year.

Keep in mind that the IRS might question some of these expenses, but they are quite legitimate. The more money your corporation earns, the more glamorous your business or profession is, and the more you do business in your office, the more reasonable it is for your corporation to have and maintain a certain "standard of living." I'm not advocating corporate yachts or planes—simply small touches to make your work more pleasant, productive, and profitable.

DEPRECIATION AND RECAPTURE

Sometimes, however, it makes good business sense to recapture—or "give back"—some of your depreciation gains. This is a good place to differentiate between *realization* and *recognition* of a gain or loss. Realization is an *economic* concept; recognition, a *tax* concept. It's as though you owned 100 shares of IBM. You might *realize* a paper profit or loss every day, with each fluctuation of the stock price. You would *recognize* that profit or loss only when you actually sold the stock. In the case of depreciable property, you recognize any profit or loss when you sell, dispose of, junk, or lose the asset.

Let's take the case of a personal computer that your corporation has completely depreciated. Your corporation sells it for $1,000. Your recognized profit is $1,000 – $0 adjusted cost basis), which is taxed as *ordinary income*. If your corporation is in the 15 percent federal income-tax bracket, the tax on the sale of your PC is $150. Besides any actual business benefits and increases in productivity you've achieved through your PC, you've received substantial tax benefits: the depreciated cost plus a cash profit of $850 ($1,000 sale price – $150 federal income tax) that you wouldn't have received if your corporation had not bought the computer and placed it in service.

What if you sell your asset before its depreciable life is over? Whether you have a gain or a loss—and how they are taxed—will depend on the difference between the price you sell it for and your adjusted cost basis.

Let's take the business car your corporation bought for $10,000 this year at a police or U.S. Treasury auction. You plan to sell it next year, after having written off $2,560 in depreciation. The adjusted cost basis of the car is $7,440.

(1) You sell the car for $7,400. Your corporation has an ordinary loss of $40 ($7,440 – $7,400). There is no recapture of depreciation.

(2) You sell the car for $7,440. Obviously, your corporation has no gain or loss.

(3) You sell the car for $8,000. Your corporation has an ordinary gain of $560 ($8,000 – $7,440) because $560 of depreciation was recaptured.

(4) You sell the car for $11,000—not unlikely for a car picked up at auction. Your corporation has a profit of $3,560 ($11,000 – $7,440). Of that $3,560, your corporation must first recapture its depreciation, so $2,560 is treated as ordinary income. The remaining $1,000 is treated as a long-term capital gain if gains exceed losses.

This is a good place to discuss treatment of long-term capital gains. At press time, the most likely legislation to be passed had your corporation's capital-gains rate calculated as 70 percent of its ordinary-income rate:

Normal Tax Bracket	Capital-Gains Rate
15%	10.5%
25	17.5
34	23.8

While how long your corporation has held the asset will affect the depreciation you have received and the price for which you can sell the asset, what's crucial is not how long your corporation has held the asset, but whether it has been sold at a profit or loss, based on the adjusted cost basis. Here's a simple working formula:

Total depreciation = potential recapture
Selling price − adjusted cost basis = profit or loss
If you have sold the asset at a loss, it's an ordinary loss.
If you have sold the asset at a profit, is the profit greater or less than the potential recapture?
If it is less, the amount of profit is treated as a recapture of depreciation and is treated as an ordinary gain (Example 3 above).
If it is greater, the amount of potential recapture is treated as an ordinary gain; the remaining profit is a long-term capital gain (if it exceeds capital losses) and receives favorable tax treatment (Example 4 above).

In putting new equipment into service, your corporation gains an additional advantage, based on the present value of money. Just as a dollar today is worth more than a dollar next year, so is a dollar in depreciation or other deductions worth more today than next year. Remember all these benefits when you are considering buying equipment for your corporation—especially toward year-end, when buying that equipment and placing it in service even in late December can provide first-year §179 deductions for the entire year, as long as you have been incorporated since January 1.

CHOOSING YOUR DEPRECIATION STRATEGY

If your corporation is going to have lots of income, take the largest deduction possible and *reduce your income immediately.*
Other factors to consider:

- Your corporation's present and future tax brackets
- The present value of money
- Present and future interest/inflation rate projections
- Whether you plan to dispose of the asset before its benefits have been earned. If you are planning to—or think you might—you are generally better off deducting as much of the asset as you can ($10,000 in 1991), rather than taking the MACRS depreciation, because of the time value of money.
- Whether you think your corporation's use of the asset will increase or decline. Remember that if your corporation's business or professional use will decline, your corporation might recapture a portion of the depreciation from the preceding year. Thus, if you use the asset for

business 30 percent this year and 80 percent next year, you might be better off deferring its purchase to next year in order to take advantage of MACRS, which your 30 percent business use would preclude your using this year.

Use the worksheets on the following pages to calculate how buying corporate assets and expensing or depreciating them can benefit your corporation and save it thousands of tax dollars every year:

ASSET #1

Asset to be acquired	_____
Cost	_____
Class life (see pp. 40–41)	_____-year property
§179 deduction?	
(up to a maximum of $10,000)	_____
Depreciation method	
(MACRS, straight-line, auto)	_____
Depreciable base	_____
Year 1 depreciation	_____
Year 2 "	_____
Year 3 "	_____
Year 4 "	_____
Year 5 "	_____
Year 6 "	_____
Year 7 "	_____
Year 8 "	_____
Year 9 "	_____
Year 10 "	_____
Year 11 "	_____

ASSET #2

Asset to be acquired	_____
Cost	_____
Class life (see pp. 40–41)	_____-year property
§179 deduction?	
(up to a maximum of $10,000)	_____
Depreciation method	
(MACRS, straight-line, auto)	_____
Depreciable base	_____
Year 1 depreciation	_____
Year 2 "	_____
Year 3 "	_____
Year 4 "	_____
Year 5 "	_____
Year 6 "	_____
Year 7 "	_____
Year 8 "	_____
Year 9 "	_____
Year 10 "	_____
Year 11 "	_____

5

How to Profit from Leasing

Just a few years ago, leasing created enormous tax incentives. You and your spouse could give one of your kids $20,000 as a nontaxable gift to establish a Clifford trust. The trust could then buy equipment you needed and lease the equipment to your corporation at a juicy profit—say, $500 a month, $6,000 a year, $30,000 over the equipment's five-year life. And how much income tax would your kid pay on that $30,000? *Zero.*

Those glorious goodies are gone. Clifford trusts, which lost their tax benefits with the advent of the "kiddie tax," have been destroyed. Leasing has lost its tax attractiveness, but its economic attractiveness remains.

No matter what the asset, some corporate owners prefer to buy and some to lease—just as some people prefer to pay cash and some to use credit cards. It's generally wiser, however, to lease those assets whose design or technological life is short and thereby to avoid the stigma or problems of obsolescence. As a corporate head, it may be good business strategy to drive a new car. And just think of all the premature computer buyers of 1987 who are sitting with obsolete equipment they'd love to dump—but can't afford to!

This is a good place to examine the advantages and disadvantages of leasing versus buying:

LEASING

Advantages
- Deductibility of payments (except car payments, which are subject to special rules)

- Cash-flow preservation
- Ability to keep abreast of state-of-the-art technology
- Financing arranged
- Simplicity of setting up lease
- Minimal recordkeeping
- No risks of ownership—e.g., breakdown or repossession of asset
- Ability to walk away when lease expires

Disadvantages
- No depreciation
- No ownership of asset at expiration of lease without further payment
- No possible appreciation

BUYING

Advantages
- Depreciation
- Deductions for maintenance, repairs
- Possible appreciation of asset and profit when it is sold

Disadvantages
- Large cash outflow
- Financing may be difficult or expensive
- Risks of ownership—e.g., repairs to asset, possible repossession
- Obsolescence of asset
- Complicated recordkeeping
- Possible depreciation recapture if asset is sold

WHAT YOU GET WHEN YOU LEASE

A lease is a contract under which your corporation (the lessee) obtains use of an asset for a specified period of time, in exchange for a sum of money. For example, your corporation might negotiate a two-year lease on a new car, with monthly payments of $700. Depending on the terms of the lease, insurance and repairs might be included in the package, and your corporation might be able to walk away from the car upon expiration of the lease.

Sounds pretty straightforward, doesn't it? Nevertheless, there are pitfalls.

LEASING PITFALLS

Beware of lease agreements containing language that states "the car must be returned in mint condition." That's virtually impossible in large cities. Also, beware of leases that require enormous balloon payments.

And be aware that the car "lemon law" does not apply to cars used by businesses.

Sometimes the lessor would rather look like a seller for tax purposes: He wants to call your lease a sale so that he can take the gain or loss this year rather than spread it out over the life of the lease. You, on the other hand, want a lease. Your corporation doesn't want to depreciate the gizmo, it wants to write off payments as rent.

To satisfy both parties, some creative types have drawn up some very ambiguous-looking documents. Some contracts are titled "Sale of Gizmo," but the language in the body of the document refers only to the *lease*.

Beware! As far as the IRS is concerned, the deal is either a sale or a lease. Advantageous as it may be for the owner to call the deal a sale and your corporation to call it a lease, such a construction is strictly illegal. If you want the tax benefits of deducting your lease payments as your corporation makes them, make sure that the structure and language of the contract indicate *throughout* that it is indeed a *lease*.

Here are some indications that although you are calling the contract a lease, it is really a sale:

You lease the asset for a period of time that is around 90 percent or more of its useful life, and/or *you get to keep the asset at the end of the lease, or to buy it for a pittance*. No matter what the language surrounding the terms of payment of the lease, the IRS can construe the contract as a sale because you will get the property back at the end of the lease, or you will get to buy it at a bargain price.

IBM was famous for this strategy. It would rent you an electronic typewriter for three years. Then you would give IBM $1 and you would "buy" the typewriter. The IRS took the position that the contract was really a sale, not a lease.

Similarly, *if the value of the lease payments discounted for present value is equal to at least 90 percent of the fair market value of the asset at the inception of the lease,* the IRS can hold that the contract is probably a sale, rather than a lease.

If your contract is truly a lease, you can deduct the rental payments; but if it is a sale disguised as a lease, the rental payments will be subject to the depreciation rules.

One major test of a true lease is your ability to lease the asset for just one year, and to have the freedom to walk away from the lease and the asset at the end of the year, or to renegotiate the lease for another year.

LEASING CHECKLIST

☐ You, the lessee, will have not only the possession, but also the use of the lessor's property in exchange for your periodic payments of rent and any other agreed-upon charges—e.g., for a service contract.

☐ To avoid characterization of the lease as a sale, make sure that the term of the lease is shorter than the property's economic or useful life. Such short-term leases are rarely attacked by the IRS as installment sales, cast in the form of leases.

☐ Your lease should require little or no money down; it should be similar to 100 percent financing.

☐ Because rent obligations generally do not appear on the lessee's balance sheet as a liability, equipment may be leased frequently without violating your corporation's capital budget restrictions (if any).

☐ Check the costs of your lease. Leasing should be a less expensive way of obtaining the use of the equipment or property.

If you are leasing equipment patented by the lessor, make sure that the lessor will be responsible for inspecting, repairing , maintaining, and servicing the equipment. You will benefit from reduced paperwork—you won't need separate maintenance and insurance contracts. You will have reduced liability for loss or damage to the equipment and increased negotiating leverage if the lessor does not maintain the equipment properly.

SAMPLE LEASE

The sample lease shown below is a flat-rate lease, one of the most traditional forms of lease. It is most suitable for equipment that is not patented or high-tech. You, the lessee, pay a flat monthly payment and agree to (a) maintain the leased property at your own expense; (b) pay for repairs and replacement parts when necessary, and (c) pay insurance premiums and other expenses related to the use or operation of the property. *The lessor assumes the entire risk of loss of the equipment's economic value.*

LEASE

AGREEMENT made March 15, 1991 between Megacorp Equipment Company, Inc., a New York corporation having its principal place of business at 512 Fifth Avenue, New York, New York (the "Lessor"), and Just Desserts, Inc., a New York corporation having its principal place of business at 79 Madison Avenue, New York, New York (the "Lessee").

The Lessor has delivered to the Lessee at its office located at 79 Madison Avenue, New York, New York, the following articles of office equipment (the "Equipment"):
[Insert description]
all of which is to be used by the Lessee only at the office maintained by him at that address.

It is therefore agreed:

1. *Lease of equipment.* The Lessor leases to the Lessee, and the Lessee rents from the Lessor, the Equipment for a term of two years commencing April 1, 1991.

2. *Rental.* The Lessee shall pay to the Lessor as rent for the use of the Equipment, $500 per month, payable on the first day of each month, the first payment to be made upon the execution of the lease. Should the rent or any part thereof be at any time unpaid, the Lessee shall pay to the Lessor interest on such arrears at the rate of 12 percent per annum from the date of default until the arrears shall be paid, together with all reasonable collection charges and expenses. These charges shall be in addition to all other remedies at law or in equity, which the Lessor may have against the Lessee for default in the payment of rent.

3. *Ownership and use.* (a) The Equipment shall at all times be the sole and exclusive property of the Lessor. The Lessee shall have no rights or property interest in the leased property, except for the right to use it in the normal operation of the office maintained by the Lessee at the address set forth above.

(a) The Equipment is and shall remain the personal property even if installed in or attached to real property. The Lessor shall be permitted to display notice of its ownership on each article of Equipment by means of a suitable stencil, label, or plaque affixed thereto. The Lessee shall promptly notify the Lessor if any stencil, label, or plaque becomes damaged or illegible, and shall permit access to the leased property by the Lessor or its agents to repair or replace any damaged or illegible item.

(b) The Lessee shall keep the Equipment at all times free and clear from all claims, levies, liens, encumbrances, and process. The Lessee shall give the Lessor immediate notice of any such attachment or other judicial process affecting any article of Equipment leased hereunder.

(c) The Lessee shall not pledge, lend, create a security interest in, sublet, or part with possession of the Equipment or any part thereof or attempt in any other manner to dispose of the Equipment, or remove the Equipment or any part thereof, without the Lessor's permission, from the Lessee's branch office at the address set forth above.

(d) The Lessee shall cause the Equipment to be operated, in accordance with the applicable vendor's or manufacturer's manual of instructions, by competent and qualified personnel.

4. *Repairs and replacements.* The Lessee shall keep the Equipment in good condition and, at its own cost and expense, make all repairs and replacements necessary for its preservation. All such replacements shall immediately become the property of the Lessor.

5. *Insurance.* The Lessee, at its own cost and expense, shall insure the Equipment against burglary, theft, fire, and vandalism in the amount of $10,000 and obtain public liability insurance with minimum limits of $100,000/$300,000 for bodily injury and $25,000 for property damage in such form and with such insurance companies as shall be satisfactory to the Lessor. All insurance policies shall name both the Lessee and the Lessor as insureds and copies of the policies and the receipts for the payment of premiums shall be furnished to the Lessor upon demand. Each damage policy shall provide for payment of all losses directly to the Lessor. Each liability policy shall provide that all losses be paid on behalf of the Lessee and the Lessor as their respective interests appear.

6. *Indemnity.* The Lessee assumes liability for and shall indemnify and hold harmless the Lessor, its agents, and servants from and against all losses, damages,

penalties, claims, actions, suits, costs, expenses, and disbursements, including legal expenses of any kind and nature imposed upon, incurred by, or asserted against the Lessor in any way relating to or arising out of this lease or of the use of the Equipment. The indemnities contained in this Section shall continue in full force and effect, notwithstanding the termination of this lease.

7. *Inspection.* Lessor's agents may, at any time, enter the Lessee's premises for the purpose of inspecting the Equipment and the manner in which it is being used.

8. *Return.* At the end of the term of this lease, the Lessee shall at its own expense return the Equipment to the Lessor at the Lessor's place of business in as good condition as when received, reasonable wear and tear excepted.

9. *Liability for damage.* The Lessee shall be responsible for any damage to the Equipment while in his possession, and shall pay to the Lessor the value of so much of the Equipment, or any part thereof, as may be damaged or destroyed. Upon receipt of such payment, the Lessor shall, to the extent of the amount paid, assign to the Lessee any rights it may have with respect to the damaged or destroyed article of Equipment under any insurance, together with all of the Lessor's right, title, and interest in the article of Equipment.

10. *Breach.* The Lessor may terminate this lease, without notice or demand, if any of the following events shall occur: (a) upon default in the payment of any installment of rent; (b) upon a breach of any other condition of this lease to be performed or observed by the Lessee; (c) if during the term of this lease bankruptcy or insolvency proceedings are commenced by or against the Lessee; (d) if a receiver is appointed for the Lessee's business; or (e) if the Lessee discontinues business at the office address set forth above. Such termination, however, shall not release the Lessee from the payment of damages sustained by the Lessor. If upon any termination of this lease the Lessee fails or refuses forthwith to deliver the Equipment to the Lessor, the Lessor may enter the Lessee's premises, or any other premises where the Equipment may be found, forcibly if necessary, and take possession of and remove the Equipment without legal process. The Lessee releases any claim or right of action for trespass or damages caused by reason of such entry and removal; nor shall the Lessor be prejudiced from pursuing all other remedies to which it otherwise might be entitled on account of arrears of rent or breach of any other conditions of this lease.

11. *Entire agreement.* This agreement supersedes all agreements previously made between the Lessor and the Lessee relating to its subject matter. There are no other understandings or agreements between them.

12. *Notices.* All notices or other documents under this lease shall be in writing and delivered personally or mailed by certified mail, postage prepaid, addressed to the parties at their last known addresses.

13. *Non-waiver.* No delay or failure by either party to exercise any right under this agreement, and no partial or single exercise of that right, shall constitute a waiver of that or any other right, unless otherwise expressly provided herein.

14. *Headings.* Headings in this lease are for convenience only and shall not be used to interpret or construe its provisions.

15. *Governing law.* This agreement shall be construed in accordance with and governed by the laws of the State of New York.

16. *Counterparts.* This lease may be executed in two or more counterparts, each of which shall be deemed an original but all of which together shall constitute one and the same instrument.

17. *Binding effect*. The provisions of this agreement shall be binding upon and inure to the benefit of the Lessor and the Lessee and their respective legal representatives, successors, and assigns.

In witness whereof the parties have executed this agreement.

Corporate Seal   Megacorp Equipment Company, Inc.

Attest: _____   by _____
                     Secretary   President

Corporate Seal   Just Desserts, Inc.

Attest: _____   By _____
                     Secretary   President

6

How to Profit from a Net Operating Loss and from Tax Credits

Profiting from tax credits sounds logical, but profiting from a loss? It sounds paradoxical, doesn't it? These losses are actually good for your corporation. They offset past and future profits and even let you collect refunds from the IRS!

WHAT IS A NET OPERATING LOSS?

Generally, a net operating loss is the excess of deductible business expenses over gross income from all sources. For example, if your corporation had gross income of $40,000 and deductible business expenses of $45,000, it would have a net operating loss of $5,000. Unlike individuals, corporations do not calculate adjusted gross income and then net income.

HOW YOUR CORPORATION GETS A NET OPERATING LOSS

Your corporation can wind up with a net operating loss in its first year simply from having heavier expenses in that year. Many small corporations do.

Or it can just have a bad year.

Very often, though, your corporation can find itself with a net operating loss because it has invested in equipment that will pay off handsomely in future years.

Suppose your corporation had net income of $40,000. It paid you a salary of $30,000 and contributed $7,500 to your defined-contribution pension plan, leaving net income of $2,500. And then it bought a computer for $5,000, which you expensed. Your corporation now has a net operating loss of $2,500. Does your loss mean that you and your corporation are failures? Of course not! It means that you have probably made a wise business decision that will help build long-term profits. Meanwhile, your corporation can enjoy juicy tax write-offs.

As explained in Chapter 4, your corporation can carry this loss back three years and then forward 15 years. Moreover, your corporation may benefit from a stream of losses created by this purchase. There's a strong argument that if your corporation had a net operating loss from depreciation in Year 1, it may have net operating losses in Years 2 and 3 or in Years 2–5 simply because the amount of depreciation on that asset—if it costs more than $12,000 and must be depreciated as well as expensed—may be even higher in those years.

HOW TO USE YOUR NET OPERATING LOSS

First check whether your corporation is permitted to use the net operating loss. Only C corporations can. Subchapter S corporations are not permitted to use a net operating loss because all losses automatically flow through to the corporation's shareholder(s).

(For more on Subchapter S corporations, see Chapter 2, "How to Choose Between a General Business Corporation and a Subchapter S Corporation" and Chapter 8, "How to Profit Even More from Your Subchapter S Corporation.")

Next, calculate your net operating loss, using this general formula:

Net operating loss = Excess of deductions over income from trade or business

Example: $40,000 income

$20,000	salary
10,000	expense
12,000	MACRS depreciation
$42,000	

Net operating loss =
$42,000–$40,000 = $2,000

Note: Losses must come from *operations.* Capital losses—from investments—are not net operating losses and are treated differently.

As mentioned earlier, first apply your net operating loss to any taxable income from three years ago—even if that year may have lasted only four months because it was the year in which you incorporated. (Start-up expenses, however, must be amortized over 60 months.) You must recompute that year's income because a net operating loss is a deduction, not a credit.

You may use the net operating loss to reduce taxable income to $0. What happens if you had tax credits for that year? You've lost them for that year, but you can use them in another year.

Let's see how this would work:

In Year 1, your corporation had income of $50,000, a tax liability of $7,500, and a targeted-jobs credit of $7,500. After applying the $7,500 credit against the tax, your corporation owed $0.

Three years from now, your corporation has a net operating loss of $10,000. It's carried back to Year 1 and applied as a deduction. Your corporate income is $40,000 ($50,000 – $10,000). If we assume that the tax liability becomes $6,000 and the $7,500 targeted-jobs credit is applied, you have to carry the remaining $1,500 credit into the next tax year.

But what if that targeted-jobs credit was a carryover and Year 1 was the last year of the carryover? No problem—you won't lose it. In that case, you can elect to not carry back, but only carry forward your net operating loss—to Year 5 and beyond.

Let your expiration dates for net operating losses and targeted-jobs credits dictate your strategy. For example, suppose that your corporate income pattern looks like this:

Year 1	Net operating loss
Year 2	Profit
Year 3	Net operating loss

Which net operating loss do you use? *Always use the oldest first.* It's simply common sense; your Year 1 loss will expire before the Year 3 loss. Remember that you can elect not to carry back a loss, but only to carry it forward, and that it will still last for 15 years.

MORE SOURCES OF POTENTIAL BENEFIT AND REFUNDS

Other sources of potential benefit and tax refunds are capital-loss carrybacks, JOBS credits, WIN (Work INcentive) credits, and their successor, the targeted-jobs credits. There's a hierarchy in the order in which your corporation should use them:

(1) The credits that will expire in the current year
(2) Capital-loss carryback—to the extent that it does not increase or produce a net operating loss in the tax year to which you carry it

(3) Targeted-jobs credits
(4) Alcohol fuels credit
(5) Research credit
(6) Former WIN credit
(7) Other credits

Example: Your company has a $7,500 targeted-jobs credit and an old $2,500 research credit. Your corporation income tax is $5,000. If neither credit expires this year, you use $5,000 of your company's targeted-jobs credit and are left with a $2,500 targeted-jobs credit and a $2,500 research credit to use in future years. If the research credit were due to expire this year, your corporation would use it first, followed by $2,500 of the targeted-jobs credit. leaving a $5,000 targeted-jobs credit to be used in the future. (The Tax Reform Act of 1984 lumped together many of these credits as a "general business credit.")

HOW TO GET YOUR REFUND

If you know that your corporation will have a net operating loss, you can file the very short and simple IRS Form 1139, "Corporation Application for Tentative Refund," shown on the next page. It saves on paperwork and gets your corporation a quick refund. The IRS should send you a check within six weeks, and you'll surely be able to use the cash in your corporation.

Form **1139** — Corporation Application for Tentative Refund

Rev. November 1987)
(See Instruction D for When To File)

Department of the Treasury
nternal Revenue Service

Do Not Attach to Your Income Tax Return—Mail in a Separate Envelope

OMB No. 1545-0582
Expires 11-30-90

Name — EASY, INC

Employer identification number — 00-0000000

Number and street — 123 MARKET STREET

Date of incorporation — 1/1/77

City or town, state, and ZIP code — SAN FRANCISCO, CA 94103

Telephone no. (optional) — (   )

1. This application is filed to carryback:
   (a) Net operating loss (attach computation) . . . $ 10,000
   (b) Net capital loss (attach computation) . . . $ —
   (c) Unused general business credit . . . $

2. Return for year of loss, unused credit, or overpayment under section 1341(b)(1)
   (a) Tax year ended ►
   (b) Date filed ► 3/15/91
   (c) Service center where filed ► FRESNO, CA

3. If this application is for an unused credit created by another carryback, give year of the first carryback ►

4. Was a consolidated return filed for any year covered on this application? . . . ☐ Yes ☑ No
   If "Yes," identify the year and enter the employer identification number if different from above ►

5. If Form 1138 (Extension of Time for Payment of Taxes by a Corporation Expecting a Net Operating Loss Carryback) has been filed, was an extension of time granted for filing the return for the year of the net operating loss? . . . ☐ Yes ☑ No
   If "Yes," give date to which extension was granted ► .... Give date Form 1138 was filed ► ....
   Unpaid tax for which Form 1138 is in effect ►

6. If you changed your accounting period, give date permission to change was granted ► —

7. If this is an application of a dissolved corporation, give date of dissolution ► -----------

8. Have you filed a petition in Tax Court for the year or years to which the carryback is to be applied? . . . ☐ Yes ☑ No

9. Does this carryback include a loss or credit from a tax shelter required to be registered? . . . ☐ Yes ☑ No

Computation of Decrease in Tax	3rd preceding tax year ended ► 1987		2nd preceding tax year ended ► 1988		1st preceding tax year ended ► 1989	
(If no entry in 1(a) or (b), skip lines 10 to 14)	(a) Before carryback	(b) After carryback	(c) Before carryback	(d) After carryback	(e) Before carryback	(f) After carryback
10 Taxable income from tax return	50,000	40,000				
11 Capital gains offset by capital loss carryback		—				
12 Subtract line 11 from line 10	50,000	40,000				
13 Net operating loss deduction after carryback						
14 Taxable income (subtract line 13 from line 12)	50,000	40,000				
15 Income tax	7,500	6,000				
16 General business credit	—	—				
17 Other credits (identify)	—	—				
18 Total credits (add lines 16 and 17)	—	—				
19 Subtract line 18 from line 15	7,500	6,000				
20 Personal holding company tax (Sch. PH 1120)	—	—				
21 Recapture of investment credit	—	—				
22 Minimum tax	—	—				
23 Total tax liability (add lines 19 through 22)	7,500	6,000				
24 Enter amounts from line 23, cols. (b), (d) and (f)	6,000					
25 Decrease in tax (subtract line 24 from line 23)	1,500					

26. Overpayment of tax due to a claim of right adjustment under section 1341(b)(1)—attach computation . . .

Under penalties of perjury, I declare that I have examined this application, and accompanying schedules and statements, and to the best of my knowledge and belief they are true, correct, and complete.

Date _____
Signature of officer _____
Title — PRESIDENT
Date ►

Preparer other than taxpayer (name and address) ►

Instructions

(Section references are to the Internal Revenue Code.)

Paperwork Reduction Act Notice.—We ask for this information to carry out the Internal Revenue laws of the United States. We need it to ensure that taxpayers are complying with these laws and to allow us to figure and collect the right amount of tax. You are required to give us this information.

A. Purpose of Form.—If you are a corporation (other than an S corporation), use Form 1139 to apply for:

● A quick refund of taxes from carryback of a net operating loss, net capital loss, or unused general business credit.

● A quick refund of taxes from an overpayment of tax due to a claim of right adjustment under section 1341(b)(1).

Note: You may elect to carryover a net operating loss instead of first carrying it back by attaching a statement to that effect on a return filed on time (including any extensions) for the year of the loss. Once you make such an election, it is irrevocable for that tax year. The carryover is limited to 15 years, whether or not you first carry it back.

If your refund for any carryback year is one million dollars or more, you may elect to

7

How to Juggle Your Fiscal Year for Minimum Taxes

Should a one-person or mom-and-pop corporation go to the trouble and possible expense of using a fiscal year rather than a calendar year? Absolutely! This strategy can defer thousands of tax dollars a year. Although it's certainly easier and more mechanical to run a small corporation on a calendar-year basis, there are substantial advantages to choosing a fiscal year that ends in March, April, or even January. This chapter will discuss those advantages and show you how to apply for—and obtain— IRS approval for your choice of fiscal year and will detail the tax savings that result from switching to fiscal-year accounting.

By deferring tax payments, your corporation can make money through:

• The interest it receives by putting those deferred taxes to work as time deposits
• The reduction of the actual value of the payments by any inflation factors

The second feature is usually called "the time value of money" and means simply that $1 today is worth more than $1 tomorrow or a year from now. The rate of inflation—especially over the long term—is a major factor; the cost of missed opportunity is minor but significant.

The accrual system of accounting is one way to defer taxes.

CASH/ACCRUAL

You already know the *cash system;* we all use it in our personal finances. When you actually *receive* the money, you declare it as income. When you actually *pay out* money, you deduct it.

The *accrual system* is a little more complicated. It focuses on when *you are owed* the money—not when you receive it, and when *you owe* the money, not when you actually pay it. Receivables count as income, and accounts payable count as deductions, even though your corporation may not have received or spent any money.

The potential danger of the accrual system is that if you sign a contract for $100,000 to be paid next year, your corporation must recognize the $100,000 now—even though it won't receive a penny until next year.

The beauty of the accrual system is its expense side. As long as you know that your corporation will have a certain expense at some point in the future, *you can write it off immediately*. Rent, leasing, and interest payments, however, can be deducted only one year in advance. Otherwise, claims the IRS, you might be tempted to write off your corporation's twenty-year lease all in the first year.

The Tax Reform Act of 1984 tightened the accrual rule to defer deductions until "economic performance" occurs—e.g., when property or services are provided or used—in order to limit the extent by which a full deduction today for an amount to be paid in the future will overstate the true value of the expense. According to the Big Six accounting firm of Deloitte & Touche:

> Exceptions are also provided for certain recurring items, which may still be treated as incurred . . . in a year if (1) economic performance occurs within a reasonable time, but no longer than 8½ months after year-end, (2) such item is recurring in nature and is consistently accrued by the taxpayer in the year the all-events test is met, and (3) the item is either immaterial, or accrual in the year results in a better matching against the related income. Treatment on the financial statements will be a factor in measuring materiality and matching.

Given these limitations of the cash/accrual game, it may be much easier to achieve the same result of deferring taxes—without the hazard of having to declare corporate income before it is received—simply by choosing a fiscal year other than the calendar year. By doing so, you will combine the advantages of juggling income with the simplicity of the cash method of accounting.

TAXABLE YEARS

There are three types of taxable years:

(1) The calendar year, which ends on December 31
(2) The 52/53-week year, which always ends on the same day of the week—e.g., the last Saturday in January—and is used primarily by retailers
(3) The fiscal year, which ends on the last day of any month from January to November

Under the calendar year, which is by far the most common method, your corporation files its tax return for the year ending December 31, 1991 on March 15, 1992. You file your individual income-tax return for the year ending December 31, 1991 on April 15, 1992. Obviously, it's more advantageous for your corporation and you to have different fiscal years so that your corporation can take its deductions for your salary and bonus in Year 1, while you don't have to declare this income from your corporation until Year 2. This one-year deferral can be extremely profitable.

CONGRESS MAKES IT TOUGHER

Naturally, Congress felt that corporate owner-employees' ability to defer the recognition of income from one calendar year to another by using timing differences between the individual's tax year (usually the calendar year) and the corporation's fiscal year was abusive. The owner-employees' creative tax planning generated a one-year-or-more rolling deferral of a portion of their income—usually a bonus paid *before the fiscal year-end* but *after the calendar year-end*. If their compensation (including bonus), deductions, and tax rates remained constant, their annual tax would not vary and they would enjoy a continuing deferral. If their bonuses were increased, the tax on that increase would also be deferred.

Accordingly, the Tax Reform Act of 1986 stopped this deferral by requiring most personal service corporations and S corporations to switch to a calendar year. Perhaps surprisingly, as a result of mass pressure by the accounting profession, the Revenue Act of 1987 permitted some S corporations and personal service corporations to retain their prior fiscal years and allowed others limited choices of fiscal years, although increased withholding payments may have to be made. Section 444 of the Revenue Act details the new rules.

Note: If the IRS gave your corporation written approval for a grandfathered fiscal year which results in a deferral of more than three months, your corporation may retain its current fiscal year without being subject to the limitations or payments compelled by Section 444.

STRATEGIES AND TACTICS

Clearly your maximum advantage will come from the widest spread between your corporation's fiscal year—e.g., January 31—and your individual taxpayer's calendar year, ending the preceding December 31. This choice gives you a free ride of 15½ months between your corporation's paying you your 1991 salary or year-end bonus in January 1992 and your not having to pay taxes on them until April 15, 1993.

But this strategy will work only for certain C corporations. To prevent S corporations from "playing the deferral float" to the maximum, the IRS will not permit them to elect a fiscal year that would create more than three months of deferral. They can still elect September 30, October 31, or November 30 fiscal years. In fact, any corporation may elect one of these fiscal years and enjoy up to a three-month deferral.

There are three major areas for owner-employees to explore with their tax professionals in order to see whether they may qualify for a fiscal year offering a deferral longer than three months:

1. *The 25 percent test* is the simplest stated, but may be the most difficult to conform to. It requires that 25 percent of your corporation's gross receipts are received consistently during the same two-month period for three consecutive years, immediately after which there is a lull in business activity. Christmas-tree farmers or gingerbread-house makers will have no difficulty meeting these requirements. However, other retailers might run into trouble because their level of business activity might remain high owing to postholiday sales.

2. *The "natural business year" test* is an accounting concept that is frequently accepted by the IRS even though your corporation may not meet the 25 percent test. In his article "How Can a Client Retain Its Fiscal Year After TRA '86" (*The Journal of Taxation,* December 1987), Virginia tax and business consultant D. Alden Newland points out that "[a]dopting a natural business year can result in some or all of the following advantages:

(1) Inventory counting and errors can be kept to a minimum.
(2) Accounts receivable/payable are low and can be verified more easily.
(3) There will be fewer adjusting journal entries because activities are low and the client's [your] personnel will have more time to get the accounting entries entered on the books.
(4) Year-end reports can be prepared more quickly.
(5) The audit will be more efficient since there will be time to talk with the client's [your] staff.
(6) Saving audit time will allow for increased time to look into internal controls, management services, and tax planning.
(7) The client [your corporation] should be more liquid, thus having a better annual report and credit rating.

(8) The report will be comparable to other reports in the industry (assuming all businesses in an industry will be on the same fiscal year).
(9) The client [your corporation] should find it easier to pay taxes because of liquidity factors discussed above.
(10) The accountant's overtime and costs will be reduced, thus reducing fees.
(11) Cash flow will be more evenly spread throughout the year."

3. *Issues raised by the "personal service corporation" definition.* The Tax Reform Act of 1986 defines a personal service corporation as "a corporation the principal activity of which is the performance of personal services that are substantially performed by employee-owners." According to the IRS, those services are substantial if the total time spent by owner-employees in performing them is *10 percent or more of the total time spent by all employees (including owner-employees) in performing those services.*

Clearly, most of us can't win on that "substantial performance" issue.

But you may be able to win on the issue of precisely what "personal services" are. On the one hand, the Tax Reform Act of 1986 states that the services Congress had in mind are "health, law, engineering, architecture, accounting, actuarial science, performing arts, and consulting." Nevertheless, Newland points out that "the net created by the present personal service corporation legislation is broad and catches many corporations that have nothing to do with professional service corporations, the perceived abusers of pre-Tax Reform Act '86 law."

Perhaps the best strategy is to emphasize the *product* that may accompany your corporate services—especially if some of those services might remotely be defined as consulting. For example, the IRS might want to pigeonhole you as a financial consultant. But you could prove that you are a financial *planner,* and that the fees paid by your clients are for the *written plans and documents* that your corporation prepares for them. In the case of an insurance agency doing estate planning but not charging separately for these services, show that your agency is selling a product— the insurance policy. Any bit of consulting is simply tangential to selling the policy.

Strategy: Word the "nature of business or principal source of income" on Form 1128 line 3 (pp.77–79) to emphasize your product. Taking this approach on a filed document will strengthen your position with the IRS.

Even several years after the Tax Reform Act of 1986 and the Revenue Act of 1987, many of these issues are still being negotiated and resolved. As a general piece of advice, try to show that your corporation provides a product and therefore is not a personal service corporation in order to increase your opportunity to choose a favorable fiscal year with the maximum deferral possible. If large amounts of income are involved, consulting your tax adviser will be worthwhile.

Since, for most entrepreneurs, the key to IRS approval of your fiscal year is having at least 25 percent of your corporate income fall into two consecutive months—e.g., December and January—here's a good argument to use:

"Most of my corporation's clients pay in January for work that was done in the preceding calendar year. More than one-third of my corporation's income is received in December and January. It makes both economic and tax sense not to separate the time period in which the income was received from the time period in which the work was done." Note that this reason appears in abbreviated form on page 3 of IRS Form 1128, "Application for Change in Accounting Period," shown on pages 77–79.

This logical argument should convince the IRS. Just make sure that your up-to-date books prove your point if the IRS ever audits your corporation.

Although the January fiscal year is the most profitable for you as an individual, it may be more prudent for your corporation to select a March 31 fiscal year and file its corporate income-tax returns on June 15. That three-month gap between December and March can be extremely valuable for shrewd tax planning because you, as an individual, have closed your books for the year, but your corporation has not. Any income your corporation pays you in January does not get reported by you until the following year. If your corporation pays you $50,000 as salary or bonus in January 1992, it takes a $50,000 deduction for its fiscal year ending March 31, 1992 and files its taxes on June 15, 1992. You have that income of $50,000 for 11 months of 1992 but don't report it or have to pay taxes on it (aside from possible withholding requirements) until April 15, 1993.

Now let's enhance *your* revenue with this further strategy: Suppose that you take that $50,000 received in January 1992 and invest it in tax-free bonds on February 1. Assuming that they mature or that you sell them on April 15, 1993, when your income taxes fall due, you'll have received free use of $50,000 for 15½ months, which should produce tax-free income of at least $3,500.

In order to make the right choice, get good professional tax advice before you decide on the best, most appropriate, and safest fiscal year for your own corporation.

FISCAL YEAR FOR SUBCHAPTER S CORPORATIONS

As mentioned earlier in this chapter, if you have a Subchapter S corporation, you no longer have much flexibility in choosing a tax year. Your corporation must use a calendar year unless you have a clear, documented business reason for choosing another fiscal year. For example, if your corporation is in the Christmas-tree business, and most of its income is received in January for sales made in December, you have an excellent business reason for choosing a January fiscal year so that income and expenses fall in the same year.

Therefore, since income from your Subchapter S corporation is included in the shareholder income as of the end of your corporation's tax year, you and your fellow shareholders cannot defer reporting income from the corporation by electing a tax year for your corporation that ends after the tax year of the shareholder/taxpayer.

HOW TO MAKE THE SWITCH

If your corporation has always been on a calendar year and you wish to switch to a fiscal year, simply file IRS Form 1128 in triplicate (shown on pp. 77–79) with your 1120 or 1120A corporate income-tax return on the new filing date and treat the matter as a *fait accompli*.

In most cases, the IRS will grant your request within 6–8 weeks. However, if, by electing a new fiscal year, your corporation would have one very short year (e.g., from December 31, 1991 to January 31–March 31, 1992), or a large difference in the amount of your corporation's income by switching to the new fiscal year, the IRS may claim that the short period is a distortion and require that your corporation deduct only 10 percent of the difference each year over the next ten years in order to average out the difference over the long term.

MORE CASH/ACCURAL AND FISCAL/CALENDAR STRATEGIES

This cash/accrual strategy is a bit more baroque and complex than earlier strategies discussed in this chapter, but many owner-employees will find the extra manipulation of income and expense well worth their while.

Let's start simply. When your corporate year-end comes, says one savvy corporate head, "Lose any checks that come in in your desk drawer and don't deposit them for a couple of weeks. If there are any questions, say you went skiing and that the checks came in while you were away." (However, many tax advisers frown on this practice because technically you had constructive receipt of funds.)

Form **1128** (Rev. January 1989) Department of the Treasury Internal Revenue Service	**Application for Change in Accounting Period** ▶ **For Paperwork Reduction Act Notice, see page 1 of separate instructions.**	OMB No. 1545-0134 Expires 9-30-91

			Check one:
Name of applicant (if joint return is filed, also show your spouse s name) JUST DESSERTS, INC.	Identifying number (See Specific Instructions) 33-0000000		☐ Individual
Number and street (P.O. box number if mail is not delivered to street address) 123 MAIN STREET	Service Center where return will be filed FRESNO CA		☐ Partnership
City or town, state, and ZIP code LARKSPUR, CA 94939	Applicant's telephone number (415) 123-4567		☐ Estate ☐ Trust
Name of person to contact (see Specific Instructions)	Telephone number of contact person (415) 123-4567		☑ Corporation ☐ S Corporation ☐ Personal Service Corporation

DO NOT FILE FORM 1128 IF YOU MEET ANY OF THE EXCEPTIONS UNDER GENERAL INSTRUCTION B.

DO NOT CHANGE YOUR TAX YEAR UNTIL THE COMMISSIONER HAS APPROVED YOUR REQUEST.

Check one (continued):
☐ IC-DISC
☐ Cooperative (Sec. 1381(a))
☐ Tax-Exempt Organization
☐ Controlled Foreign Corp.
☐ FSC
☐ Foreign Corp.

SECTION A.—All Filers

1a Present tax year ends 12/31/91	1b Permission is requested to change to a tax year ending 1/31/92	1c Permission is requested to adopt a tax year ending

1d Permission is requested to retain a tax year ending (see items (e) and (f) in Exceptions under General Instruction B).

2 The tax year change or adoption will require a return for a short period beginning JANUARY 1, 1991 ending JANUARY 31, 1991

3 Nature of business or principal source of income
GOURMET COOKIES

4 What is your overall method of accounting? ☑ Cash receipts and disbursements ☐ Accrual
☐ Other (explain) ▶

	Yes	No
5 Are you an individual requesting a change from a fiscal year to a calendar year under Rev. Proc. 66-50, 1966-2 C.B. 1260? (If "Yes," file Form 1128 with the applicable Service Center.)		✓
6 In the last 6 years have you changed or requested permission to change your accounting period, your overall method of accounting or the accounting treatment of any item?		✓

If "Yes" and there was a ruling letter issued granting permission to make the change, attach a copy. If a copy of the ruling letter is not available, explain and give the date permission was granted. If a ruling letter was not required, e.g., corporations using Rev. Proc. 84-34, 1984-1 C.B. 508, or Regulations section 1.442-1(c), explain the facts and give the date the change was implemented.

If a change in accounting period was granted within the last 6 years, explain in detail the unusual circumstances requiring this change.

	Yes	No
7 Do you have pending any accounting method, accounting period, ruling, or technical advice request in the National Office?		✓

If "Yes," attach a statement explaining the type of request (method, period, etc.) and the specific issues involved in each request.

8 Enter the taxable income* or (loss) for the 3 tax years immediately before the short period and for the short period. If necessary, estimate the amount for the short period.

Third preceding year	Second preceding year	First preceding year	Short period
$ N/A	$ N/A	$ 20,000	$ 7,500

*Individuals enter adjusted gross income. Partnerships and S corporations enter ordinary income. Section 501(c) organizations enter unrelated business taxable income.

	Yes	No
9 Are you a U.S. shareholder in a controlled foreign corporation (CFC)?		✓

If "Yes," attach a statement for each CFC stating the name, address, identifying number, tax year, your percentage of total combined voting power, and the amount of income included in your gross income under section 951 for the 3 tax years immediately before the short period and for the short period.

	Yes	No
10 Are you a member of a partnership, a beneficiary of a trust or estate, a shareholder of an S corporation, or a shareholder of an Interest Charge Domestic International Sales Corporation (IC-DISC) or a shareholder in a Foreign Sales Corporation (FSC)?		✓

If "Yes," attach a statement showing the name, address, identifying number, tax year, percentage of interest in capital and profits, or percentage of interest of each IC-DISC and the amount of income received from each partnership, trust, estate, S corporation, IC-DISC, or FSC for the first preceding year and the short period.

Form **1128** (Rev. 1-89)

Form 1128 (Rev. 1-89)   Page 2

SECTION A.—All Filers (continued)

		Yes	No
11	Are you an unincorporated syndicate, group, pool, or joint venture that has elected, under the provisions of Regulations section 1.761-2(b), not to be treated as a partnership?.		✓
	If "Yes," provide a copy of the statement described in Regulations section 1.761-2(b). If no formal election was made, describe in detail why you are not considered a partnership for Federal income tax purposes.		
12 a	Are you an S corporation whose shareholders hold more than half of the shares of stock (as of the first day of the tax year to which the request relates) of the corporation and have: (1) the same tax year, or (2) are concurrently changing to the tax year that the corporation retains or changes to per Section A, item 1b or 1d?		✓
b	Is the corporation described in section 3.01(2) of Revenue Procedure 87-32?		✓
13 a	Are you a partnership, S corporation, or a personal service corporation that is retaining or changing to a tax year that coincides with its natural business year as defined in section 4.01(1) of Rev. Proc. 87-32 and as verified by its satisfaction of the requirements of section 4.02(1) of Rev. Proc. 87-32?		✓
b	If the partnership, S corporation, or personal service corporation is changing to a natural business year as defined in section 4.01(1), do you represent that such tax year results in less deferral of income to the partners or shareholders than your present tax year?.		✓
c	Is the partnership, S corporation, or personal service corporation described in section 3.01(2) of Rev. Proc. 87-32? (See General Instruction G. "Rev. Proc. 87-32" for necessary attachments)		✓
14	State the reasons for requesting the change. (Attach a separate sheet if you need more space.)		

BULK OF BUSINESS TAKES PLACE IN NOVEMBER AND DECEMBER, AND MOST OF
RELATED INCOME IS RECEIVED DURING THE FOLLOWING JANUARY.

....

....

....

....

....

SECTION B.—Partnerships N/A

1	Date business began. (See specific instructions for Section B.) ▶	
2	Is any partner applying for a corresponding change in accounting period?	
3	Attach a statement showing each partner's name, type of partner (e.g., individual, partnership, estate, trust, corporation, S corporation, IC-DISC, etc.), address, identifying number, tax year, the percentage of interest in capital and profits, and how the interest was acquired.	
4	Is any partner of this partnership a member of a personal service corporation as defined in Temporary Regulations section 1.441-4T(d)(1)?	
	If "Yes," attach a separate sheet providing the name, address, identifying number, tax year, percentage of interest in capital and profits, and the amount of income received from each personal service corporation for the first preceding year and the short period.	

SECTION C.—All Corporations

		Yes	No
1	Date of incorporation ▶ 1/2/90		
2	Is the change being requested by a subsidiary who became a member of an affiliated group to join with the parent corporation in the filing of a consolidated return for the short period?		✓
	If "Yes," DO NOT FILE THIS FORM. SEE "EXCEPTIONS" IN GENERAL INSTRUCTION B.		
3	Is the corporation a member of an affiliated group filing a consolidated return?		✓
	If "Yes," attach a statement showing (a) the name, address, identifying number used on the consolidated return, the tax year, and the Internal Revenue Service Center where the taxpayer files the return; and (b) the name, address, and identifying number of each member of the affiliated group. Designate the parent corporation and the taxable income (loss) of each member for the 3 years immediately before the short period and for the short period.		
4	Did the corporation pay any dividends to its shareholders during the short period?		✓
	If "Yes," furnish the following information:		
	(a) Taxable dividends	$	
	(b) Nontaxable dividends (explain how determined)	$	
5	Are you requesting a change for a corporation under Rev. Proc. 84-34? (If "Yes," file Form 1128 with the applicable Service Center.)		✓
6	If you are a personal service corporation, attach a statement showing each shareholder's name, address, identifying number, tax year, percentage of ownership, and type of entity (e.g., individual, partnership, corporation, etc.)		

Form 1128 (Rev 1-89)   Page 3

SECTION D.—S Corporations N/A

		Yes	No
1	Date of election ▶		
2	Attach a statement showing each shareholder's name, address, identifying number, tax year, percentage of ownership, and type of entity (e.g., individual, estate, trust, or qualified Subchapter S Trust as defined in section 1361(d)(3)).		
3	Has the newly electing S corporation filed **Form 2553**, Election by a Small Business Corporation, to adopt, retain, or change its accounting period? . . . . If "Yes," do not file this form.		

SECTION E.—Tax-Exempt Organizations N/A

1 Form of organization: ☐ Corporation   ☐ Trust   ☐ Other (specify) ▶

2 Date of organization ▶

3 Code section under which you are exempt ▶

4 Are you required to file an annual return on Form 990, 990-C, 990-PF, 990-T, 1120-H, or 1120-POL? . . . .

5 Date exemption was granted ▶ .... Attach a copy of the ruling letter granting exemption. If a copy of the letter is not available, attach explanation.

6 If a private foundation, is the foundation terminating its status under section 507? . . . .

7 Are you requesting a change for a tax-exempt organization under Rev. Proc. 85-58, 1985-2 C.B. 740, or Rev. Proc. 76-10, 1976-1 C.B. 548? (If "Yes," see instructions for Section E.) . . . .

SECTION F.—Interest Charge Domestic International Sales Corporations or Foreign Sales Corporations N/A

1 Date of election ▶

2 Attach a statement stating the name, address, identifying number, tax year, and the percentage of ownership and percentage of voting power of each shareholder.

SECTION G.—Controlled Foreign Corporation N/A

1 Enter the tax year that was used for tax purposes ▶

2 Attach a statement for each U.S. shareholder (as defined in section 951(b)) stating the name, address, identifying number, tax year, percentage of total combined voting power, and the amount of income included in the gross income under section 951 for the 3 tax years immediately before the short period and for the short period.

SIGNATURE—All Filers (See Specific Instructions)

Under penalties of perjury, I declare that I have examined this application, including accompanying schedules and statements, and to the best of my knowledge and belief it is true, correct, and complete. Declaration of preparer (other than applicant) is based on all information of which preparer has any knowledge.

JUST DESSERTS, INC.
Applicant's name

3/1/91
Date

Mary Smith
Signature

PRESIDENT
Title

MARY SMITH
Signing official's name (Please print or type)

Date

Signature of officer of the parent corporation, if applicable

Title

Signature of individual or firm (other than applicant) preparing the application

Date

Firm or preparer's name

This strategy can be elaborated on so that you become very creative with payables and receivables—say, every third year—if your corporation tends to get large chunks of income at the end of the year. Annual contract payments are a good example. Instead of declaring $60,000 income every year, your corporation may be able to declare nearly $0 one year and $120,000 the next. Because federal, state, and local corporate and personal income-tax rates will affect your structuring of how much money you want your corporation to receive or defer every year, no general strategy can be recommended. An aggressive accountant can be your corporation's best friend.

One way of creating those big swings in income is by having your corporation borrow large chunks of money for very short periods of time—say one to six months—perhaps just to offset unusually high income that your corporation looks as though it might earn this year. Such borrowing will not only let your corporation write off all the interest this year, but also will let your company look as though it has much more debt than it actually has, and correspondingly less income because of high interest payments.

Fiscal/calendar strategies take advantage of the fact that your corporation pays you in what is your Year 2 but your company's Year 1 because it is on a fiscal year while you are on a calendar year.

The simplest and most popular fiscal/calendar strategy even permits your corporation to deduct next year's pension-fund contribution as well as bonus before it pays them to the fund and to you. Your corporation's position is "We expect to pay our key employee a bonus at the end of our fiscal year, so we are deducting not only the amount of the bonus, but also the 25 percent defined-contribution pension money based on that bonus." (This strategy does not work with defined-benefit pension plans because their funding is not based on salaries and bonuses, but in most cases some partial contributions may still be made.)

Actually, it's a good idea for your corporation to contribute at least some of that pension money at the beginning of the year, on the grounds that its management (you) knows what your minimum salary will be that year. In that way, your pension fund is getting the use of that money for an additional 11 months or so, before the payment is actually due.

In fact, it's a great idea used alone! Why shouldn't your corporation take the position that, since it knows it will be paying you at least $50,000 this year, it will make a $12,500 defined-contribution payment in January, rather than waiting until December?

CAN YOU STILL PROFIT AFTER PAYING ESTIMATED TAXES?

At this point, critics may complain: "If you have to pay estimated taxes, what do you really gain from all this finagling?" Surprisingly, you *don't* have to pay estimated taxes as high as you might have thought.

Here is one key strategy for paying minimum estimated income taxes without being penalized by the IRS. It's most suitable for sole owner-employees of young corporations:

The withholding rules state that you need pay in—or have withheld—only as much as your last year's income-tax liability. *It doesn't matter how much more you make this year: you're still safe*—even if you win the lottery or pay yourself an enormous, but well-deserved, bonus. (If you were unemployed last year while setting up your corporation or had investment losses or other deductions that wiped out your income, play it safe and send the IRS $300–$500 anyway. Underwithholding penalties can be stiff.)

So, in Year 1, your corporation pays you a small salary. Year 2 is great. Your corporation pays you a generous salary and a bonus in the beginning of the year—but *after the first quarter*—e.g., on April 1. You pay estimated income taxes *based on last year's tiny salary,* plus an extra $300–$500 just to be on the safe side. In Year 3, your corporation pays you a modest salary again, as in Year 1, and you pay the basic estimated tax or withholding based on that year's salary. In Year 4, you repeat Year 2, paying withholding and estimated income taxes based on the unusually low Year 3 salary.

You can repeat this alternation of low-high-low-high salary/bonus as long as you like. Just remember that the size of your pension contribution will probably depend on your salary.

Will the IRS argue: "This strategy is a setup. We're going to audit your books"? It's remote and unlikely in a one-or two-person corporation. In fact, the probability of your small corporation's being audited by the IRS is far smaller than the probability of your unincorporated business or professional return's being audited by "Uncle."

And here's your counterargument: You can defend your salary strategy by showing that your corporation often has sales or chunks of income that come in all at once, so you pay yourself a bonus. Or, if you're a writer, artist, or entertainer, you might reverse the argument, showing that you might have a very good year, so that your corporation pays you a high salary plus bonus, followed by a year of burnout, in which you have to take it easy, so that your corporation pays you a much lower salary and no bonus.

8

How to Profit Even More from Your Subchapter S Corporation

Now that you know the basics of Subchapter S corporations, here are some more advanced strategies:

SALARY VS. INCOME

In an S corporation, you can decide whether to take out money as salary or as your share of corporate income. Unlike a C corporation, where dividends are taxed at both the corporate level (because your corporation cannot deduct them) and at the personal level, on your individual tax return, S corporation income flows through to the shareholders and is taxed only once, at their level.

Why do you want to pay yourself a salary, which is subject to high Social Security taxes? You may not want to, but you have to in order to make a pension-fund contribution. You must differentiate between your salary and your share of S corporation income. For example, if your share of your S corporation income is $100,000, you can declare $40,000 to be salary and $60,000 to be S corporation income, or any other reasonable combination that adds up to $100,000. The trade-off is that the higher your salary is, the greater your pension-fund contribution can be, but the higher your FICA tax will be (up to whatever maximum salary limit is in force).

On the other hand, in order to build your pension fund rapidly, you may choose a salary far above the Social Security tax limit—e.g., $72,000—because there is no difference in FICA tax deductions between a salary of $51,300 (the 1990 FICA maximum) and one of $72,000.

Harold Glassberg, senior partner of the Spring Valley, New York, CPA firm of Glassberg, Holden & Mermer, suggests an alternate strategy. To avoid paying a total of 15.3 percent in Social Security taxes (7.65 percent each deducted from your salary and matched by your S corporation), instead of taking $50,000 in salary take $20,000 in salary and $30,000 in S corporation dividends. You, the owner-employee, will save $4,590 ($30,000 × 15.3 percent) per year in Social Security taxes, based on 1990 rates.

> Owner-employees who utilize this strategy will also be able to put $2,000 per year into an IRA account. Higher-paid owner-employees will not be eligible for the IRA deduction.

Glassberg points out that owner-employees who choose a low salary should cover gaps in their Social Security coverage by increasing their life insurance and disability insurance coverage. "They will still come out ahead," he emphasizes.

> You can have it both ways. If you want to receive maximum Social Security benefits when you retire, pay yourself the maximum salary taxed by Social Security for the last five years that you work—e.g., age 60–65. *You need be on maximum salary for only those five years in order to collect maximum benefits.*

If your state, like Connecticut, Tennessee, and several others, does not tax salaries but does tax shareholder income, you will probably want to pay yourself more in salary and less in shareholder income to minimize your state income taxes.

WHAT I NEED TO DO TO IMPLEMENT THIS STRATEGY (such as: Calculate three or four salaries your corporation might pay you and the Social Security tax and pension contribution for each salary. Check whether your state taxes salaries or only shareholder income. Choose the optimum combination and plan

to pay yourself this salary and to make this contribution to your
pension fund. Set up a tax-deductible IRA, if you are entitled to.)

_____

_____

_____

ESTIMATED TAX SAVINGS: $_____

PASSIVE INCOME? NO PROBLEM

An S corporation can collect all the investment income its owner-
employees desire without being nailed as a personal holding company and
having to pay punitive taxes. But since income flows through to shareholders and is taxed at the same individual rates, why bother with the
extra layers of corporate paperwork necessary to set up and run an S
corporation?

The answer is simple: to create legitimate retirement plans, and to
offset any passive investment losses that the shareholders might have.

Consider executives in their midfifties who have been casualties of
"corporate downsizing"—for example, the 10,000 IBM employees fired in
1990. Many of them have some kind of investment portfolio and also
pension assets from their former employer that they could roll over into
their own shiny new pension plan, if they were savvy enough to incorporate.

Forming an S corporation lets them place their personal stockhold-
ings into an investment company which they can manage, much as they
had managed their investments in the past. *But here's the crucial difference:* this way they can be the owner-employees of that company,
*earning a salary and thus the right to keep on contributing to their
pension funds.* As individual investors, they had no such rights.

WHAT I NEED TO DO TO IMPLEMENT THIS STRATEGY
(such as: calculate the size of your investment portfolio, your
potential salary, the size of your pension fund and estimated
annual contributions.) _____

_____

ESTIMATED TAX SAVINGS: $_____

SHARING THE WEALTH

This strategy is similar to the one discussed in Chapter 18, "How to
Profit from Putting Your Relatives on the Payroll." It is one of the few that
works as well with an S corporation as with a C corporation.

By moving income around among the members of your family, you
can shift income from *your maximum bracket* (presently 33 percent) to

their minimum bracket (presently 15 percent). If your children are over the age of 14, any income they receive as shareholders of your S corporation is taxed at their own bracket—usually the minimum.

Similarly, if you are supporting your retired parents, you can use your S corporation shares to make gifts to them. In this way, you will be supporting them with pretax dollars (their share of income from your S corporation) rather than after-tax dollars: They are receiving income directly, without your getting the money, paying tax on it, and then giving them the remainder.

> Use a shareholders' agreement to make sure that your children or parents can't transfer their shares, except to you or your corporation. The agreement will prevent Great-aunt Helen, whom you can't stand, or your kids' friends, whom you don't even know, but who might win the stock in a poker game, from getting their mitts on the stock.
>
> Other effective strategies to include in the agreement are
>
> ☐ that your parents or children have to offer their stock first to the corporation
> • that no compensation will be paid for their shares for the first 15 years that they hold it.

WHAT I NEED TO DO TO IMPLEMENT THIS STRATEGY (such as: Calculate the amount of money your corporation considers switching to each relative, the amount of income tax the relative would pay, and the amount of income tax you would pay if you received those funds. _____ _____ _____ _____

ESTIMATED TAX SAVINGS: $_____

9

How to Avoid the Double Whammy in Switching from a C Corporation to a Subchapter S Corporation

WARNING:
DO NOT ATTEMPT TO SWITCH FROM A C CORPORATION TO A SUBCHAPTER S CORPORATION WITHOUT OBTAINING THE BEST TAX ADVICE YOU CAN FIND.

Converting your existing C corporation into an S corporation can provide significant tax advantages for its shareholder-employees. However, a potential "double whammy" exists for those C corporations which hold appreciated assets—usually real estate or securities. In response to a perceived abuse whereby C corporations would avoid a corporate-level tax on the disposition of appreciated assets by electing S corporation status just prior to the sale of those assets, the IRS enacted Internal Revenue Code §1374, which imposed a corporate-level tax on the "built-in gain" of appreciated assets sold within *10 years following the S corporation election*.

As a result, your assets would be taxed twice: at the corporate level, for a maximum of 34 percent, and then, when your S corporation sold them and distributed the profits to its shareholders, for a maximum marginal rate of 33 percent, for a total of 55.8 percent.

EXAMPLE: $100,000 profit on asset
                  × .34   corporate tax rate
              $ 34,000 corporate tax

              $ 66,000 net profit on asset
                  × .33   S corporation shareholder's tax rate
              $ 21,780 S corporation shareholder's tax

              $ 55,780 total tax on profit on asset

However, you can avoid the tax on built-in gains by offsetting them with losses. The rule is strict: The loss asset cannot have been contributed to the C corporation within two years of either the first tax year as an S corporation or the filing of the S corporation election, whichever is earlier. In this way, the IRS has severely limited the extent to which built-in gains can be offset by built-in unrealized losses.

To avoid the corporate-level tax on built-in gains, start planning now if you are considering switching from a C corporation to an S corporation and have substantial assets. *Specifically identify all assets* held by your C corporation as of the date you plan to make your S corporation election, and analyze the potential built-in gain or loss you would have if you sold the asset. Your list should look like this:

Asset	Date of Purchase	Cost	Fair Market Value	Gain or (Loss)
		$	$	$

The key issue is whether the asset has a gain or a loss as of the date of the S corporation election. If there is no gain as of that date, the asset can rise astronomically thereafter and your S corporation will not owe any tax on the gain.

Realize that your new S corporation does not have to sell the asset in order to have a built-in gain or loss. Therefore you do not have to sell a favorite piece of office equipment or furniture which has become obsolete and is worth very little money just so that you can declare a needed loss to offset the gain in another asset.

When you list your assets with built-in gains, there will doubtless be some that you don't think you will mind hanging onto for 10 years. Blue-chip stocks are a good example—expecially if they are paying high dividends. *But remember: When you switch to an S corporation, those dividends will no longer be 70 percent tax-free.*

Make a separate list of securities, if you like, and consider it separately from your other assets that have built-in gains or losses. You may be able to use certain options strategies—buying puts, for example—that will cushion your risk in keeping the stocks for such a long period of time without "stopping the clock" and wiping out their holding period.

Another strategy is to offset your built-in gains with your net operating losses (NOLs) and NOL carry-forwards. Here's where they can really come in handy and save you from double taxation. For a complete description of how to profit from your corporation's NOLs, please review Chapter 6, "How to Profit from a Net Operating Loss and from Tax Credits."

SUMMING UP

The best general advice I can give you in this complex but potentially profitable area is to keep things in perspective. Weigh the possible gains and losses over one, three, five, and ten years. Use a variety of scenarios; that's what spread sheets—or even pencil and paper—are for. I wouldn't let a built-in gain of $1,000–$10,000 stop me from switching from a C corporation to an S corporation. But I certainly would think twice and would have my accountant crunch numbers until they squeaked if I had a built-in gain of $25,000 or more.

10

How to Set Up *Your* Best Pension Fund

Because corporate owner-employees come in all ages and income levels, pension funds work best and most profitably when they are designed individually for the entrepreneurs and professionals who own and run their small corporations. Key variables include whether the corporation employs people other than the owner and his or her family, and how many years of service are available in which to fund retirement benefits.

For how to legally avoid covering your employees, see pp. 102–03.

Is setting up a pension fund complicated? Not with the step-by-step instructions and worksheets in this chapter. Is it time-consuming? Well, maybe a little, at the beginning, but no more so than is researching and shopping for your ideal car or vacation. Surely choosing your optimum pension fund will be more rewarding than either, and it will be able to provide you with many years of perfect cars and vacations.

IMPORTANT: If you want your S corporation to set up a pension fund for you, it will have to pay you a salary on which its pension-fund contribution will be based. (Any profits in excess of your salary can be paid to you as profits.)

89

IRAs, SEP/IRAs, AND 401(k)s

You've probably heard a lot about this pension-fund alphabet soup. Except for IRAs, which may be reinstated for the millions of us who lost our tax-deductible benefits in 1987, these plans do not provide benefits as attractive as those offered by defined-contribution and defined-benefit plans.

The SEP/IRA (Simplified Employee Pension) plan lets your company contribute up to 15 percent of employee compensation, up to a maximum of $30,000 per employee. While it's a very easy plan to set up and administer—there are no IRS or Department of Labor reporting requirements—the 15 percent/$30,000 maximum contribution won't give you as much as the 25 percent contribution of a defined-contribution plan or a possible $50,000+ contribution to a defined-benefit plan.

The 401(k) plan, in which you can set aside as much as 15 percent of your yearly compensation (a maximum of $7,979 in 1990), and to which your employer can make matching contributions, works best if you are *someone else's employee*. Only then do you actually benefit from your employer's contribution.

The most profitable strategy, therefore, is to choose between a defined-contribution pension plan and a defined-benefit pension plan.

DEFINED-CONTRIBUTION PENSION PLANS

Defined-contribution pension plans let your corporation contribute a percentage of your annual compensation—salary plus bonus—every year, limited to the lesser of 25 percent of compensation, or $30,000. There are three types of defined-contribution plans: the money-purchase plan, the profit-sharing plan, and the integrated defined-contribution plan.

Money-purchase plans have a specific contribution formula, and contributions must be made each year, *whether or not your corporation has a profit*. Its contribution can range from less than 1 percent of compensation up to 25 percent, if the money-purchase plan is used alone. It can also be combined with a profit-sharing or defined-benefit plan, as explained later in this chapter.

Profit-sharing plans let your corporation make pension-fund contributions *only in years that it has had a profit*. Contributions can range from less than 1 percent to 15 percent of compensation, but probably should not exceed 60 percent of corporate profits. (The IRS wants some profits left in your corporation so that it can tax them.) Therefore, in wording its Trust Agreement and Adoption Agreement, your corporation should spell out limits on profit-sharing contributions first on the basis of your corporation's profits and second on the basis of the desired contribution as a percentage of compensation.

The simplest wording, with the greatest flexibility, is: "The employer shall contribute such amount to the profit-sharing plan as annually determined by its Board of Directors." (Translation: *You* will decide how much you want to contribute to your profit-sharing plan.)

There are advantages and disadvantages in choosing the simple 25 percent money-purchase pension plan over the 10 percent money-purchase pension plan *plus* the 0–15 percent profit-sharing plan.

Advantages	*Disadvantages*
Your corporation doesn't have to show a profit in order to make the 25 percent contribution. This is especially important in the first few years of corporate life when it can make contributions that it could not make if it were bound by profit-sharing rules. Your corporation might have to borrow money to make those contributions, but both it and you would benefit from those contributions.	Your corporation is locked into a fixed liability and has no flexibility. It must make set-percentage contributions every year.
One pension plan is easier to set up and administer than two.	

In general, as long as your corporation has only you or your family as employees, it's a good idea to adopt the forced-saving element of the 25 percent money-purchase plan. Otherwise you might find that your company is contributing only the mandatory 10 percent in its money-purchase plan.

Salting away as much money as you can is a major advantage of defined-contribution plans. *There is no limit to the size of your pension fund.*

It's easy to set up a profit-sharing plan. Most mutual funds offer a Model Profit-Sharing Plan which the IRS has already approved. Many brokerage houses do, too. You'll also need to file IRS Form 5307, "Short Form Application for Determination for Employee Benefit Plan."

If this model plan does not suit your purposes, your lawyer will have to draft a profit-sharing plan and submit it to the IRS for approval. Have this plan submitted shortly after you incorporate; the IRS usually has a very large backlog of plans to approve, and you want its approval before your corporation files its taxes and makes its pension-fund contribution the following April. Your lawyer will need to draw up a money-purchase plan, which is slightly more complex.

The Trust Agreement and Adoption Agreement are integral parts of the Model Profit-Sharing Plan, which sets the rules that bind your corporation. The Trust Agreement further discusses the areas in which your corporate pension fund may invest and how the investments will be made and administered. (It reads a lot more complicated than it actually is— especially for a one-person pension fund.) The Adoption Agreement, commonly used by mutual funds, can be used to target exactly which employees are covered, how contributions are calculated, how vesting is achieved, and many other crucial details.

If you have many employees who are paid much less than you are, you may wish to elect an *integrated defined-contribution plan,* under which your corporation is obligated to cover only those employees earning amounts above the Social Security maximum ($51,300 in 1990). Your corporation pays only the Social Security tax for employees earning $51,300 or less and contributes 5.7 percent of salaries over $51,300 to the defined-contribution plan.

Example: You earn $81,300, and your employees earn less than $51,300. Your corporation can contribute $1,710 to your retirement plan (5.7 percent × $30,000).

Obviously, this is a ridiculously small pension contribution. You can increase it *only* by contributing to your employees' pension fund as well.

Example: As earlier, you earn $81,300, and your employees earn less than $51,300. Your corporation contributes 4 percent to the retirement fund of employees earning less than $51,300. Now it can contribute $5,663 to your retirement account (4 percent × $30,000 plus 8.7 percent × $51,300).

> In comparing these three defined-contribution plans,
> the IRS message is clear: If you want a generous
> pension plan for yourself, you have to provide one for
> your employees. Nevertheless, there are useful
> loopholes—as shown on pp. 102–04.

DEFINED-BENEFIT PENSION PLANS

In effect, defined-benefit pension plans start with the "answer"—the amount of pension-fund benefits you wish to receive every month—and work backward to the variables of the equation—how many years you and your employees have until retirement—to come up with the "question": How much money will your corporation have to contribute each year to fund these benefits?

Retirement benefits are usually stated as an annual amount: (a) a percentage of compensation—usually defined as the average of the highest 3 or 5 *consecutive* years of compensation multiplied by years of service; (b) a fixed dollar amount; (c) a dollar amount per month multiplied by the number of years of service; (d) an annual percentage of compensation multiplied by years of service.

The annual benefit is limited to the lesser of $102,582 in 1990, increased annually by a cost-of-living adjustment, or 100 percent of compensation based on a straight-life annuity. It is decreased for employees who have less than 10 years of service at normal retirement age. A minimum benefit of $10,000 per year is also reduced for employees with less than 10 years of service.

Traditional defined-benefit plans are expensive to set up and administer. They require the work of a licensed actuary because they are based on such individual variables as the participants' ages, the number of years until retirement, and the retirement benefits they desire. First-year costs for designing defined-benefit plans can run as high as $3,000–$5,000 per participant; annual costs for administering the plan can run as high as $800–$1,500. A licensed actuary must sign the forms that are filed with the IRS and the Department of Labor.

These plans work best for executives of one-person or family-only corporations who are in their forties or older and whose compensation is at least $50,000. As you can see from the tables below, furnished by Michael Sonnenberg, CFP, CLU, ChFC president of Dollar Concepts, Inc., and Robert G. Hahn, president of Red Bank Pension Services, Inc., defined-benefit pension-plan contributions rise sharply with the employee's age. The real difference begins at about age 49.

A revival of an old type of defined-benefit plan is simpler and less costly to design and administer. In a 412(i) plan (named for the relevant Internal Revenue Code section), all pension assets are invested in life insurance and annuity contracts. Because these plans are fully insured, they do not need to file Schedule B, Actuarial Information, along with their ERISA pension-reporting forms, and therefore do not need to be certified by a licensed actuary.

And, because the IRS permits these plans to use an assumed 5 percent rate of return rather than the 8 percent rate of return shown above, you will be able to sock away thousands of dollars more into your pension fund every year.

	Salary $50,000		Salary $80,000	
Age	Defined Contrib.	Defined Benefit*	Defined Contrib.	Defined Benefit*
35	$12,500	$1,749	$20,000	$2,359
36	12,500	2,131	20,000	2,875
37	12,500	2,514	20,000	3,391
38	12,500	2,796	20,000	3,907
39	12,500	3,179	20,000	4,423
45	12,500	5,574	20,000	7,518
46	12,500	7,314	20,000	10,278
47	12,500	9,054	20,000	13,038
48	12,500	10,794	20,000	15,798
49	12,500	12,534	20,000	18,558
55	12,500	22,973	20,000	30,696
56	12,500	30,619	20,000	44,141
57	12,500	38,625	20,000	57,586
58	12,500	45,911	20,000	71,031
59	12,500	53,557	20,000	84,476

*Critical assumptions: retirement at age 65, 8 percent compounded annual rate of return, annual retirement benefits of $50,000/$80,000.

		Salary $50,000	
Age	Defined Contribution Plan	Defined Benefit Plan: 8% Rate of Return	412(i) D.B. Plan: 5% Rate of Return
35	$12,500	$ 1,749	$ 7,526
45	12,500	5,574	15,122
55	12,500	22,973	39,752

		Salary $80,000	
Age	Defined Contribution Plan	Defined Benefit Plan: 8% Rate of Return	412(i) D.B. Plan: 5% Rate of Return
35	20,000	2,359	12,041
45	20,000	7,518	24,194
55	20,000	30,696	63,603

These insurance-based pension plans are the only pension plans permitted to use an assumed rate of return of 5 percent. At present, the IRS makes other defined-benefit plans use an assumed rate of return of 8 percent. In early 1990, the IRS cracked down on small-company defined-benefit plans using an assumed rate of return lower than 8 percent, disallowing contributions made using the lower percentage and penalizing the corporations which established these plans.

INVESTING YOUR PENSION FUND

In addition to life insurance and annuity contracts, your pension fund can invest in certificates of deposit, money-market funds, bonds, stocks, and mutual funds and, under some circumstances, antiques and works of art.

Certificates of deposit and *money-market funds* share several characteristics: The amount of money your fund invests (its principal) is the same at the end of the investment period as at the beginning, and the interest rate is known at the beginning of the investment period. However, certificates of deposit have fixed maturities—the most common are 3 months, 6 months, 1 year, 2 years, and 5 years—and most offer a fixed rate of interest over the life of the CD. (*A few banks reserve the right to lower the interest rate without notice; read the CD's fine print very carefully before committing your funds.*)

Money-market funds are more flexible. There is no maturity to wait for; investors can get in and out of the money market with virtually no restrictions (although some funds may penalize them for making more than five or six switches a year). However, interest rates are more flexible, too, and investors cannot count on a guaranteed rate of return.

Do not invest your pension fund in a *tax-free* money-market fund. There is no tax advantage to your pension fund, because it is a tax-deferred investment vehicle, and a tax-free fund's interest rates are much lower than a taxable money-market fund's.

Over the long term (5–30 + years), certificates of deposit and money-market funds are bad investments because they do not keep up with inflation, preserve purchasing power, or provide true growth. Nevertheless, CDs and money-market funds can be excellent short-term investments when interest rates are high (as in the early 1980s, when the prime rate was over 20 percent), and you can lock in a virtually riskless profit; or during bear markets, when you want to preserve your pension fund's capital. Fortunately for amateur investors, high interest rates and bear markets usually coincide and receive ample press. They are hard to miss, easy to profit from.

Even before the Great American Junk Bond Debacle, bonds of any type were poor investments for pension funds under $5 million. Bonds are a very illiquid investment. Even when bought or sold in 50-bond lots ($50,000 face value), it's not unusual for buyers to find that the asking price is now 1 point more; or sellers to find that the bid price is now 1 point less ($10 per bond). In contrast, buying or selling 500 shares of a $100 stock sold on the New York Stock Exchange usually doesn't change the price of the stock at all.

Unlike certificates of deposit and money-market funds, the price of the bond is not guaranteed unless it is held to maturity. Bond prices can rise and fall—mostly fall—on changes in interest rates, balance-of-payment statistics, foreign-exchange statistics, and rumors about whether the chairman of the Federal Reserve Board has had a heart attack, or the sniffles.

Convertible bonds—which can be exchanged for shares of stock—belong in a different category, but usually investors pay far too much for the conversion privilege.

In general, while undoubtedly there are undervalued bonds that can reward investors handsomely, bonds are investments best suited to the professional investor managing portfolios in excess of $5 million.

Stocks and *stock mutual funds* are the most rewarding long-term financial assets. If you are familiar with the stock market or have specific knowledge about an industry or a company, you may wish to build your own pension-fund portfolio by selecting individual stocks.

> To manage your portfolio professionally, buy at least 200 shares of any stock you choose in order to save on commissions. Choose no more than 5–6 stocks for a pension fund of $100,000 or less, 10–12 stocks for a $250,000 pension fund, and 18–20 for a $500,000 pension fund.

There are many excellent stock mutual funds that will provide even more diversification (see following section). Allocate your fund's assets among the three or four you think best, and plan to replace the worst-performing fund with a better-performing fund once a year. Make sure that you choose a mutual fund that is part of a family of funds containing a top-performing money-market fund, so that you can switch between equities and a money market as market and economic conditions dictate.

DO YOUR OWN RESEARCH?

Admittedly, I've been fascinated by the stock market ever since I was a teenager. Even before I worked in Wall Street as a portfolio analyst, I realized that investments—not savings—were the road to wealth.

Happily, you don't have to be an MBA to run your pension plan successfully. All it takes is two or three hours a week, time which will also help you become more proficient in investing your corporate and personal funds.

For choosing stocks, I recommend reading *Investor's Daily,* which has very concise, useful information and statistics. The table on page 2, showing the 60 New York Stock Exchange stocks with the greatest percentage rise in volume (which often precedes rise in price), is especially useful and can generate investment leads, or stocks to research further. The newspaper has two rankings that are especially useful. The earnings-per-share ranking compares the stock's earnings-per-share growth in the past five years and the stability of that growth. The relative strength compares the stock's trading action to that of the Standard & Poor's 500 Stock Index. Both are shown as percentile numbers. You can create a list of potential investments by noting those stocks that rank 90 or better (in the top tenth of stocks traded) in each category.

For the most condensed information, I prefer the *Daily Graphs Option Guide,* which is published weekly by William O'Neil & Co., Inc., and is delivered on Sunday in most cities. Over 650 stocks are displayed in one-year charts, along with 58 statistics for each stock. Two of the most useful are the indication of a five-year earnings growth rate higher than 20 percent, shown by an asterisk next to the stock's name, and the five-year earnings growth rate, shown as a percentage. As the price of a company's stock rises when earnings rise, choosing stocks with a history of consistent profitability and increases in earnings is one way for you to invest successfully.

When you have a list of 20 or 30 names, get the Standard & Poor's sheets on these companies from a broker, or consult them in a business library. These sheets, which are published quarterly, contain a great deal of current and long-term information about the companies and their prospects.

Although there are over 600 mutual funds that invest in stocks, you should find it fairly easy to choose the best three or four for your needs, because business magazines have done most of the number crunching for you. *Barron's* ranks mutual funds quarterly; *Business Week, Forbes, Fortune,* and *Money* rank funds annually. Pick up the most recent back issues and compare rankings. Different magazines will give greater weight to different variables, or will analyze the funds' performances in differing time periods, but ratings should still be fairly close.

Magazine graphics will speed your search. In *Business Week's* 1990 annual mutual funds ratings (February 19, 1990 issue) for example, three red arrows pointing upward indicated superior performance. Only 30 funds earned this top ranking. Each fund's performance compared to all other funds for each of four 30-month periods from January 1, 1980 through December 31, 1989 is shown as a string of four boxes, ranging from colorless for no ranking (new fund) to one-quarter red for bottom-quartile performance, up to completely red for top-quartile performance.

Other criteria that are important to your choosing a mutual fund are the fund's total return on investment over 1, 5, and 10 years, its potential risk factor (usually compared to the rate of return on Treasury bills), and the fund's load (sales charge). Most funds charge a front-end load, upon purchase; some impose back-end loads, when the fund is sold. Sometimes back-end loads decrease over time and end after a five-year holding period.

There has always been controversy over whether load mutual funds perform better than no-load funds and therefore are worth buying even though they impose hefty 4.50–8.75 percent sales charges. With a little hunting, you should be able to find some no-load funds that offer superior performance. If, however, you find load funds that offer returns that are consistently 12 percent higher than those of the best no-load funds, it makes sense to choose these load funds, as their net rate of return is higher than their no-load competitors'.

HOW TO INCREASE YOUR RETURNS

There are three investment strategies you can use to increase your pension fund's performance:

(1) *Make your pension-fund contribution as early in the year as you can, in order to take advantage of receiving maximum interest on your pension fund.*

"That's great," says Ernie, a St. Louis importer. "But how do I know what I'm going to pay myself as salary until near the end of the year?"

Even though Ernie doesn't know exactly how much he's going to pay himself as salary, he *does* know at the beginning of the year that it will be at least $40,000. That means that he can put a $10,000 contribution into his money-purchase pension fund now, based on his minimum salary of $40,000. If he has a good year and pays himself $60,000, he can put another $5,000 into his pension fund later in the year.

What's the advantage of making your pension-fund contribution early, rather than at the last minute? Think of 8 percent interest on $10,000 every year for 20 or 30 years. It really adds up!

(2) *Realize that your pension fund is not subject to capital-gains taxes.* Therefore your pension fund can take quick profits. If your fund owns 200 shares of XYZ, which rises 10 points in one week, you need have no second thoughts about grabbing a quick $2,000 profit. (Chances are, in the next week or two, XYZ will give up some of its rise anyway.) If you are a consummate stock picker, you can trade your pension-fund portfolio as often as you like, gloating because your defined-contribution pension fund has no IRS or Department of Labor limitations on its growth or profits.

(3) *Sell call options on the stocks held in your pension fund.* Now you're hedging like a professional investor or money manager. It's often been said that amateurs buy calls, professionals sell them. That's because most options expire worthless, leaving the option sellers to pocket the premiums.

Here's a basic primer on options:

Options are listed securities that give the purchaser the right—but not the obligation—to buy (call option) or sell (put option) 100 shares of stock at a predetermined price (the strike price) by a certain date (the expiration date), usually the third Friday of the month. For this privilege, the option purchaser pays a premium, which is expressed in dollars per share, but which must be multiplied by 100 to get the actual price. If a call on XYZ stock is trading at 3½, a call purchaser will have to pay $350 for a call on 100 shares.

Option premiums are composed of two elements. The *intrinsic value* is the distance from the strike price. If you own a call on XYZ stock at 40 and the stock is trading at 35, 5 points below the strike price, there will be little intrinsic value in the option premium. If XYZ is trading at 40, right at the strike price, there will usually be about 1–2 points in intrinsic value in the option premium. If XYZ is trading at 45, 5 points above the strike price, there will usually be 4½–5 points in intrinsic value in the option premium. *Note:* "In-the-money" calls rarely rise or fall precisely point-for-point with their stock, since intrinsic value is only one element of the option price.

Time value is the second, equally important element in option premiums. Naturally, an option with only a week before expiration is worth much less than an option with three or four months to run. The decay in the time value of an option as its expiration approaches is generally responsible for most options expiring worthless, with the option writer (seller) pocketing the premium, rather than the option's being sold or executed (exchanged for stock at the strike price) at a profit.

While successful options trading deserves its own book, strategies for writing calls on the stocks in your pension-fund portfolio are fairly simple and can enhance its rate of return substantially.

Let's look at XYZ again. It's not a dynamic new growth stock and it's not very volatile, so it's an ideal candidate for selling calls. Food and beverage, retailing, and utilities stocks are some good examples. Ideally, XYZ will not rise to its strike price, so your stock won't get called away from you, and you will be able to write a new call and collect a new premium every three months.

In January 1991, with your 200 shares of XYZ trading around 38–40, and paying $3.00 per share in annual dividends, you sell 2 March 45 calls at 3. On March 15, 1991, the expiration date, XYZ has advanced to 42, so your stock is not called away. You write 2 June 45 calls at 4¼. So far you have collected $1,450 in option premiums (net of commissions) and $300 in dividends, and the year's only half over!

On June 21, 1991, the expiration date, XYZ has advanced to 44, and again your stock is not called away. Then, anticipating a summer rally and wanting to hold onto your stock, you wait a week until XYZ hits 45 and you can write the September *50* calls, which began trading when XYZ touched 45. You sell 2 calls at 3½ and are happy to see that call premiums are rising, reflecting Wall Street's expectations for a summer rally.

The summer rally produces a 10 percent rise in the market. XYZ, an average stock, rises exactly 10 percent—from 45 to 49½, and again your stock is not called away. And now, fearing a market downturn, you write 2 December 50 calls at 5.

This time you're wrong. On December 20, XYZ closes at 51-1/2 and your stock is called at 50. Has it been a profitable holding for your pension fund? Let's see how you made out:

2 March	45 calls at 3	$ 600
2 June	45 calls at 4¼	850
2 September	50 calls at 3½	700
2 December	50 calls at 5	1,000
	Call-writing income	$3,150
	Dividend income	600
	Total income	$3,750

For calculation of rates of return

Average price per share	45
Average value of 200 XYZ	$9,000

For calculation of capital gain

January average price	39
December sale price	50
Sale price of 200 XYZ	$10,000
Capital gain (assuming purchase price of 39)	$2,200

Option return on average value of XYZ	35.0%
Dividend return on average value of XYZ	6.7
Capital gain return on average value of XYZ	28.2
Total return	69.9%

Assuming no calls written	
Dividend return on average value of XYZ	6.7%
Price increase on average value of XYZ	
(from 39 to 51½ = 12½ points)	32.1
Total return	38.8%

By selling options on XYZ, your performance for this stock was 80 percent higher than if you had done nothing but collect dividends—that's two-and-a-half times better than the stock's dramatic rise of 32 percent in one year!

Does this strategy work in the real world? It certainly does. Over a five-year period in the 1980s, I steadily wrote calls on 200 shares of Ralston Purina and 300 shares of Phelps Dodge in my pension fund. Writing the Ralston Purina calls was easier, but the premiums received were lower because the stock was not very volatile.

Phelps Dodge was another story. As the price of copper swung dramatically as it moved from $0.65 to $1.35 to $1.00 per pound, the price of Phelps Dodge and its options moved like a roller coaster. I added about $5,000 to my pension fund in profits from writing Philps Dodge premiums alone, and also added about 5,000 white hairs.

Right now, about half the stocks in my defined-contribution pension fund have calls written against them, and I expect their premiums to add at least 15–20 percent to my fund's performance every year. For the entrepreneur or professional who enjoys investments, I'd recommend buying stocks on which listed options are traded–there are presently over 650 of them–in order to enjoy the flexibility of strategy and increased rate of return that call writing can provide.

Put options can also be used to protect your pension fund's profits or limit its losses. Think of a put as an insurance policy. For the payment of a small premium, you are able to sell your stock at a certain price until your chosen expiration date, no matter how badly the stock may fall. (Investors who held UAL puts as well as stock certainly fared better, when the stock plummeted from 280 to 135 in the fall of 1989, than those who held the stock without protective puts.)

OTHER LEGAL INVESTMENTS

In addition to securities and insurance vehicles, you may invest your defined-contribution pension fund in real estate, art, antiques—in fact, anything of value that a "prudent trustee" would invest in. This is the so-called "prudent-man rule."

However, there are some practical caveats and some IRS caveats. First, even if you are an expert in one of these esoteric fields, it makes sense to limit your investment to 40–50 percent of your pension fund— keeping the rest in stocks or mutual funds—and then only if your corporation and pension fund are limited to family employees. With the ballyhoo accompanying record prices for Impressionist, Post-impressionist, and Modern art, many people forget that there are entire schools of painting selling for a fraction of the price they fetched in the Victorian era or in the 1920s. Chinese porcelain, Japanese prints, Roman bronzes, 19th-century photographs—all and more are suitable pension-fund investments, *if* you know what you are doing, and *if* you can prove it to the IRS if you, as trustee of your pension fund, are ever audited. (A good library and many years' worth of auction catalogs will be helpful in demonstrating your expertise.)

Nevertheless, *too much knowledge* can run you afoul of the IRS. If you are an art dealer specializing in American paintings, you can get in trouble with the IRS if you collect American paintings in your pension fund and trade them frequently. The IRS has taken the position that such a frequently traded pension fund is simply an extension of the owner-employee's business and therefore should not receive the tax deduction for pension contributions available to other pension funds.

Accordingly, says an IRS source, you would fare much better by having your pension fund invest in another area of art or antiques: American or English silver, European paintings, musical instruments, rare coins, Japanese prints—anything but American paintings.

Remember that art, antiques, and real estate are notoriously illiquid. No one knows what your investments will be worth when you retire, or whether they will be able to fund your retirement comfortably—even if you have chosen them well.

HOW TO AVOID COVERING YOUR EMPLOYEES

There *are* legal ways of having your corporate pension fund not cover your employees. They work best in small corporations, when it's just you—or you and your spouse—and one or two assistants.

First, if your business or profession lends itself to hiring freelancers to work on specific projects, you don't have to cover these people in your pension fund. Just make sure that they are true freelancers: they can choose their workplace (your office or theirs), they choose their hours, they choose the sequence in which they perform the work, they use their own equipment, and they are hired on a project basis. *If they do not meet most of these criteria, the IRS can insist that they are employees, not freelancers.* Then you will have to pay Social Security tax for them and may have to include them in your pension plan.

> Make sure that you send freelancers 1099 forms at the
> end of the year if you have paid them more than $600.
> Assignment letters stating the details of the project
> also strengthen your position that these people are
> freelancers.

If you require more steady help or hours, here are two more strategies. Your pension fund does not have to include employees before their twenty-first birthday. If you hire 18- or 19-year-olds, it is very likely that they will move to another job before you have to include them in your pension plan.

Or consider job sharing: hiring two employees to fill one job. As long as employees work fewer than 1,000 hours a year (an average of 20 hours a week for 50 weeks), they do not have to be covered by your pension plan. There are great advantages to job sharing for both you and your employees. By choosing employees who can work only part-time—college or graduate students, mothers with young children, or retirees—you will be able to find more intelligent, more talented, and more motivated help. They will find more interesting work that accommodates their schedules.

HOW TO COVER YOUR EMPLOYEES MINIMALLY

If these strategies don't fit your needs, how about a pension fund that will let you sock away $30,000 for yourself, but as little as $450 for some of your employees?

Bennett H. Pearl, senior pension consultant of the National Life Insurance Company of Vermont, suggests using a target-benefit plan. "Regardless of their similarities to defined-benefit plans," says Pearl, "target-benefit plans are, by law, defined-contribution plans. Target-benefit plans are weighted in favor of older participants. Furthermore, service can be a 'weighting' factor. Each contribution accumulates in an individual account, with all interest and earnings accruing to the participant's account, as in any other defined-contribution plan."

According to Pearl, the key difference between a target-benefit plan and other defined-contribution plans is that the percentage of contribution varies, with older participants with long service (past and future) getting a higher percentage of contribution than younger participants with long service (past and future).

Let's look at Dr. Me, age 55, earning $120,000; Nurse Jones, age 38, earning $25,000; Receptionist Smith, age 30, earning $18,000; and Technician White, age 25, earning $15,000. Under both a 25 percent money-purchase plan and a target-benefit plan, the doctor gets a $30,000 contribution—but look at the difference in what he contributes for his employees:

	Contribution Under 25% Money-Purchase Plan	Contribution Under Target-Benefit Plan
Dr. Me	$30,000	$30,000
Nurse Jones	6,250	1,362
Receptionist Smith	4,500	564
Technician White	3,750	450*
Total	$44,500	$32,376
Amount Contributed for Employees	$14,500	$ 2,376
Percentage Contributed for Dr. Me	67.4%	92.7%

*A minimum 3% contribution is necessary to satisfy top-heavy pension-plan requirements.

Obviously, the target-benefit plan can be very attractve for professionals over the age of 45 who have a staff of younger, lower-paid employees.

REPORTING REQUIREMENTS

If you have a one-person or family-only corporation and the assets in your defined-contribution pension plan total less than $100,000, *you do not have to file any pension-reporting forms with the IRS.* If plan assets exceed $100,000, file IRS Form 5500EZ annually.

If your corporate defined-contribution pension fund covers nonfamily employees, or if you have a defined-benefit pension plan, check with the IRS to find out which forms you must file annually.

WHICH PENSION PLAN IS BEST FOR YOU?

The following questions are designed to help you choose the best pension plan for your needs.

(If 25 percent of your salary does exceed $30,000, consider choosing a defined-benefit plan; if it does not, a defined-contribution plan.)

What is your age?
Years before assumed retirement at age 65? _____
(If you are younger than 45, you will do better with a defined-contribution plan; if you are older, with a defined-benefit plan.)

Estimate your corporation's income and your salary:

Year	Corporate Income	Salary	Does 25% of Your Salary Exceed $30,000?
1991	$	$	
1992			
1993			
1994			
1995			

I enjoy picking stocks or mutual funds, and consider myself to be a successful investor.
(If your answer is yes, you will do better with a defined-contribution plan.)

I have specialized knowledge in art or antiques.
(If your answer is yes, you will do better with a defined-contribution plan.)

I prefer accepting a guaranteed rate of return.
(If your answer is yes, you will do better with a defined-benefit plan.)

I want my pension plan to provide set annual benefits.
(If your answer is yes, choose a defined-benefit plan.)
OR
I want there to be no limit on the size to which my pension fund can grow.
(If your answer is yes, choose a defined-contribution plan.)

My corporation has no employees (or only family employees) and does not expect to hire any (or any nonfamily employees) before 1995.
(If your answer is yes, you can choose either a defined-benefit or a defined-contribution plan. If you have or plan to hire nonfamily employees, consult a pension expert, or you may wish to choose a target-benefit plan.)

Maximum Number of *Defined-Benefit Answers* 5	Your Number of *Defined-Benefit Answers*

Maximum Number of *Defined-Contribution Answers* 6	Your Number of *Defined-Contribution Answers* _____

IF YOU HAVE 4 OR MORE ANSWERS IN EITHER CATE-
GORY, CHOOSE THAT PLAN. IF YOUR ANSWERS ARE
DIVIDED BETWEEN THE CATEGORIES, CONSULT A
PENSION EXPERT.

11

How to Profit from Your Pension Fund *Before* You Retire

Sophisticated corporate owner-employees know how to treat their pension funds as their own private banks. You, too, can borrow legally from your pension fund, and you should probably use it, rather than turning to banks or other lenders. *Remember that you can borrow from your pension fund only if you have a C corporation—not an S corporation.* As you will see in this chapter, you will also profit more from borrowing from your pension fund if you have a defined-contribution plan than if you have a defined-benefit plan.

WHY USE YOUR PENSION FUND?

There are three basic reasons to borrow from your pension fund rather than from other lenders. First, you'll find a friendlier, faster banker: yourself. Second, you'll have more flexibility in setting the repayment terms of the loan. Third, your pension fund will benefit by collecting a high rate of interest.

In contrast to your friendly neighborhood banker, who might take a month to approve a loan and provide you with the money, you, as trustee of your pension fund, can arrange the loan in less than a week—often in only two or three days. Where banks usually call for a *monthly* repayment schedule, you can set up an easier *quarterly* repayment schedule. And, rather than your bank's collecting a hefty rate of interest, your pension fund can earn that high rate of return which, in many years, can be much greater than that provided by stocks, bonds, or other conventional pension-fund investments.

LEGAL PURPOSES AND LIMITATIONS

Sorry, you can't borrow from your pension fund to take a well-earned vacation, not even if you've been working 100-hour weeks. In fact, according to the IRS, there are three purposes for which you can borrow from your pension fund without the loan's being treated as a distribution and your being taxed accordingly:

(1) to acquire, construct, or reconstruct your personal residence;
(2) to pay tuition for the next semester or quarter of postsecondary college or graduate school for yourself (the employee), your spouse, child, or dependent;

> You may not borrow from your pension fund to pay for private elementary or high schools—only for college or graduate school.

(3) to pay for your, your spouse's, child's, or dependent's medical treatment that meets the requirement of "immediate and heavy financial need."

If the loan is for your *principal* residence, it may run for more than five years. Other loans must be repaid within five years, or they will be treated automatically as distributions, and you will be taxed accordingly.

According to the Internal Revenue Code §72(p), the following conditions must be satisfied:

(1) The loan must be available to all participant/beneficiaries on a reasonable equivalent basis.
(2) The loan must not be more available to highly compensated employees, officers, or shareholders than to other employees. (Obviously, this is not a problem if you and your family are the only employees.) The pension plan must have a specific loan provision, and the loan must bear a reasonable rate of interest and be adequately secured.

Generally the amount of the loan is determinable from the parameters discussed in Internal Revenue Code §72(p)(2): a loan that does not exceed

(a) the lesser of $50,000, reduced by any outstanding loans within the prior year; or (b) the greater of $10,000, or half the participant's accrued benefit under the plan, is permitted.

For purposes of determining whether the loan satisfies the size limitations:

(1) all the outstanding loan balances are aggregated;
(2) loans from all plans of an employer are treated as loans from a single plan. Additionally, the maximum ($50,000) must be reduced by (a) the highest outstanding balance of loans from the plan during the one-year period ending on the day before the date on which the loan is made over: and (b) the outstanding balance of loans from the plan on the date on which such loan was made.

The loan must be amortized in level payments (principal + interest) not less frequently than quarterly over the term of the loan.

WHY YOU SHOULD PAY MAXIMUM INTEREST RATES

As I write this chapter, 30-year fixed-mortgage interest rates in the tri-state New York metropolitan area are running 10.00 percent–10.50 percent. Some lenders also charge points or origination fees. Banks are charging 12 percent–15 percent on personal loans. Household Finance Corporation is charging 23.9 percent interest for a $10,000 or $15,000 loan, repayable over five years.

Ordinarily, if you were shopping for a mortgage or a loan, you would choose the *lowest* interest rates because you were paying someone else. But now, since you are borrowing from your own pension fund, the more interest that you can repay legally, the better. All this interest will swell the coffers of your pension fund without decreasing the amount of your permitted annual contributions *if you have a defined-contribution pension plan*.

Let's assume that, for the next few years, interest rates remain where they were in mid-1990. If you paid yourself $40,000 in salary and borrowed $15,000 from your pension fund for Junior's freshman year at Ivy U. on January 1, 1992, at an interest rate of 23 percent, slightly lower than that of Household Finance Corporation, and repaid the loan on December 31, 1992, you would have been able to add $3,450 in interest payments to your pension fund without decreasing the $10,000 contribution your corporation could make to your pension fund ($40,000 × 25 percent).

However, if you had a defined-benefit pension plan, the 23 percent interest earned would surely be high enough to reduce the 1992 pension contribution your corporation could make for you, and your actuary would have to recalculate the reduced contribution.

THE PAPERWORK

Even if you have a one-person corporation and the odds against your being audited are very high, you still should have a corporate resolution authorizing the loan from your pension fund. And, if your pension fund's assets are being held at a brokerage house or bank, you will surely need a copy of that corporate resolution in order to get the brokerage house or bank to release those funds to you.

Here is a corporate resolution that you can adapt:

MINUTES OF A SPECIAL MEETING OF SHAREHOLDERS
of
JUST DESSERTS, INC.

MINUTES of a special meeting of shareholders held at 123 Easy Street, New York City, in the State of New York, on the first day of April, 1991, at ten o'clock in the morning.

The meeting was duly called to order by the President and sole stockholder, who stated the object of the meeting.

On motion duly made, seconded, and unanimously carried, the following resolutions were adopted:

WHEREAS, the President is entitled to borrow funds from her corporate pension plan for the purpose of buying a principal residence, which she plans to do later this year, and

WHEREAS, the President is entitled to borrow funds from her corporate pension plan for the purpose of paying her daughter's college tuition, it is

RESOLVED, that she may borrow up to $50,000 from her pension plan for either or both of these purposes. If she borrows to purchase a principal residence, she may borrow for a period of up to thirty years at the rate of 11 percent simple interest. If she borrows to pay for her daughter's college tuition, she may borrow for a period of up to five years at the rate of 23 percent simple interest, and it is

FURTHER RESOLVED, that she will file notes on those terms, showing quarterly repayment schedules, if she chooses to borrow the funds from her corporate pension fund for either of these purposes.

There being no further business, the meeting was adjourned. Dated the first day of April, 1991.

_____
Secretary

_____
President

Happy borrowing!

12

How to Invest Your Corporate Surplus for Enormous Profits

Knowledgeable corporate owner-employees use their C corporations as investment vehicles. They use their corporate earnings to purchase stocks whose dividends are 70 percent tax-free. For most small corporations— those whose net corporate income is $50,000 or less—the effective tax rate is only 4.5 percent: *the dividends are 95.5 percent tax-free!*

YOUR GOAL: TAX-FREE DIVIDENDS

When a U.S. corporation receives dividends from another U.S. corporation on stock held at least 45 days, 70 percent of those dividends received are free of federal income taxes. It's true for a major insurance company or bank, and it's true for your profitable little corporation *if it's a C corporation*, because only a C corporation can split income between your salary and its retained corporate earnings.

The effective corporate tax rates on dividends are gratifying enough to turn any squanderer into a saver and investor:

111

1991 Corporate Tax Rates		Taxable Percent of Dividend	Effective Tax Rate on Dividend	Tax-free Portion of Dividend
$ 0–$50,000	15%	30%	4.5%	95.5%
$50,000–$75,000	25%	30%	7.5%	92.5%
$75,000+	34%	30%	10.2%	89.8%

Thus, at its worst, 89.8 percent of a dividend received by your corporation will be tax-free. In comparison, if you own the stock personally, the dividend will be 72 percent tax-free if you are in the 28 percent bracket and 67 percent tax-free if you are in the 33 percent bracket. (When you liquidate your corporation, you'll have to pay tax on the accumulated tax-deferred dividends, but those dividends will have profited from tax-deferred compounding for many, many years.)

How much is this feature actually worth? With the usual hedge clauses about the following not being regarded as stock recommendations, let me mention the two stocks that my corporation currently holds:

No. Shares	Company	Recent Price	Recent Value	Dividend	Annual Income	Yield
200	Texas Utilities	35¾	$ 7,150	$2.96	$ 592	8.28%
500	Zweig Fund	11	5,500	1.12	560	10.18%
			$12,600		$1,152	9.14%

Annual income	$1,142
Tax-free portion	799
Taxable portion	343
Corporate tax (15%)	51
Tax-free dividends	$1,091

This $12,000 portfolio and $1,100 a year in dividends is just a beginning. My business plan calls for my corporation's buying $5,000–$10,000 worth of stock each year, paying at least 8 percent in dividends. Assuming an average annual stock purchase of $7,500, asset growth rate of 5 percent, reinvestment of tax-free dividends, and recognizing that there is no tax on unrealized gains, the table below illustrates the growth of a modest, steady investment strategy over a ten-year period:

Year No.	Portfolio Value	Annual Contribution	Total	8% Dividends	After-tax Dividends	Assume 5% Growth Rate	Total Value (Portfolio + After-tax Dividends)
Starting Point	$12,000	$ —	$12,000	$ 960	$ 917	$12,600	$ 13,517
1	13,517	7,500	21,017	1,681	1,605	22,068	23,673
2	23,673	7,500	31,173	2,494	2,382	32,732	35,114
3	35,114	7,500	42,614	3,409	3,256	44,745	48,001
4	48,001	7,500	55,501	4,440	4,240	58,276	62,516
5	62,516	7,500	70,016	5,601	5,349	73,517	78,866
6*	78,866	7,500	86,366	6,909	6,391*	90,684	97,075
7	97,075	7,500	104,575	8,366	7,739	109,804	117,543
8	117,543	7,500	125,043	10,003	9,253	131,295	140,548
9	140,548	7,500	148,048	11,844	10,956	155,450	166,406
10	166,406	7,500	173,906	13,912	12,869	182,601	195,470**
		$75,000		$ 69,619	$ 64,957		

*At this point, corporate tax rates may rise from 15 percent to 25 percent; therefore after-tax dividends might fall from 95.5 percent to 92.5 percent of total dividends received.

**Note that despite the rapid growth of this portfolio, my corporation is still far away from the $250,000 accumulated earnings trap. (See p. 120 for details on this tax trap.)

At the risk of belaboring the obvious, let me point out some of the juicy benefits of this investment plan. With contributions of only $7,500 per year, my corporate portfolio can grow to nearly $200,000 at the end of ten years. During that period, dividends on the stocks held in the portfolio total $69,619, nearly equaling the ten-year contribution. And, best of all, taxes on those dividends are a mere $4,662! I know I'll have to pay more tax when I liquidate my portfolio, but I may not sell it until I retire. Meanwhile, I'm just going to enjoy letting my corporate investments grow on a tax-deferred basis.

By the seventh year, dividends received will outstrip my annual contribution and, under the critical assumptions outlined earlier, the portfolio's value will increase by over $20,000. And, in the tenth year, the portfolio's value will increase by nearly $30,000. To summarize, over ten years this portfolio will grow from $13,517 to $195,470—an increase of more than 1,300 percent.

Oh, and did I mention that it's more pleasant to have your money working for you than vice versa—even in your own corporation?

Yes, it's often been called "the miracle of compounding," and it is indeed miraculous. This strategy lets entrepreneurs use their own corporations to get rich by creating their own minimally taxed and tax-deferred investment programs.

But enough preaching! You are either a disciplined saver and investor, or you're not. (In all fairness, some entrepreneurs can't afford to be—they have to plow all their money back into the business.) Why don't you work out the numbers yourself and see how you can use your own corporation to get rich?

Year No.	Portfolio Value	Annual Contrib.	Total	8% Divs.	After-tax Divs. (× .955)	Portfolio: Assume 5% Growth Rate (Total × 1.05)	Total Value (Portfolio + After-tax Divs.)
1	$ 0	$ ____	$ ____	$ ____	$ ____	$ ____	$ ____
2							
3							
4							
5							
6							
7							
8							
9							
10							

ON A SCALE FROM 1 (LOWEST) TO 10 (HIGHEST), HOW IMPORTANT IS THE TAX-FREE DIVIDEND FEATURE OF THE C CORPORATION TO YOU?

_____ points

HOW TO CHOOSE STOCKS FOR YOUR CORPORATE PORTFOLIO

Investing for your corporate portfolio is a little different from investing for your pension fund. In your corporate portfolio, dividend yield and stability of dividends is more important than superior growth. Put that high-tech cutting edge stock with an earnings growth rate of 50 percent a year but no dividend in your pension-fund portfolio, not in your corporate portfolio. Your corporate portfolio is the right place for those comfortable—perhaps even boring—stocks which yield 9 percent in bear markets, 5 percent in bull markets, which may take as long as seven years to double in price, and *whose dividends are increased every year.*

Remember that your corporation pays a capital-gains tax (currently at the same rate as its income tax) whenever it sells a stock it owns at a profit. Your pension fund does not pay capital-gains taxes and therefore can trade almost with impunity, but the stocks in your corporate portfolio should be sold only when the outlook for their companies changes drastically.

One easy way of minimizing this risk is to buy only stocks with a minimum Standard & Poor's rating of B+—ask your broker or consult a public business library. Sell a stock in your corporate portfolio:

• when Standard & Poor's lowers its rating—shown by a downward arrow for three consecutive months in the S & P Monthly Stock Guide

• when the dividend is not increased during the year.

TARGETING YOUR RETURN ON INVESTMENT

Now that you know the basics, let me start you off with a list of 130 stocks that have passed several tight screens that I have constructed. All of them have minimum Standard & Poor's ratings of B+, all of them have paid cash dividends every year since 1985 (a few go back to the turn of the century), all of them have increased their dividends each year from 1985 through 1989, and the minimum five-year dividend increase was 48 percent, for a minimum compound annual rate of 8.2 percent. (To put the numbers in perspective, a dividend that doubled in five years—an increase of 100 percent—equaled a compound annual rate of 14.9 percent.)

Why did I choose the 48 percent/8.2 percent compound annual rate of dividend growth as a cutoff point? It's double the annual rate of inflation. Corporate investors in these stocks did much better than the annual inflation rate—*before the 70 percent dividend exclusion!*

Before presenting this list, let me go over the Standard & Poor's stock ranking system, which is based on companies' growth and stability of earnings and dividends:

A+	Highest	B	Below average
A	High	B−	Lower
A−	Above average	C	Lowest
B+	Average	D	In reorganization

DIVIDEND STOCKS

COMPANY	S+P RATING	'85 DIVIDENDS	'89 DIVIDENDS	INCREASE	COMPOUND %
ABBOTT LABS	A+	0.68	1.35	99%	14.7%
ALBERTSON'S	A+	0.34	0.74	118%	16.8%
AMER. GENERAL	A	1.00	1.50	50%	8.4%
AM. WATER WKS	A+	0.50	0.74	48%	8.2%
AMETEK	A−	0.43	0.64	49%	8.3%
AMP, INC.	A−	0.72	1.70	136%	18.7%
ANGELICA	A	0.52	0.76	46%	7.9%
ANHEUSER-BUSCH	A+	0.37	0.80	116%	16.7%
ATLANTA GAS LIGHT	B+	1.26	1.90	51%	8.6%
AUTOMATIC DATA	A+	0.32	0.56	75%	11.8%
AVERY INTL.	A	0.31	0.54	74%	11.7%
BAIRNCO	B+	0.55	0.95	73%	11.6%
BALL CORP.	A−	0.68	1.10	62%	10.1%
BANC ONE	A+	0.63	1.01	60%	9.9%
BANDAG	A+	0.60	0.90	50%	8.4%
BANKERS TRUST	A−	1.38	2.08	51%	8.6%
BARNETT BANKS	A+	0.67	1.12	67%	10.8%
BAXTER INTL.	A−	0.37	0.55	49%	8.3%
H AND R BLOCK	A	0.58	1.10	90%	13.7%
BRISTOL-MYERS SQUIBB	A+	0.94	2.00	113%	16.3%
BROWNING-FERRIS	A+	0.27	0.56	107%	15.7%
BRUNSWICK	B+	0.25	0.44	76%	12.0%
CAMPBELL SOUP	A−	0.61	0.92	51%	8.6%
CAROLINA FRT.	B+	0.40	0.60	50%	8.4%
CENTEL CORP.	A	1.06	2.24	111%	16.1%
CHUBB CORP.	B+	1.51	2.28	51%	8.6%
CINCINN. BELL	A+	0.39	0.65	67%	10.8%
CLOROX	A+	0.62	1.19	92%	13.9%
COMMUN. PSYCH.	A	0.17	0.36	112%	16.2%
CONAGRA, INC.	A+	0.28	0.54	93%	14.0%
CONSOL. NAT. GAS	A	1.16	1.76	52%	8.7%
CROMPTON AND KN.	A	0.30	0.58	93%	14.1%
DAYTON HUDSON	A+	0.67	1.12	67%	10.8%
DEAN FOODS	A+	0.36	0.62	72%	11.5%
DELUXE CORP.	A+	0.49	0.98	100%	14.9%
DEXTER CORP.	B+	0.53	0.80	51%	8.6%
R.R. DONNELLEY	A+	0.58	0.88	52%	8.7%
DOVER CORP.	A−	0.43	0.70	63%	10.2%
DUN AND BRADST.	A+	1.06	1.94	83%	12.8%
ECHLIN	A−	0.41	0.64	56%	9.3%
ENNIS BUS. FORMS	A	0.12	0.59	392%	37.5%
FAMILY DOLLAR	A−	0.17	0.35	106%	15.5%

COMPANY	S+P RATING	'85 DIVIDENDS	'89 DIVIDENDS	INCREASE	COMPOUND %
FIRSTAR CORP.	B+	0.64	1.09	70%	11.2%
FIRST UNION	A	0.58	1.00	72%	11.5%
FIRST WACHOV.	A	0.82	1.39	70%	11.1%
FLEET/NORSTAR	A+	0.68	1.38	103%	15.2%
FLIGHTSAFETY	A−	0.10	0.17	70%	11.2%
FLOWERS INDS.	A	0.26	0.55	112%	16.2%
GAP, INC.	A−	0.13	0.64	392%	37.5%
GEICO CORP.	A−	1.00	1.80	80%	12.5%
GENERAL CINEMA	A	0.21	0.41	95%	14.3%
GENERAL ELECT.	A+	1.12	1.64	46%	7.9%
GENERAL MILLS	A	1.12	2.04	82%	12.7%
GENERAL RE CORP.	A−	0.78	1.36	74%	11.8%
W.W. GRAINGER	A	0.67	1.00	49%	8.3%
GRT. LAKES CHEM.	B+	0.23	0.38	65%	10.6%
HANNAFORD	A+	0.24	0.36	50%	8.4%
(JOHN) HARLAND	A+	0.28	0.68	143%	19.4%
(H.J.) HEINZ	A+	0.38	0.75	97%	14.6%
HERSHEY FOODS	A+	0.48	0.74	54%	9.0%
HILLENBRAND	A+	0.27	0.50	85%	13.1%
HUMANA INC.	A−	0.66	0.98	48%	8.2%
HUNT MFG.	A−	0.15	0.27	80%	12.5%
ILLINOIS TOOL	A−	0.34	0.54	59%	9.7%
INTL. FLAV AND FR.	A	1.13	1.92	70%	11.2%
JOHNSON & JOHN.	A	0.64	1.12	75%	11.8%
JOSTENS INC.	A+	0.39	0.66	69%	11.1%
K MART	A−	0.80	1.56	95%	14.3%
KELLOGG CO.	A+	0.90	1.72	91%	13.8%
KEYSTONE INT.	B+	0.35	0.53	51%	8.7%
KIMBERLY-CLK.	A+	1.16	2.35	103%	15.2%
KNIGHT-RIDDER	A+	0.79	1.22	54%	9.1%
LEE ENTERPR.	A	0.45	0.68	51%	8.6%
LEGGETT AND PLATT	A	0.33	0.71	115%	16.6%
(ELI) LILLY	A+	0.80	1.35	69%	11.0%
LONGS DRUG STR.	A	0.62	0.92	48%	8.2%
LORAL CORP.	A+	0.47	0.74	57%	9.5%
LUBY'S CAFET.	A	0.36	0.58	61%	10.0%
MARRIOTT CORP.	A+	0.11	0.24	118%	16.9%
MAY DEPT. STRS.	A+	0.78	1.39	78%	12.3%
MCDONALD'S	A+	0.20	0.31	55%	9.2%
MCDONNELL-DG.	A−	1.84	2.76	50%	8.4%
MCGRAW-HILL	NR*	1.30	2.05	58%	9.5%
MEDTRONIC	A	0.38	0.71	87%	13.3%
MELVILLE CORP.	A+	0.72	0.81	13%	2.4%
MERCK AND CO.	A+	0.55	1.64	198%	24.4%

COMPANY	S+P RATING	'85 DIVIDENDS	'89 DIVIDENDS	INCREASE	COMPOUND %
MILLIPORE	A	0.24	0.38	58%	9.6%
MINNESOTA MNG.	A	1.75	2.60	49%	8.2%
(J.P.) MORGAN	A−	1.13	1.66	47%	8.0%
NACCO INDUSTS.	A	0.36	0.58	61%	10.0%
NAT'L SVCE. IND.	A+	0.49	0.84	71%	11.4%
NBD BANCORP	A	0.45	1.13	151%	20.2%
NCNB CORP.	A	0.69	1.10	59%	9.8%
NCR CORP.	A+	0.38	1.30	242%	27.9%
NUCOR CORP.	B+	0.27	0.43	59%	9.8%
PEPSICO, INC.	A	0.59	0.92	56%	9.3%
PFIZER INC.	A+	1.38	2.20	59%	9.8%
PHILIP MORRIS	A+	0.50	1.18	136%	18.7%
PHILIPS INDS.	A	0.23	0.56	143%	19.5%
PNC FINANCIAL	A−	1.28	2.00	56%	9.3%
PPG INDUSTRIES	A+	0.82	1.38	68%	11.0%
PREMIER IND'L.	A	0.23	0.48	109%	15.9%
QUAKER OATS	A	0.62	1.25	102%	15.1%
RALSTON PURINA	A+	0.98	1.65	68%	11.0%
RITE AID CORP.	A	0.43	0.82	91%	13.8%
RUBBERMAID	A+	0.23	0.46	100%	14.9%
SARA LEE	A+	0.35	0.72	106%	15.5%
SECURITY PACIF.	A	1.31	2.20	68%	10.9%
SERVICE CP.INT.	A	0.21	0.52	148%	19.9%
(J.M.) SMUCKER	A	0.48	1.00	108%	15.8%
STANDARD COMM.	A−	0.21	0.50	138%	18.9%
STANLEY WORKS	A	0.67	1.02	52%	8.8%
SUPER VALU ST.	A+	0.33	0.56	70%	11.2%
SYNTEX CORP.	A	0.44	1.45	230%	26.9%
SYSCO CORP.	A+	0.10	0.19	90%	13.7%
TIMES MIRROR	A−	0.68	1.00	47%	8.0%
TORCHMARK CP.	A+	0.53	1.25	136%	18.7%
UNIVERSAL CORP.	A+	0.96	1.40	46%	7.8%
UPJOHN CO.	A	0.44	0.91	107%	15.6%
UST INC.	A+	0.43	0.92	114%	16.4%
V. F. CORP.	A+	0.58	0.91	57%	9.4%
WALGREEN CO.	A+	0.44	0.71	61%	10.0%
WALLACE COMPUTER	A+	0.22	0.42	91%	13.8%
WAL-MART STRS.	A+	0.05	0.21	320%	33.2%
WARNER-LAMBERT	A−	1.50	2.56	71%	11.3%
WASTE MGMT.	A	0.11	0.27	145%	19.7%
WITCO CORP.	B+	0.99	1.60	62%	10.1%
ZERO CORP.	A−	0.19	0.38	100%	14.9%

*McGraw-Hill is not rated because Standard & Poor's is a subsidiary of McGraw-Hill.

TAX TRAPS AND HOW TO AVOID THEM

The three potential tax traps associated with investing your corporate surplus are all easy to avoid, so I shall discuss them briefly here and in greater detail in Chapters 16 and 17.

THE TAX ON SWITCHING

Unlike your pension fund, which pays no capital-gains tax on its trades when they are made, your corporation pays a capital-gains tax (presently at the same rate as its income tax) any time it sells a security in its portfolio at a profit. Selling stocks at a profit is often desirable—think of the summer and early fall of 1987, when the stock market peaked before the October crash—but it can turn into a counterproductive habit of trading your portfolio too frequently and paying a capital-gains tax on every successful trade.

The tax on switching is not a tax trap in the way the next two tax problems are, because it doesn't generate tax penalties. But too much switching can easily become portfolio churning, and the capital-gains taxes and high commissions caused by frequent trading can erode your profits just as surely as a tax penalty can.

THE PERSONAL HOLDING COMPANY TRAP

The Internal Revenue Code defines a personal holding company as any corporation where at least 60 percent of adjusted ordinary gross income is considered "personal holding company income." For the purposes of this chapter, we'll consider dividend income from your corporate portfolio, which might run as high as $10,000–$15,000 a year after five or ten years of successful investing. (More complete rules will be found in Chapter 17.)

Generally, there are only two types of owner-employees who might be at risk: (1) authors or artists who take several years to complete a major work and who receive chunks of earned income in one year, followed by a year or two of little or no earned income; and (2) women who take maternity leaves. If you fall into one of these categories or think that you will within the next few years, remember that as long as your corporation receives 59 percent or less of its income from interest and dividends, you won't fall into the trap and be liable for tax penalties.

If you expect your corporation's dividend income to be at least 60 percent of its adjusted gross income, you can use any of the following strategies, or a combination of them:

(1) increase your corporation's earned income—often
as little as $500–$1,000 will bring the dividend
figure down from 60 percent or more to 59 percent
or less
(2) sell as much stock as you need to reduce
dividends to 59 percent and reinvest the proceeds
in municipal bonds, whose interest is excluded in
calculating personal holding company percentages
(3) sell as much stock as you need to reduce
dividends to 59 percent and reinvest the proceeds
in growth stocks paying no dividends

For more detailed strategies, please see pp. 263–66.

THE ACCUMULATED EARNINGS TAX TRAP

For most owner-employees, the accumulated earnings tax trap is a
potential pitfall either five or ten years down the road, or never. At present,
your corporation is allowed to accumulate earnings of $150,000 if its
principal function, according to the IRS, is "services in the field of law,
health, engineering, architecture, accounting, actuarial science, performing arts, or consulting"; and earnings of $250,000 if it escapes that classi-
fication. If your corporation exceeds those $150,000/$250,000 limitations,
the IRS may impose a punitive tax that can go as high as 38½ percent of
your excessive accumulated earnings, or a total of 84½ percent (46 percent maximum bracket + 38½ percent).

For these reasons, it makes sense to retain no more than $100,000–
$125,000 in your corporation to generate dividends that are 70 percent tax-
free. You'll be able to retain as much money as possible in your corporation without skating close to the edge of the $150,000/$250,000 accumulated earnings limit.

At this time in your corporate life, it's probably sufficient to be aware
that, at some point in the future, you may have to plan strategies to
sidestep the accumulated earnings trap. Four of those strategies will be
found on pp. 249–52.

CHECKLIST

Here's a quick checklist to help you focus on what you'll need to
become a successful corporate investor, enjoying dividends that are 70
percent tax-free:

- For significant returns, plan to invest at least $5,000 a year; that's only $1,250 quarterly.
- Don't be deterred by having to buy odd lots (less than 100 shares). Over the years, they'll add up to hundreds of shares.
- Don't confuse the company with the stock. Tiffany may make beautiful things, but in 1989–90 the price of its stock was cut nearly in half—from 61 to 32—because its sales and earnings are too dependent on U.S. and Japanese consumer prosperity. Ralston Purina makes delicious cereals and pet foods, but in 1989–90 its stock plunged from 102 to 77 because of narrowing profit margins and a lowering of price/earnings ratios among packaged-food stocks.
- Be a disciplined investor. Stick to your investment strategy of selling a stock only when (a) its dividend has not been increased during the year; (b) the outlook for the stock has weakened; (c) the stock market is topping out or has started declining, and you think that if you sell the stock now, you can repurchase it later at a significantly lower price and pyramid your position. Von Clausewitz may have said it best: "Everything in strategy is very simple, but that does not mean everything is very easy."

13

How to Use Your C Corporation to Beat the Taxmen: How to Pay Minimum Corporate and Personal Federal, State, and Local Income Taxes

This chapter has two purposes. First, it will show you, the C corporation owner, how to beat *all* the taxmen—federal, state, and local—at their own games by giving you strategies for various net taxable income levels. It will show you how to make that crucial split: choosing a reasonable salary for your corporation to pay you and retaining income in your corporation so that you and your corporation pay minimum taxes no matter where you incorporate and live.

State and local income taxes can increase your already heavy tax burden substantially. In New York City—the most heavily taxed locality—single taxpayers whose net taxable income is $45,000 and who are in the 33 percent federal tax bracket have to pay an additional 11.275 percent in state and city income taxes. (While these percentages appear lower than the 42 percent federal tax bracket and 18.5 percent state and city brackets of five years ago, many deductions have been curtailed or eliminated, resulting in higher taxes than before.) In contrast to New York City, five states impose no personal or corporate income tax: Nevada, South Dakota, Texas, Washington, and Wyoming. Other states, like Connecticut and Florida, impose no personal income tax, or do not tax earned income.

These discrepancies in state and local tax rates lead to the second purpose of this chapter: how to find the lowest-taxed corporate home. There are several metropolitan areas of the United States in whch it is possible to choose from among two or three states. In the New York City metropolitan area, entrepreneurs can have their corporate homes in New York City, New York State (Long Island, Westchester, or Rockland counties, for example), New Jersey, or Connecticut. All have vastly different personal and corporate tax rates, as the examples in this chapter demonstrate clearly. Similarly, in the Washington, D.C., metropolitan area, entrepreneurs can choose to incorporate in the District of Columbia, in Maryland, or in Virginia—all with different tax rates.

This chapter will also be useful for entrepreneurs who are considering larger geographical areas. Suppose you are thinking of setting up shop in the Pacific Northwest. A quick flip of the pages will show you the tax differences between incorporating in northern California, with its 9.3 percent corporate and personal income taxes; Oregon, with its 9 percent corporate and 6.6 percent personal income taxes; and Washington, with no corporate or personal income taxes. *These differences can save you $5,000, $10,000 a year and more!*

HOW TO USE THIS CHAPTER

This chapter makes a number of assumptions which you can modify in your worksheet calculations in order to obtain figures that better fit your own personal circumstances. Two assumptions virtually balance each other (or cancel each other out): First, that state and local personal exemptions are equal to federal personal exemptions (presently $2,000) and that the state and local standard deduction is equal to the federal standard deduction (presently $3,100 for single taxpayers, $5,200 for married taxpayers filing jointly). This assumption tends to understate state and local individual income taxes slightly. Second, for ease of comparison, state taxes have not been deducted from federal taxes. This assumption tends to overstate federal corporate and individual taxes slightly.

This chapter also assumes that single and married corporate owners have no additional income and that married corporate heads have nonworking spouses and no children. Thus, if a single corporate owner-employee takes a salary of $40,000, his or her net taxable income would be $34,900 ($40,000 – $2,000 exemption – $3,100 standard deduction). A married owner-employee would have a net taxable income of $30,800 ($40,000 – $4,000 exemptions – $5,200 standard deduction).

We'll also assume that the corporate income to be split is gross corporate income less all expenses except salary, pension contribution, and corporate income taxes, and that our owner-employee has chosen a simple 25 percent defined-contribution plan for his or her pension and profit-sharing account.

In the tables that follow, you will see the best way to split corporate income between your salary and earnings retained in the corporation so that you and your corporation will pay minimum taxes and still benefit from advantageous pension contributions and corporate investments whose dividends are 70 percent tax-free.

After you review these tables and the notes that show you the best way to split income between your salary and retained corporate income in your state or locality, use the tax tables at the end of this chapter for your worksheet calculations, and *you will be able to save thousands of dollars a year, every year!*

TABLES—
STATE BY STATE

ALABAMA

Single—$35,000 Individual/Corporate

Income Split	**$20,000** $15,000	**$23,000** $12,000	**$26,000** $9,000
Less Pension Contribution	$5,000	$5,750	$6,500
Net Income	$10,000	$6,250	$2,500
Federal Taxes	**$2,239** $1,500	**$2,689** $938	**$3,448** $375
State Taxes	**$345** $500	**$855** $313	**$1,005** $125
Totals	**$2,584** $2,000	**$3,544** $1,251	**$4,453** $500
Grand Total	**$4,584**	**$4,795**	**$4,953**

Single—$60,000 Individual/Corporate

Income Split	**$30,000** $30,000	**$35,000** $25,000	**$40,000** $20,000	**$45,000** $15,000
Less Pension Contribution	$7,500	$8,750	$10,000	$11,250
Net Income	$22,500	$16,250	$10,000	$3,750
Federal Taxes	**$4,568** $3,375	**$5,968** $2,438	**$7,368** $1,500	**$8,768** $563
State Taxes	**$1,205** $1,125	**$1,455** $813	**$1,705** $500	**$1,955** $188
Totals	**$5,773** $4,500	**$7,423** $3,251	**$9,073** $2,000	**$10,723** $751
Grand Total	**$10,273**	**$10,674**	**$11,073**	**$11,474**

Your Estimates

Corporate Income from income split	$ _____
Less Pension contribution	− _____
Net corp. income	$ _____
Federal corp. tax	$ _____
State corp. tax	$ _____
Individual income from income split	$ _____
Less exemptions (number × $2,000 or correct amount for your state)	− _____
	$ _____
Less standard deduction ($3,100 if single, $5,200 if married) or Itemized total	− _____
Taxable income	$ _____
Federal income tax	$ _____
State income tax	$ _____

Insert numbers on worksheet into box at right; add for totals

TAX RATES

Corporate—5%
Individual—
  Single—$110 + 5% of excess over $3,000
  Married—$220 + 5% of excess over $3,000

COMMENT

For single individuals in the $35,000 category, the $20,000/$15,000 income split is best; in the $60,000 category, the $30,000/$30,000 split is best.

For married individuals in the $50,000 category, the $38,000/$12,000 income split offers the lowest taxes and provides the greatest tax-sheltered pension contribution. In the $75,000 category, the $38,000/$37,000 split offers the lowest taxes.

ALABAMA

Married—$50,000 Individual/Corporate

Income Split	$25,000 $25,000	$32,000 $18,000	$38,000 $12,000
Less Pension Contribution	$6,250	$8,000	$9,500
Net Income	$18,750	$10,000	$2,500
Federal Taxes	$2,374 $2,813	$3,424 $1,500	$4,324 $375
State Taxes	$710 $938	$1,060 $500	$1,360 $125
Totals	$3,084 $3,751	$4,484 $2,000	$5,684 $500
Grand Total	$6,835	$6,484	$6,184

Married—$75,000 Individual/Corporate

Income Split	$30,000 $45,000	$38,000 $37,000	$45,000 $30,000	$55,000 $20,000
Less Pension Contribution	$7,500	$9,500	$11,250	$13,750
Net Income	$37,500	$27,500	$18,750	$6,250
Federal Taxes	$3,124 $5,625	$4,324 $4,125	$6,008 $2,813	$8,808 $938
State Taxes	$960 $1,875	$1,360 $1,375	$1,710 $938	$2,210 $313
Totals	$4,084 $7,500	$5,684 $5,500	$7,718 $3,751	$11,018 $1,251
Grand Total	$11,584	$11,184	$11,469	$12,269

Individual/Corporate

Income split	$ $
Less Pension contribution	$
Net Income	$
Federal Taxes	$ $
State Taxes	$ $
Totals	$ $
Grand Total	$

Corp. funds available for investment (corp. net income-corp. taxes) $ _____

127

ALASKA

Single—$35,000 **Individual**/Corporate

Income Split	$20,000 $15,000	$23,000 $12,000	$26,000 $9,000
Less Pension Contribution	$5,000	$5,750	$6,500
Net Income	$10,000	$6,250	$2,500
Federal Taxes	$2,239 $1,500	$2,689 $938	$3,448 $375
State Taxes	$0 $100	$0 $63	$0 $25
Totals	$2,239 $1,600	$2,689 $1,001	$3,448 $400
Grand Total	$3,839	$3,690	$3,848

Single—$60,000 **Individual**/Corporate

Income Split	$30,000 $30,000	$35,000 $25,000	$40,000 $20,000	$45,000 $15,000
Less Pension Contribution	$7,500	$8,750	$10,000	$11,250
Net Income	$22,500	$16,250	$10,000	$3,750
Federal Taxes	$4,568 $3,375	$5,968 $2,438	$7,368 $1,500	$8,768 $563
State Taxes	$0 $375	$0 $225	$0 $100	$0 $38
Totals	$4,568 $3,750	$5,968 $2,663	$7,368 $1,600	$8,768 $601
Grand Total	$8,318	$8,631	$8,968	$9,369

Your Estimates

Corporate Income from income split	$ _____
Less Pension contribution	− _____
Net corp. income	$ _____
Federal corp. tax	$ _____
State corp. tax	$ _____
Individual income from income split	$ _____
Less exemptions (number × $2,000 or correct amount for your state)	− _____
	$ _____
Less standard deduction ($3,100 if single, $5,200 if married) or Itemized total	− _____
Taxable income	$ _____
Federal income tax	$ _____
State income tax	$ ____0_____

Insert numbers on worksheet into box at right; add for totals

TAX RATES

Corporate—1st $10,000   1%
      Next $10,000   2
      Next $10,000   3
      Next $10,000   4
Individual—0

COMMENT

Because Alaska imposes no personal income tax and a minimal corporate income tax, the $23,000/12,000 income split is best for single individuals in the $35,000 category. At $60,000, the best choice is the $30,000/$30,000 split.

For married individuals in the $50,000 category, the $38,000/$12,000 income split offers the lowest taxes while providing the greatest tax-sheltered pension contribution. At $75,000, the $38,000/$37,000 split offers the lowest taxes. However, the $45,000/$30,000 split provides $7,000 more in salary and $1,750 in pension contributions for only $122 in additional taxes.

ALASKA

Married—$50,000 Individual/Corporate

Income Split	$25,000 $25,000	$32,000 $18,000	$38,000 $12,000
Less Pension Contribution	$6,250	$8,000	$9,500
Net Income	$18,750	$10,000	$2,500
Federal Taxes	$2,374 $2,813	$3,424 $1,500	$4,324 $375
State Taxes	$0 $275	$0 $100	$0 $25
Totals	$2,374 $3,088	$3,424 $1,600	$4,324 $400
Grand Total	$5,462	$5,024	$4,724

Married—$75,000 Individual/Corporate

Income Split	$30,000 $45,000	$38,000 $37,000	$45,000 $30,000	$55,000 $20,000
Less Pension Contribution	$7,500	$9,500	$11,250	$13,750
Net Income	$37,500	$27,500	$18,750	$6,250
Federal Taxes	$3,124 $5,625	$4,324 $4,125	$6,008 $2,813	$8,808 $938
State Taxes	$0 $900	$0 $525	$0 $275	$0 $63
Totals	$3,124 $6,525	$4,324 $4,650	$6,008 $3,088	$8,808 $1,001
Grand Total	$9,649	$8,974	$9,096	$9,809

Individual/Corporate

Income split	$ $
Less Pension contribution	$
Net Income	$
Federal Taxes	$ $
State Taxes	$ 0 $
Totals	$ $
Grand Total	$

Corp. funds available for investment (corp. net income-corp. taxes) $ _____

ARIZONA

Single—$35,000 Individual/Corporate

Income Split	$20,000 $15,000	$23,000 $12,000	$26,000 $9,000
Less Pension Contribution	$5,000	$5,750	$6,500
Net Income	$10,000	$6,250	$2,500
Federal Taxes	$2,239 $1,500	$2,689 $938	$3,448 $375
State Taxes	$921 $770	$1,161 $376	$1,401 $90
Totals	$3,160 $2,270	$3,850 $1,314	$4,849 $465
Grand Total	$5,430	$5,164	$5,314

Single—$60,000 Individual/Corporate

Income Split	$30,000 $30,000	$35,000 $25,000	$40,000 $20,000	$45,000 $15,000
Less Pension Contribution	$7,500	$8,750	$10,000	$11,250
Net Income	$22,500	$16,250	$10,000	$3,750
Federal Taxes	$4,568 $3,375	$5,968 $2,438	$7,368 $1,500	$8,768 $563
State Taxes	$1,721 $2,083	$2,121 $1,426	$2,521 $770	$2,921 $164
Totals	$6,289 $5,458	$8,089 $3,864	$9,889 $2,270	$11,689 $727
Grand Total	$11,747	$11,953	$12,159	$12,416

Your Estimates

Corporate Income from income split	$ _____
Less Pension contribution	− _____
Net corp. income	$ _____
Federal corp. tax	$ _____
State corp. tax	$ _____
Individual income from income split	$ _____
Less exemptions (number × $2,000 or correct amount for your state)	− _____
	$ _____
Less standard deduction ($3,100 if single, $5,200 if married) or Itemized total	− _____
Taxable income	$ _____
Federal income tax	$ _____
State income tax	$ _____

Insert numbers on worksheet into box at right; add for totals

TAX RATES

Corporate	—	1st $1,000	2.5%
		2nd $1,000	4.0
		3rd $1,000	5.0
		4th $1,000	6.5
		5th $1,000	8.0
		6th $1,000	9.0
		Over $6,000	10.5

Individual—
  Single—over $7,740 = 8%−$271
  Married—over $15,480 = 8%−$542

COMMENT

For single individuals in the $35,000 category, the $23,000/$12,000 income split offers the lowest taxes. At $60,000, the $30,000/$30,000 split is clearly the best choice.

For married entrepreneurs in the $50,000 category, the $38,000/$12,000 income split offers both the highest salary and pension contribution *and* the lowest taxes. At $75,000, the $38,000/$37,000 split offers the lowest taxes, but the $45,000/$30,000 split provides $7,000 more in salary and $1,750 more in pension contributions for *a mere $13 in additional taxes.*

ARIZONA

Married—$50,000 Individual/Corporate

Income Split	$25,000 $25,000	$32,000 $18,000	$38,000 $12,000
Less Pension Contribution	$6,250	$8,000	$9,500
Net Income	$18,750	$10,000	$2,500
Federal Taxes	$2,374 $2,813	$3,424 $1,500	$4,324 $375
State Taxes	$722 $1,689	$1,282 $770	$1,762 $90
Totals	$3,096 $4,502	$4,706 $2,270	$6,086 $465
Grand Total	$7,598	$6,976	$6,551

Married—$75,000 Individual/Corporate

Income Split	$30,000 $45,000	$38,000 $37,000	$45,000 $30,000	$55,000 $20,000
Less Pension Contribution	$7,500	$9,500	$11,250	$13,750
Net Income	$37,500	$27,500	$18,750	$6,250
Federal Taxes	$3,124 $5,625	$4,324 $4,125	$6,008 $2,813	$8,808 $938
State Taxes	$1,122 $3,658	$1,762 $2,608	$2,322 $1,689	$3,122 $376
Totals	$4,246 $9,283	$6,086 $6,733	$8,330 $4,502	$11,930 $1,314
Grand Total	$13,529	$12,819	$12,832	$13,244

Individual/Corporate

Income split	$ $
Less Pension contribution	$
Net Income	$
Federal Taxes	$ $
State Taxes	$ $
Totals	$ $
Grand Total	$

Corp. funds available for investment (corp. net income-corp. taxes) $ _____

ARKANSAS

Single—$35,000 **Individual**/Corporate

Income Split	$20,000 $15,000	$23,000 $12,000	$26,000 $9,000
Less Pension Contribution	$5,000	$5,750	$6,500
Net Income	$10,000	$6,250	$2,500
Federal Taxes	$2,239 $1,500	$2,689 $938	$3,448 $375
State Taxes	$476 $210	$654 $98	$834 $25
Totals	$2,715 $1,710	$3,343 $1,036	$4,282 $400
Grand Total	$4,425	$4,379	$4,682

Single—$60,000 **Individual**/Corporate

Income Split	$30,000 $30,000	$35,000 $25,000	$40,000 $20,000	$45,000 $15,000
Less Pension Contribution	$7,500	$8,750	$10,000	$11,250
Net Income	$22,500	$16,250	$10,000	$3,750
Federal Taxes	$4,568 $3,375	$5,968 $2,438	$7,368 $1,500	$8,768 $563
State Taxes	$1,074 $815	$1,423 $503	$1,773 $210	$2,123 $45
Totals	$5,642 $4,190	$7,391 $2,941	$9,141 $1,710	$10,891 $608
Grand Total	$9,832	$10,332	$10,851	$11,499

Your Estimates

Corporate Income from income split	$ _____
Less Pension contribution	
Net corp. income	$ _____
Federal corp. tax	$ _____
State corp. tax	$ _____
Individual income from income split	$ _____
Less exemptions (number × $2,000 or correct amount for your state)	− _____
	$ _____
Less standard deduction ($3,100 if single, $5,200 if married) or Itemized total	− _____
Taxable income	$ _____
Federal income tax	$ _____
State income tax	$ _____

Insert numbers on worksheet into box at right; add for totals

TAX RATES

Corporate—— 1st $3,000 1%
Next $3,000 2
Next $5,000 3
Next $14,000 5
Next $25,000 6

Individual —
$ 9,000–$14,999 $210 + 4.5% of excess over $9,000
15,000–24,999 $480 + 6% of excess over $15,000
25,000 + $1,080 + 7% of excess over $25,000

COMMENT

For single individuals in the $35,000 category, the $23,000/$12,000 income split is best; in the $60,000 category, the $30,000/$30,000 split is clearly the best choice.

For married individuals in the $50,000 category, the $38,000/$12,000 income split offers the lowest taxes and provides the greatest tax-sheltered pension contribution. At $75,000, the $38,000/$37,000 split offers the lowest taxes.

ARKANSAS

Married—$50,000 Individual/Corporate

Income Split	$25,000 $25,000	$32,000 $18,000	$38,000 $12,000
Less Pension Contribution	$6,250	$8,000	$9,500
Net Income	$18,750	$10,000	$2,500
Federal Taxes	$2,374 $2,813	$3,424 $1,500	$4,324 $375
State Taxes	$528 $628	$948 $210	$1,346 $25
Totals	$2,902 $3,441	$4,372 $1,710	$5,670 $400
Grand Total	$6,343	$6,082	$6,070

Married—$75,000 Individual/Corporate

Income Split	$30,000 $45,000	$38,000 $37,000	$45,000 $30,000	$55,000 $20,000
Less Pension Contribution	$7,500	$9,500	$11,250	$13,750
Net Income	$37,500	$27,500	$18,750	$6,250
Federal Taxes	$3,124 $5,625	$4,324 $4,125	$6,008 $2,813	$8,808 $938
State Taxes	$828 $1,690	$1,346 $1,090	$1,836 $628	$2,536 $98
Totals	$3,952 $7,315	$5,670 $5,215	$7,844 $3,441	$11,344 $1,036
Grand Total	$11,267	$10,885	$11,285	$12,380

Individual/Corporate

Income split	$ $
Less Pension contribution	$
Net Income	$
Federal Taxes	$ $
State Taxes	$ $
Totals	$ $
Grand Total	$

Corp. funds available for investment (corp. net income-corp. taxes) $ _____

CALIFORNIA

Single—$35,000 **Individual**/Corporate

Income Split	$20,000 $15,000	$23,000 $12,000	$26,000 $9,000
Less Pension Contribution	$5,000	$5,750	$6,500
Net Income	$10,000	$6,250	$2,500
Federal Taxes	$2,239 $1,500	$2,689 $938	$3,448 $375
State Taxes	$365 $930	$543 $800	$723 $800
Totals	$2,604 $2,430	$3,232 $1,738	$4,171 $1,175
Grand Total	$5,034	$4,970	$5,346

Single—$60,000 **Individual**/Corporate

Income Split	$30,000 $30,000	$35,000 $25,000	$40,000 $20,000	$45,000 $15,000
Less Pension Contribution	$7,500	$8,750	$10,000	$11,250
Net Income	$22,500	$16,250	$10,000	$3,750
Federal Taxes	$4,568 $3,375	$5,968 $2,438	$7,368 $1,500	$8,768 $563
State Taxes	$1,043 $2,093	$1,488 $1,511	$1,953 $930	$2,418 $800
Totals	$5,611 $5,468	$7,456 $3,949	$9,321 $2,430	$11,186 $1,363
Grand Total	$11,079	$11,405	$11,751	$12,549

Your Estimates

Corporate Income from income split	$ _____
Less Pension contribution	− _____
Net corp. income	$ _____
Federal corp. tax	$ _____
State corp. tax	$ _____
Individual income from income split	$ _____
Less exemptions (number × $2,000 or correct amount for your state)	− _____
Less standard deduction ($3,100 if single, $5,200 if married) or Itemized total	− _____
Taxable income	$ _____
Federal income tax	$ _____
State income tax	$ _____

Insert numbers on worksheet into box at right; add for totals

TAX RATES

Corporate—9.3%, with a minimum of $800
Individual—

Single—$	9,528–$15,035	$150 + 4% of excess over $9,528
	$15,035–$20,873	$371 + 6% of excess over $15,035
	$20,873–$26,380	$721 + 8% of excess over $20,873
	Over $26,380	$1,168 + 9.3% of excess over $26,380
Married—$	8,040–$19,056	$80 + 2% of excess over $8,040
	$19,056–$30,070	$301 + 4% of excess over $19,056
	$30,070–$41,746	$741 + 6% of excess over $30,070
	$41,746–$52,760	$1,442 + 9.3% of excess over $41,746

COMMENT

For single entrepreneurs in the $35,000 category, the $23,000/$12,000 income split offers the lowest taxes. At $60,000, the $30,000/$30,000 split is clearly the best choice.

For married individuals in the $50,000 category, the $38,000/$12,000 income split offers both the highest salary and pension contribution *and* lowest taxes. At $75,000, the $38,000/$37,000 and $45,000/$30,000 splits offer nearly equal low taxes. Therefore the choice is a trade-off between lower salary and pension contribution but higher tax-free investment income vs. higher salary and pension contributions but lower corporate tax-free investment income.

CALIFORNIA

Married—$50,000 **Individual**/Corporate

Income Split	**$25,000** $25,000	**$32,000** $18,000	**$38,000** $12,000
Less Pension Contribution	$6,250	$8,000	$9,500
Net Income	$18,750	$10,000	$2,500
Federal Taxes	**$2,374** $2,813	**$3,424** $1,500	**$4,324** $375
State Taxes	**$235** $1,744	**$451** $930	**$691** $800
Totals	**$2,609** $4,557	**$3,875** $2,430	**$5,015** $1,175
Grand Total	**$7,166**	**$6,305**	**$6,190**

Married—$75,000 **Individual**/Corporate

Income Split	**$30,000** $45,000	**$38,000** $37,000	**$45,000** $30,000	**$55,000** $20,000
Less Pension Contribution	$7,500	$9,500	$11,250	$13,750
Net Income	$37,500	$27,500	$18,750	$6,250
Federal Taxes	**$3,124** $5,625	**$4,324** $4,125	**$6,008** $2,813	**$8,808** $938
State Taxes	**$371** $3,488	**$691** $2,558	**$1,085** $1,744	**$1,766** $800
Totals	**$3,495** $9,113	**$5,015** $6,683	**$7,093** $4,557	**$10,574** $1,738
Grand Total	**$12,608**	**$11,698**	**$11,650**	**$12,312**

Individual/Corporate

Income split	$ $
Less Pension contribution	$
Net Income	$
Federal Taxes	$ $
State Taxes	$ $
Totals	$ $
Grand Total	$

Corp. funds available for investment (corp. net income-corp. taxes) $ _____

COLORADO

Single—$35,000 Individual/Corporate

Income Split	$20,000 $15,000	$23,000 $12,000	$26,000 $9,000
Less Pension Contribution	$5,000	$5,750	$6,500
Net Income	$10,000	$6,250	$2,500
Federal Taxes	$2,239 $1,500	$2,689 $938	$3,448 $375
State Taxes	$1,361 $500	$895 $313	$1,045 $125
Totals	$3,600 $2,000	$3,584 $1,251	$4,493 $500
Grand Total	$5,600	$4,835	$4,993

Single—$60,000 Individual/Corporate

Income Split	$30,000 $30,000	$35,000 $25,000	$40,000 $20,000	$45,000 $15,000
Less Pension Contribution	$7,500	$8,750	$10,000	$11,250
Net Income	$22,500	$16,250	$10,000	$3,750
Federal Taxes	$4,568 $3,375	$5,968 $2,438	$7,368 $1,500	$8,768 $563
State Taxes	$1,245 $1,125	$1,495 $813	$1,745 $500	$1,995 $188
Totals	$5,813 $4,500	$7,463 $3,251	$9,113 $2,000	$10,763 $751
Grand Total	$10,313	$10,714	$11,113	$11,514

Your Estimates

Corporate Income from income split	$ _____
Less Pension contribution	− _____
Net corp. income	$ _____
Federal corp. tax	$ _____
State corp. tax	$ _____
Individual income from income split	$ _____
Less exemptions (number × $2,000 or correct amount for your state)	− _____
Less standard deduction ($3,100 if single, $5,200 if married) or Itemized total	$ _____ − _____
Taxable income	$ _____
Federal income tax	$ _____
State income tax	$ _____

Insert numbers on worksheet into box at right; add for totals

COMMENT

Because corporate and individual rates are an equal flat 5%, they weigh less heavily on your decision making than do federal rates, which are graduated.

TAX RATES

Corporate—5%
Individual—5%

For single individuals in the $35,000 category, the $23,000/$12,000 income split is best; in the $60,000 category, the $30,000/$30,000 split is best.

For married individuals in the $50,000 category, the $38,000/$12,000 income split offers both the highest salary and pension contribution *and* the lowest taxes. At $75,000, the $38,000/$37,000 split is clearly the best choice.

136

COLORADO

Married—$50,000 Individual/Corporate

Income Split	$25,000 $25,000	$32,000 $18,000	$38,000 $12,000
Less Pension Contribution	$6,250	$8,000	$9,500
Net Income	$18,750	$10,000	$2,500
Federal Taxes	$2,374 $2,813	$3,424 $1,500	$4,324 $375
State Taxes	$790 $938	$1,140 $500	$1,440 $125
Totals	$3,164 $3,751	$4,564 $2,000	$5,764 $500
Grand Total	$6,915	$6,564	$6,264

Married—$75,000 Individual/Corporate

Income Split	$30,000 $45,000	$38,000 $37,000	$45,000 $30,000	$55,000 $20,000
Less Pension Contribution	$7,500	$9,500	$11,250	$13,750
Net Income	$37,500	$27,500	$18,750	$6,250
Federal Taxes	$3,124 $5,625	$4,324 $4,125	$6,008 $2,813	$8,808 $938
State Taxes	$1,040 $1,875	$1,440 $1,375	$1,790 $938	$2,290 $313
Totals	$4,164 $7,500	$5,764 $5,500	$7,798 $3,751	$11,098 $1,251
Grand Total	$11,664	$11,264	$11,549	$12,349

Individual/Corporate

Income split	$ $
Less Pension contribution	$
Net Income	$
Federal Taxes	$ $
State Taxes	$ $
Totals	$ $
Grand Total	$

Corp. funds available for investment (corp. net income-corp. taxes) $ _____

CONNECTICUT

Single—$35,000 Individual/Corporate

Income Split	$20,000 $15,000	$23,000 $12,000	$26,000 $9,000
Less Pension Contribution	$5,000	$5,750	$6,500
Net Income	$10,000	$6,250	$2,500
Federal Taxes	$2,239 $1,500	$2,689 $938	$3,448 $375
State Taxes	$0 $1,380	$0 $876	$0 $345
Totals	$2,239 $2,880	$2,689 $1,814	$3,448 $720
Grand Total	$5,119	$4,503	$4,168

Single—$60,000 Individual/Corporate

Income Split	$30,000 $30,000	$35,000 $25,000	$40,000 $20,000	$45,000 $15,000
Less Pension Contribution	$7,500	$8,750	$10,000	$11,250
Net Income	$22,500	$16,250	$10,000	$3,750
Federal Taxes	$4,568 $3,375	$5,968 $2,438	$7,368 $1,500	$8,768 $563
State Taxes	$0 $3,105	$0 $2,243	$0 $1,380	$0 $518
Totals	$4,568 $6,480	$5,968 $4,681	$7,368 $2,880	$8,768 $1,081
Grand Total	$11,048	$10,649	$10,248	$9,849

Your Estimates

Corporate Income from income split	$ _____
Less Pension contribution	− _____
Net corp. income	$ _____
Federal corp. tax	$ _____
State corp. tax	$ _____
Individual income from income split	$ _____
Less exemptions (number × $2,000 or correct amount for your state)	− _____
	$ _____
Less standard deduction ($3,100 if single, $5,200 if married) or Itemized total	− _____
Taxable income	$ _____
Federal income tax	$ _____
State income tax (none on earned income)	$ _____

Insert numbers on worksheet into box at right; add for totals

TAX RATES

Corporate—11.5% + 20% surtax = 13.8% total
Individual— 0 on earned income

COMMENT

Because Connecticut has the highest differential between corporate and individual rates (13.8%), the *highest-salary income splits* in all categories will produce the *lowest taxes* as well as the *greatest pension contributions*.

CONNECTICUT

Married—$50,000 Individual/Corporate

Income Split	$25,000 $25,000	$32,000 $18,000	$38,000 $12,000
Less Pension Contribution	$6,250	$8,000	$9,500
Net Income	$18,750	$10,000	$2,500
Federal Taxes	$2,374 $2,813	$3,424 $1,500	$4,324 $375
State Taxes	$0 $2,588	$0 $1,380	$0 $345
Totals	$2,374 $5,401	$3,424 $2,880	$4,324 $720
Grand Total	$7,775	$6,304	$5,044

Married—$75,000 Individual/Corporate

Income Split	$30,000 $45,000	$38,000 $37,000	$45,000 $30,000	$55,000 $20,000
Less Pension Contribution	$7,500	$9,500	$11,250	$13,750
Net Income	$37,500	$27,500	$18,750	$6,250
Federal Taxes	$3,124 $5,625	$4,324 $4,125	$6,008 $2,813	$8,808 $938
State Taxes	$0 $5,175	$0 $3,975	$0 $2,588	$0 $876
Totals	$3,124 $10,800	$4,324 $8,100	$6,008 $5,401	$8,808 $1,814
Grand Total	$13,924	$12,424	$11,409	$10,622

Individual/Corporate

Income split	$ $
Less Pension contribution	$
Net Income	$
Federal Taxes	$ $
State Taxes	$ $
Totals	$ $
Grand Total	$

Corp. funds available for investment (corp. net income-corp. taxes) $ _____

DELAWARE

Single—$35,000 Individual/Corporate

Income Split	$20,000 $15,000	$23,000 $12,000	$26,000 $9,000
Less Pension Contribution	$5,000	$5,750	$6,500
Net Income	$10,000	$6,250	$2,500
Federal Taxes	$2,239 $1,500	$2,689 $938	$3,448 $375
State Taxes	$704 $870	$884 $544	$1,069 $218
Totals	$2,943 $2,370	$3,573 $1,482	$4,517 $593
Grand Total	$5,313	$5,055	$5,110

Single—$60,000 Individual/Corporate

Income Split	$30,000 $30,000	$35,000 $25,000	$40,000 $20,000	$45,000 $15,000
Less Pension Contribution	$7,500	$8,750	$10,000	$11,250
Net Income	$22,500	$16,250	$10,000	$3,750
Federal Taxes	$4,568 $3,375	$5,968 $2,438	$7,368 $1,500	$8,768 $563
State Taxes	$1,333 $1,958	$1,683 $1,414	$2,062 $870	$2,442 $326
Totals	$5,901 $5,333	$7,651 $3,852	$9,430 $2,370	$11,210 $889
Grand Total	$11,234	$11,503	$11,800	$12,099

Your Estimates

Corporate Income from income split	$ _____
Less Pension contribution	– _____
Net corp. income	$ _____
Federal corp. tax	$ _____
State corp. tax	$ _____
Individual income from income split	$ _____
Less exemptions	
(number × $2,000 or correct amount for your state)	– _____
	$ _____
Less standard deduction ($3,100 if single, $5,200 if married) or Itemized total	– _____
Taxable income	$ _____
Federal income tax	$ _____
State income tax	$ _____

Insert numbers on worksheet into box at right; add for totals

TAX RATES

Corporate—8.7%
Individual—

$10,000–$20,000	$410	+ 6% of excess over $10,000
$20,000–$25,000	$1,010	+ 6.6% of excess over $20,000
$25,000–$30,000	$1,340	+ 7% of excess over $25,000
$30,000–$40,000	$1,690	+ 7.6% of excess over $30,000
$40,000–$50,000	$2,450	+ 7.7% of excess over $40,000

COMMENT

For single individuals in the $35,000 category, the $23,000/$12,000 income split is the best choice, although the $26,000/$9,000 split provides $3,000 more in salary and $750 more in pension contributions for only $55 more in taxes. At $60,000, the $30,000/$30,000 split is clearly the best choice for lowest taxes and highest tax-free corporate investment income.

For married individuals in the $50,000 category, the $38,000/$12,000 income split offers the lowest taxes and provides the highest salary and pension contribution. In the $75,000 category, the $38,000/$37,000 split produces the lowest taxes.

DELAWARE

Married—$50,000 **Individual**/Corporate

Income Split	$25,000 $25,000	$32,000 $18,000	$38,000 $12,000
Less Pension Contribution	$6,250	$8,000	$9,500
Net Income	$18,750	$10,000	$2,500
Federal Taxes	$2,374 $2,813	$3,424 $1,500	$4,324 $375
State Taxes	$758 $1,641	$1,178 $870	$1,606 $218
Totals	$3,132 $4,454	$4,602 $2,370	$5,930 $593
Grand Total	$7,586	$6,972	$6,523

Married—$75,000 **Individual**/Corporate

Income Split	$30,000 $45,000	$38,000 $37,000	$45,000 $30,000	$55,000 $20,000
Less Pension Contribution	$7,500	$9,500	$11,250	$13,750
Net Income	$37,500	$27,500	$18,750	$6,250
Federal Taxes	$3,124 $5,625	$4,324 $4,125	$6,008 $2,813	$8,808 $938
State Taxes	$1,063 $3,263	$1,606 $2,393	$2,131 $1,641	$2,897 $544
Totals	$4,187 $8,888	$5,930 $6,518	$8,139 $4,454	$11,705 $1,482
Grand Total	$13,075	$12,448	$12,593	$13,187

Individual/Corporate

Income split	$ $
Less Pension contribution	$
Net Income	$
Federal Taxes	$ $
State Taxes	$ $
Totals	$ $
Grand Total	$

Corp. funds available for investment (corp. net income-corp. taxes) $ _____

141

DISTRICT OF COLUMBIA

Single—$35,000 **Individual**/Corporate

Income Split	$20,000 $15,000	$23,000 $12,000	$26,000 $9,000
Less Pension Contribution	$5,000	$5,750	$6,500
Net Income	$10,000	$6,250	$2,500
Federal Taxes	$2,239 $1,500	$2,689 $938	$3,448 $375
State Taxes	$992 $1,050	$1,232 $656	$1,486 $263
Totals	$3,231 $2,550	$3,921 $1,594	$4,934 $638
Grand Total	$5,781	$5,515	$5,572

Single—$60,000 **Individual**/Corporate

Income Split	$30,000 $30,000	$35,000 $25,000	$40,000 $20,000	$45,000 $15,000
Less Pension Contribution	$7,500	$8,750	$10,000	$11,250
Net Income	$22,500	$16,250	$10,000	$3,750
Federal Taxes	$4,568 $3,375	$5,968 $2,438	$7,368 $1,500	$8,768 $563
State Taxes	$1,866 $2,363	$2,341 $1,706	$2,816 $1,050	$3,291 $394
Totals	$6,434 $5,738	$8,309 $4,144	$10,184 $2,550	$12,059 $957
Grand Total	$12,172	$12,453	$12,734	$13,016

Your Estimates

Corporate Income from income split	$ _____
Less Pension contribution	– _____
Net corp. income	$ _____
Federal corp. tax	$ _____
State corp. tax	$ _____
Individual income from income split	$ _____
Less exemptions (number × $2,000 or correct amount for your state)	– _____
	$ _____
Less standard deduction ($3,100 if single, $5,200 if married) or Itemized total	– _____
Taxable income	$ _____
Federal income tax	$ _____
State income tax	$ _____

Insert numbers on worksheet into box at right; add for totals

TAX RATES

Corporate—10% + .5% surtax = 10.5% total
Individual—

$10,000–$20,000	$600 + 8% of excess over $10,000
Over $20,000	$1,400 + 9.5% of excess over $20,000

COMMENT

For single entrepreneurs in the $35,000 category, the $23,000/$12,000 income split offers the lowest taxes. However, the $26,000/$9,000 split is probably more desirable: it offers $3,000 more in salary and $750 more in pension contributions for a *mere $57 in additional taxes*. At $60,000, the $30,000/$30,000 split is clearly the best choice.

For married individuals in the $50,000 category, the $38,000/$12,000 income split offers both the highest salary and pension contribution *and* the lowest taxes. At $75,000, the $38,000/$37,000 split produces the lowest taxes.

DISTRICT OF COLUMBIA

Married—$50,000 Individual/Corporate

Income Split	$25,000 $25,000	$32,000 $18,000	$38,000 $12,000
Less Pension Contribution	$6,250	$8,000	$9,500
Net Income	$18,750	$10,000	$2,500
Federal Taxes	$2,374 $2,813	$3,424 $1,500	$4,324 $375
State Taxes	$1,064 $1,969	$1,666 $1,050	$2,236 $263
Totals	$3,438 $4,782	$5,090 $2,550	$6,560 $638
Grand Total	$8,220	$7,640	$7,198

Married—$75,000 Individual/Corporate

Income Split	$30,000 $45,000	$38,000 $37,000	$45,000 $30,000	$55,000 $20,000
Less Pension Contribution	$7,500	$9,500	$11,250	$13,750
Net Income	$37,500	$27,500	$18,750	$6,250
Federal Taxes	$3,124 $5,625	$4,324 $4,125	$6,008 $2,813	$8,808 $938
State Taxes	$1,476 $3,938	$2,236 $2,888	$2,901 $1,969	$3,851 $656
Totals	$4,600 $9,563	$6,560 $7,013	$8,909 $4,782	$12,659 $1,594
Grand Total	$14,163	$13,573	$13,691	$14,253

Individual/Corporate

Income split	$ $
Less Pension contribution	$
Net Income	$
Federal Taxes	$ $
State Taxes	$ $
Totals	$ $
Grand Total	$

Corp. funds available for investment (corp. net income-corp. taxes) $ _____

FLORIDA

Single—$35,000 **Individual**/Corporate

Income Split	**$20,000** $15,000	**$23,000** $12,000	**$26,000** $9,000
Less Pension Contribution	$5,000	$5,750	$6,500
Net Income	$10,000	$6,250	$2,500
Federal Taxes	**$2,239** $1,500	**$2,689** $938	**$3,448** $375
State Taxes	**$0** $550	**$0** $344	**$0** $138
Totals	**$2,239** $2,050	**$2,689** $1,282	**$3,448** $513
Grand Total	**$4,289**	**$3,971**	**$3,961**

Single—$60,000 **Individual**/Corporate

Income Split	**$30,000** $30,000	**$35,000** $25,000	**$40,000** $20,000	**$45,000** $15,000
Less Pension Contribution	$7,500	$8,750	$10,000	$11,250
Net Income	$22,500	$16,250	$10,000	$3,750
Federal Taxes	**$4,568** $3,375	**$5,968** $2,438	**$7,368** $1,500	**$8,768** $563
State Taxes	**$0** $1,238	**$0** $894	**$0** $550	**$0** $206
Totals	**$4,568** $4,613	**$5,968** $3,332	**$7,368** $2,050	**$8,768** $769
Grand Total	**$9,181**	**$9,300**	**$9,418**	**$9,537**

Your Estimates

Corporate Income from income split	$ _____
Less Pension contribution	− _____
Net corp. income	$ _____
Federal corp. tax	$ _____
State corp. tax	$ _____
Individual income from income split	$ _____
Less exemptions (number × $2,000 or correct amount for your state)	− _____ $ _____
Less standard deduction ($3,100 if single, $5,200 if married) or Itemized total	− _____
Taxable income	$ _____
Federal income tax	$ _____
State income tax	$ ____0____

Insert numbers on worksheet into box at right; add for totals

TAX RATES

Corporate—5.5%
Individual—0

COMMENT

Because Florida does not impose a personal income tax, the $26,000/$9,000 income split offers both the highest salary *and* the lowest taxes for single entrepreneurs in the $35,000 category. At $60,000, the $30,000/$30,000 split is clearly the best choice.

For married individuals in the $50,000 category, the $38,000/$12,000 income split offers both the highest salary and pension contribution *and* the lowest taxes. At $75,000, the $45,000/$30,000 split produces the lowest taxes, but the $55,000/$20,000 split provides $10,000 more in salary and $2,500 more in pension contributions for a *mere $138 in additional taxes.*

FLORIDA

Married—$50,000 Individual/Corporate

Income Split	$25,000 $25,000	$32,000 $18,000	$38,000 $12,000
Less Pension Contribution	$6,250	$8,000	$9,500
Net Income	$18,750	$10,000	$2,500
Federal Taxes	$2,374 $2,813	$3,424 $1,500	$4,324 $375
State Taxes	$0 $1,031	$0 $550	$0 $138
Totals	$2,374 $3,844	$3,424 $2,050	$4,324 $513
Grand Total	$6,218	$5,474	$4,837

Married—$75,000 Individual/Corporate

Income Split	$30,000 $45,000	$38,000 $37,000	$45,000 $30,000	$55,000 $20,000
Less Pension Contribution	$7,500	$9,500	$11,250	$13,750
Net Income	$37,500	$27,500	$18,750	$6,250
Federal Taxes	$3,124 $5,625	$4,324 $4,125	$6,008 $2,813	$8,808 $938
State Taxes	$0 $2,063	$0 $1,513	$0 $1,031	$0 $344
Totals	$3,124 $7,688	$4,324 $5,638	$6,008 $3,844	$8,808 $1,282
Grand Total	$10,812	$9,962	$9,852	$10,090

Individual/Corporate

Income split	$ $
Less Pension contribution	$
Net Income	$
Federal Taxes	$ $
State Taxes	$ $ 0
Totals	$ $
Grand Total	$

Corp. funds available for investment (corp. net income-corp. taxes) $ _____

GEORGIA

Single—$35,000 Individual/Corporate

Income Split	$20,000 $15,000	$23,000 $12,000	$26,000 $9,000
Less Pension Contribution	$5,000	$5,750	$6,500
Net Income	$10,000	$6,250	$2,500
Federal Taxes	$2,239 $1,500	$2,689 $938	$3,448 $375
State Taxes	$704 $600	$884 $375	$1,064 $150
Totals	$2,943 $2,100	$3,573 $1,313	$4,512 $525
Grand Total	$5,043	$4,886	$5,037

Single—$60,000 Individual/Corporate

Income Split	$30,000 $30,000	$35,000 $25,000	$40,000 $20,000	$45,000 $15,000
Less Pension Contribution	$7,500	$8,750	$10,000	$11,250
Net Income	$22,500	$16,250	$10,000	$3,750
Federal Taxes	$4,568 $3,375	$5,968 $2,438	$7,368 $1,500	$8,768 $563
State Taxes	$1,304 $1,350	$1,604 $975	$1,904 $600	$2,204 $225
Totals	$5,872 $4,725	$7,572 $3,413	$9,272 $2,100	$10,972 $788
Grand Total	$10,597	$10,985	$11,372	$11,760

Your Estimates

Corporate Income from income split	$ _____
Less Pension contribution	– _____
Net corp. income	$ _____
Federal corp. tax	$ _____
State corp. tax	$ _____
Individual income from income split	$ _____
Less exemptions (number × $2,000 or correct amount for your state)	– _____
	$ _____
Less standard deduction ($3,100 if single, $5,200 if married) or Itemized total	– _____
Taxable income	$ _____
Federal income tax	$ _____
State income tax	$ _____

Insert numbers on worksheet into box at right; add for totals

TAX RATES

Corporate—6%
Individual—
  Single—$230 + 6% of excess over $7,000
  Married—$340 + 6% of excess over $10,000

COMMENT

For single individuals in the $35,000 category, the $23,000/$12,000 income split offers the lowest taxes. In the $60,000 category, the $30,000/$30,000 split is clearly the best choice.

For married individuals in the $50,000 category, the $32,000/$18,000 income split offers the lowest taxes. At $75,000, the $45,000/$30,000 split produces the lowest taxes and is the best choice for most entrepreneurs.

146

GEORGIA

Married—$50,000 Individual/Corporate

Income Split	$25,000 $25,000	$32,000 $18,000	$38,000 $12,000
Less Pension Contribution	$6,250	$8,000	$9,500
Net Income	$18,750	$10,000	$2,500
Federal Taxes	$2,374 $2,813	$3,424 $1,500	$4,324 $375
State Taxes	$688 $1,125	$1,108 $600	$2,068 $150
Totals	$3,062 $3,938	$4,532 $2,100	$6,392 $525
Grand Total	$7,000	$6,632	$6,917

Married—$75,000 Individual/Corporate

Income Split	$30,000 $45,000	$38,000 $37,000	$45,000 $30,000	$55,000 $20,000
Less Pension Contribution	$7,500	$9,500	$11,250	$13,750
Net Income	$37,500	$27,500	$18,750	$6,250
Federal Taxes	$3,124 $5,625	$4,324 $4,125	$6,008 $2,813	$8,808 $938
State Taxes	$988 $2,250	$2,068 $1,650	$1,888 $1,125	$2,488 $375
Totals	$4,112 $7,875	$6,392 $5,775	$7,896 $3,938	$11,296 $1,313
Grand Total	$11,987	$12,167	$11,834	$12,609

Individual/Corporate

Income split	$ _____ $ _____
Less Pension contribution	$ _____
Net Income	$ _____
Federal Taxes	$ _____ $ _____
State Taxes	$ _____ $ _____
Totals	$ _____ $ _____
Grand Total	$ _____

Corp. funds available for investment (corp. net income-corp. taxes) $ _____

147

HAWAII

Single—$35,000 **Individual**/Corporate

Income Split	$20,000	$23,000	$26,000
	$15,000	$12,000	$9,000
Less Pension Contribution	$5,000	$5,750	$6,500
Net Income	$10,000	$6,250	$2,500
Federal Taxes	$2,239	$2,689	$3,448
	$1,500	$938	$375
State Taxes	$1,060	$1,389	$1,678
	$440	$275	$110
Totals	$3,299	$4,078	$5,126
	$1,940	$1,213	$485
Grand Total	$5,239	$5,291	$5,611

Single—$60,000 **Individual**/Corporate

Income Split	$30,000	$35,000	$40,000	$45,000
	$30,000	$25,000	$20,000	$15,000
Less Pension Contribution	$7,500	$8,750	$10,000	$11,250
Net Income	$22,500	$16,250	$10,000	$3,750
Federal Taxes	$4,568	$5,968	$7,368	$8,768
	$3,375	$2,438	$1,500	$563
State Taxes	$2,028	$2,528	$3,028	$3,528
	$990	$715	$440	$165
Totals	$6,596	$8,496	$10,396	$12,296
	$4,365	$3,153	$1,940	$728
Grand Total	$10,961	$11,649	$12,336	$13,024

Your Estimates

Corporate Income from income split	$ _____
Less Pension contribution	
Net corp. income	$ _____
Federal corp. tax	$ _____
State corp. tax	$ _____
Individual income from income split	$ _____
Less exemptions (number × $2,000 or correct amount for your state)	− _____ $ _____
Less standard deduction ($3,100 if single, $5,200 if married) or Itemized total	− _____
Taxable income	$ _____
Federal income tax	$ _____
State income tax	$ _____

Insert numbers on worksheet into box at right; add for totals

TAX RATES

Corporate—1st $25,000 4.4%
         Next $75,000 5.4
Individual—
  Single—$10,500–$15,500 $675 + 8.75% of excess over $10,500
        $15,500–$20,500 $1,113 + 9.5% of excess over $15,500
      Over $20,500 $1,588 + 10% of excess over $20,500
  Married—$11,000–$21,000 $550 + 8% of excess over $11,000
    $21,000–$31,000 $1,350 + 8.75% of excess over $21,000
    $31,000–$41,000 $2,225 + 9.5% of excess over $31,000
    Over $41,000 $3,175 + 10% of excess over $41,000

COMMENT

Because Hawaii's corporate tax rate is approximately half the individual rate, income splits that maximize corporate income will result in lowest taxes—especially for single entrepreneurs. Those income splits are $20,000/$15,000 in the $35,000 category ($23,000/$12,000 is also attractive) and $30,000/$30,000 in the $60,000 category.

For married individuals in the $50,000 category, the $38,000/$12,000 income split offers the lowest taxes and provides the highest salary and tax-sheltered pension contribution. At $75,000, the $38,000/$37,000 split is clearly the best choice.

HAWAII

Married—$50,000 **Individual**/Corporate

Income Split	$25,000 $25,000	$32,000 $18,000	$38,000 $12,000
Less Pension Contribution	$6,250	$8,000	$9,500
Net Income	$18,750	$10,000	$2,500
Federal Taxes	$2,374 $2,813	$3,424 $1,500	$4,324 $375
State Taxes	$934 $825	$1,508 $440	$2,033 $110
Totals	$3,308 $3,638	$4,932 $1,940	$6,357 $485
Grand Total	$6,946	$6,872	$6,842

Married—$75,000 **Individual**/Corporate

Income Split	$30,000 $45,000	$38,000 $37,000	$45,000 $30,000	$55,000 $20,000
Less Pension Contribution	$7,500	$9,500	$11,250	$13,750
Net Income	$37,500	$27,500	$18,750	$6,250
Federal Taxes	$3.124 $5,625	$4,324 $4,125	$6,008 $2,813	$8,808 $938
State Taxes	$1,334 $1,775	$2,033 $1,235	$2,681 $825	$3,655 $275
Totals	$4,458 $7,400	$6,357 $5,360	$8,689 $3,638	$12,463 $1,213
Grand Total	$11,858	$11,717	$12,327	$13,676

Individual/Corporate

Income split	$ $
Less Pension contribution	$
Net Income	$
Federal Taxes	$ $
State Taxes	$ $
Totals	$ $
Grand Total	$

Corp. funds available for investment (corp. net income-corp. taxes) $ _____

IDAHO

Single—$35,000 Individual/Corporate

Income Split	$20,000	$23,000	$26,000
	$15,000	$12,000	$9,000
Less Pension Contribution	$5,000	$5,750	$6,500
Net Income	$10,000	$6,250	$2,500
Federal Taxes	$2,239	$2,689	$3,448
	$1,500	$938	$375
State Taxes	$990	$1,224	$1,461
	$810	$510	$210
Totals	$3,229	$3,913	$4,909
	$2,310	$1,448	$585
Grand Total	$5,539	$5,361	$5,494

Single—$60,000 Individual/Corporate

Income Split	$30,000	$35,000	$40,000	$45,000
	$30,000	$25,000	$20,000	$15,000
Less Pension Contribution	$7,500	$8,750	$10,000	$11,250
Net Income	$22,500	$16,250	$10,000	$3,750
Federal Taxes	$4,568	$5,968	$7,368	$8,768
	$3,375	$2,438	$1,500	$563
State Taxes	$1,790	$2,200	$2,610	$3,020
	$1,810	$1,310	$810	$310
Totals	$6,358	$8,168	$9,978	$11,788
	$5,185	$3,748	$2,310	$873
Grand Total	$11,543	$11,916	$12,288	$12,661

Your Estimates

Corporate Income from income split	$ _____
Less Pension contribution	− _____
Net corp. income	$ _____
Federal corp. tax	$ _____
State corp. tax	$ _____
Individual income from income split	$ _____
Less exemptions (number × $2,000 or correct amount for your state)	− _____
	$ _____
Less standard deduction ($3,100 if single, $5,200 if married) or Itemized total	− _____
Taxable income	$ _____
Federal income tax	$ _____
State income tax	$ _____

Insert numbers on worksheet into box at right; add for totals

TAX RATES

Corporate—8% + $10
Individual—
Single—$2,500–$20,000 $413 + 7.8% of excess over $2,500
Over $20,000 $1,388 + 8.2% of excess over $20,000
Married—twice the tax on half the aggregate taxable income

COMMENT

For single individuals in the $35,000 category, the $23,000/$12,000 income split produces the lowest taxes. At $60,000, the $30,000/$30,000 split is clearly the best choice.

For married individuals in the $50,000 category, the $38,000/$12,000 income split offers both the greatest salary and pension contribution *and* the lowest taxes. At $75,000, the $38,000/$37,000 split produces the lowest taxes, but the $45,000/$30,000 split provides $7,000 more in salary and $1,750 more in pension contributions for a *mere $218 in additional taxes*.

IDAHO

Married—$50,000 **Individual**/Corporate

Income Split	$25,000 $25,000	$32,000 $18,000	$38,000 $12,000
Less Pension Contribution	$6,250	$8,000	$9,500
Net Income	$18,750	$10,000	$2,500
Federal Taxes	$2,374 $2,813	$3,424 $1,500	$4,324 $375
State Taxes	$842 $1,510	$1,434 $810	$1,902 $210
Totals	$3,216 $4,323	$4,858 $2,310	$6,226 $585
Grand Total	$7,539	$7,168	$6,811

Married—$75,000 **Individual**/Corporate

Income Split	$30,000 $45,000	$38,000 $37,000	$45,000 $30,000	$55,000 $20,000
Less Pension Contribution	$7,500	$9,500	$11,250	$13,750
Net Income	$37,500	$27,500	$18,750	$6,250
Federal Taxes	$3,124 $5,625	$4,324 $4,125	$6,008 $2,813	$8,808 $938
State Taxes	$1,278 $3,010	$1,902 $2,210	$2,448 $1,510	$3,252 $510
Totals	$4,402 $8,635	$6,226 $6,335	$8,456 $4,323	$12,060 $1,448
Grand Total	$13,037	$12,561	$12,779	$13,508

Individual/Corporate

Income split	$ $
Less Pension contribution	$
Net Income	$
Federal Taxes	$ $
State Taxes	$ $
Totals	$ $
Grand Total	$

Corp. funds available for investment (corp. net income-corp. taxes) $ _____

151

ILLINOIS

Single—$35,000 **Individual**/Corporate

Income Split	$20,000	$23,000	$26,000
	$15,000	$12,000	$9,000
Less Pension Contribution	$5,000	$5,750	$6,500
Net Income	$10,000	$6,250	$2,500
Federal Taxes	$2,239	$2,689	$3,448
	$1,500	$938	$375
State Taxes	$447	$537	$627
	$480	$300	$120
Totals	$2,686	$3,226	$4,075
	$1,980	$1,238	$495
Grand Total	$4,666	$4,464	$4,570

Single—$60,000 **Individual**/Corporate

Income Split	$30,000	$35,000	$40,000	$45,000
	$30,000	$25,000	$20,000	$15,000
Less Pension Contribution	$7,500	$8,750	$10,000	$11,250
Net Income	$22,500	$16,250	$10,000	$3,750
Federal Taxes	$4,568	$5,968	$7,368	$8,768
	$3,375	$2,438	$1,500	$563
State Taxes	$747	$897	$1,047	$1,197
	$1,080	$780	$480	$180
Totals	$5,315	$6,865	$8,415	$9,965
	$4,455	$3,218	$1,980	$743
Grand Total	$9,770	$10,083	$10,395	$10,708

Your Estimates

Corporate Income from income split	$ _____
Less Pension contribution	− _____
Net corp. income	$ _____
Federal corp. tax	$ _____
State corp. tax	$ _____
Individual income from income split	$ _____
Less exemptions (number × $2,000 or correct amount for your state)	− _____
	$ _____
Less standard deduction ($3,100 if single, $5,200 if married) or Itemized total	− _____
Taxable income	$ _____
Federal income tax	$ _____
State income tax	$ _____

Insert numbers on worksheet into box at right; add for totals

COMMENT

For single individuals in the $35,000 category, the $23,000/$12,000 income split offers the lowest taxes. However, the $26,000/$9,000 split is probably more desirable: it offers $3,000 more in salary and $750 more in pension contributions for a *mere $106* in additional taxes.

For married entrepreneurs in the $50,000 category, the $38,000/$12,000 income split offers both the highest salary and pension contribution *and* the lowest taxes. At $75,000, the $38,000/$37,000 split offers the lowest taxes. However, the $45,000/$30,000 split, which offers $7,000 more in salary and $1,750 more in pension contributions for a *mere $162 in additional taxes*, may be more attractive to many business owners and professionals.

TAX RATES

Corporate—4.8%
Individual—3.0%

ILLINOIS

Married—$50,000 Individual/Corporate

Income Split	**$25,000** $25,000	**$32,000** $18,000	**$38,000** $12,000
Less Pension Contribution	$6,250	$8,000	$9,500
Net Income	$18,750	$10,000	$2,500
Federal Taxes	**$2,374** $2,813	**$3,424** $1,500	**$4,324** $375
State Taxes	**$474** $900	**$684** $480	**$864** $120
Totals	**$2,848** $3,713	**$4,108** $1,980	**$5,188** $495
Grand Total	**$6,561**	**$6,088**	**$5,683**

Married—$75,000 Individual/Corporate

Income Split	**$30,000** $45,000	**$38,000** $37,000	**$45,000** $30,000	**$55,000** $20,000
Less Pension Contribution	$7,500	$9,500	$11,250	$13,750
Net Income	$37,500	$27,500	$18,750	$6,250
Federal Taxes	**$3,124** $5,625	**$4,324** $4,125	**$6,008** $2,813	**$8,808** $938
State Taxes	**$624** $1,800	**$864** $1,320	**$1,074** $900	**$1,374** $300
Totals	**$3,748** $7,425	**$5,188** $5,445	**$7,082** $3,713	**$10,182** $1,238
Grand Total	**$11,173**	**$10,633**	**$10,795**	**$11,420**

Individual/Corporate

Income split	$ $
Less Pension contribution	$
Net Income	$
Federal Taxes	$ $
State Taxes	$ $
Totals	$ $
Grand Total	$

Corp. funds available for investment (corp. net income-corp. taxes) $ _____

153

INDIANA

Single—$35,000 **Individual**/Corporate

Income Split	**$20,000** $15,000	**$23,000** $12,000	**$26,000** $9,000
Less Pension Contribution	$5,000	$5,750	$6,500
Net Income	$10,000	$6,250	$2,500
Federal Taxes	**$2,239** $1,500	**$2,689** $938	**$3,448** $375
State Taxes	**$507** $340	**$609** $213	**$711** $85
Totals	**$2,746** $1,840	**$3,298** $1,151	**$4,159** $460
Grand Total	**$4,586**	**$4,449**	**$4,619**

Single—$60,000 **Individual**/Corporate

Income Split	**$30,000** $30,000	**$35,000** $25,000	**$40,000** $20,000	**$45,000** $15,000
Less Pension Contribution	$7,500	$8,750	$10,000	$11,250
Net Income	$22,500	$16,250	$10,000	$3,750
Federal Taxes	**$4,568** $3,375	**$5,968** $2,438	**$7,368** $1,500	**$8,768** $563
State Taxes	**$847** $765	**$1,017** $553	**$1,187** $340	**$1,357** $128
Totals	**$5,415** $4,140	**$6,985** $2,991	**$8,555** $1,840	**$10,125** $691
Grand Total	**$9,555**	**$9,976**	**$10,395**	**$10,816**

Your Estimates

Corporate Income from income split	$ _____
Less Pension contribution	− _____
Net corp. income	$ _____
Federal corp. tax	$ _____
State corp. tax	$ _____
Individual income from income split	$ _____
Less exemptions (number × $2,000 or correct amount for your state)	− _____
	$ _____
Less standard deduction ($3,100 if single, $5,200 if married) or Itemized total	− _____
Taxable income	$ _____
Federal income tax	$ _____
State income tax	$ _____

Insert numbers on worksheet into box at right; add for totals

TAX RATES

Corporate—3.4%
Individual—3.4%

COMMENT

For single individuals in the $35,000 category, the $23,000/$12,000 income split offers the lowest taxes. At $60,000, the $30,000/$30,000 split is clearly the best choice.

For married individuals in the $50,000 category, the $38,000/$12,000 income split provides both the highest salary and pension contribution *and* the lowest taxes. At $75,000, the $38,000/$37,000 split is best.

INDIANA

Married—$50,000 Individual/Corporate

Income Split	**$25,000** $25,000	**$32,000** $18,000	**$38,000** $12,000
Less Pension Contribution	$6,250	$8,000	$9,500
Net Income	$18,750	$10,000	$2,500
Federal Taxes	**$2,374** $2,813	**$3,424** $1,500	**$4,324** $375
State Taxes	**$537** $638	**$775** $340	**$979** $85
Totals	**$2,911** $3,451	**$4,199** $1,840	**$5,303** $460
Grand Total	**$6,362**	**$6,039**	**$5,763**

Married—$75,000 Individual/Corporate

Income Split	**$30,000** $45,000	**$38,000** $37,000	**$45,000** $30,000	**$55,000** $20,000
Less Pension Contribution	$7,500	$9,500	$11,250	$13,750
Net Income	$37,500	$27,500	$18,750	$6,250
Federal Taxes	**$3,124** $5,625	**$4,324** $4,125	**$6,008** $2,813	**$8,808** $938
State Taxes	**$707** $1,280	**$979** $935	**$1,217** $638	**$1,557** $213
Totals	**$3,831** $6,905	**$5,303** $5,060	**$7,225** $3,451	**$10,365** $1,151
Grand Total	**$10,736**	**$10,363**	**$10,676**	**$11,516**

Individual/Corporate

Income split	$ $
Less Pension contribution	$
Net Income	$
Federal Taxes	$ $
State Taxes	$ $
Totals	$ $
Grand Total	$

Corp. funds available for investment (corp. net income-corp. taxes) $ _____

IOWA

Single—$35,000 **Individual**/Corporate

Income Split	$20,000 $15,000	$23,000 $12,000	$26,000 $9,000
Less Pension Contribution	$5,000	$5,750	$6,500
Net Income	$10,000	$6,250	$2,500
Federal Taxes	$2,239 $1,500	$2,689 $938	$3,448 $375
State Taxes	$712 $600	$928 $375	$1,146 $150
Totals	$2,951 $2,100	$3,617 $1,313	$4,594 $525
Grand Total	$5,051	$4,930	$5,119

Single—$60,000 **Individual**/Corporate

Income Split	$30,000 $30,000	$35,000 $25,000	$40,000 $20,000	$45,000 $15,000
Less Pension Contribution	$7,500	$8,750	$10,000	$11,250
Net Income	$22,500	$16,250	$10,000	$3,750
Federal Taxes	$4,568 $3,375	$5,968 $2,438	$7,368 $1,500	$8,768 $563
State Taxes	$1,448 $1,350	$1,825 $975	$2,258 $600	$2,698 $225
Totals	$6,016 $4,725	$7,793 $3,413	$9,626 $2,100	$11,466 $788
Grand Total	$10,741	$11,206	$11,726	$12,254

Your Estimates

Corporate Income from income split	$ _____
Less Pension contribution	– _____
Net corp. income	$ _____
Federal corp. tax	$ _____
State corp. tax	$ _____
Individual income from income split	$ _____
Less exemptions (number × $2,000 or correct amount for your state)	– _____
	$ _____
Less standard deduction ($3,100 if single, $5,200 if married) or Itemized total	– _____
Taxable income	$ _____
Federal income tax	$ _____
State income tax	$ _____

Insert numbers on worksheet into box at right; add for totals

TAX RATES

Corporate—First $25,000   6%
         Next $75,000   8
Individual—
  $ 9,144–$15,240 $321 + 6% of excess over $9,144
  $15,240–$20,320 $736 + 7.2% of excess over $15,240
  $20,320–$30,480 $1,102 + 7.55% of excess over $20,320
  $30,480–$45,720 $1,869 + 8.8% of excess over $30,480
  Over $45,720 $3,210 + 9.98% of excess over $45,720

COMMENT

For single individuals in the $35,000 category, the $23,000/$12,000 income split is best; in the $60,000 category, the $30,000/$30,000 split is clearly the best choice.

For married individuals in the $50,000 category, the $38,000/$12,000 income split produces both the highest salary and pension contribution *and* the lowest taxes. At $75,000, the $38,000/$37,000 split offers the lowest taxes.

IOWA

Married—$50,000 **Individual**/Corporate

Income Split	$25,000 $25,000	$32,000 $18,000	$38,000 $12,000
Less Pension Contribution	$6,250	$8,000	$9,500
Net Income	$18,750	$10,000	$2,500
Federal Taxes	$2,374 $2,813	$3,424 $1,500	$4,324 $375
State Taxes	$776 $1,125	$1,289 $600	$1,742 $150
Totals	$3,150 $3,938	$4,713 $2,100	$6,066 $525
Grand Total	$7,088	$6,813	$6,591

Married—$75,000 **Individual**/Corporate

Income Split	$30,000 $45,000	$38,000 $37,000	$45,000 $30,000	$55,000 $20,000
Less Pension Contribution	$7,500	$9,500	$11,250	$13,750
Net Income	$37,500	$27,500	$18,750	$6,250
Federal Taxes	$3,124 $5,625	$4,324 $4,125	$6,008 $2,813	$8,808 $938
State Taxes	$1,138 $2,500	$1,742 $1,700	$2,337 $1,125	$3,218 $375
Totals	$4,262 $8,125	$6,066 $5,825	$8,345 $3,938	$12,026 $1,313
Grand Total	$12,387	$11,891	$12,283	$13,339

Individual/Corporate

Income split	$ $
Less Pension contribution	$
Net Income	$
Federal Taxes	$ $
State Taxes	$ $
Totals	$ $
Grand Total	$

Corp. funds available for investment (corp. net income-corp. taxes) $ _____

KANSAS

Single—$35,000 **Individual**/Corporate

Income Split	**$20,000** $15,000	**$23,000** $12,000	**$26,000** $9,000
Less Pension Contribution	$5,000	$5,750	$6,500
Net Income	$10,000	$6,250	$2,500
Federal Taxes	**$2,239** $1,500	**$2,689** $938	**$3,448** $375
State Taxes	**$671** $450	**$806** $281	**$941** $113
Totals	**$2,910** $1,950	**$3,495** $1,219	**$4,389** $488
Grand Total	**$4,860**	**$4,714**	**$4,877**

Single—$60,000 **Individual**/Corporate

Income Split	**$30,000** $30,000	**$35,000** $25,000	**$40,000** $20,000	**$45,000** $15,000
Less Pension Contribution	$7,500	$8,750	$10,000	$11,250
Net Income	$22,500	$16,250	$10,000	$3,750
Federal Taxes	**$4,568** $3,375	**$5,968** $2,438	**$7,368** $1,500	**$8,768** $563
State Taxes	**$1,121** $1,013	**$1,381** $731	**$1,678** $450	**$1,976** $169
Totals	**$5,689** $4,388	**$7,349** $3,169	**$9,046** $1,950	**$10,744** $732
Grand Total	**$10,077**	**$10,518**	**$10,996**	**$11,476**

Your Estimates

Corporate Income from income split	$ _____
Less Pension contribution	– _____
Net corp. income	$ _____
Federal corp. tax	$ _____
State corp. tax	$ _____
Individual income from income split	$ _____
Less exemptions (number × $2,000 or correct amount for your state)	– _____
	$ _____
Less standard deduction ($3,100 if single, $5,200 if married) or Itemized total	– _____
Taxable income	$ _____
Federal income tax	$ _____
State income tax	$ _____

Insert numbers on worksheet into box at right; add for totals

TAX RATES

Corporate—4.5% + 2.25% surtax on taxable income in excess of $25,000

Individual—
Single—Not over $27,500   4.5%
    Over $27,500 $1,238 + 5.95% of excess over $27,500
Married—Not over $35,000   3.65%
    Over $35,000 $1,278 + 5.15% of excess over $35,000

COMMENT

For single taxpayers in the $35,000 category, the $23,000/$12,000 income split offers the lowest taxes. At $60,000, the $30,000/$30,000 split is clearly the best choice.

For married individuals in the $50,000 category, the $38,000/$12,000 income split provides both the highest salary and pension contribution *and* the lowest taxes. At $75,000, the $38,000/$37,000 split is best.

KANSAS

Married—$50,000 Individual/Corporate

Income Split	$25,000 $25,000	$32,000 $18,000	$38,000 $12,000
Less Pension Contribution	$6,250	$8,000	$9,500
Net Income	$18,750	$10,000	$2,500
Federal Taxes	$2,374 $2,813	$3,424 $1,500	$4,324 $375
State Taxes	$577 $844	$832 $450	$1,051 $113
Totals	$2,951 $3,657	$4,256 $1,950	$5,375 $488
Grand Total	$6,608	$6,206	$5,863

Married—$75,000 Individual/Corporate

Income Split	$30,000 $45,000	$38,000 $37,000	$45,000 $30,000	$55,000 $20,000
Less Pension Contribution	$7,500	$9,500	$11,250	$13,750
Net Income	$37,500	$27,500	$18,750	$6,250
Federal Taxes	$3,124 $5,625	$4,324 $4,125	$6,008 $2,813	$8,808 $938
State Taxes	$759 $1,701	$1,051 $1,241	$1,319 $844	$1,834 $281
Totals	$3,883 $7,326	$5,375 $5,366	$7,327 $3,657	$10,642 $1,219
Grand Total	$11,209	$10,741	$10,984	$11,861

Individual/Corporate

Income split	$ $
Less Pension contribution	$
Net Income	$
Federal Taxes	$ $
State Taxes	$ $
Totals	$ $
Grand Total	$

Corp. funds available for investment (corp. net income-corp. taxes) $ _____

KENTUCKY

Single—$35,000 **Individual**/Corporate

Income Split	$20,000 $15,000	$23,000 $12,000	$26,000 $9,000
Less Pension Contribution	$5,000	$5,750	$6,500
Net Income	$10,000	$6,250	$2,500
Federal Taxes	$2,239 $1,500	$2,689 $938	$3,448 $375
State Taxes	$694 $300	$874 $188	$1,054 $75
Totals	$2,933 $1,800	$3,563 $1,126	$4,502 $450
Grand Total	$4,733	$4,689	$4,952

Single—$60,000 **Individual**/Corporate

Income Split	$30,000 $30,000	$35,000 $25,000	$40,000 $20,000	$45,000 $15,000
Less Pension Contribution	$7,500	$8,750	$10,000	$11,250
Net Income	$22,500	$16,250	$10,000	$3,750
Federal Taxes	$4,568 $3,375	$5,968 $2,438	$7,368 $1,500	$8,768 $563
State Taxes	$1,294 $675	$1,594 $488	$1,894 $300	$2,194 $113
Totals	$5,862 $4,050	$7,562 $2,926	$9,262 $1,800	$10,962 $676
Grand Total	$9,912	$10,488	$11,062	$11,638

Your Estimates

Corporate Income from income split $ _____
Less Pension contribution − _____
Net corp. income $ _____
Federal corp. tax $ _____
State corp. tax $ _____
Individual income from income split $ _____
Less exemptions
(number × $2,000 or correct amount for your state) − _____
$ _____
Less standard deduction ($3,100 if single,
$5,200 if married) or Itemized total − _____
Taxable income $ _____
Federal income tax $ _____
State income tax $ _____

Insert numbers on worksheet into box at right; add for totals

TAX RATES

Corporate—First $25,000   3%
           Next $25,000   4
Individual—Over $8,000 $280 + 6% of excess over $8,000

COMMENT

For single individuals in the $35,000 category, the $23,000/$12,000 income split offers the lowest taxes. In the $60,000 category, the $30,000/$30,000 split is clearly the best choice.

For married individuals in the $50,000 category, the $38,000/$12,000 income split offers both the highest salary and pension contribution *and* lowest taxes. At $75,000, the $38,000/$37,000 split is best for most entrepreneurs and professionals.

KENTUCKY

Married—$50,000 **Individual**/Corporate

Income Split	**$25,000** $25,000	**$32,000** $18,000	**$38,000** $12,000
Less Pension Contribution	$6,250	$8,000	$9,500
Net Income	$18,750	$10,000	$2,500
Federal Taxes	**$2,374** $2,813	**$3,424** $1,500	**$4,324** $375
State Taxes	**$748** $563	**$1,168** $300	**$1,528** $75
Totals	**$3,122** $3,376	**$4,592** $1,800	**$5,852** $450
Grand Total	**$6,498**	**$6,392**	**$6,302**

Married—$75,000 **Individual**/Corporate

Income Split	**$30,000** $45,000	**$38,000** $37,000	**$45,000** $30,000	**$55,000** $20,000
Less Pension Contribution	$7,500	$9,500	$11,250	$13,750
Net Income	$37,500	$27,500	$18,750	$6,250
Federal Taxes	**$3,124** $5,625	**$4,324** $4,125	**$6,008** $2,813	**$8,808** $938
State Taxes	**$1,048** $1,250	**$1,528** $850	**$1,948** $563	**$2,548** $188
Totals	**$4,172** $6,875	**$5,852** $4,975	**$7,956** $3,376	**$11,356** $1,126
Grand Total	**$11,047**	**$10,827**	**$11,332**	**$12,482**

Individual/Corporate

Income split	$ $
Less Pension contribution	$
Net Income	$
Federal Taxes	$ $
State Taxes	$ $
Totals	$ $
Grand Total	$

Corp. funds available for investment (corp. net income-corp. taxes) $ _____

LOUISIANA

Single—$35,000 Individual/Corporate

Income Split	$20,000 $15,000	$23,000 $12,000	$26,000 $9,000
Less Pension Contribution	$5,000	$5,750	$6,500
Net Income	$10,000	$6,250	$2,500
Federal Taxes	$2,239 $1,500	$2,689 $938	$3,448 $375
State Taxes	$396 $400	$516 $250	$636 $100
Totals	$2,635 $1,900	$3,205 $1,188	$4,084 $475
Grand Total	$4,535	$4,393	$4,559

Single—$60,000 Individual/Corporate

Income Split	$30,000 $30,000	$35,000 $25,000	$40,000 $20,000	$45,000 $15,000
Less Pension Contribution	$7,500	$8,750	$10,000	$11,250
Net Income	$22,500	$16,250	$10,000	$3,750
Federal Taxes	$4,568 $3,375	$5,968 $2,438	$7,368 $1,500	$8,768 $563
State Taxes	$796 $900	$996 $650	$1,196 $400	$1,396 $150
Totals	$5,364 $4,275	$6,964 $3,088	$8,564 $1,900	$10,164 $713
Grand Total	$9,639	$10,052	$10,464	$10,877

Your Estimates

Corporate Income from income split	$ _____
Less Pension contribution	− _____
Net corp. income	$ _____
Federal corp. tax	$ _____
State corp. tax	$ _____
Individual income from income split	$ _____
Less exemptions (number × $2,000 or correct amount for your state)	− _____
	$ _____
Less standard deduction ($3,100 if single, $5,200 if married) or Itemized total	− _____
Taxable income	$ _____
Federal income tax	$ _____
State income tax	$ _____

Insert numbers on worksheet into box at right; add for totals

TAX RATES

Corporate—First $25,000   4%
        Next $25,000   5
Individual—
  Single—$10,000–$50,000 $200 + 4% of
                excess over $10,000
  Married—twice the tax on half the aggregate
                taxable income

COMMENT

For single individuals in the $35,000 category, the $23,000/$12,000 income split offers the lowest taxes. However, the $26,000/$9,000 split may be more attractive to some entrepreneurs: it provides $3,000 more in salary and $750 more in pension contributions for only $166 more in taxes.

For married individuals in the $50,000 category, the $38,000/$12,000 income split produces both the highest salary and pension contribution *and* the lowest taxes. At $75,000, the $38,000/$37,000 split is clearly the best choice.

LOUISIANA

Married—$50,000 **Individual**/Corporate

Income Split	$25,000 $25,000	$32,000 $18,000	$38,000 $12,000
Less Pension Contribution	$6,250	$8,000	$9,500
Net Income	$18,750	$10,000	$2,500
Federal Taxes	$2,374 $2,813	$3,424 $1,500	$4,324 $375
State Taxes	$304 $750	$512 $400	$752 $100
Totals	$2,678 $3,563	$3,936 $1,900	$5,076 $475
Grand Total	$6,241	$5,836	$5,551

Married—$75,000 **Individual**/Corporate

Income Split	$30,000 $45,000	$38,000 $37,000	$45,000 $30,000	$55,000 $20,000
Less Pension Contribution	$7,500	$9,500	$11,250	$13,750
Net Income	$37,500	$27,500	$18,750	$6,250
Federal Taxes	$3,124 $5,625	$4,324 $4,125	$6,008 $2,813	$8,808 $938
State Taxes	$432 $1,625	$752 $1,125	$1,032 $750	$1,432 $250
Totals	$3,556 $7,250	$5,076 $5,250	$7,040 $3,563	$10,240 $1,188
Grand Total	$10,806	$10,326	$10,603	$11,428

Individual/Corporate

Income split	$ $
Less Pension contribution	$
Net Income	$
Federal Taxes	$ $
State Taxes	$ $
Totals	$ $
Grand Total	$

Corp. funds available for investment (corp. net income-corp. taxes) $ _____

MAINE

Single—$35,000 **Individual**/Corporate

Income Split	$20,000 $15,000	$23,000 $12,000	$26,000 $9,000
Less Pension Contribution	$5,000	$5,750	$6,500
Net Income	$10,000	$6,250	$2,500
Federal Taxes	$2,239 $1,500	$2,689 $938	$3,448 $375
State Taxes	$763 $350	$1,002 $219	$1,257 $88
Totals	$3,002 $1,850	$3,691 $1,157	$4,705 $463
Grand Total	$4,852	$4,848	$5,168

Single—$60,000 **Individual**/Corporate

Income Split	$30,000 $30,000	$35,000 $25,000	$40,000 $20,000	$45,000 $15,000
Less Pension Contribution	$7,500	$8,750	$10,000	$11,250
Net Income	$22,500	$16,250	$10,000	$3,750
Federal Taxes	$4,568 $3,375	$5,968 $2,438	$7,368 $1,500	$8,768 $563
State Taxes	$1,597 $788	$2,022 $569	$2,447 $350	$2,872 $131
Totals	$6,165 $4,163	$7,990 $3,007	$9,815 $1,850	$11,640 $694
Grand Total	$10,328	$10,997	$11,665	$12,334

Your Estimates

Corporate Income from income split	$ _____
Less Pension contribution	− _____
Net corp. income	$ _____
Federal corp. tax	$ _____
State corp. tax	$ _____
Individual income from income split	$ _____
Less exemptions (number × $2,000 or correct amount for your state)	− _____
	$ _____
Less standard deduction ($3,100 if single, $5,200 if married) or Itemized total	− _____
Taxable income	$ _____
Federal income tax	$ _____
State income tax	$ _____

Insert numbers on worksheet into box at right; add for totals

TAX RATES

Corporate—First $25,000   3.5 %
    Next $50,000   7.93
Individual—
  Single—Over $16,000 $840 + 8.5% of excess over $16,000
  Married—$16,001–$32,000 $520 + 7% of excess over $16,000
     Over $32,000 $1,640 + 8.5% of excess over $32,000

COMMENT

For single individuals in the $35,000 category, the $23,000/ $12,000 income split is best. At $60,000, the $30,000/$30,000 split is clearly the best choice.

For married individuals in the $50,000 category, the $38,000/$12,000 income split provides both the highest salary and pension contribution *and* lowest taxes. At $75,000, the $38,000/$37,000 split is the best choice for most entrepreneurs and professionals.

MAINE

Married—$50,000 Individual/Corporate

Income Split	$25,000 $25,000	$32,000 $18,000	$38,000 $12,000
Less Pension Contribution	$6,250	$8,000	$9,500
Net Income	$18,750	$10,000	$2,500
Federal Taxes	$2,374 $2,813	$3,424 $1,500	$4,324 $375
State Taxes	$511 $656	$996 $350	$1,416 $88
Totals	$2,885 $3,469	$4,420 $1,850	$5,740 $463
Grand Total	$6,354	$6,270	$6,203

Married—$75,000 Individual/Corporate

Income Split	$30,000 $45,000	$38,000 $37,000	$45,000 $30,000	$55,000 $20,000
Less Pension Contribution	$7,500	$9,500	$11,250	$13,750
Net Income	$37,500	$27,500	$18,750	$6,250
Federal Taxes	$3,124 $5,625	$4,324 $4,125	$6,008 $2,813	$8,808 $938
State Taxes	$856 $1,866	$1,416 $1,073	$1,963 $656	$2,813 $219
Totals	$3,980 $7,491	$5,740 $5,198	$7,971 $3,469	$11,621 $1,157
Grand Total	$11,471	$10,938	$11,440	$12,778

Individual/Corporate

Income split	$ $
Less Pension contribution	$
Net Income	$
Federal Taxes	$ $
State Taxes	$ $
Totals	$ $
Grand Total	$

Corp. funds available for investment (corp. net income-corp. taxes) $ _____

MARYLAND

Single—$35,000 **Individual**/Corporate

Income Split	$20,000 $15,000	$23,000 $12,000	$26,000 $9,000
Less Pension Contribution	$5,000	$5,750	$6,500
Net Income	$10,000	$6,250	$2,500
Federal Taxes	$2,239 $1,500	$2,689 $938	$3,448 $375
State Taxes	$685 $700	$835 $438	$985 $175
Totals	$2,924 $2,200	$3,524 $1,376	$4,433 $550
Grand Total	$5,124	$4,900	$4,983

Single—$60,000 **Individual**/Corporate

Income Split	$30,000 $30,000	$35,000 $25,000	$40,000 $20,000	$45,000 $15,000
Less Pension Contribution	$7,500	$8,750	$10,000	$11,250
Net Income	$22,500	$16,250	$10,000	$3,750
Federal Taxes	$4,568 $3,375	$5,968 $2,438	$7,368 $1,500	$8,768 $563
State Taxes	$1,185 $1,575	$1,435 $1,138	$1,685 $700	$1,935 $263
Totals	$5,753 $4,950	$7,403 $3,576	$9,053 $2,200	$10,703 $826
Grand Total	$10,703	$10,979	$11,253	$11,529

Your Estimates

Corporate Income from income split	$ _____
Less Pension contribution	– _____
Net corp. income	$ _____
Federal corp. tax	$ _____
State corp. tax	$ _____
Individual income from income split	$ _____
Less exemptions (number × $2,000 or correct amount for your state)	– _____
	$ _____
Less standard deduction ($3,100 if single, $5,200 if married) or Itemized total	– _____
Taxable income	$ _____
Federal income tax	$ _____
State income tax	$ _____

Insert numbers on worksheet into box at right; add for totals

TAX RATES

Corporate—7%
Individual—$90 + 5% of excess over $3,000

COMMENT

For single taxpayers in the $35,000 category, the $23,000/$12,000 income split produces the lowest taxes. However, the $26,000/$9,000 split may be more attractive to some entrepreneurs and professionals: it provides $3,000 more in salary and $750 more in pension contributions for *only $83* more in taxes.

For married taxpayers in the $50,000 category, the $38,000/$12,000 income split produces both the highest salary and pension contribution *and* the lowest taxes. At $75,000, the $38,000/$37,000 split offers the lowest taxes. However, the $45,000/$30,000 split provides $7,000 more in salary and $1,750 more in pension contributions for a *mere $110* in additional taxes.

166

MARYLAND

Married—$50,000 **Individual**/Corporate

Income Split	$25,000 $25,000	$32,000 $18,000	$38,000 $12,000
Less Pension Contribution	$6,250	$8,000	$9,500
Net Income	$18,750	$10,000	$2,500
Federal Taxes	$2,374 $2,813	$3,424 $1,500	$4,324 $375
State Taxes	$730 $1,313	$1,080 $700	$1,380 $175
Totals	$3,104 $4,126	$4,504 $2,200	$5,704 $550
Grand Total	$7,230	$6,704	$6,254

Married—$75,000 **Individual**/Corporate

Income Split	$30,000 $45,000	$38,000 $37,000	$45,000 $30,000	$55,000 $20,000
Less Pension Contribution	$7,500	$9,500	$11,250	$13,750
Net Income	$37,500	$27,500	$18,750	$6,250
Federal Taxes	$3,124 $5,625	$4,324 $4,125	$6,008 $2,813	$8,808 $938
State Taxes	$980 $2,625	$1,380 $1,925	$1,730 $1,313	$2,230 $438
Totals	$4,104 $8,250	$5,704 $6,050	$7,738 $4,126	$11,038 $1,376
Grand Total	$12,354	$11,754	$11,864	$12,414

Individual/Corporate

Income split	$ $
Less Pension contribution	$
Net Income	$
Federal Taxes	$ $
State Taxes	$ $
Totals	$ $
Grand Total	$

Corp. funds available for investment (corp. net income-corp. taxes) $ _____

MASSACHUSETTS

Single—$35,000 Individual/Corporate

Income Split	$20,000 $15,000	$23,000 $12,000	$26,000 $9,000
Less Pension Contribution	$5,000	$5,750	$6,500
Net Income	$10,000	$6,250	$2,500
Federal Taxes	$2,239 $1,500	$2,689 $938	$3,448 $375
State Taxes	$857 $950	$1,029 $594	$1,202 $456
Totals	$3,096 $2,450	$3,718 $1,532	$4,650 $831
Grand Total	$5,546	$5,250	$5,481

Single—$60,000 Individual/Corporate

Income Split	$30,000 $30,000	$35,000 $25,000	$40,000 $20,000	$45,000 $15,000
Less Pension Contribution	$7,500	$8,750	$10,000	$11,250
Net Income	$22,500	$16,250	$10,000	$3,750
Federal Taxes	$4,568 $3,375	$5,968 $2,438	$7,368 $1,500	$8,768 $563
State Taxes	$1,432 $2,138	$1,719 $1,544	$2,007 $950	$2,294 $456
Totals	$6,000 $5,513	$7,687 $3,982	$9,375 $2,450	$11,062 $1,019
Grand Total	$11,513	$11,669	$11,825	$12,081

Your Estimates

Corporate Income from income split	$ _____
Less Pension contribution	– _____
Net corp. income	$ _____
Federal corp. tax	$ _____
State corp. tax	$ _____
Individual income from income split	$ _____
Less exemptions (number × $2,000 or correct amount for your state)	– _____
Less standard deduction ($3,100 if single, $5,200 if married) or Itemized total	$ _____
Taxable income	– _____
Federal income tax	$ _____
State income tax	$ _____

Insert numbers on worksheet into box at right; add for totals

TAX RATES

Corporate—9.5% of net income OR $400 + 14% surtax ($456)— whichever is greater

Individual—5.75% of earned income

COMMENT

For single individuals in the $35,000 category, the $23,000/$12,000 income split is best. At $60,000, the $30,000/$30,000 split produces the lowest taxes. However, the $35,000/$25,000 split offers $5,000 more in salary and $1,250 more in pension contributions for a *mere $156 in additional taxes*.

For married entrepreneurs and professionals in the $50,000 category, the $38,000/$12,000 income split offers both the highest salary and pension contribution *and* the lowest taxes. At $75,000, the $45,000/$30,000 split is clearly the best choice.

168

MASSACHUSETTS

Married—$50,000 **Individual**/Corporate

Income Split	**$25,000** $25,000	**$32,000** $18,000	**$38,000** $12,000
Less Pension Contribution	$6,250	$8,000	$9,500
Net Income	$18,750	$10,000	$2,500
Federal Taxes	**$2,374** $2,813	**$3,424** $1,500	**$4,324** $375
State Taxes	**$909** $1,781	**$1,311** $950	**$1,656** $456
Totals	**$3,283** $4,594	**$4,735** $2,450	**$5,980** $831
Grand Total	**$7,877**	**$7,185**	**$6,811**

Married—$75,000 **Individual**/Corporate

Income Split	**$30,000** $45,000	**$38,000** $37,000	**$45,000** $30,000	**$55,000** $20,000
Less Pension Contribution	$7,500	$9,500	$11,250	$13,750
Net Income	$37,500	$27,500	$18,750	$6,250
Federal Taxes	**$3,124** $5,625	**$4,324** $4,125	**$6,008** $2,813	**$8,808** $938
State Taxes	**$1,196** $3,563	**$1,656** $2,613	**$2,059** $1,781	**$2,634** $594
Totals	**$4,320** $9,188	**$5,980** $6,738	**$8,067** $4,594	**$11,442** $1,532
Grand Total	**$13,508**	**$12,718**	**$12,661**	**$12,974**

Individual/Corporate

Income split	$ $
Less Pension contribution	$
Net Income	$
Federal Taxes	$ $
State Taxes	$ $
Totals	$ $
Grand Total	$

Corp. funds available for investment (corp. net income-corp. taxes) $ _____

MICHIGAN

Single—$35,000 Individual/Corporate

Income Split	$20,000 $15,000	$23,000 $12,000	$26,000 $9,000
Less Pension Contribution	$5,000	$5,750	$6,500
Net Income	$10,000	$6,250	$2,500
Federal Taxes	$2,239 $1,500	$2,689 $938	$3,448 $375
State Taxes	$685 $235	$823 $147	$961 $59
Totals	$2,924 $1,735	$3,512 $1,085	$4,409 $434
Grand Total	$4,659	$4,597	$4,843

Single—$60,000 Individual/Corporate

Income Split	$30,000 $30,000	$35,000 $25,000	$40,000 $20,000	$45,000 $15,000
Less Pension Contribution	$7,500	$8,750	$10,000	$11,250
Net Income	$22,500	$16,250	$10,000	$3,750
Federal Taxes	$4,568 $3,375	$5,968 $2,438	$7,368 $1,500	$8,768 $563
State Taxes	$1,145 $529	$1,375 $382	$1,605 $235	$1,835 $88
Totals	$5,713 $3,904	$7,343 $2,820	$8,973 $1,735	$10,603 $651
Grand Total	$9,617	$10,163	$10,708	$11,254

Your Estimates

Corporate Income from income split	$ _____
Less Pension contribution	
Net corp. income	$ _____
Federal corp. tax	$ _____
State corp. tax	$ _____
Individual income from income split	$ _____
Less exemptions	
(number × $2,000 or correct amount for your state)	
	$ _____
Less standard deduction ($3,100 if single, $5,200 if married) or Itemized total	−
Taxable income	$ _____
Federal income tax	$ _____
State income tax	$ _____

Insert numbers on worksheet into box at right; add for totals

COMMENT

TAX RATES

Corporate—2.35%
Individual—4.6%

For single individuals in the $35,000 category, the $23,000/$12,000 income split is best. In the $60,000 category, the $30,000/$30,000 split is clearly the best choice.

For married individuals in the $50,000 category, the $38,000/$12,000 income split produces both the highest salary and pension contribution *and* the lowest taxes. At $75,000, the $38,000/$37,000 split is best for most professionals and entrepreneurs.

MICHIGAN

Married—$50,000 **Individual**/Corporate

Income Split	$25,000 $25,000	$32,000 $18,000	$38,000 $12,000
Less Pension Contribution	$6,250	$8,000	$9,500
Net Income	$18,750	$10,000	$2,500
Federal Taxes	$2,374 $2,813	$3,424 $1,500	$4,324 $375
State Taxes	$727 $441	$1,049 $235	$1,325 $59
Totals	$3,101 $3,254	$4,473 $1,735	$5,649 $434
Grand Total	$6,355	$6,208	$6,083

Married—$75,000 **Individual**/Corporate

Income Split	$30,000 $45,000	$38,000 $37,000	$45,000 $30,000	$55,000 $20,000
Less Pension Contribution	$7,500	$9,500	$11,250	$13,750
Net Income	$37,500	$27,500	$18,750	$6,250
Federal Taxes	$3,124 $5,625	$4,324 $4,125	$6,008 $2,813	$8,808 $938
State Taxes	$957 $881	$1,325 $646	$1,647 $441	$2,107 $147
Totals	$4,081 $6,506	$5,649 $4,771	$7,655 $3,254	$10,915 $1,085
Grand Total	$10,587	$10,420	$10,909	$12,000

Individual/Corporate

Income split	$ $
Less Pension contribution	$
Net Income	$
Federal Taxes	$ $
State Taxes	$ $
Totals	$ $
Grand Total	$

Corp. funds available for investment (corp. net income-corp. taxes) $ _____

171

MINNESOTA

Single—$35,000 Individual/Corporate

Income Split	**$20,000** $15,000	**$23,000** $12,000	**$26,000** $9,000
Less Pension Contribution	$5,000	$5,750	$6,500
Net Income	$10,000	$6,250	$2,500
Federal Taxes	**$2,239** $1,500	**$2,689** $938	**$3,448** $375
State Taxes	**$932** $950	**$1,172** $594	**$1,412** $238
Totals	**$3,171** $2,450	**$3,861** $1,532	**$4,860** $613
Grand Total	**$5,621**	**$5,393**	**$5,473**

Single—$60,000 Individual/Corporate

Income Split	**$30,000** $30,000	**$35,000** $25,000	**$40,000** $20,000	**$45,000** $15,000
Less Pension Contribution	$7,500	$8,750	$10,000	$11,250
Net Income	$22,500	$16,250	$10,000	$3,750
Federal Taxes	**$4,568** $3,375	**$5,968** $2,438	**$7,368** $1,500	**$8,768** $563
State Taxes	**$1,732** $2,138	**$2,132** $1,544	**$2,532** $950	**$2,932** $356
Totals	**$6,300** $5,513	**$8,100** $3,982	**$9,900** $2,450	**$11,700** $919
Grand Total	**$11,813**	**$12,082**	**$12,350**	**$12,619**

Your Estimates

Corporate Income from income split	$ _____
Less Pension contribution	− _____
Net corp. income	$ _____
Federal corp. tax	$ _____
State corp. tax	$ _____
Individual income from income split	$ _____
Less exemptions (number × $2,000 or correct amount for your state)	− _____ $ _____
Less standard deduction ($3,100 if single, $5,200 if married) or Itemized total	− _____
Taxable income	$ _____
Federal income tax	$ _____
State income tax	$ _____

Insert numbers on worksheet into box at right; add for totals

TAX RATES

Corporate—9.5%
Individual—
  Single—Over $13,000 $780 + 8% of excess over $13,000
  Married—Over $19,000 $1,140 + 8% of excess over $19,000

COMMENT

For single individuals in the $35,000 category, the $23,000/$12,000 income split is best. At $60,000, the $30,000/$30,000 split produces the lowest taxes.

For married individuals in the $50,000 category, the $38,000/$12,000 income split offers both the highest salary and pension contribution *and* the lowest taxes. At $75,000, the $38,000/$37,000 split produces the lowest taxes. However, the $45,000/$30,000 split, which provides $7,000 more in salary and $1,750 more in pension contributions for a *mere $100 in additional taxes*, may be more attractive to most taxpayers.

MINNESOTA

Married—$50,000 **Individual**/Corporate

Income Split	$25,000 $25,000	$32,000 $18,000	$38,000 $12,000
Less Pension Contribution	$6,250	$8,000	$9,500
Net Income	$18,750	$10,000	$2,500
Federal Taxes	$2,374 $2,813	$3,424 $1,500	$4,324 $375
State Taxes	$948 $1,781	$1,444 $950	$1,924 $238
Totals	$3,322 $4,594	$4,868 $2,450	$6,248 $613
Grand Total	$7,916	$7,318	$6,861

Married—$75,000 **Individual**/Corporate

Income Split	$30,000 $45,000	$38,000 $37,000	$45,000 $30,000	$55,000 $20,000
Less Pension Contribution	$7,500	$9,500	$11,250	$13,750
Net Income	$37,500	$27,500	$18,750	$6,250
Federal Taxes	$3,124 $5,625	$4,324 $4,125	$6,008 $2,813	$8,808 $938
State Taxes	$1,284 $3,563	$1,924 $2,613	$2,484 $1,781	$3,284 $594
Totals	$4,408 $9,188	$6,248 $6,738	$8,492 $4,594	$12,092 $1,532
Grand Total	$13,596	$12,986	$13,086	$13,624

Individual/Corporate

Income split	$ $
Less Pension contribution	$
Net Income	$
Federal Taxes	$ $
State Taxes	$ $
Totals	$ $
Grand Total	$

Corp. funds available for investment (corp. net income-corp. taxes) $ _____

MISSISSIPPI

Single—$35,000 Individual/Corporate

Income Split	$20,000 $15,000	$23,000 $12,000	$26,000 $9,000
Less Pension Contribution	$5,000	$5,750	$6,500
Net Income	$10,000	$6,250	$2,500
Federal Taxes	$2,239 $1,500	$2,689 $938	$3,448 $375
State Taxes	$595 $350	$745 $200	$895 $75
Totals	$2,834 $1,850	$3,434 $1,138	$4,343 $450
Grand Total	$4,684	$4,572	$4,793

Single—$60,000 Individual/Corporate

Income Split	$30,000 $30,000	$35,000 $25,000	$40,000 $20,000	$45,000 $15,000
Less Pension Contribution	$7,500	$8,750	$10,000	$11,250
Net Income	$22,500	$16,250	$10,000	$3,750
Federal Taxes	$4,568 $3,375	$5,968 $2,438	$7,368 $1,500	$8,768 $563
State Taxes	$1,095 $975	$1,345 $663	$1,595 $350	$1,845 $113
Totals	$5,663 $4,350	$7,313 $3,101	$8,963 $1,850	$10,613 $676
Grand Total	$10,013	$10,414	$10,813	$11,289

Your Estimates

Corporate Income from income split	$ _____
Less Pension contribution	− _____
Net corp. income	$ _____
Federal corp. tax	$ _____
State corp. tax	$ _____
Individual income from income split	$ _____
Less exemptions (number × $2,000 or correct amount for your state)	− _____
	$ _____
Less standard deduction ($3,100 if single, $5,200 if married) or Itemized total	− _____
Taxable income	$ _____
Federal income tax	$ _____
State income tax	$ _____

Insert numbers on worksheet into box at right; add for totals

TAX RATES

Corporate—First $5,000   3%
Next $5,000   4
Over $10,000   5
Individual—Over $10,000 $350 + 5% of excess over $10,000

COMMENT

For single individuals in the $35,000 category, the $23,000/$12,000 income split is best. At $60,000, the $30,000/$30,000 split is clearly the best choice.

For married individuals in the $50,000 category, the $38,000/$12,000 income split produces both the highest salary and pension contribution *and* the lowest taxes. At $75,000, the $38,000/$37,000 split is the best choice.

MISSISSIPPI

Married—$50,000 **Individual**/Corporate

Income Split	$25,000 $25,000	$32,000 $18,000	$38,000 $12,000
Less Pension Contribution	$6,250	$8,000	$9,500
Net Income	$18,750	$10,000	$2,500
Federal Taxes	$2,374 $2,813	$3,424 $1,500	$4,324 $375
State Taxes	$640 $788	$990 $350	$1,290 $75
Totals	$3,014 $3,601	$4,414 $1,850	$5,614 $450
Grand Total	$6,615	$6,264	$6,064

Married—$75,000 **Individual**/Corporate

Income Split	$30,000 $45,000	$38,000 $37,000	$45,000 $30,000	$55,000 $20,000
Less Pension Contribution	$7,500	$9,500	$11,250	$13,750
Net Income	$37,500	$27,500	$18,750	$6,250
Federal Taxes	$3,124 $5,625	$4,324 $4,125	$6,008 $2,813	$8,808 $938
State Taxes	$890 $1,725	$1,290 $1,225	$1,640 $788	$2,140 $200
Totals	$4,014 $7,350	$5,614 $5,350	$7,648 $3,601	$10,948 $1,138
Grand Total	$11,364	$10,964	$11,249	$12,086

Individual/Corporate

Income split	$ $
Less Pension contribution	$
Net Income	$
Federal Taxes	$ $
State Taxes	$ $
Totals	$ $
Grand Total	$

Corp. funds available for investment (corp. net income-corp. taxes) $ _____

175

MISSOURI

Single—$35,000 **Individual**/Corporate

Income Split	**$20,000** $15,000	**$23,000** $12,000	**$26,000** $9,000
Less Pension Contribution	$5,000	$5,750	$6,500
Net Income	$10,000	$6,250	$2,500
Federal Taxes	**$2,239** $1,500	**$2,689** $938	**$3,448** $375
State Taxes	**$669** $500	**$849** $313	**$1,029** $125
Totals	**$2,908** $2,000	**$3,538** $1,251	**$4,477** $500
Grand Total	**$4,908**	**$4,789**	**$4,977**

Single—$60,000 **Individual**/Corporate

Income Split	**$30,000** $30,000	**$35,000** $25,000	**$40,000** $20,000	**$45,000** $15,000
Less Pension Contribution	$7,500	$8,750	$10,000	$11,250
Net Income	$22,500	$16,250	$10,000	$3,750
Federal Taxes	**$4,568** $3,375	**$5,968** $2,438	**$7,368** $1,500	**$8,768** $563
State Taxes	**$1,269** $1,125	**$1,569** $813	**$1,869** $500	**$2,169** $188
Totals	**$5,837** $4,500	**$7,537** $3,251	**$9,237** $2,000	**$10,937** $751
Grand Total	**$10,337**	**$10,788**	**$11,237**	**$11,688**

Your Estimates

Corporate Income from income split	$ _____
Less Pension contribution	− _____
Net corp. income	$ _____
Federal corp. tax	$ _____
State corp. tax	$ _____
Individual income from income split	$ _____
Less exemptions (number × $2,000 or correct amount for your state)	− _____
	$ _____
Less standard deduction ($3,100 if single, $5,200 if married) or Itemized total	− _____
Taxable income	$ _____
Federal income tax	$ _____
State income tax	$ _____

Insert numbers on worksheet into box at right; add for totals

TAX RATES

Corporate—5%
Individual—Over $9,000 $315 + 6% of excess over $9,000

COMMENT

For single individuals in the $35,000 category, the $23,000/$12,000 income split produces the lowest taxes. At $60,000, the $30,000/$30,000 split is clearly the best choice.

For married entrepreneurs and professionals in the $50,000 category, the $38,000/$12,000 income split offers both the greatest salary and pension contribution *and* the lowest taxes. At $75,000, the $38,000/$37,000 split produces the lowest taxes and is the best choice.

MISSOURI

Married—$50,000 Individual/Corporate

Income Split	**$25,000** $25,000	**$32,000** $18,000	**$38,000** $12,000
Less Pension Contribution	$6,250	$8,000	$9,500
Net Income	$18,750	$10,000	$2,500
Federal Taxes	**$2,374** $2,813	**$3,424** $1,500	**$4,324** $375
State Taxes	**$723** $938	**$1,143** $500	**$1,503** $125
Totals	**$3,097** $3,751	**$4,567** $2,000	**$5,827** $500
Grand Total	**$6,848**	**$6,567**	**$6,327**

Married—$75,000 Individual/Corporate

Income Split	**$30,000** $45,000	**$38,000** $37,000	**$45,000** $30,000	**$55,000** $20,000
Less Pension Contribution	$7,500	$9,500	$11,250	$13,750
Net Income	$37,500	$27,500	$18,750	$6,250
Federal Taxes	**$3,124** $5,625	**$4,324** $4,125	**$6,008** $2,813	**$8,808** $938
State Taxes	**$1,023** $1,875	**$1,503** $1,375	**$1,923** $938	**$2,523** $313
Totals	**$4,147** $7,500	**$5,827** $5,500	**$7,931** $3,751	**$11,331** $1,251
Grand Total	**$11,647**	**$11,327**	**$11,682**	**$12,582**

Individual/Corporate

Income split	$ $
Less Pension contribution	$
Net Income	$
Federal Taxes	$ $
State Taxes	$ $
Totals	$ $
Grand Total	$

Corp. funds available for investment (corp. net income-corp. taxes) $ _____

MONTANA

Single—$35,000 **Individual**/Corporate

Income Split	$20,000 $15,000	$23,000 $12,000	$26,000 $9,000
Less Pension Contribution	$5,000	$5,750	$6,500
Net Income	$10,000	$6,250	$2,500
Federal Taxes	$2,239 $1,500	$2,689 $938	$3,448 $375
State Taxes	$764 $675	$1,016 $422	$1,268 $169
Totals	$3,003 $2,175	$3,705 $1,360	$4,716 $544
Grand Total	$5,178	$5,065	$5,260

Single—$60,000 **Individual**/Corporate

Income Split	$30,000 $30,000	$35,000 $25,000	$40,000 $20,000	$45,000 $15,000
Less Pension Contribution	$7,500	$8,750	$10,000	$11,250
Net Income	$22,500	$16,250	$10,000	$3,750
Federal Taxes	$4,568 $3,375	$5,968 $2,438	$7,368 $1,500	$8,768 $563
State Taxes	$1,645 $1,519	$2,117 $1,097	$2,642 $675	$3,167 $253
Totals	$6,213 $4,894	$8,085 $3,535	$10,010 $2,175	$11,935 $816
Grand Total	$11,107	$11,620	$12,185	$12,751

Your Estimates

Corporate Income from income split	$ _____
Less Pension contribution	− _____
Net corp. income	$ _____
Federal corp. tax	$ _____
State corp. tax	$ _____
Individual income from income split	$ _____
Less exemptions (number × $2,000 or correct amount for your state)	− _____
	$ _____
Less standard deduction ($3,100 if single, $5,200 if married) or Itemized total	− _____
Taxable income	$ _____
Federal income tax	$ _____
State income tax	$ _____

Insert numbers on worksheet into box at right; add for totals

TAX RATES

Corporate—6.75%
Individual—

$15,000–$21,000	$772 + 8.40% of excess over $15,000
$21,000–$30,000	$1,276 + 9.45% of excess over $21,000
$30,000–$52,500	$2,127 + 10.50% of excess over $30,000

(includes 5% education surcharge)

COMMENT

For single individuals in the $35,000 category, the $23,000/$12,000 income split is best. At $60,000, the $30,000/$30,000 split is clearly the best choice.

For married individuals in the $50,000 category, the $38,000/$12,000 income split offers both the greatest salary and pension contribution *and* the lowest taxes. At $75,000, the $38,000/$37,000 split produces the lowest taxes.

MONTANA

Married—$50,000 Individual/Corporate

Income Split	$25,000 $25,000	$32,000 $18,000	$38,000 $12,000
Less Pension Contribution	$6,250	$8,000	$9,500
Net Income	$18,750	$10,000	$2,500
Federal Taxes	$2,374 $2,813	$3,424 $1,500	$4,324 $375
State Taxes	$839 $1,266	$1,446 $675	$2,013 $169
Totals	$3,213 $4,079	$4,870 $2,175	$6,337 $544
Grand Total	$7,292	$7,045	$6,881

Married—$75,000 Individual/Corporate

Income Split	$30,000 $45,000	$38,000 $37,000	$45,000 $30,000	$55,000 $20,000
Less Pension Contribution	$7,500	$9,500	$11,250	$13,750
Net Income	$37,500	$27,500	$18,750	$6,250
Federal Taxes	$3,124 $5,625	$4,324 $4,125	$6,008 $2,813	$8,808 $938
State Taxes	$1,259 $2,531	$2,013 $1,856	$2,736 $1,266	$3,786 $422
Totals	$4,383 $8,156	$6,337 $5,981	$8,744 $4,079	$12,594 $1,360
Grand Total	$12,539	$12,318	$12,823	$13,954

Individual/Corporate

Income split	$ $
Less Pension contribution	$
Net Income	$
Federal Taxes	$ $
State Taxes	$ $
Totals	$ $
Grand Total	$

Corp. funds available for investment (corp. net income-corp. taxes) $ _____

179

NEBRASKA

Single—$35,000 **Individual**/Corporate

Income Split	$20,000 $15,000	$23,000 $12,000	$26,000 $9,000
Less Pension Contribution	$5,000	$5,750	$6,500
Net Income	$10,000	$6,250	$2,500
Federal Taxes	$2,239 $1,500	$2,689 $938	$3,448 $375
State Taxes	$452 $475	$564 $297	$714 $119
Totals	$2,691 $1,975	$3,253 $1,235	$4,162 $494
Grand Total	$4,666	$4,488	$4,656

Single—$60,000 **Individual**/Corporate

Income Split	$30,000 $30,000	$35,000 $25,000	$40,000 $20,000	$45,000 $15,000
Less Pension Contribution	$7,500	$8,750	$10,000	$11,250
Net Income	$22,500	$16,250	$10,000	$3,750
Federal Taxes	$4,568 $3,375	$5,968 $2,438	$7,368 $1,500	$8,768 $563
State Taxes	$914 $1,069	$1,191 $772	$1,485 $475	$1,780 $178
Totals	$5,482 $4,444	$7,159 $3,210	$8,853 $1,975	$10,548 $741
Grand Total	$9,926	$10,369	$10,828	$11,289

Your Estimates

Corporate Income from income split	$ _____
Less Pension contribution	_____
Net corp. income	$ _____
Federal corp. tax	$ _____
State corp. tax	$ _____
Individual income from income split	$ _____
Less exemptions (number × $2,000 or correct amount for your state)	− _____
	$ _____
Less standard deduction ($3,100 if single, $5,200 if married) or Itemized total	− _____
Taxable income	$ _____
Federal income tax	$ _____
State income tax	$ _____

Insert numbers on worksheet into box at right; add for totals

TAX RATES

Corporate—First $50,000   4.75%
Individual—
Single— $16,800–$27,000 $509 + 5% of
                   excess over $16,800
    Over $27,000 $1,019 + 5.9%
                of excess over $27,000
Married—$ 3,000–$28,000 $60 + 3.5% of
                   excess over $3,000
    $28,000–$45,000 $848 + 5% of
                   excess over $28,000
    Over $45,000 $1,698 + 5.9%
                of excess over $45,000

COMMENT

For single individuals in the $35,000 category, the $23,000/$12,000 income split is best. At $60,000, the $30,000/$30,000 split is clearly the best choice.

For married individuals in the $50,000 category, the $38,000/$12,000 income split offers both the highest salary and pension contribution *and* the lowest taxes. At $75,000, the $38,000/$37,000 split produces the lowest taxes and is the best choice for most entrepreneurs and professionals.

NEBRASKA

Married—$50,000 Individual/Corporate

Income Split	**$25,000** $25,000	**$32,000** $18,000	**$38,000** $12,000
Less Pension Contribution	$6,250	$8,000	$9,500
Net Income	$18,750	$10,000	$2,500
Federal Taxes	**$2,374** $2,813	**$3,424** $1,500	**$4,324** $375
State Taxes	**$463** $891	**$684** $475	**$888** $119
Totals	**$2,837** $3,704	**$4,108** $1,975	**$5,212** $494
Grand Total	**$6,541**	**$6,083**	**$5,706**

Married—$75,000 Individual/Corporate

Income Split	**$30,000** $45,000	**$38,000** $37,000	**$45,000** $30,000	**$55,000** $20,000
Less Pension Contribution	$7,500	$9,500	$11,250	$13,750
Net Income	$37,500	$27,500	$18,750	$6,250
Federal Taxes	**$3,124** $5,625	**$4,324** $4,125	**$6,008** $2,813	**$8,808** $938
State Taxes	**$621** $1,781	**$888** $1,306	**$1,238** $891	**$1,745** $297
Totals	**$3,745** $7,406	**$5,212** $5,431	**$7,246** $3,704	**$10,553** $1,235
Grand Total	**$11,151**	**$10,643**	**$10,950**	**$11,788**

Individual/Corporate

Income split	$ $
Less Pension contribution	$
Net Income	$
Federal Taxes	$ $
State Taxes	$ $
Totals	$ $
Grand Total	$

Corp. funds available for investment (corp. net income-corp. taxes) $ _____

NEVADA

Single—$35,000 **Individual**/Corporate

Income Split	$20,000	$23,000	$26,000
	$15,000	$12,000	$9,000
Less Pension Contribution	$5,000	$5,750	$6,500
Net Income	$10,000	$6,250	$2,500
Federal Taxes	$2,239	$2,689	$3,448
	$1,500	$938	$375
State Taxes	$0	$0	$0
	$0	$0	$0
Totals	$2,239	$2,689	$3,448
	$1,500	$938	$375
Grand Total	$3,739	$3,627	$3,823

Single—$60,000 **Individual**/Corporate

Income Split	$30,000	$35,000	$40,000	$45,000
	$30,000	$25,000	$20,000	$15,000
Less Pension Contribution	$7,500	$8,750	$10,000	$11,250
Net Income	$22,500	$16,250	$10,000	$3,750
Federal Taxes	$4,568	$5,968	$7,368	$8,768
	$3,375	$2,438	$1,500	$563
State Taxes	$0	$0	$0	$0
	$0	$0	$0	$0
Totals	$4,568	$5,968	$7,368	$8,768
	$3,375	$2,438	$1,500	$563
Grand Total	$7,943	$8,406	$8,868	$9,331

Your Estimates

Corporate Income from income split	$ _____
Less Pension contribution	_____
Net corp. income	$ _____
Federal corp. tax	$ _____
State corp. tax	$ _____0_____
Individual income from income split	$ _____
Less exemptions (number × $2,000 or correct amount for your state)	− _____
	$ _____
Less standard deduction ($3,100 if single, $5,200 if married) or Itemized total	− _____
Taxable income	$ _____
Federal income tax	$ _____
State income tax	$ _____0_____

Insert numbers on worksheet into box at right; add for totals

COMMENT

TAX RATES

Corporate—0
Individual—0

Because Nevada imposes no personal or corporate income tax, the $23,000/$12,000 income split is best for single individuals in the $35,000 category. At $60,000, the $30,000/$30,000 split is clearly the best choice.

For married individuals in the $50,000 category, the $38,000/$12,000 income split provides both the highest salary and pension contribution *and* the lowest taxes. At $75,000, the $38,000/$37,000 split offers the lowest taxes.

NEVADA

Married—$50,000 **Individual**/Corporate

Income Split	$25,000 $25,000	$32,000 $18,000	$38,000 $12,000
Less Pension Contribution	$6,250	$8,000	$9,500
Net Income	$18,750	$10,000	$2,500
Federal Taxes	$2,374 $2,813	$3,424 $1,500	$4,324 $375
State Taxes	$0 $0	$0 $0	$0 $0
Totals	$2,374 $2,813	$3,424 $1,500	$4,324 $375
Grand Total	$5,187	$4,924	$4,699

Married—$75,000 **Individual**/Corporate

Income Split	$30,000 $45,000	$38,000 $37,000	$45,000 $30,000	$55,000 $20,000
Less Pension Contribution	$7,500	$9,500	$11,250	$13,750
Net Income	$37,500	$27,500	$18,750	$6,250
Federal Taxes	$3,124 $5,625	$4,324 $4,125	$6,008 $2,813	$8,808 $938
State Taxes	$0 $0	$0 $0	$0 $0	$0 $0
Totals	$3,124 $5,625	$4,324 $4,125	$6,008 $2,813	$8,808 $938
Grand Total	$8,749	$8,449	$8,821	$9,746

Individual/Corporate

Income split	$ $
Less Pension contribution	$
Net Income	$
Federal Taxes	$ $
State Taxes	$ 0 $ 0
Totals	$ $
Grand Total	$

Corp. funds available for investment (corp. net income-corp. taxes) $ _____

NEW HAMPSHIRE

Single—$35,000 Individual/Corporate

Income Split	$20,000 $15,000	$23,000 $12,000	$26,000 $9,000
Less Pension Contribution	$5,000	$5,750	$6,500
Net Income	$10,000	$6,250	$2,500
Federal Taxes	$2,239 $1,500	$2,689 $938	$3,448 $375
State Taxes	$0 $800	$0 $500	$0 $200
Totals	$2,239 $2,300	$2,689 $1,438	$3,448 $575
Grand Total	$4,539	$4,127	$4,023

Single—$60,000 Individual/Corporate

Income Split	$30,000 $30,000	$35,000 $25,000	$40,000 $20,000	$45,000 $15,000
Less Pension Contribution	$7,500	$8,750	$10,000	$11,250
Net Income	$22,500	$16,250	$10,000	$3,750
Federal Taxes	$4,568 $3,375	$5,968 $2,438	$7,368 $1,500	$8,768 $563
State Taxes	$0 $1,800	$0 $1,300	$0 $800	$0 $300
Totals	$4,568 $5,175	$5,968 $3,738	$7,368 $2,300	$8,768 $863
Grand Total	$9,743	$9,706	$9,668	$9,631

Your Estimates

Corporate Income from income split	$ _____
Less Pension contribution	_____
Net corp. income	$ _____
Federal corp. tax	$ _____
State corp. tax	$ _____
Individual income from income split	$ _____
Less exemptions (number × $2,000 or correct amount for your state)	− $ _____
Less standard deduction ($3,100 if single, $5,200 if married) or Itemized total	− _____
Taxable income	$ _____
Federal income tax	$ _____
State income tax (none on salaries)	$ _____

Insert numbers on worksheet into box at right; add for totals

TAX RATES

Corporate—8%
Individual—0 on salaries

COMMENT

Because New Hampshire does not tax salaries, the *highest-salary income splits* in all categories will produce the *lowest taxes* as well as the *highest pension contributions*.

NEW HAMPSHIRE

Married—$50,000 **Individual**/Corporate

Income Split	$25,000 $25,000	$32,000 $18,000	$38,000 $12,000
Less Pension Contribution	$6,250	$8,000	$9,500
Net Income	$18,750	$10,000	$2,500
Federal Taxes	$2,374 $2,813	$3,424 $1,500	$4,324 $375
State Taxes	$0 $1,500	$0 $800	$0 $200
Totals	$2,374 $4,313	$3,424 $2,300	$4,324 $575
Grand Total	$6,687	$5,724	$4,899

Married—$75,000 **Individual**/Corporate

Income Split	$30,000 $45,000	$38,000 $37,000	$45,000 $30,000	$55,000 $20,000
Less Pension Contribution	$7,500	$9,500	$11,250	$13,750
Net Income	$37,500	$27,500	$18,750	$6,250
Federal Taxes	$3,124 $5,625	$4,324 $4,125	$6,008 $2,813	$8,808 $938
State Taxes	$0 $3,000	$0 $2,200	$0 $1,500	$0 $500
Totals	$3,124 $8,625	$4,324 $6,325	$6,008 $4,313	$8,808 $1,438
Grand Total	$11,749	$10,649	$10,321	$10,246

Individual/Corporate

Income split	$ $
Less Pension contribution	$
Net Income	$
Federal Taxes	$ $
State Taxes	$ 0 $
Totals	$ $
Grand Total	$

Corp. funds available for investment (corp. net income-corp. taxes) $ _____

NEW JERSEY

Single—$35,000 Individual/Corporate

Income Split	$20,000 $15,000	$23,000 $12,000	$26,000 $9,000
Less Pension Contribution	$5,000	$5,750	$6,500
Net Income	$10,000	$6,250	$2,500
Federal Taxes	$2,239 $1,500	$2,689 $938	$3,448 $375
State Taxes	$298 $900	$358 $563	$423 $225
Totals	$2,537 $2,400	$3,047 $1,501	$3,871 $600
Grand Total	$4,937	$4,548	$4,471

Single—$60,000 Individual/Corporate

Income Split	$30,000 $30,000	$35,000 $25,000	$40,000 $20,000	$45,000 $15,000
Less Pension Contribution	$7,500	$8,750	$10,000	$11,250
Net Income	$22,500	$16,250	$10,000	$3,750
Federal Taxes	$4,568 $3,375	$5,968 $2,438	$7,368 $1,500	$8,768 $563
State Taxes	$523 $2,025	$648 $1,463	$773 $900	$898 $338
Totals	$5,091 $5,400	$6,616 $3,901	$8,141 $2,400	$9,666 $901
Grand Total	$10,491	$10,517	$10,541	$10,567

Your Estimates

Corporate Income from income split	$ _____
Less Pension contribution	− _____
Net corp. income	$ _____
Federal corp. tax	$ _____
State corp. tax	$ _____
Individual income from income split	$ _____
Less exemptions (number × $2,000 or correct amount for your state)	− _____
	$ _____
Less standard deduction ($3,100 if single, $5,200 if married) or Itemized total	− _____
Taxable income	$ _____
Federal income tax	$ _____
State income tax	$ _____

Insert numbers on worksheet into box at right; add for totals

TAX RATES

Corporate—9%
Individual—First $20,000   2%
    $20,000–$50,000 $400 + 2.5% of
               excess over $20,000

COMMENT

Because New Jersey's individual income tax is so low, the *highest-salary income splits* in the $35,000 and $50,000 categories will produce the *lowest taxes* as well as the *highest pension contributions*.

For single entrepreneurs in the $60,000 category, the $30,000/$30,000 income split generates the lowest taxes. However, the $45,000/$15,000 split may be more attractive: it provides $15,000 more in salary and $3,750 more in pension contributions for a *mere $76 in additional taxes*.

For married entrepreneurs and professionals in the $75,000 category, the *$55,000/$20,000 split is a best bet*. For *only $50 in additional taxes*, it provides $10,000 more in salary and $2,500 in pension contributions than the lowest-taxes choice.

NEW JERSEY

Married—$50,000 **Individual**/Corporate

Income Split	$25,000 $25,000	$32,000 $18,000	$38,000 $12,000
Less Pension Contribution	$6,250	$8,000	$9,500
Net Income	$18,750	$10,000	$2,500
Federal Taxes	$2,374 $2,813	$3,424 $1,500	$4,324 $375
State Taxes	$316 $1,688	$470 $900	$620 $225
Totals	$2,690 $4,501	$3,894 $2,400	$4,944 $600
Grand Total	$7,191	$6,294	$5,544

Married—$75,000 **Individual**/Corporate

Income Split	$30,000 $45,000	$38,000 $37,000	$45,000 $30,000	$55,000 $20,000
Less Pension Contribution	$7,500	$9,500	$11,250	$13,750
Net Income	$37,500	$27,500	$18,750	$6,250
Federal Taxes	$3,124 $5,625	$4,324 $4,125	$6,008 $2,813	$8,808 $938
State Taxes	$420 $3,375	$620 $2,475	$795 $1,688	$1,045 $563
Totals	$3,544 $9,000	$4,944 $6,600	$6,803 $4,501	$9,853 $1,501
Grand Total	$12,544	$11,544	$11,304	$11,354

Individual/Corporate

Income split	$ $
Less Pension contribution	$
Net Income	$
Federal Taxes	$ $
State Taxes	$ $
Totals	$ $
Grand Total	$

Corp. funds available for investment (corp. net income-corp. taxes) $ _____

NEW MEXICO

Single—$35,000 Individual/Corporate

Income Split	**$20,000** $15,000	**$23,000** $12,000	**$26,000** $9,000
Less Pension Contribution	$5,000	$5,750	$6,500
Net Income	$10,000	$6,250	$2,500
Federal Taxes	**$2,239** $1,500	**$2,689** $938	**$3,448** $375
State Taxes	**$453** $480	**$617** $300	**$791** $120
Totals	**$2,692** $1,980	**$3,306** $1,238	**$4,239** $495
Grand Total	**$4,672**	**$4,544**	**$4,734**

Single—$60,000 Individual/Corporate

Income Split	**$30,000** $30,000	**$35,000** $25,000	**$40,000** $20,000	**$45,000** $15,000
Less Pension Contribution	$7,500	$8,750	$10,000	$11,250
Net Income	$22,500	$16,250	$10,000	$3,750
Federal Taxes	**$4,568** $3,375	**$5,968** $2,438	**$7,368** $1,500	**$8,768** $563
State Taxes	**$1,040** $1,080	**$1,385** $780	**$1,759** $480	**$2,144** $180
Totals	**$5,608** $4,455	**$7,353** $3,218	**$9,127** $1,980	**$10,912** $743
Grand Total	**$10,063**	**$10,571**	**$11,107**	**$11,655**

Your Estimates

Corporate Income from income split	$ _____
Less Pension contribution	− _____
Net corp. income	$ _____
Federal corp. tax	$ _____
State corp. tax	$ _____
Individual income from income split	$ _____
Less exemptions (number × $2,000 or correct amount for your state)	− _____
	$ _____
Less standard deduction ($3,100 if single, $5,200 if married) or Itemized total	− _____
Taxable income	$ _____
Federal income tax	$ _____
State income tax	$ _____

Insert numbers on worksheet into box at right; add for totals

TAX RATES

Corporate—First $500,000   4.8%

Individual—
Single—

$15,600–$23,400	$484 + 5.8% of excess over $15,600
$23,400–$31,200	$936 + 6.9% of excess over $23,400
$31,200–$41,600	$1,474 + 7.7% of excess over $31,200

Married—

$16,000–$24,000	$496 + 4.8% of excess over $16,000
$24,000–$36,000	$880 + 5.9% of excess over $24,000
$36,000–$48,000	$1,588 + 6.9% of excess over $36,000

COMMENT

For single individuals in the $35,000 category, the $23,000/$12,000 income split is best. At $60,000, the $30,000/$30,000 split is clearly the best choice.

For married individuals in the $50,000 category, the $38,000/$12,000 income split offers both the highest salary and pension contribution *and* the lowest taxes. At $75,000, the $38,000/$37,000 split is the best option for most professionals and entrepreneurs.

NEW MEXICO

Married—$50,000 **Individual**/Corporate

Income Split	$25,000	$32,000	$38,000
	$25,000	$18,000	$12,000
Less Pension Contribution	$6,250	$8,000	$9,500
Net Income	$18,750	$10,000	$2,500
Federal Taxes	$2,374	$3,424	$4,324
	$2,813	$1,500	$375
State Taxes	$488	$822	$1,163
	$900	$480	$120
Totals	$2,862	$4,246	$5,487
	$3,713	$1,980	$495
Grand Total	$6,575	$6,226	$5,982

Married—$75,000 **Individual**/Corporate

Income Split	$30,000	$38,000	$45,000	$55,000
	$45,000	$37,000	$30,000	$20,000
Less Pension Contribution	$7,500	$9,500	$11,250	$13,750
Net Income	$37,500	$27,500	$18,750	$6,250
Federal Taxes	$3,124	$4,324	$6,008	$8,808
	$5,625	$4,125	$2,813	$938
State Taxes	$726	$1,163	$1,576	$2,264
	$1,800	$1,320	$900	$300
Totals	$3,850	$5,487	$7,584	$11,072
	$7,425	$5,445	$3,713	$1,238
Grand Total	$11,275	$10,932	$11,297	$12,310

Individual/Corporate

Income split	$
	$
Less Pension contribution	$
Net Income	$
Federal Taxes	$
	$
State Taxes	$
	$
Totals	$
	$
Grand Total	$

Corp. funds available for investment (corp. net income-corp. taxes) $ _____

NEW YORK STATE

Single—$35,000 **Individual**/Corporate

Income Split	$20,000 $15,000	$23,000 $12,000	$26,000 $9,000
Less Pension Contribution	$5,000	$5,750	$6,500
Net Income	$10,000	$6,250	$2,500
Federal Taxes	$2,239 $1,500	$2,689 $938	$3,448 $375
State Taxes	$838 $800	$1,055 $500	$1,276 $325
Totals	$3,077 $2,300	$3,744 $1,438	$4,724 $700
Grand Total	$5,377	$5,182	$5,424

Single—$60,000 **Individual**/Corporate

Income Split	$30,000 $30,000	$35,000 $25,000	$40,000 $20,000	$45,000 $15,000
Less Pension Contribution	$7,500	$8,750	$10,000	$11,250
Net Income	$22,500	$16,250	$10,000	$3,750
Federal Taxes	$4,568 $3,375	$5,968 $2,438	$7,368 $1,500	$8,768 $563
State Taxes	$1,571 $1,800	$1,940 $1,300	$2,309 $800	$2,678 $325
Totals	$6,139 $5,175	$7,908 $3,738	$9,677 $2,300	$11,446 $888
Grand Total	$11,314	$11,646	$11,977	$12,334

Your Estimates

Corporate Income from income split	$ _____
Less Pension contribution	– _____
Net corp. income	$ _____
Federal corp. tax	$ _____
State corp. tax	$ _____
Individual income from income split	$ _____
Less exemptions (number × $2,000 or correct amount for your state)	– _____
	$ _____
Less standard deduction ($3,100 if single, $5,200 if married) or Itemized total	– _____
Taxable income	$ _____
Federal income tax	$ _____
State income tax	$ _____

Insert numbers on worksheet into box at right; add for totals

TAX RATES

Corporate—8%, $325 minimum
　　　(17% surtax expired 12/31/89)
Individual—
　Single—Over $16,000 $915 + 7.375% of ex-
　　　　　cess over $16,000
　Married—$25,000–$32,000 $1,340 + 7% of
　　　　　excess over $25,000
　　Over $32,000 $1,830 + 7.375% of
　　　　　excess over $32,000

COMMENT

For single individuals in the $35,000 category, the $23,000/$12,000 income split is best. At $60,000, the $30,000/$30,000 split is clearly the best choice.

For married entrepreneurs and professionals in the $50,000 category, the $38,000/$12,000 income split generates both the highest salary and pension contribution *and* the lowest taxes. At $75,000, the $38,000/$37,000 split offers the lowest taxes. However, the $45,000/$30,000 split may be more attractive: it provides $7,000 more in salary and $1,750 more in pension contributions for *only $176 in additional taxes.*

NEW YORK STATE

Married—$50,000 Individual/Corporate

Income Split	**$25,000**	**$32,000**	**$38,000**
	$25,000	$18,000	$12,000
Less Pension Contribution	$6,250	$8,000	$9,500
Net Income	$18,750	$10,000	$2,500
Federal Taxes	**$2,374**	**$3,424**	**$4,324**
	$2,813	$1,500	$375
State Taxes	**$790**	**$1,208**	**$1,606**
	$1,500	$800	$325
Totals	**$3,164**	**$4,632**	**$5,930**
	$4,313	$2,300	$700
Grand Total	**$7,477**	**$6,932**	**$6,630**

Married—$75,000 Individual/Corporate

Income Split	**$30,000**	**$38,000**	**$45,000**	**$55,000**
	$45,000	$37,000	$30,000	$20,000
Less Pension Contribution	$7,500	$9,500	$11,250	$13,750
Net Income	$37,500	$27,500	$18,750	$6,250
Federal Taxes	**$3,124**	**$4,324**	**$6,008**	**$8,808**
	$5,625	$4,125	$2,813	$938
State Taxes	**$1,088**	**$1,606**	**$2,110**	**$2,848**
	$3,000	$2,200	$1,500	$500
Totals	**$4,212**	**$5,930**	**$8,118**	**$11,656**
	$8,625	$6,325	$4,313	$1,438
Grand Total	**$12,837**	**$12,255**	**$12,431**	**$13,094**

Individual/Corporate

Income split	$
	$
Less Pension contribution	$
Net Income	$
Federal Taxes	$
	$
State Taxes	$
	$
Totals	$
	$
Grand Total	$

Corp. funds available for investment (corp. net income-corp. taxes) $ _____

NEW YORK CITY

Single—$35,000 Individual/Corporate

Income Split	**$20,000** / $15,000	**$23,000** / $12,000	**$26,000** / $9,000
Less Pension Contribution	$5,000	$5,750	$6,500
Net Income	$10,000	$6,250	$2,500
Federal Taxes	**$2,239** / $1,500	**$2,689** / $938	**$3,448** / $375
State Taxes	**$838** / $800	**$1,055** / $500	**$1,276** / $325
City Taxes	**$363** / $885	**$459** / $553	**$651** / $300
Totals	**$3,440** / $3,185	**$4,203** / $1,991	**$5,375** / $1,000
Grand Total	**$6,625**	**$6,194**	**$6,375**

Single—$60,000 Individual/Corporate

Income Split	**$30,000** / $30,000	**$35,000** / $25,000	**$40,000** / $20,000	**$45,000** / $15,000
Less Pension Contribution	$7,500	$8,750	$10,000	$11,250
Net Income	$22,500	$16,250	$10,000	$3,750
Federal Taxes	**$4,568** / $3,375	**$5,968** / $2,438	**$7,368** / $1,500	**$8,768** / $563
State Taxes	**$1,571** / $1,800	**$1,940** / $1,300	**$2,309** / $800	**$2,678** / $325
City Taxes	**$683** / $1,991	**$850** / $1,438	**$1,017** / $885	**$1,185** / $332
Totals	**$6,822** / $7,166	**$8,758** / $5,176	**$10,694** / $3,185	**$12,631** / $1,220
Grand Total	**$13,988**	**$13,934**	**$13,879**	**$13,851**

Your Estimates

Corporate Income from income split	$ _____
Less Pension contribution	− _____
Net corp. income	$ _____
Federal corp. tax	$ _____
State corp. tax	$ _____
City corp. tax	$ _____
Individual income from income split	$ _____
Less exemptions (number × $2,000 or correct amount for your state)	− _____
Less standard deduction ($3,100 if single, $5,200 if married) or Itemized total	− _____
Taxable income	$ _____
Federal income tax	$ _____
State income tax	$ _____
City income tax	$ _____

Insert numbers on worksheet into box at right; add for totals

TAX RATES

Corporate—8.85%, $300 minimum
Individual—$16,500–$27,500 $402 + 3.2% of excess over $16,500
$27,500–$66,000 $754 + 3.35% of excess over $27,500

COMMENT

As in the past decade, New York City once again earns the dubious distinction of imposing the heaviest taxes in the nation. Because individual tax rates are much lower than corporate rates, the highest income split generates the lowest taxes in three out of four income categories.

For single entrepreneurs in the $35,000 category, the $23,000/$12,000 income split is clearly the best choice.

NEW YORK CITY

Married—$50,000 **Individual**/Corporate

Income Split	**$25,000** $25,000	**$32,000** $18,000	**$38,000** $12,000
Less Pension Contribution	$6,250	$8,000	$9,500
Net Income	$18,750	$10,000	$2,500
Federal Taxes	**$2,374** $2,813	**$3,424** $1,500	**$4,324** $375
State Taxes	**$790** $1,500	**$1,208** $800	**$1,606** $325
City Taxes	**$355** $1,659	**$544** $885	**$715** $300
Totals	**$3,519** $5,972	**$5,176** $3,185	**$6,645** $1,000
Grand Total	**$9,491**	**$8,361**	**$7,645**

Married—$75,000 **Individual**/Corporate

Income Split	**$30,000** $45,000	**$38,000** $37,000	**$45,000** $30,000	**$55,000** $20,000
Less Pension Contribution	$7,500	$9,500	$11,250	$13,750
Net Income	$37,500	$27,500	$18,750	$6,250
Federal Taxes	**$3,124** $5,625	**$4,324** $4,125	**$6,008** $2,813	**$8,808** $938
State Taxes	**$1,088** $3,000	**$1,606** $2,200	**$2,110** $1,500	**$2,848** $500
City Taxes	**$490** $3,319	**$715** $2,434	**$939** $1,659	**$1,259** $553
Totals	**$4,702** $11,944	**$6,645** $8,759	**$9,057** $5,972	**$12,915** $1,991
Grand Total	**$16,646**	**$15,404**	**$15,029**	**$14,906**

Individual/Corporate

Income split	$ $
Less Pension contribution	$
Net Income	$
Federal Taxes	$ $
State Taxes	$ $
City Taxes	$
Totals	$ $
Grand Total	$

Corp. funds available for investment (corp. net income-corp. taxes) $ _____

NORTH CAROLINA

Single—$35,000 Individual/Corporate

Income Split	$20,000 $15,000	$23,000 $12,000	$26,000 $9,000
Less Pension Contribution	$5,000	$5,750	$6,500
Net Income	$10,000	$6,250	$2,500
Federal Taxes	$2,239 $1,500	$2,689 $938	$3,448 $375
State Taxes	$916 $700	$1,126 $438	$1,336 $175
Totals	$3,155 $2,200	$3,815 $1,376	$4,784 $550
Grand Total	$5,355	$5,191	$5,334

Single—$60,000 Individual/Corporate

Income Split	$30,000 $30,000	$35,000 $25,000	$40,000 $20,000	$45,000 $15,000
Less Pension Contribution	$7,500	$8,750	$10,000	$11,250
Net Income	$22,500	$16,250	$10,000	$3,750
Federal Taxes	$4,568 $3,375	$5,968 $2,438	$7,368 $1,500	$8,768 $563
State Taxes	$1,616 $1,575	$1,966 $1,138	$2,316 $700	$2,666 $263
Totals	$6,184 $4,950	$7,934 $3,576	$9,684 $2,200	$11,434 $826
Grand Total	$11,134	$11,510	$11,884	$12,260

Your Estimates

Corporate Income from income split $ _____
Less Pension contribution   − _____
Net corp. income $ _____
Federal corp. tax $ _____
State corp. tax $ _____
Individual income from income split $ _____
Less exemptions
(number × $2,000 or correct amount for your state)
                                                     $ _____

Less standard deduction ($3,100 if single,
$5,200 if married) or Itemized total   − _____
Taxable income $ _____
Federal income tax $ _____
State income tax $ _____

Insert numbers on worksheet into box at right; add for totals

TAX RATES

Corporate—7%
Individual—
  Single—Over $12,750 $765 + 7% of excess
                          over $12,750
  Married—Over $21,250 $1,275 + 7% of ex-
                          cess over $21,250

COMMENT

For single individuals in the $35,000 category, the $23,000/$12,000 income split is best. At $60,000, the $30,000/$30,000 split is clearly the best choice.

For married professionals and entrepreneurs in the $50,000 category, the $38,000/$12,000 income split produces both the highest salary and pension contribution *and* the lowest taxes. At $75,000, the $38,000/$37,000 split is the best option for most people.

NORTH CAROLINA

Married—$50,000 **Individual**/Corporate

Income Split	**$25,000** $25,000	**$32,000** $18,000	**$38,000** $12,000
Less Pension Contribution	$6,250	$8,000	$9,500
Net Income	$18,750	$10,000	$2,500
Federal Taxes	**$2,374** $2,813	**$3,424** $1,500	**$4,324** $375
State Taxes	**$948** $1,313	**$1,349** $700	**$1,769** $175
Totals	**$3,322** $4,126	**$4,773** $2,200	**$6,093** $550
Grand Total	**$7,448**	**$6,973**	**$6,643**

Married—$75,000 **Individual**/Corporate

Income Split	**$30,000** $45,000	**$38,000** $37,000	**$45,000** $30,000	**$55,000** $20,000
Less Pension Contribution	$7,500	$9,500	$11,250	$13,750
Net Income	$37,500	$27,500	$18,750	$6,250
Federal Taxes	**$3,124** $5,625	**$4,324** $4,125	**$6,008** $2,813	**$8,808** $938
State Taxes	**$1,248** $2,625	**$1,769** $1,925	**$2,259** $1,313	**$2,959** $438
Totals	**$4,372** $8,250	**$6,093** $6,050	**$8,267** $4,126	**$11,767** $1,376
Grand Total	**$12,622**	**$12,143**	**$12,393**	**$13,143**

Individual/Corporate

Income split	$ $
Less Pension contribution	$
Net Income	$
Federal Taxes	$ $
State Taxes	$ $
Totals	$ $
Grand Total	$

Corp. funds available for investment (corp. net income-corp. taxes) $ _____

NORTH DAKOTA

Single—$35,000 Individual/Corporate

Income Split	$20,000 $15,000	$23,000 $12,000	$26,000 $9,000
Less Pension Contribution	$5,000	$5,750	$6,500
Net Income	$10,000	$6,250	$2,500
Federal Taxes	$2,239 $1,500	$2,689 $938	$3,448 $375
State Taxes	$313 $435	$376 $236	$483 $75
Totals	$2,552 $1,935	$3,065 $1,174	$3,931 $450
Grand Total	$4,487	$4,239	$4,381

Single—$60,000 Individual/Corporate

Income Split	$30,000 $30,000	$35,000 $25,000	$40,000 $20,000	$45,000 $15,000
Less Pension Contribution	$7,500	$8,750	$10,000	$11,250
Net Income	$22,500	$16,250	$10,000	$3,750
Federal Taxes	$4,568 $3,375	$5,968 $2,438	$7,368 $1,500	$8,768 $563
State Taxes	$640 $1,114	$836 $810	$1,032 $435	$1,228 $124
Totals	$5,208 $4,489	$6,804 $3,248	$8,400 $1,935	$9,996 $687
Grand Total	$9,697	$10,052	$10,335	$10,683

Your Estimates

Corporate Income from income split	$ _____
Less Pension contribution	− _____
Net corp. income	$ _____
Federal corp. tax	$ _____
State corp. tax	$ _____
Individual income from income split	$ _____
Less exemptions (number × $2,000 or correct amount for your state)	− _____ $ _____
Less standard deduction ($3,100 if single, $5,200 if married) or Itemized total	− _____
Taxable income	$ _____
Federal income tax	$ _____
State income tax	$ _____

Insert numbers on worksheet into box at right; add for totals

TAX RATES

Corporate—First $3,000   3 %
           Next $5,000   4.5
           Next $12,000   6
           Next $10,000   7.5
           Next $20,000   9
Individual—
   Optional simplified method = 14% of federal
      income tax

COMMENT

For single individuals in the $35,000 category, the $23,000/$12,000 income split is best; in the $60,000 category, the $30,000/$30,000 split is clearly the best choice.

For married individuals in the $50,000 category, the $38,000/$12,000 income split produces both the highest salary and pension contribution *and* the lowest taxes. At $75,000, the $38,000/$37,000 split generates the lowest taxes. However, the $45,000/$30,000 split, which offers $7,000 more in salary and $1,750 more in pension contributions for a *mere $160 in additional taxes,* may be more attractive to many entrepreneurs and professionals.

NORTH DAKOTA

Married—$50,000 Individual/Corporate

Income Split	$25,000 $25,000	$32,000 $18,000	$38,000 $12,000
Less Pension Contribution	$6,250	$8,000	$9,500
Net Income	$18,750	$10,000	$2,500
Federal Taxes	$2,374 $2,813	$3,424 $1,500	$4,324 $375
State Taxes	$332 $960	$479 $435	$605 $75
Totals	$2,706 $3,773	$3,903 $1,935	$4,929 $450
Grand Total	$6,479	$5,838	$5,379

Married—$75,000 Individual/Corporate

Income Split	$30,000 $45,000	$38,000 $37,000	$45,000 $30,000	$55,000 $20,000
Less Pension Contribution	$7,500	$9,500	$11,250	$13,750
Net Income	$37,500	$27,500	$18,750	$6,250
Federal Taxes	$3,124 $5,625	$4,324 $4,125	$6,008 $2,813	$8,808 $938
State Taxes	$437 $2,370	$605 $1,508	$841 $960	$1,233 $236
Totals	$3,561 $7,995	$4,929 $5,633	$6,849 $3,773	$10,041 $1,174
Grand Total	$11,556	$10,562	$10,622	$11,215

Individual/Corporate

Income split	$ $
Less Pension contribution	$
Net Income	$
Federal Taxes	$ $
State Taxes	$ $
Totals	$ $
Grand Total	$

Corp. funds available for investment (corp. net income-corp. taxes) $ _____

OHIO

Single—$35,000 Individual/Corporate

Income Split	$20,000 $15,000	$23,000 $12,000	$26,000 $9,000
Less Pension Contribution	$5,000	$5,750	$6,500
Net Income	$10,000	$6,250	$2,500
Federal Taxes	$2,239 $1,500	$2,689 $938	$3,448 $375
State Taxes	$257 $510	$368 $319	$486 $128
Totals	$2,496 $2,010	$3,057 $1,257	$3,934 $503
Grand Total	$4,506	$4,314	$4,437

Single—$60,000 Individual/Corporate

Income Split	$30,000 $30,000	$35,000 $25,000	$40,000 $20,000	$45,000 $15,000
Less Pension Contribution	$7,500	$8,750	$10,000	$11,250
Net Income	$22,500	$16,250	$10,000	$3,750
Federal Taxes	$4,568 $3,375	$5,968 $2,438	$7,368 $1,500	$8,768 $563
State Taxes	$664 $1,148	$887 $829	$1,110 $510	$1,333 $191
Totals	$5,232 $4,523	$6,855 $3,267	$8,478 $2,010	$10,101 $754
Grand Total	$9,755	$10,122	$10,488	$10,855

Your Estimates

Corporate Income from income split	$ _____
Less Pension contribution	– _____
Net corp. income	$ _____
Federal corp. tax	$ _____
State corp. tax	$ _____
Individual income from income split	$ _____
Less exemptions (number × $2,000 or correct amount for your state)	– _____
	$ _____
Less standard deduction ($3,100 if single, $5,200 if married) or Itemized total	– _____
Taxable income	$ _____
Federal income tax	$ _____
State income tax	$ _____

Insert numbers on worksheet into box at right; add for totals

TAX RATES

Corporate—First $50,000 5.1%
Individual—$20,000–$40,000 $446 + 4.457%
of excess over $20,000
$40,000–$80,000 $1,337 +
5.201% of excess over $40,000

COMMENT

For single individuals in the $35,000 category, the $23,000/$12,000 income split is best. At $60,000, the $30,000/$30,000 split is clearly the best choice.

For married individuals in the $50,000 category, the $38,000/$12,000 income split produces both the highest salary and pension contribution *and* the lowest taxes. At $75,000, the $38,000/$37,000 split generates the lowest taxes.

198

OHIO

Married—$50,000 Individual/Corporate

Income Split	$25,000 $25,000	$32,000 $18,000	$38,000 $12,000
Less Pension Contribution	$6,250	$8,000	$9,500
Net Income	$18,750	$10,000	$2,500
Federal Taxes	$2,374 $2,813	$3,424 $1,500	$4,324 $375
State Taxes	$254 $956	$571 $510	$838 $128
Totals	$2,628 $3,769	$3,995 $2,010	$5,162 $503
Grand Total	$6,397	$6,005	$5,665

Married—$75,000 Individual/Corporate

Income Split	$30,000 $45,000	$38,000 $37,000	$45,000 $30,000	$55,000 $20,000
Less Pension Contribution	$7,500	$9,500	$11,250	$13,750
Net Income	$37,500	$27,500	$18,750	$6,250
Federal Taxes	$3,124 $5,625	$4,324 $4,125	$6,008 $2,813	$8,808 $938
State Taxes	$482 $1,913	$838 $1,403	$1,150 $956	$1,639 $319
Totals	$3,606 $7,538	$5,162 $5,528	$17,158 $3,769	$10,447 $1,257
Grand Total	$11,144	$10,690	$20,927	$11,704

Individual/Corporate

Income split	$ $
Less Pension contribution	$
Net Income	$
Federal Taxes	$ $
State Taxes	$ $
Totals	$ $
Grand Total	$

Corp. funds available for investment (corp. net income-corp. taxes) $ _____

199

OKLAHOMA

Single—$35,000 **Individual**/Corporate

Income Split	$20,000 $15,000	$23,000 $12,000	$26,000 $9,000
Less Pension Contribution	$5,000	$5,750	$6,500
Net Income	$10,000	$6,250	$2,500
Federal Taxes	$2,239 $1,500	$2,689 $938	$3,448 $375
State Taxes	$639 $500	$819 $313	$999 $125
Totals	$2,878 $2,000	$3,508 $1,251	$4,447 $500
Grand Total	$4,878	$4,759	$4,947

Single—$60,000 **Individual**/Corporate

Income Split	$30,000 $30,000	$35,000 $25,000	$40,000 $20,000	$45,000 $15,000
Less Pension Contribution	$7,500	$8,750	$10,000	$11,250
Net Income	$22,500	$16,250	$10,000	$3,750
Federal Taxes	$4,568 $3,375	$5,968 $2,438	$7,368 $1,500	$8,768 $563
State Taxes	$1,239 $1,125	$1,539 $813	$1,839 $500	$2,139 $188
Totals	$5,807 $4,500	$7,507 $3,251	$9,207 $2,000	$10,907 $751
Grand Total	$10,307	$10,758	$11,207	$11,658

Your Estimates

Corporate Income from income split	$ _____
Less Pension contribution	− _____
Net corp. income	$ _____
Federal corp. tax	$ _____
State corp. tax	$ _____
Individual income from income split	$ _____
Less exemptions (number × $2,000 or correct amount for your state)	− _____
	$ _____
Less standard deduction ($3,100 if single, $5,200 if married) or Itemized total	− _____
Taxable income	$ _____
Federal income tax	$ _____
State income tax	$ _____

Insert numbers on worksheet into box at right; add for totals

TAX RATES

Corporate—7%

Individual—
Single—Over $7,500 $195 + 6% of excess over $7,500
Married—Over $15,000 $390 + 6% of excess over $15,000

COMMENT

For single individuals in the $35,000 category, the $23,000/$12,000 income split is best. At $60,000, the $30,000/$30,000 split is clearly the best choice.

For married individuals in the $50,000 category, the $38,000/$12,000 income split provides both the highest salary and pension contribution *and* the lowest taxes. At $75,000, the $38,000/$37,000 split produces the lowest taxes.

OKLAHOMA

Married—$50,000 Individual/Corporate

Income Split	**$25,000** $25,000	**$32,000** $18,000	**$38,000** $12,000
Less Pension Contribution	$6,250	$8,000	$9,500
Net Income	$18,750	$10,000	$2,500
Federal Taxes	**$2,374** $2,813	**$3,424** $1,500	**$4,324** $375
State Taxes	**$438** $938	**$858** $500	**$1,218** $125
Totals	**$2,812** $3,751	**$4,282** $2,000	**$5,542** $500
Grand Total	**$6,563**	**$6,282**	**$6,042**

Married—$75,000 Individual/Corporate

Income Split	**$30,000** $45,000	**$38,000** $37,000	**$45,000** $30,000	**$55,000** $20,000
Less Pension Contribution	$7,500	$9,500	$11,250	$13,750
Net Income	$37,500	$27,500	$18,750	$6,250
Federal Taxes	**$3,124** $5,625	**$4,324** $4,125	**$6,008** $2,813	**$8,808** $938
State Taxes	**$738** $1,875	**$1,218** $1,375	**$1,638** $938	**$2,238** $313
Totals	**$3,862** $7,500	**$5,542** $5,500	**$7,646** $3,751	**$11,046** $1,251
Grand Total	**$11,362**	**$11,042**	**$11,397**	**$12,297**

Individual/Corporate

Income split	$ $
Less Pension contribution	$
Net Income	$
Federal Taxes	$ $
State Taxes	$ $
Totals	$ $
Grand Total	$

Corp. funds available for investment (corp. net income-corp. taxes) $ _____

OREGON

Single—$35,000 Individual/Corporate

Income Split	**$20,000** $15,000	**$23,000** $12,000	**$26,000** $9,000
Less Pension Contribution	$5,000	$5,750	$6,500
Net Income	$10,000	$6,250	$2,500
Federal Taxes	**$2,239** $1,500	**$2,689** $938	**$3,448** $375
State Taxes	**$1,201** $660	**$1,471** $413	**$1,741** $165
Totals	**$3,440** $2,160	**$4,160** $1,351	**$5,189** $540
Grand Total	**$5,600**	**$5,511**	**$5,729**

Single—$60,000 Individual/Corporate

Income Split	**$30,000** $30,000	**$35,000** $25,000	**$40,000** $20,000	**$45,000** $15,000
Less Pension Contribution	$7,500	$8,750	$10,000	$11,250
Net Income	$22,500	$16,250	$10,000	$3,750
Federal Taxes	**$4,568** $3,375	**$5,968** $2,438	**$7,368** $1,500	**$8,768** $563
State Taxes	**$2,101** $1,485	**$2,551** $1,073	**$3,001** $660	**$3,451** $248
Totals	**$6,669** $4,860	**$8,519** $3,511	**$10,369** $2,160	**$12,219** $811
Grand Total	**$11,529**	**$12,030**	**$12,529**	**$13,030**

Your Estimates

Corporate Income from income split	$ _____
Less Pension contribution	_____
Net corp. income	$ _____
Federal corp. tax	$ _____
State corp. tax	$ _____
Individual income from income split	$ _____
Less exemptions (number × $2,000 or correct amount for your state)	— _____ $ _____
Less standard deduction ($3,100 if single, $5,200 if married) or Itemized total	— _____
Taxable income	$ _____
Federal income tax	$ _____
State income tax	$ _____

Insert numbers on worksheet into box at right; add for totals

TAX RATES

Corporate—6.6%
Individual—
Single—$310 + 9.9% of excess over $5,000
Married—twice the tax on half the aggregate taxable income

COMMENT

For single individuals in the $35,000 category, the $23,000/$12,000 income split is best; in the $60,000 category, the $30,000/$30,000 split is clearly the best choice.

For married entrepreneurs and professionals in the $50,000 category, the $38,000/$12,000 income split offers both the lowest taxes and the highest salary and pension contribution. At $75,000, the $38,000/$37,000 split produces the lowest taxes.

OREGON

Married—$50,000 Individual/Corporate

Income Split	$25,000 $25,000	$32,000 $18,000	$38,000 $12,000
Less Pension Contribution	$6,250	$8,000	$9,500
Net Income	$18,750	$10,000	$2,500
Federal Taxes	$2,374 $2,813	$3,424 $1,500	$4,324 $375
State Taxes	$1,088 $1,238	$1,772 $660	$2,312 $165
Totals	$3,462 $4,051	$5,196 $2,160	$6,636 $540
Grand Total	$7,513	$7,356	$7,176

Married—$75,000 Individual/Corporate

Income Split	$30,000 $45,000	$38,000 $37,000	$45,000 $30,000	$55,000 $20,000
Less Pension Contribution	$7,500	$9,500	$11,250	$13,750
Net Income	$37,500	$27,500	$18,750	$6,250
Federal Taxes	$3,124 $5,625	$4,324 $4,125	$6,008 $2,813	$8,808 $938
State Taxes	$1,592 $2,475	$2,312 $1,815	$2,942 $1,238	$3,842 $413
Totals	$4,716 $8,100	$6,636 $5,940	$8,950 $4,051	$12,650 $1,351
Grand Total	$12,816	$12,576	$13,001	$14,001

Individual/Corporate

Income split	$ $
Less Pension contribution	$
Net Income	$
Federal Taxes	$ $
State Taxes	$ $
Totals	$ $
Grand Total	$

Corp. funds available for investment (corp. net income-corp. taxes) $ _____

PENNSYLVANIA

Single—$35,000 Individual/Corporate

Income Split	$20,000 $15,000	$23,000 $12,000	$26,000 $9,000
Less Pension Contribution	$5,000	$5,750	$6,500
Net Income	$10,000	$6,250	$2,500
Federal Taxes	$2,239 $1,500	$2,689 $938	$3,448 $375
State Taxes	$313 $850	$376 $531	$439 $213
Totals	$2,552 $2,350	$3,065 $1,469	$3,887 $588
Grand Total	$4,902	$4,534	$4,475

Single—$60,000 Individual/Corporate

Income Split	$30,000 $30,000	$35,000 $25,000	$40,000 $20,000	$45,000 $15,000
Less Pension Contribution	$7,500	$8,750	$10,000	$11,250
Net Income	$22,500	$16,250	$10,000	$3,750
Federal Taxes	$4,568 $3,375	$5,968 $2,438	$7,368 $1,500	$8,768 $563
State Taxes	$523 $1,913	$628 $1,381	$733 $850	$838 $319
Totals	$5,091 $5,288	$6,596 $3,819	$8,101 $2,350	$9,606 $882
Grand Total	$10,379	$10,415	$10,451	$10,488

Your Estimates

Corporate Income from income split	$ _____
Less Pension contribution	
Net corp. income	$ _____
Federal corp. tax	$ _____
State corp. tax	$ _____
Individual income from income split	$ _____
Less exemptions (number × $2,000 or correct amount for your state)	− $ _____
Less standard deduction ($3,100 if single, $5,200 if married) or Itemized total	−
Taxable income	$ _____
Federal income tax	$ _____
State income tax	$ _____

Insert numbers on worksheet into box at right; add for totals

COMMENT

TAX RATES

Corporate—8.5%
Individual—2.1%

For single entrepreneurs and professionals in the $35,000 category, the $26,000/$9,000 income split provides both the lowest taxes and the highest salary and pension contribution. At $60,000, the $30,000/$30,000 split offers the lowest taxes. However, the $35,000/$25,000, $40,000/$20,000, and $45,000/$15,000 splits may be more attractive: they offer as much as $15,000 more in salary and $3,750 more in pension contributions for *as little as $109 in additional taxes.*

For married individuals in the $50,000 category, the $38,000/$12,000 income split is the best choice. At $75,000, the $45,000/$30,000 income split produces the lowest taxes, but the $55,000/$20,000 split may be more attractive to many entrepreneurs and professionals.

PENNSYLVANIA

Married—$50,000 Individual/Corporate

Income Split	$25,000 $25,000	$32,000 $18,000	$38,000 $12,000
Less Pension Contribution	$6,250	$8,000	$9,500
Net Income	$18,750	$10,000	$2,500
Federal Taxes	$2,374 $2,813	$3,424 $1,500	$4,324 $375
State Taxes	$332 $1,594	$479 $850	$605 $213
Totals	$2,706 $4,407	$3,903 $2,350	$4,929 $588
Grand Total	$7,113	$6,253	$5,517

Married—$75,000 Individual/Corporate

Income Split	$30,000 $45,000	$38,000 $37,000	$45,000 $30,000	$55,000 $20,000
Less Pension Contribution	$7,500	$9,500	$11,250	$13,750
Net Income	$37,500	$27,500	$18,750	$6,250
Federal Taxes	$3,124 $5,625	$4,324 $4,125	$6,008 $2,813	$8,808 $938
State Taxes	$437 $3,188	$605 $2,338	$752 $1,594	$962 $531
Totals	$3,561 $8,813	$4,929 $6,463	$6,760 $4,407	$9,770 $1,469
Grand Total	$12,374	$11,392	$11,167	$11,239

Individual/Corporate

Income split	$ $
Less Pension contribution	$
Net Income	$
Federal Taxes	$ $
State Taxes	$ $
Totals	$ $
Grand Total	$

Corp. funds available for investment (corp. net income-corp. taxes) $ _____

RHODE ISLAND

Single—$35,000 Individual/Corporate

Income Split	$20,000 $15,000	$23,000 $12,000	$26,000 $9,000
Less Pension Contribution	$5,000	$5,750	$6,500
Net Income	$10,000	$6,250	$2,500
Federal Taxes	$2,239 $1,500	$2,689 $938	$3,448 $375
State Taxes	$514 $900	$617 $563	$792 $225
Totals	$2,753 $2,400	$3,306 $1,501	$4,240 $600
Grand Total	$5,153	$4,807	$4,840

Single—$60,000 Individual/Corporate

Income Split	$30,000 $30,000	$35,000 $25,000	$40,000 $20,000	$45,000 $15,000
Less Pension Contribution	$7,500	$8,750	$10,000	$11,250
Net Income	$22,500	$16,250	$10,000	$3,750
Federal Taxes	$4,568 $3,375	$5,968 $2,438	$7,368 $1,500	$8,768 $563
State Taxes	$1,049 $2,025	$1,370 $1,463	$1,692 $900	$2,013 $338
Totals	$5,617 $5,400	$7,338 $3,901	$9,060 $2,400	$10,781 $901
Grand Total	$11,017	$11,239	$11,460	$11,682

Your Estimates

Corporate Income from income split $ _____
Less Pension contribution − _____
Net corp. income $ _____
Federal corp. tax $ _____
State corp. tax $ _____
Individual income from income split $ _____
Less exemptions
(number × $2,000 or correct amount for your state) − _____
$ _____
Less standard deduction ($3,100 if single,
$5,200 if married) or Itemized total − _____
Taxable income $ _____
Federal income tax $ _____
State income tax $ _____

Insert numbers on worksheet into box at right; add for totals

TAX RATES

Corporate—9%
Individual—22.96% of federal income tax

COMMENT

For single individuals in the $35,000 category, the $23,000/$12,000 income split produces the lowest taxes; but the $26,000/$9,000 split offers $3,000 more in salary and $750 more in pension contributions for a *mere $33 in additional taxes*. At $60,000, the $30,000/$30,000 split produces the lowest taxes.

For married individuals in the $50,000 category, the $38,000/$12,000 income split provides both the highest salary and pension contribution *and* the lowest taxes. At $75,000, the $45,000/$30,000 split is clearly the best choice.

RHODE ISLAND

Married—$50,000 Individual/Corporate

Income Split	$25,000 $25,000	$32,000 $18,000	$38,000 $12,000
Less Pension Contribution	$6,250	$8,000	$9,500
Net Income	$18,750	$10,000	$2,500
Federal Taxes	$2,374 $2,813	$3,424 $1,500	$4,324 $375
State Taxes	$545 $1,688	$786 $900	$993 $225
Totals	$2,919 $4,501	$4,210 $2,400	$5,317 $600
Grand Total	$7,420	$6,610	$5,917

Married—$75,000 Individual/Corporate

Income Split	$30,000 $45,000	$38,000 $37,000	$45,000 $30,000	$55,000 $20,000
Less Pension Contribution	$7,500	$9,500	$11,250	$13,750
Net Income	$37,500	$27,500	$18,750	$6,250
Federal Taxes	$3,124 $5,625	$4,324 $4,125	$6,008 $2,813	$8,808 $938
State Taxes	$717 $3,375	$993 $2,475	$1,379 $1,688	$2,022 $563
Totals	$3,841 $9,000	$5,317 $6,600	$7,387 $4,501	$10,830 $1,501
Grand Total	$12,841	$11,917	$11,888	$12,331

Individual/Corporate

Income split	$ $
Less Pension contribution	$
Net Income	$
Federal Taxes	$ $
State Taxes	$ $
Totals	$ $
Grand Total	$

Corp. funds available for investment (corp. net income-corp. taxes) $ _____

207

SOUTH CAROLINA

Single—$35,000 **Individual**/Corporate

Income Split	$20,000 $15,000	$23,000 $12,000	$26,000 $9,000
Less Pension Contribution	$5,000	$5,750	$6,500
Net Income	$10,000	$6,250	$2,500
Federal Taxes	$2,239 $1,500	$2,689 $938	$3,448 $375
State Taxes	$753 $500	$963 $313	$1,173 $125
Totals	$2,992 $2,000	$3,652 $1,251	$4,621 $500
Grand Total	$4,992	$4,903	$5,121

Single—$60,000 **Individual**/Corporate

Income Split	$30,000 $30,000	$35,000 $25,000	$40,000 $20,000	$45,000 $15,000
Less Pension Contribution	$7,500	$8,750	$10,000	$11,250
Net Income	$22,500	$16,250	$10,000	$3,750
Federal Taxes	$4,568 $3,375	$5,968 $2,438	$7,368 $1,500	$8,768 $563
State Taxes	$1,453 $1,125	$1,803 $813	$2,153 $500	$3,203 $188
Totals	$6,021 $4,500	$7,771 $3,251	$9,521 $2,000	$11,971 $751
Grand Total	$10,521	$11,022	$11,521	$12,722

Your Estimates

Corporate Income from income split	$ _____
Less Pension contribution	− _____
Net corp. income	$ _____
Federal corp. tax	$ _____
State corp. tax	$ _____
Individual income from income split	$ _____
Less exemptions	
(number × $2,000 or correct amount for your state)	− _____
	$ _____
Less standard deduction ($3,100 if single, $5,200 if married) or Itemized total	− _____
Taxable income	$ _____
Federal income tax	$ _____
State income tax	$ _____

Insert numbers on worksheet into box at right; add for totals

TAX RATES

Corporate—5%
Individual—Over $10,000 $410 + 7% of excess over $10,000

COMMENT

For single individuals in the $35,000 category, the $23,000/$12,000 income split is best. At $60,000, the $30,000/$30,000 split is clearly the best choice.

For married individuals in the $50,000 category, the $38,000/$12,000 income split offers both the highest salary and pension contribution *and* the lowest taxes. At $75,000, the $38,000/$37,000 split produces the lowest taxes.

SOUTH CAROLINA

Married—$50,000 **Individual**/Corporate

Income Split	$25,000 $25,000	$32,000 $18,000	$38,000 $12,000
Less Pension Contribution	$6,250	$8,000	$9,500
Net Income	$18,750	$10,000	$2,500
Federal Taxes	$2,374 $2,813	$3,424 $1,500	$4,324 $375
State Taxes	$1,516 $938	$2,006 $500	$2,426 $125
Totals	$3,890 $3,751	$5,430 $2,000	$6,750 $500
Grand Total	$7,641	$7,430	$7,250

Married—$75,000 **Individual**/Corporate

Income Split	$30,000 $45,000	$38,000 $37,000	$45,000 $30,000	$55,000 $20,000
Less Pension Contribution	$7,500	$9,500	$11,250	$13,750
Net Income	$37,500	$27,500	$18,750	$6,250
Federal Taxes	$3,124 $5,625	$4,324 $4,125	$6,008 $2,813	$8,808 $938
State Taxes	$1,866 $1,875	$2,426 $1,375	$2,916 $938	$3,616 $313
Totals	$4,990 $7,500	$6,750 $5,500	$8,924 $3,751	$12,424 $1,251
Grand Total	$12,490	$12,250	$12,675	$13,675

Individual/Corporate

Income split	$ $
Less Pension contribution	$
Net Income	$
Federal Taxes	$ $
State Taxes	$ $
Totals	$ $
Grand Total	$

Corp. funds available for investment (corp. net income-corp. taxes) $ _____

SOUTH DAKOTA

Single—$35,000 **Individual**/Corporate

Income Split	$20,000 $15,000	$23,000 $12,000	$26,000 $9,000
Less Pension Contribution	$5,000	$5,750	$6,500
Net Income	$10,000	$6,250	$2,500
Federal Taxes	$2,239 $1,500	$2,689 $938	$3,448 $375
State Taxes	$0 $0	$0 $0	$0 $0
Totals	$2,239 $1,500	$2,689 $938	$3,448 $375
Grand Total	$3,739	$3,627	$3,823

Single—$60,000 **Individual**/Corporate

Income Split	$30,000 $30,000	$35,000 $25,000	$40,000 $20,000	$45,000 $15,000
Less Pension Contribution	$7,500	$8,750	$10,000	$11,250
Net Income	$22,500	$16,250	$10,000	$3,750
Federal Taxes	$4,568 $3,375	$5,968 $2,438	$7,368 $1,500	$8,768 $563
State Taxes	$0 $0	$0 $0	$0 $0	$0 $0
Totals	$4,568 $3,375	$5,968 $2,438	$7,368 $1,500	$8,768 $563
Grand Total	$7,943	$8,406	$8,868	$9,331

Your Estimates

Corporate Income from income split	$ _____
Less Pension contribution	− _____
Net corp. income	$ _____
Federal corp. tax	$ _____
State corp. tax	$ ___0___
Individual income from income split	$ _____
Less exemptions (number × $2,000 or correct amount for your state)	− _____
	$ _____
Less standard deduction ($3,100 if single, $5,200 if married) or Itemized total	− _____
Taxable income	$ _____
Federal income tax	$ _____
State income tax	$ ___0___

Insert numbers on worksheet into box at right; add for totals

COMMENT

TAX RATES

Corporate—0
Individual—0

Because South Dakota imposes no personal or corporate income tax, the $23,000/$12,000 income split is best for single individuals in the $35,000 category. At $60,000, the $30,000/$30,000 split is clearly the best choice.

For married individuals in the $50,000 category, the $38,000/$12,000 income split provides the highest salary and pension contribution *and* the lowest taxes. At $75,000, the $38,000/$37,000 split offers the lowest taxes.

SOUTH DAKOTA

Married—$50,000 **Individual**/Corporate

Income Split	$25,000 $25,000	$32,000 $18,000	$38,000 $12,000
Less Pension Contribution	$6,250	$8,000	$9,500
Net Income	$18,750	$10,000	$2,500
Federal Taxes	$2,374 $2,813	$3,424 $1,500	$4,324 $375
State Taxes	$0 $0	$0 $0	$0 $0
Totals	$2,374 $2,813	$3,424 $1,500	$4,324 $375
Grand Total	$5,187	$4,924	$4,699

Married—$75,000 **Individual**/Corporate

Income Split	$30,000 $45,000	$38,000 $37,000	$45,000 $30,000	$55,000 $20,000
Less Pension Contribution	$7,500	$9,500	$11,250	$13,750
Net Income	$37,500	$27,500	$18,750	$6,250
Federal Taxes	$3,124 $5,625	$4,324 $4,125	$6,008 $2,813	$8,808 $938
State Taxes	$0 $0	$0 $0	$0 $0	$0 $0
Totals	$3,124 $5,625	$4,324 $4,125	$6,008 $2,813	$8,808 $938
Grand Total	$8,749	$8,449	$8,821	$9,746

Individual/Corporate

Income split	$ $
Less Pension contribution	$
Net Income	$
Federal Taxes	$ $
State Taxes	$ 0 $ 0
Totals	$ $
Grand Total	$

Corp. funds available for investment (corp. net income-corp. taxes) $ _____

TENNESSEE

Single—$35,000 Individual/Corporate

Income Split	$20,000 $15,000	$23,000 $12,000	$26,000 $9,000
Less Pension Contribution	$5,000	$5,750	$6,500
Net Income	$10,000	$6,250	$2,500
Federal Taxes	$2,239 $1,500	$2,689 $938	$3,448 $375
State Taxes	$0 $600	$0 $375	$0 $150
Totals	$2,239 $2,100	$2,689 $1,313	$3,448 $525
Grand Total	$4,339	$4,002	$3,973

Single—$60,000 Individual/Corporate

Income Split	$30,000 $30,000	$35,000 $25,000	$40,000 $20,000	$45,000 $15,000
Less Pension Contribution	$7,500	$8,750	$10,000	$11,250
Net Income	$22,500	$16,250	$10,000	$3,750
Federal Taxes	$4,568 $3,375	$5,968 $2,438	$7,368 $1,500	$8,768 $563
State Taxes	$0 $1,350	$0 $975	$0 $600	$0 $225
Totals	$4,568 $4,725	$5,968 $3,413	$7,368 $2,100	$8,768 $788
Grand Total	$9,293	$9,381	$9,468	$9,556

Your Estimates

Corporate Income from income split	$ _____
Less Pension contribution	− _____
Net corp. income	$ _____
Federal corp. tax	$ _____
State corp. tax	$ _____
Individual income from income split	$ _____
Less exemptions (number × $2,000 or correct amount for your state)	− _____
Less standard deduction ($3,100 if single, $5,200 if married) or Itemized total	− _____
Taxable income	$ _____
Federal income tax	$ _____
State income tax	$ _____

Insert numbers on worksheet into box at right; add for totals

COMMENT

TAX RATES

Corporate—6%
Individual—0 (on salaries)

Because Tennessee does not tax salaries, the *highest-salary income splits* in the $35,000 and $50,000 categories will produce the *lowest taxes* as well as the highest pension contributions.

For single entrepreneurs in the $60,000 category, the $30,000/$30,000 income split provides the lowest taxes. However, the $35,000/$25,000 split may be more attractive: it provides $5,000 more in salary and $1,250 in pension contributions for *only $88 in additional taxes.*

For married entrepreneurs in the $75,000 category, the *$55,000/ $20,000 split is a best bet.* For only $175 in additional taxes, it provides $10,000 more in salary and $2,500 more in pension contributions than the lowest-taxed income split.

212

TENNESSEE

Married—$50,000 **Individual**/Corporate

Income Split	**$25,000** $25,000	**$32,000** $18,000	**$38,000** $12,000
Less Pension Contribution	$6,250	$8,000	$9,500
Net Income	$18,750	$10,000	$2,500
Federal Taxes	**$2,374** $2,813	**$3,424** $1,500	**$4,324** $375
State Taxes	**$0** $1,125	**$0** $600	**$0** $150
Totals	**$2,374** $3,938	**$3,424** $2,100	**$4,324** $525
Grand Total	**$6,312**	**$5,524**	**$4,849**

Married—$75,000 **Individual**/Corporate

Income Split	**$30,000** $45,000	**$38,000** $37,000	**$45,000** $30,000	**$55,000** $20,000
Less Pension Contribution	$7,500	$9,500	$11,250	$13,750
Net Income	$37,500	$27,500	$18,750	$6,250
Federal Taxes	**$3,124** $5,625	**$4,324** $4,125	**$6,008** $2,813	**$8,808** $938
State Taxes	**$0** $2,250	**$0** $1,650	**$0** $1,125	**$0** $375
Totals	**$3,124** $7,875	**$4,324** $5,775	**$6,008** $3,938	**$8,808** $1,313
Grand Total	**$10,999**	**$10,099**	**$9,946**	**$10,121**

Individual/Corporate

Income split	$ $
Less Pension contribution	$
Net Income	$
Federal Taxes	$ $
State Taxes	$ $
Totals	$ $
Grand Total	$

Corp. funds available for investment (corp. net income-corp. taxes) $ _____

TEXAS

Single—$35,000 Individual/Corporate

Income Split	$20,000 $15,000	$23,000 $12,000	$26,000 $9,000
Less Pension Contribution	$5,000	$5,750	$6,500
Net Income	$10,000	$6,250	$2,500
Federal Taxes	$2,239 $1,500	$2,689 $938	$3,448 $375
State Taxes	$0 $0	$0 $0	$0 $0
Totals	$2,239 $1,500	$2,689 $938	$3,448 $375
Grand Total	$3,739	$3,627	$3,823

Single—$60,000 Individual/Corporate

Income Split	$30,000 $30,000	$35,000 $25,000	$40,000 $20,000	$45,000 $15,000
Less Pension Contribution	$7,500	$8,750	$10,000	$11,250
Net Income	$22,500	$16,250	$10,000	$3,750
Federal Taxes	$4,568 $3,375	$5,968 $2,438	$7,368 $1,500	$8,768 $563
State Taxes	$0 $0	$0 $0	$0 $0	$0 $0
Totals	$4,568 $3,375	$5,968 $2,438	$7,368 $1,500	$8,768 $563
Grand Total	$7,943	$8,406	$8,868	$9,331

Your Estimates

Corporate Income from income split	$ _____
Less Pension contribution	− _____
Net corp. income	$ _____
Federal corp. tax	$ _____
State corp. tax	$ ____0____
Individual income from income split	$ _____
Less exemptions (number × $2,000 or correct amount for your state)	− _____
	$ _____
Less standard deduction ($3,100 if single, $5,200 if married) or Itemized total	− _____
Taxable income	$ _____
Federal income tax	$ _____
State income tax	$ ____0____

Insert numbers on worksheet into box at right; add for totals

TAX RATES

Corporate—0
Individual—0

COMMENT

Because Texas imposes no personal or corporate income tax, the $23,000/$12,000 income split is best for single individuals in the $35,000 category. At $60,000, the $30,000/$30,000 split is clearly the best choice.

For married individuals in the $50,000 category, the $38,000/$12,000 income split offers both the highest salary and pension contribution *and* the lowest taxes. At $75,000, the $38,000/$37,000 split offers the lowest taxes.

TEXAS

Married—$50,000 **Individual**/Corporate

Income Split	$25,000 $25,000	$32,000 $18,000	$38,000 $12,000
Less Pension Contribution	$6,250	$8,000	$9,500
Net Income	$18,750	$10,000	$2,500
Federal Taxes	$2,374 $2,813	$3,424 $1,500	$4,324 $375
State Taxes	$0 $0	$0 $0	$0 $0
Totals	$2,374 $2,813	$3,424 $1,500	$4,324 $375
Grand Total	$5,187	$4,924	$4,699

Married—$75,000 **Individual**/Corporate

Income Split	$30,000 $45,000	$38,000 $37,000	$45,000 $30,000	$55,000 $20,000
Less Pension Contribution	$7,500	$9,500	$11,250	$13,750
Net Income	$37,500	$27,500	$18,750	$6,250
Federal Taxes	$3,124 $5,625	$4,324 $4,125	$6,008 $2,813	$8,808 $938
State Taxes	$0 $0	$0 $0	$0 $0	$0 $0
Totals	$3,124 $5,625	$4,324 $4,125	$6,008 $2,813	$8,808 $938
Grand Total	$8,749	$8,449	$8,821	$9,746

Individual/Corporate

Income split	$ $
Less Pension contribution	$
Net Income	$
Federal Taxes	$ $
State Taxes	$ 0 $ 0
Totals	$ $
Grand Total	$

Corp. funds available for investment (corp. net income-corp. taxes) $ _____

215

UTAH

Single—$35,000 **Individual**/Corporate

Income Split	$20,000	$23,000	$26,000
	$15,000	$12,000	$9,000
Less Pension Contribution	$5,000	$5,750	$6,500
Net Income	$10,000	$6,250	$2,500
Federal Taxes	$2,239	$2,689	$3,448
	$1,500	$938	$375
State Taxes	$968	$1,184	$1,400
	$500	$313	$125
Totals	$3,207	$3,873	$4,848
	$2,000	$1,251	$500
Grand Total	$5,207	$5,124	$5,348

Single—$60,000 **Individual**/Corporate

Income Split	$30,000	$35,000	$40,000	$45,000
	$30,000	$25,000	$20,000	$15,000
Less Pension Contribution	$7,500	$8,750	$10,000	$11,250
Net Income	$22,500	$16,250	$10,000	$3,750
Federal Taxes	$4,568	$5,968	$7,368	$8,768
	$3,375	$2,438	$1,500	$563
State Taxes	$3,178	$2,048	$2,408	$2,768
	$1,125	$813	$500	$188
Totals	$7,746	$8,016	$9,776	$11,536
	$4,500	$3,251	$2,000	$751
Grand Total	$12,246	$11,267	$11,776	$12,287

Your Estimates

Corporate Income from income split	$ _____
Less Pension contribution	– _____
Net corp. income	$ _____
Federal corp. tax	$ _____
State corp. tax	$ _____
Individual income from income split	$ _____
Less exemptions (number × $2,000 or correct amount for your state)	– _____
	$ _____
Less standard deduction ($3,100 if single, $5,200 if married) or Itemized total	– _____
Taxable income	$ _____
Federal income tax	$ _____
State income tax	$ _____

Insert numbers on worksheet into box at right; add for totals

TAX RATES

Corporate—5%, min. $100
Individual—
Single—Over $3,750 $165.50 + 7.2% of excess over $3,750
Married—Over $7,500 $330.75 + 7.2% of excess over $7,500

COMMENT

For single individuals in the $35,000 category, the $23,000/$12,000 income split is best. At $60,000, the $35,000/$25,000 split is clearly the best choice.

For married individuals in the $50,000 category, the $38,000/$12,000 income split generates both the highest salary and pension contribution *and* the lowest taxes. At $75,000, the $38,000/$37,000 split offers the lowest taxes.

UTAH

Married—$50,000 Individual/Corporate

Income Split	$25,000 $25,000	$32,000 $18,000	$38,000 $12,000
Less Pension Contribution	$6,250	$8,000	$9,500
Net Income	$18,750	$10,000	$2,500
Federal Taxes	$2,374 $2,813	$3,424 $1,500	$4,324 $375
State Taxes	$928 $938	$1,432 $500	$1,864 $125
Totals	$3,302 $3,751	$4,856 $2,000	$6,188 $500
Grand Total	$7,053	$6,856	$6,688

Married—$75,000 Individual/Corporate

Income Split	$30,000 $45,000	$38,000 $37,000	$45,000 $30,000	$55,000 $20,000
Less Pension Contribution	$7,500	$9,500	$11,250	$13,750
Net Income	$37,500	$27,500	$18,750	$6,250
Federal Taxes	$3,124 $5,625	$4,324 $4,125	$6,008 $2,813	$8,808 $938
State Taxes	$1,288 $1,875	$1,864 $1,375	$2,368 $938	$3,088 $313
Totals	$4,412 $7,500	$6,188 $5,500	$8,376 $3,751	$11,896 $1,251
Grand Total	$11,912	$11,688	$12,127	$13,147

Individual/Corporate

Income split	$ $
Less Pension contribution	$
Net Income	$
Federal Taxes	$ $
State Taxes	$ $
Totals	$ $
Grand Total	$

Corp. funds available for investment (corp. net income-corp. taxes) $ _____

217

VERMONT

Single—$35,000 Individual/Corporate

Income Split	$20,000 $15,000	$23,000 $12,000	$26,000 $9,000
Less Pension Contribution	$5,000	$5,750	$6,500
Net Income	$10,000	$6,250	$2,500
Federal Taxes	$2,239 $1,500	$2,689 $938	$3,448 $375
State Taxes	$560 $550	$672 $344	$862 $138
Totals	$2,799 $2,050	$3,361 $1,282	$4,310 $513
Grand Total	$4,849	$4,643	$4,823

Single—$60,000 Individual/Corporate

Income Split	$30,000 $30,000	$35,000 $25,000	$40,000 $20,000	$45,000 $15,000
Less Pension Contribution	$7,500	$8,750	$10,000	$11,250
Net Income	$22,500	$16,250	$10,000	$3,750
Federal Taxes	$4,568 $3,375	$5,968 $2,438	$7,368 $1,500	$8,768 $563
State Taxes	$1,142 $1,375	$1,492 $963	$1,842 $550	$2,192 $206
Totals	$5,710 $4,750	$7,460 $3,401	$9,210 $2,050	$10,960 $769
Grand Total	$10,460	$10,861	$11,260	$11,729

Your Estimates

Corporate Income from income split	$ _____
Less Pension contribution	− _____
Net corp. income	$ _____
Federal corp. tax	$ _____
State corp. tax	$ _____
Individual income from income split	$ _____
Less exemptions (number × $2,000 or correct amount for your state)	− _____
	$ _____
Less standard deduction ($3,100 if single, $5,200 if married) or Itemized total	− _____
Taxable income	$ _____
Federal income tax	$ _____
State income tax	$ _____

Insert numbers on worksheet into box at right; add for totals

TAX RATES

Corporate—First $10,000   5.5%
        Next $15,000   6.6
        Next $225,000   7.7
Individual—25% of federal income
        tax

COMMENT

For single individuals in the $35,000 category, the $23,000/$12,000 income split is best. At $60,000, the $30,000/$30,000 split is clearly the best choice.

For married individuals in the $50,000 category, the $38,000/$12,000 income split produces both the highest salary and pension contribution *and* the lowest taxes. At $75,000, the $38,000/$37,000 split is the best option for most entrepreneurs and professionals.

VERMONT

Married—$50,000 Individual/Corporate

Income Split	$25,000	$32,000	$38,000
	$25,000	$18,000	$12,000
Less Pension Contribution	$6,250	$8,000	$9,500
Net Income	$18,750	$10,000	$2,500
Federal Taxes	$2,374	$3,424	$4,324
	$2,813	$1,500	$375
State Taxes	$594	$856	$1,081
	$1,128	$550	$138
Totals	$2,968	$4,280	$5,405
	$3,941	$2,050	$513
Grand Total	$6,909	$6,330	$5,918

Married—$75,000 Individual/Corporate

Income Split	$30,000	$38,000	$45,000	$55,000
	$45,000	$37,000	$30,000	$20,000
Less Pension Contribution	$7,500	$9,500	$11,250	$13,750
Net Income	$37,500	$27,500	$18,750	$6,250
Federal Taxes	$3,124	$4,324	$6,008	$8,808
	$5,625	$4,125	$2,813	$938
State Taxes	$781	$1,081	$1,502	$2,202
	$2,503	$1,733	$1,128	$344
Totals	$3,905	$5,405	$7,510	$11,010
	$8,128	$5,858	$3,941	$1,282
Grand Total	$12,033	$11,263	$11,451	$12,292

Individual/Corporate

Income split	$
	$
Less Pension contribution	$
Net Income	$
Federal Taxes	$
	$
State Taxes	$
	$
Totals	$
	$
Grand Total	$

Corp. funds available for investment (corp. net income-corp. taxes) $ _____

VIRGINIA

Single—$35,000 Individual/Corporate

Income Split	$20,000 $15,000	$23,000 $12,000	$26,000 $9,000
Less Pension Contribution	$5,000	$5,750	$6,500
Net Income	$10,000	$6,250	$2,500
Federal Taxes	$2,239 $1,500	$2,689 $938	$3,448 $375
State Taxes	$615 $600	$772 $375	$944 $150
Totals	$2,854 $2,100	$3,461 $1,313	$4,392 $525
Grand Total	$4,954	$4,774	$4,917

Single—$60,000 Individual/Corporate

Income Split	$30,000 $30,000	$35,000 $25,000	$40,000 $20,000	$45,000 $15,000
Less Pension Contribution	$7,500	$8,750	$10,000	$11,250
Net Income	$22,500	$16,250	$10,000	$3,750
Federal Taxes	$4,568 $3,375	$5,968 $2,438	$7,368 $1,500	$8,768 $563
State Taxes	$1,174 $1,350	$1,462 $975	$1,749 $600	$2,037 $225
Totals	$5,742 $4,725	$7,430 $3,413	$9,117 $2,100	$10,805 $788
Grand Total	$10,467	$10,843	$11,217	$11,593

Your Estimates

Corporate Income from income split	$ _____
Less Pension contribution	− _____
Net corp. income	$ _____
Federal corp. tax	$ _____
State corp. tax	$ _____
Individual income from income split	$ _____
Less exemptions (number × $2,000 or correct amount for your state)	− _____
	$ _____
Less standard deduction ($3,100 if single, $5,200 if married) or Itemized total	− _____
Taxable income	$ _____
Federal income tax	$ _____
State income tax	$ _____

Insert numbers on worksheet into box at right; add for totals

TAX RATES

Corporate—6%
Individual—Over $17,000 $720 + 5.75% of excess over $17,000

COMMENT

For single individuals in the $35,000 category, the $23,000/$12,000 income split is best. In the $60,000 category, the $30,000/$30,000 split is clearly the best choice.

For married professionals and entrepreneurs in the $50,000 category, the $38,000/$12,000 income split offers both the highest salary and pension contribution *and* the lowest taxes. At $75,000, the $38,000/$37,000 split produces the lowest taxes.

VIRGINIA

Married—$50,000 **Individual**/Corporate

Income Split	$25,000 $25,000	$32,000 $18,000	$38,000 $12,000
Less Pension Contribution	$6,250	$8,000	$9,500
Net Income	$18,750	$10,000	$2,500
Federal Taxes	$2,374 $2,813	$3,424 $1,500	$4,324 $375
State Taxes	$660 $1,125	$1,054 $600	$1,399 $150
Totals	$3,034 $3,938	$4,478 $2,100	$5,723 $525
Grand Total	$6,972	$6,578	$6,248

Married—$75,000 **Individual**/Corporate

Income Split	$30,000 $45,000	$38,000 $37,000	$45,000 $30,000	$55,000 $20,000
Less Pension Contribution	$7,500	$9,500	$11,250	$13,750
Net Income	$37,500	$27,500	$18,750	$6,250
Federal Taxes	$3,124 $5,625	$4,324 $4,125	$6,008 $2,813	$8,808 $938
State Taxes	$939 $2,250	$1,399 $1,650	$1,801 $1,125	$2,376 $375
Totals	$4,063 $7,875	$5,723 $5,775	$7,809 $3,938	$11,184 $1,313
Grand Total	$11,938	$11,498	$11,747	$12,497

Individual/Corporate

Income split	$ $
Less Pension contribution	$
Net Income	$
Federal Taxes	$ $
State Taxes	$ $
Totals	$ $
Grand Total	$

Corp. funds available for investment (corp. net income-corp. taxes) $ _____

WASHINGTON

Single—$35,000 **Individual**/Corporate

Income Split	$20,000	$23,000	$26,000
	$15,000	$12,000	$9,000
Less Pension Contribution	$5,000	$5,750	$6,500
Net Income	$10,000	$6,250	$2,500
Federal Taxes	$2,239	$2,689	$3,448
	$1,500	$938	$375
State Taxes	$0	$0	$0
	$0	$0	$0
Totals	$2,239	$2,689	$3,448
	$1,500	$938	$375
Grand Total	$3,739	$3,627	$3,823

Single—$60,000 **Individual**/Corporate

Income Split	$30,000	$35,000	$40,000	$45,000
	$30,000	$25,000	$20,000	$15,000
Less Pension Contribution	$7,500	$8,750	$10,000	$11,250
Net Income	$22,500	$16,250	$10,000	$3,750
Federal Taxes	$4,568	$5,968	$7,368	$8,768
	$3,375	$2,438	$1,500	$563
State Taxes	$0	$0	$0	$0
	$0	$0	$0	$0
Totals	$4,568	$5,968	$7,368	$8,768
	$3,375	$2,438	$1,500	$563
Grand Total	$7,943	$8,406	$8,868	$9,331

Your Estimates

Corporate Income from income split	$	
Less Pension contribution	−	
Net corp. income	$	
Federal corp. tax	$	
State corp. tax	$	0
Individual income from income split	$	
Less exemptions (number × $2,000 or correct amount for your state)	−	
	$	
Less standard deduction ($3,100 if single, $5,200 if married) or Itemized total	−	
Taxable income	$	
Federal income tax	$	
State income tax	$	0

Insert numbers on worksheet into box at right; add for totals

COMMENT

TAX RATES

Corporate—0
Individual—0

Because Washington imposes no personal or corporate income tax, the $23,000/$12,000 income split is best for single individuals in the $35,000 category. At $60,000, the $30,000/$30,000 split is clearly the best choice. For married individuals in the $50,000 category, the $38,000/$12,000 income split provides both the highest salary and pension contribution *and* the lowest taxes. At $75,000, the $38,000/$37,000 split offers the lowest taxes.

222

WASHINGTON

Married—$50,000 **Individual**/Corporate

Income Split	**$25,000** $25,000	**$32,000** $18,000	**$38,000** $12,000
Less Pension Contribution	$6,250	$8,000	$9,500
Net Income	$18,750	$10,000	$2,500
Federal Taxes	**$2,374** $2,813	**$3,424** $1,500	**$4,324** $375
State Taxes	**$0** $0	**$0** $0	**$0** $0
Totals	**$2,374** $2,813	**$3,424** $1,500	**$4,324** $375
Grand Total	**$5,187**	**$4,924**	**$4,699**

Married—$75,000 **Individual**/Corporate

Income Split	**$30,000** $45,000	**$38,000** $37,000	**$45,000** $30,000	**$55,000** $20,000
Less Pension Contribution	$7,500	$9,500	$11,250	$13,750
Net Income	$37,500	$27,500	$18,750	$6,250
Federal Taxes	**$3,124** $5,625	**$4,324** $4,125	**$6,008** $2,813	**$8,808** $938
State Taxes	**$0** $0	**$0** $0	**$0** $0	**$0** $0
Totals	**$3,124** $5,625	**$4,324** $4,125	**$6,008** $2,813	**$8,808** $938
Grand Total	**$8,749**	**$8,449**	**$8,821**	**$9,746**

Individual/Corporate

Income split	$ $
Less Pension contribution	$
Net Income	$
Federal Taxes	$ $
State Taxes	$ 0 $ 0
Totals	$ $
Grand Total	$

Corp. funds available for investment (corp. net income-corp. taxes) $ _____

223

WEST VIRGINIA

Single—$35,000 Individual/Corporate

Income Split	$20,000	$23,000	$26,000
	$15,000	$12,000	$9,000
Less Pension Contribution	$5,000	$5,750	$6,500
Net Income	$10,000	$6,250	$2,500
Federal Taxes	$2,239	$2,689	$3,448
	$1,500	$938	$375
State Taxes	$496	$616	$736
	$915	$572	$229
Totals	$2,735	$3,305	$4,184
	$2,415	$1,510	$604
Grand Total	$5,150	$4,815	$4,788

Single—$60,000 Individual/Corporate

Income Split	$30,000	$35,000	$40,000	$45,000
	$30,000	$25,000	$20,000	$15,000
Less Pension Contribution	$7,500	$8,750	$10,000	$11,250
Net Income	$22,500	$16,250	$10,000	$3,750
Federal Taxes	$4,568	$5,968	$7,368	$8,768
	$3,375	$2,438	$1,500	$563
State Taxes	$896	$1,121	$1,346	$1,571
	$2,059	$1,487	$915	$343
Totals	$5,464	$7,089	$8,714	$10,339
	$5,434	$3,925	$2,415	$906
Grand Total	$10,898	$11,014	$11,129	$11,245

Your Estimates

Corporate Income from income split	$ _____
Less Pension contribution	– _____
Net corp. income	$ _____
Federal corp. tax	$ _____
State corp. tax	$ _____
Individual income from income split	$ _____
Less exemptions (number × $2,000 or correct amount for your state)	– _____
	$ _____
Less standard deduction ($3,100 if single, $5,200 if married) or Itemized total	– _____
Taxable income	$ _____
Federal income tax	$ _____
State income tax	$ _____

Insert numbers on worksheet into box at right; add for totals

TAX RATES

Corporate—9.15%

Individual—$10,000–$25,000 $300 + 4% of excess over $10,000

$25,000–$40,000 $900 + 4.5% of excess over $25,000

$40,000–$60,000 $1,575 + 6% of excess over $40,000

COMMENT

For single individuals in the $35,000 category, the $26,000/$9,000 income split offers both the highest salary and pension contribution *and* the lowest taxes. At $60,000, the $30,000/$30,000 split is clearly the best choice.

For married individuals in the $50,000 category, the $38,000/$12,000 income split produces both the highest salary and pension contribution *and* the lowest taxes. At $75,000, the $45,000/$30,000 split offers a generous salary and the lowest taxes.

WEST VIRGINIA

Married—$50,000 **Individual**/Corporate

Income Split	$25,000 $25,000	$32,000 $18,000	$38,000 $12,000
Less Pension Contribution	$6,250	$8,000	$9,500
Net Income	$18,750	$10,000	$2,500
Federal Taxes	$2,374 $2,813	$3,424 $1,500	$4,324 $375
State Taxes	$532 $1,716	$812 $915	$1,071 $229
Totals	$2,906 $4,529	$4,236 $2,415	$5,395 $604
Grand Total	$7,435	$6,651	$5,999

Married—$75,000 **Individual**/Corporate

Income Split	$30,000 $45,000	$38,000 $37,000	$45,000 $30,000	$55,000 $20,000
Less Pension Contribution	$7,500	$9,500	$11,250	$13,750
Net Income	$37,500	$27,500	$18,750	$6,250
Federal Taxes	$3,124 $5,625	$4,324 $4,125	$6,008 $2,813	$8,808 $938
State Taxes	$732 $3,431	$1,071 $2,516	$1,386 $1,716	$1,923 $572
Totals	$3,856 $9,056	$5,395 $6,641	$7,394 $4,529	$10,731 $1,510
Grand Total	$12,912	$12,036	$11,923	$12,241

Individual/Corporate

Income split	$ $
Less Pension contribution	$
Net Income	$
Federal Taxes	$ $
State Taxes	$ $
Totals	$ $
Grand Total	$

Corp. funds available for investment (corp. net income-corp. taxes) $ _____

WISCONSIN

Single—$35,000 **Individual**/Corporate

Income Split	**$20,000** $15,000	**$23,000** $12,000	**$26,000** $9,000
Less Pension Contribution	$5,000	$5,750	$6,500
Net Income	$10,000	$6,250	$2,500
Federal Taxes	**$2,239** $1,500	**$2,689** $938	**$3,448** $375
State Taxes	**$853** $790	**$1,060** $494	**$1,268** $198
Totals	**$3,092** $2,290	**$3,749** $1,432	**$4,716** $573
Grand Total	**$5,382**	**$5,181**	**$5,289**

Single—$60,000 **Individual**/Corporate

Income Split	**$30,000** $30,000	**$35,000** $25,000	**$40,000** $20,000	**$45,000** $15,000
Less Pension Contribution	$7,500	$8,750	$10,000	$11,250
Net Income	$22,500	$16,250	$10,000	$3,750
Federal Taxes	**$4,568** $3,375	**$5,968** $2,438	**$7,368** $1,500	**$8,768** $563
State Taxes	**$1,545** $1,778	**$1,892** $1,284	**$2,238** $790	**$2,585** $296
Totals	**$6,113** $5,153	**$7,860** $3,722	**$9,606** $2,290	**$11,353** $859
Grand Total	**$11,266**	**$11,582**	**$11,896**	**$12,212**

Your Estimates

Corporate Income from income split	$ _____
Less Pension contribution	− _____
Net corp. income	$ _____
Federal corp. tax	$ _____
State corp. tax	$ _____
Individual income from income split	$ _____
Less exemptions (number × $2,000 or correct amount for your state)	− _____
	$ _____
Less standard deduction ($3,100 if single, $5,200 if married) or Itemized total	− _____
Taxable income	$ _____
Federal income tax	$ _____
State income tax	$ _____

Insert numbers on worksheet into box at right; add for totals

TAX RATES

Corporate—7.9%
Individual—
Single— Over $15,000 $859 + 6.93% of excess over $15,000
Married—Over $20,000 $1,145 + 6.93% of excess over $20,000

COMMENT

For single individuals in the $35,000 category, the $23,000/$12,000 income split is best. At $60,000, the $30,000/$30,000 split is clearly the best choice.

For married individuals in the $50,000 category, the $38,000/$12,000 income split offers both the highest salary and pension contribution *and* the lowest taxes. At $75,000, the $38,000/$37,000 split produces the lowest taxes.

WISCONSIN

Married—$50,000 **Individual**/Corporate

Income Split	$25,000 $25,000	$32,000 $18,000	$38,000 $12,000
Less Pension Contribution	$6,250	$8,000	$9,500
Net Income	$18,750	$10,000	$2,500
Federal Taxes	$2,374 $2,813	$3,424 $1,500	$4,324 $375
State Taxes	$870 $1,481	$1,339 $790	$1,755 $198
Totals	$3,244 $4,294	$4,763 $2,290	$6,079 $573
Grand Total	$7,538	$7,053	$6,652

Married—$75,000 **Individual**/Corporate

Income Split	$30,000 $45,000	$38,000 $37,000	$45,000 $30,000	$55,000 $20,000
Less Pension Contribution	$7,500	$9,500	$11,250	$13,750
Net Income	$37,500	$27,500	$18,750	$6,250
Federal Taxes	$3,124 $5,625	$4,324 $4,125	$6,008 $2,813	$8,808 $938
State Taxes	$1,200 $2,963	$1,755 $2,173	$2,240 $1,481	$2,933 $494
Totals	$4,324 $8,588	$6,079 $6,298	$8,248 $4,294	$11,741 $1,432
Grand Total	$12,912	$12,377	$12,542	$13,173

Individual/Corporate

Income split	$ $
Less Pension contribution	$
Net Income	$
Federal Taxes	$ $
State Taxes	$ $
Totals	$ $
Grand Total	$

Corp. funds available for investment (corp. net income-corp. taxes) $ _____

227

WYOMING

Single—$35,000 Individual/Corporate

Income Split	$20,000 $15,000	$23,000 $12,000	$26,000 $9,000
Less Pension Contribution	$5,000	$5,750	$6,500
Net Income	$10,000	$6,250	$2,500
Federal Taxes	$2,239 $1,500	$2,689 $938	$3,448 $375
State Taxes	$0 $0	$0 $0	$0 $0
Totals	$2,239 $1,500	$2,689 $938	$3,448 $375
Grand Total	$3,739	$3,627	$3,823

Single—$60,000 Individual/Corporate

Income Split	$30,000 $30,000	$35,000 $25,000	$40,000 $20,000	$45,000 $15,000
Less Pension Contribution	$7,500	$8,750	$10,000	$11,250
Net Income	$22,500	$16,250	$10,000	$3,750
Federal Taxes	$4,568 $3,375	$5,968 $2,438	$7,368 $1,500	$8,768 $563
State Taxes	$0 $0	$0 $0	$0 $0	$0 $0
Totals	$4,568 $3,375	$5,968 $2,438	$7,368 $1,500	$8,768 $563
Grand Total	$7,943	$8,406	$8,868	$9,331

Your Estimates

Corporate Income from income split	$ _____
Less Pension contribution	_____
Net corp. income	$ _____
Federal corp. tax	$ _____
State corp. tax	$ ___0___
Individual income from income split	$ _____
Less exemptions (number × $2,000 or correct amount for your state)	– _____
	$ _____
Less standard deduction ($3,100 if single, $5,200 if married) or Itemized total	– _____
Taxable income	$ _____
Federal income tax	$ _____
State income tax	$ ___0___

Insert numbers on worksheet into box at right; add for totals

COMMENT

Because Wyoming imposes no personal or corporate income tax, the $23,000/$12,000 income split is best for single individuals in the $35,000 category. At $60,000, the $30,000/$30,000 split is clearly the best choice. For married individuals in the $50,000 category, the $38,000/$12,000 income split provides both the highest salary and pension contribution *and* the lowest taxes. At $75,000, the $38,000/$37,000 split offers the lowest taxes.

TAX RATES

Corporate—0
Individual—0

WYOMING

Married—$50,000 Individual/Corporate

Income Split	**$25,000** $25,000	**$32,000** $18,000	**$38,000** $12,000
Less Pension Contribution	$6,250	$8,000	$9,500
Net Income	$18,750	$10,000	$2,500
Federal Taxes	**$2,374** $2,813	**$3,424** $1,500	**$4,324** $375
State Taxes	**$0** $0	**$0** $0	**$0** $0
Totals	**$2,374** $2,813	**$3,424** $1,500	**$4,324** $375
Grand Total	**$5,187**	**$4,924**	**$4,699**

Married—$75,000 Individual/Corporate

Income Split	**$30,000** $45,000	**$38,000** $37,000	**$45,000** $30,000	**$55,000** $20,000
Less Pension Contribution	$7,500	$9,500	$11,250	$13,750
Net Income	$37,500	$27,500	$18,750	$6,250
Federal Taxes	**$3,124** $5,625	**$4,324** $4,125	**$6,008** $2,813	**$8,808** $938
State Taxes	**$0** $0	**$0** $0	**$0** $0	**$0** $0
Totals	**$3,124** $5,625	**$4,324** $4,125	**$6,008** $2,813	**$8,808** $938
Grand Total	**$8,749**	**$8,449**	**$8,821**	**$9,746**

Individual/Corporate

Income split	$ $
Less Pension contribution	$
Net Income	$
Federal Taxes	$ $
State Taxes	$ 0 $ 0
Totals	$ $
Grand Total	$

Corp. funds available for investment (corp. net income-corp. taxes) $ _____

1989 Tax Table—Continued

If taxable income is—		And you are—			
At least	But less than	Single	Married filing jointly *	Married filing separately	Head of a household
		Your tax is—			
14,000					
14,000	14,050	2.104	2.104	2.104	2.104
14,050	14,100	2.111	2.111	2.111	2.111
14,100	14,150	2.119	2.119	2.119	2.119
14,150	14,200	2.126	2.126	2.126	2.126
14,200	14,250	2.134	2.134	2.134	2.134
14,250	14,300	2.141	2.141	2.141	2.141
14,300	14,350	2.149	2.149	2.149	2.149
14,350	14,400	2.156	2.156	2.156	2.156
14,400	14,450	2.164	2.164	2.164	2.164
14,450	14,500	2.171	2.171	2.171	2.171
14,500	14,550	2.179	2.179	2.179	2.179
14,550	14,600	2.186	2.186	2.186	2.186
14,600	14,650	2.194	2.194	2.194	2.194
14,650	14,700	2.201	2.201	2.201	2.201
14,700	14,750	2.209	2.209	2.209	2.209
14,750	14,800	2.216	2.216	2.216	2.216
14,800	14,850	2.224	2.224	2.224	2.224
14,850	14,900	2.231	2.231	2.231	2.231
14,900	14,950	2.239	2.239	2.239	2.239
14,950	15,000	2.246	2.246	2.246	2.246
15,000					
15,000	15,050	2.254	2.254	2.254	2.254
15,050	15,100	2.261	2.261	2.261	2.261
15,100	15,150	2.269	2.269	2.269	2.269
15,150	15,200	2.276	2.276	2.276	2.276
15,200	15,250	2.284	2.284	2.284	2.284
15,250	15,300	2.291	2.291	2.291	2.291
15,300	15,350	2.299	2.299	2.299	2.299
15,350	15,400	2.306	2.306	2.306	2.306
15,400	15,450	2.314	2.314	2.314	2.314
15,450	15,500	2.321	2.321	2.321	2.321
15,500	15,550	2.329	2.329	2.335	2.329
15,550	15,600	2.336	2.336	2.349	2.336
15,600	15,650	2.344	2.344	2.363	2.344
15,650	15,700	2.351	2.351	2.377	2.351
15,700	15,750	2.359	2.359	2.391	2.359
15,750	15,800	2.366	2.366	2.405	2.366
15,800	15,850	2.374	2.374	2.419	2.374
15,850	15,900	2.381	2.381	2.433	2.381
15,900	15,950	2.389	2.389	2.447	2.389
15,950	16,000	2.396	2.396	2.461	2.396
16,000					
16,000	16,050	2.404	2.404	2.475	2.404
16,050	16,100	2.411	2.411	2.489	2.411
16,100	16,150	2.419	2.419	2.503	2.419
16,150	16,200	2.426	2.426	2.517	2.426
16,200	16,250	2.434	2.434	2.531	2.434
16,250	16,300	2.441	2.441	2.545	2.441
16,300	16,350	2.449	2.449	2.559	2.449
16,350	16,400	2.456	2.456	2.573	2.456
16,400	16,450	2.464	2.464	2.587	2.464
16,450	16,500	2.471	2.471	2.601	2.471
16,500	16,550	2.479	2.479	2.615	2.479
16,550	16,600	2.486	2.486	2.629	2.486
16,600	16,650	2.494	2.494	2.643	2.494
16,650	16,700	2.501	2.501	2.657	2.501
16,700	16,750	2.509	2.509	2.671	2.509
16,750	16,800	2.516	2.516	2.685	2.516
16,800	16,850	2.524	2.524	2.699	2.524
16,850	16,900	2.531	2.531	2.713	2.531
16,900	16,950	2.539	2.539	2.727	2.539
16,950	17,000	2.546	2.546	2.741	2.546

If taxable income is—		And you are—			
At least	But less than	Single	Married filing jointly *	Married filing separately	Head of a household
		Your tax is—			
17,000					
17,000	17,050	2.554	2.554	2.755	2.554
17,050	17,100	2.561	2.561	2.769	2.561
17,100	17,150	2.569	2.569	2.783	2.569
17,150	17,200	2.576	2.576	2.797	2.576
17,200	17,250	2.584	2.584	2.811	2.584
17,250	17,300	2.591	2.591	2.825	2.591
17,300	17,350	2.599	2.599	2.839	2.599
17,350	17,400	2.606	2.606	2.853	2.606
17,400	17,450	2.614	2.614	2.867	2.614
17,450	17,500	2.621	2.621	2.881	2.621
17,500	17,550	2.629	2.629	2.895	2.629
17,550	17,600	2.636	2.636	2.909	2.636
17,600	17,650	2.644	2.644	2.923	2.644
17,650	17,700	2.651	2.651	2.937	2.651
17,700	17,750	2.659	2.659	2.951	2.659
17,750	17,800	2.666	2.666	2.965	2.666
17,800	17,850	2.674	2.674	2.979	2.674
17,850	17,900	2.681	2.681	2.993	2.681
17,900	17,950	2.689	2.689	3.007	2.689
17,950	18,000	2.696	2.696	3.021	2.696
18,000					
18,000	18,050	2.704	2.704	3.035	2.704
18,050	18,100	2.711	2.711	3.049	2.711
18,100	18,150	2.719	2.719	3.063	2.719
18,150	18,200	2.726	2.726	3.077	2.726
18,200	18,250	2.734	2.734	3.091	2.734
18,250	18,300	2.741	2.741	3.105	2.741
18,300	18,350	2.749	2.749	3.119	2.749
18,350	18,400	2.756	2.756	3.133	2.756
18,400	18,450	2.764	2.764	3.147	2.764
18,450	18,500	2.771	2.771	3.161	2.771
18,500	18,550	2.779	2.779	3.175	2.779
18,550	18,600	2.786	2.786	3.189	2.786
18,600	18,650	2.804	2.794	3.203	2.794
18,650	18,700	2.818	2.801	3.217	2.801
18,700	18,750	2.832	2.809	3.231	2.809
18,750	18,800	2.846	2.816	3.245	2.816
18,800	18,850	2.860	2.824	3.259	2.824
18,850	18,900	2.874	2.831	3.273	2.831
18,900	18,950	2.888	2.839	3.287	2.839
18,950	19,000	2.902	2.846	3.301	2.846
19,000					
19,000	19,050	2.916	2.854	3.315	2.854
19,050	19,100	2.930	2.861	3.329	2.861
19,100	19,150	2.944	2.869	3.343	2.869
19,150	19,200	2.958	2.876	3.357	2.876
19,200	19,250	2.972	2.884	3.371	2.884
19,250	19,300	2.986	2.891	3.385	2.891
19,300	19,350	3.000	2.899	3.399	2.899
19,350	19,400	3.014	2.906	3.413	2.906
19,400	19,450	3.028	2.914	3.427	2.914
19,450	19,500	3.042	2.921	3.441	2.921
19,500	19,550	3.056	2.929	3.455	2.929
19,550	19,600	3.070	2.936	3.469	2.936
19,600	19,650	3.084	2.944	3.483	2.944
19,650	19,700	3.098	2.951	3.497	2.951
19,700	19,750	3.112	2.959	3.511	2.959
19,750	19,800	3.126	2.966	3.525	2.966
19,800	19,850	3.140	2.974	3.539	2.974
19,850	19,900	3.154	2.981	3.553	2.981
19,900	19,950	3.168	2.989	3.567	2.989
19,950	20,000	3.182	2.996	3.581	2.996

If taxable income is—		And you are—			
At least	But less than	Single	Married filing jointly *	Married filing separately	Head of a household
		Your tax is—			
20,000					
20,000	20,050	3.196	3.004	3.595	3.004
20,050	20,100	3.210	3.011	3.609	3.011
20,100	20,150	3.224	3.019	3.623	3.019
20,150	20,200	3.238	3.026	3.637	3.026
20,200	20,250	3.252	3.034	3.651	3.034
20,250	20,300	3.266	3.041	3.665	3.041
20,300	20,350	3.280	3.049	3.679	3.049
20,350	20,400	3.294	3.056	3.693	3.056
20,400	20,450	3.308	3.064	3.707	3.064
20,450	20,500	3.322	3.071	3.721	3.071
20,500	20,550	3.336	3.079	3.735	3.079
20,550	20,600	3.350	3.086	3.749	3.086
20,600	20,650	3.364	3.094	3.763	3.094
20,650	20,700	3.378	3.101	3.777	3.101
20,700	20,750	3.392	3.109	3.791	3.109
20,750	20,800	3.406	3.116	3.805	3.116
20,800	20,850	3.420	3.124	3.819	3.124
20,850	20,900	3.434	3.131	3.833	3.131
20,900	20,950	3.448	3.139	3.847	3.139
20,950	21,000	3.462	3.146	3.861	3.146
21,000					
21,000	21,050	3.476	3.154	3.875	3.154
21,050	21,100	3.490	3.161	3.889	3.161
21,100	21,150	3.504	3.169	3.903	3.169
21,150	21,200	3.518	3.176	3.917	3.176
21,200	21,250	3.532	3.184	3.931	3.184
21,250	21,300	3.546	3.191	3.945	3.191
21,300	21,350	3.560	3.199	3.959	3.199
21,350	21,400	3.574	3.206	3.973	3.206
21,400	21,450	3.588	3.214	3.987	3.214
21,450	21,500	3.602	3.221	4.001	3.221
21,500	21,550	3.616	3.229	4.015	3.229
21,550	21,600	3.630	3.236	4.029	3.236
21,600	21,650	3.644	3.244	4.043	3.244
21,650	21,700	3.658	3.251	4.057	3.251
21,700	21,750	3.672	3.259	4.071	3.259
21,750	21,800	3.686	3.266	4.085	3.266
21,800	21,850	3.700	3.274	4.099	3.274
21,850	21,900	3.714	3.281	4.113	3.281
21,900	21,950	3.728	3.289	4.127	3.289
21,950	22,000	3.742	3.296	4.141	3.296
22,000					
22,000	22,050	3.756	3.304	4.155	3.304
22,050	22,100	3.770	3.311	4.169	3.311
22,100	22,150	3.784	3.319	4.183	3.319
22,150	22,200	3.798	3.326	4.197	3.326
22,200	22,250	3.812	3.334	4.211	3.334
22,250	22,300	3.826	3.341	4.225	3.341
22,300	22,350	3.840	3.349	4.239	3.349
22,350	22,400	3.854	3.356	4.253	3.356
22,400	22,450	3.868	3.364	4.267	3.364
22,450	22,500	3.882	3.371	4.281	3.371
22,500	22,550	3.896	3.379	4.295	3.379
22,550	22,600	3.910	3.386	4.309	3.386
22,600	22,650	3.924	3.394	4.323	3.394
22,650	22,700	3.938	3.401	4.337	3.401
22,700	22,750	3.952	3.409	4.351	3.409
22,750	22,800	3.966	3.416	4.365	3.416
22,800	22,850	3.980	3.424	4.379	3.424
22,850	22,900	3.994	3.431	4.393	3.431
22,900	22,950	4.008	3.439	4.407	3.439
22,950	23,000	4.022	3.446	4.421	3.446

* This column must also be used by a qualifying widow(er).

Continued on next page

1989 Tax Table— *Continued*

If line 37 (taxable income) is— At least	But less than	Single	Married filing jointly *	Married filing separately	Head of a household
23,000					
23,000	23,050	4,036	3,454	4,435	3,454
23,050	23,100	4,050	3,461	4,449	3,461
23,100	23,150	4,064	3,469	4,463	3,469
23,150	23,200	4,078	3,476	4,477	3,476
23,200	23,250	4,092	3,484	4,491	3,484
23,250	23,300	4,106	3,491	4,505	3,491
23,300	23,350	4,120	3,499	4,519	3,499
23,350	23,400	4,134	3,506	4,533	3,506
23,400	23,450	4,148	3,514	4,547	3,514
23,450	23,500	4,162	3,521	4,561	3,521
23,500	23,550	4,176	3,529	4,575	3,529
23,550	23,600	4,190	3,536	4,589	3,536
23,600	23,650	4,204	3,544	4,603	3,544
23,650	23,700	4,218	3,551	4,617	3,551
23,700	23,750	4,232	3,559	4,631	3,559
23,750	23,800	4,246	3,566	4,645	3,566
23,800	23,850	4,260	3,574	4,659	3,574
23,850	23,900	4,274	3,581	4,673	3,581
23,900	23,950	4,288	3,589	4,687	3,589
23,950	24,000	4,302	3,596	4,701	3,596
24,000					
24,000	24,050	4,316	3,604	4,715	3,604
24,050	24,100	4,330	3,611	4,729	3,611
24,100	24,150	4,344	3,619	4,743	3,619
24,150	24,200	4,358	3,626	4,757	3,626
24,200	24,250	4,372	3,634	4,771	3,634
24,250	24,300	4,386	3,641	4,785	3,641
24,300	24,350	4,400	3,649	4,799	3,649
24,350	24,400	4,414	3,656	4,813	3,656
24,400	24,450	4,428	3,664	4,827	3,664
24,450	24,500	4,442	3,671	4,841	3,671
24,500	24,550	4,456	3,679	4,855	3,679
24,550	24,600	4,470	3,686	4,869	3,686
24,600	24,650	4,484	3,694	4,883	3,694
24,650	24,700	4,498	3,701	4,897	3,701
24,700	24,750	4,512	3,709	4,911	3,709
24,750	24,800	4,526	3,716	4,925	3,716
24,800	24,850	4,540	3,724	4,939	3,724
24,850	24,900	4,554	3,731	4,953	3,735
24,900	24,950	4,568	3,739	4,967	3,749
24,950	25,000	4,582	3,746	4,981	3,763
25,000					
25,000	25,050	4,596	3,754	4,995	3,777
25,050	25,100	4,610	3,761	5,009	3,791
25,100	25,150	4,624	3,769	5,023	3,805
25,150	25,200	4,638	3,776	5,037	3,819
25,200	25,250	4,652	3,784	5,051	3,833
25,250	25,300	4,666	3,791	5,065	3,847
25,300	25,350	4,680	3,799	5,079	3,861
25,350	25,400	4,694	3,806	5,093	3,875
25,400	25,450	4,708	3,814	5,107	3,889
25,450	25,500	4,722	3,821	5,121	3,903
25,500	25,550	4,736	3,829	5,135	3,917
25,550	25,600	4,750	3,836	5,149	3,931
25,600	25,650	4,764	3,844	5,163	3,945
25,650	25,700	4,778	3,851	5,177	3,959
25,700	25,750	4,792	3,859	5,191	3,973
25,750	25,800	4,806	3,866	5,205	3,987
25,800	25,850	4,820	3,874	5,219	4,001
25,850	25,900	4,834	3,881	5,233	4,015
25,900	25,950	4,848	3,889	5,247	4,029
25,950	26,000	4,862	3,896	5,261	4,043

If line 37 (taxable income) is— At least	But less than	Single	Married filing jointly *	Married filing separately	Head of a household
26,000					
26,000	26,050	4,876	3,904	5,275	4,057
26,050	26,100	4,890	3,911	5,289	4,071
26,100	26,150	4,904	3,919	5,303	4,085
26,150	26,200	4,918	3,926	5,317	4,099
26,200	26,250	4,932	3,934	5,331	4,113
26,250	26,300	4,946	3,941	5,345	4,127
26,300	26,350	4,960	3,949	5,359	4,141
26,350	26,400	4,974	3,956	5,373	4,155
26,400	26,450	4,988	3,964	5,387	4,169
26,450	26,500	5,002	3,971	5,401	4,183
26,500	26,550	5,016	3,979	5,415	4,197
26,550	26,600	5,030	3,986	5,429	4,211
26,600	26,650	5,044	3,994	5,443	4,225
26,650	26,700	5,058	4,001	5,457	4,239
26,700	26,750	5,072	4,009	5,471	4,253
26,750	26,800	5,086	4,016	5,485	4,267
26,800	26,850	5,100	4,024	5,499	4,281
26,850	26,900	5,114	4,031	5,513	4,295
26,900	26,950	5,128	4,039	5,527	4,309
26,950	27,000	5,142	4,046	5,541	4,323
27,000					
27,000	27,050	5,156	4,054	5,555	4,337
27,050	27,100	5,170	4,061	5,569	4,351
27,100	27,150	5,184	4,069	5,583	4,365
27,150	27,200	5,198	4,076	5,597	4,379
27,200	27,250	5,212	4,084	5,611	4,393
27,250	27,300	5,226	4,091	5,625	4,407
27,300	27,350	5,240	4,099	5,639	4,421
27,350	27,400	5,254	4,106	5,653	4,435
27,400	27,450	5,268	4,114	5,667	4,449
27,450	27,500	5,282	4,121	5,681	4,463
27,500	27,550	5,296	4,129	5,695	4,477
27,550	27,600	5,310	4,136	5,709	4,491
27,600	27,650	5,324	4,144	5,723	4,505
27,650	27,700	5,338	4,151	5,737	4,519
27,700	27,750	5,352	4,159	5,751	4,533
27,750	27,800	5,366	4,166	5,765	4,547
27,800	27,850	5,380	4,174	5,779	4,561
27,850	27,900	5,394	4,181	5,793	4,575
27,900	27,950	5,408	4,189	5,807	4,589
27,950	28,000	5,422	4,196	5,821	4,603
28,000					
28,000	28,050	5,436	4,204	5,835	4,617
28,050	28,100	5,450	4,211	5,849	4,631
28,100	28,150	5,464	4,219	5,863	4,645
28,150	28,200	5,478	4,226	5,877	4,659
28,200	28,250	5,492	4,234	5,891	4,673
28,250	28,300	5,506	4,241	5,905	4,687
28,300	28,350	5,520	4,249	5,919	4,701
28,350	28,400	5,534	4,256	5,933	4,715
28,400	28,450	5,548	4,264	5,947	4,729
28,450	28,500	5,562	4,271	5,961	4,743
28,500	28,550	5,576	4,279	5,975	4,757
28,550	28,600	5,590	4,286	5,989	4,771
28,600	28,650	5,604	4,294	6,003	4,785
28,650	28,700	5,618	4,301	6,017	4,799
28,700	28,750	5,632	4,309	6,031	4,813
28,750	28,800	5,646	4,316	6,045	4,827
28,800	28,850	5,660	4,324	6,059	4,841
28,850	28,900	5,674	4,331	6,073	4,855
28,900	28,950	5,688	4,339	6,087	4,869
28,950	29,000	5,702	4,346	6,101	4,883

If line 37 (taxable income) is— At least	But less than	Single	Married filing jointly *	Married filing separately	Head of a household
29,000					
29,000	29,050	5,716	4,354	6,115	4,897
29,050	29,100	5,730	4,361	6,129	4,911
29,100	29,150	5,744	4,369	6,143	4,925
29,150	29,200	5,758	4,376	6,157	4,939
29,200	29,250	5,772	4,384	6,171	4,953
29,250	29,300	5,786	4,391	6,185	4,967
29,300	29,350	5,800	4,399	6,199	4,981
29,350	29,400	5,814	4,406	6,213	4,995
29,400	29,450	5,828	4,414	6,227	5,009
29,450	29,500	5,842	4,421	6,241	5,023
29,500	29,550	5,856	4,429	6,255	5,037
29,550	29,600	5,870	4,436	6,269	5,051
29,600	29,650	5,884	4,444	6,283	5,065
29,650	29,700	5,898	4,451	6,297	5,079
29,700	29,750	5,912	4,459	6,311	5,093
29,750	29,800	5,926	4,466	6,325	5,107
29,800	29,850	5,940	4,474	6,339	5,121
29,850	29,900	5,954	4,481	6,353	5,135
29,900	29,950	5,968	4,489	6,367	5,149
29,950	30,000	5,982	4,496	6,381	5,163
30,000					
30,000	30,050	5,996	4,504	6,395	5,177
30,050	30,100	6,010	4,511	6,409	5,191
30,100	30,150	6,024	4,519	6,423	5,205
30,150	30,200	6,038	4,526	6,437	5,219
30,200	30,250	6,052	4,534	6,451	5,233
30,250	30,300	6,066	4,541	6,465	5,247
30,300	30,350	6,080	4,549	6,479	5,261
30,350	30,400	6,094	4,556	6,493	5,275
30,400	30,450	6,108	4,564	6,507	5,289
30,450	30,500	6,122	4,571	6,521	5,303
30,500	30,550	6,136	4,579	6,535	5,317
30,550	30,600	6,150	4,586	6,549	5,331
30,600	30,650	6,164	4,594	6,563	5,345
30,650	30,700	6,178	4,601	6,577	5,359
30,700	30,750	6,192	4,609	6,591	5,373
30,750	30,800	6,206	4,616	6,605	5,387
30,800	30,850	6,220	4,624	6,619	5,401
30,850	30,900	6,234	4,631	6,633	5,415
30,900	30,950	6,248	4,639	6,647	5,429
30,950	31,000	6,262	4,650	6,661	5,443
31,000					
31,000	31,050	6,276	4,664	6,675	5,457
31,050	31,100	6,290	4,678	6,689	5,471
31,100	31,150	6,304	4,692	6,703	5,485
31,150	31,200	6,318	4,706	6,717	5,499
31,200	31,250	6,332	4,720	6,731	5,513
31,250	31,300	6,346	4,734	6,745	5,527
31,300	31,350	6,360	4,748	6,759	5,541
31,350	31,400	6,374	4,762	6,773	5,555
31,400	31,450	6,388	4,776	6,787	5,569
31,450	31,500	6,402	4,790	6,801	5,583
31,500	31,550	6,416	4,804	6,815	5,597
31,550	31,600	6,430	4,818	6,829	5,611
31,600	31,650	6,444	4,832	6,843	5,625
31,650	31,700	6,458	4,846	6,857	5,639
31,700	31,750	6,472	4,860	6,871	5,653
31,750	31,800	6,486	4,874	6,885	5,667
31,800	31,850	6,500	4,888	6,899	5,681
31,850	31,900	6,514	4,902	6,913	5,695
31,900	31,950	6,528	4,916	6,927	5,709
31,950	32,000	6,542	4,930	6,941	5,723

* This column must also be used by a qualifying widow(er).

Continued on next page

1989 Tax Table—*Continued*

If taxable income is— At least	But less than	Single	Married filing jointly *	Married filing separately	Head of a household
32,000					
32,000	32,050	6,556	4,944	6,955	5,737
32,050	32,100	6,570	4,958	6,969	5,751
32,100	32,150	6,584	4,972	6,983	5,765
32,150	32,200	6,598	4,986	6,997	5,779
32,200	32,250	6,612	5,000	7,011	5,793
32,250	32,300	6,626	5,014	7,025	5,807
32,300	32,350	6,640	5,028	7,039	5,821
32,350	32,400	6,654	5,042	7,053	5,835
32,400	32,450	6,668	5,056	7,067	5,849
32,450	32,500	6,682	5,070	7,081	5,863
32,500	32,550	6,696	5,084	7,095	5,877
32,550	32,600	6,710	5,098	7,109	5,891
32,600	32,650	6,724	5,112	7,123	5,905
32,650	32,700	6,738	5,126	7,137	5,919
32,700	32,750	6,752	5,140	7,151	5,933
32,750	32,800	6,766	5,154	7,165	5,947
32,800	32,850	6,780	5,168	7,179	5,961
32,850	32,900	6,794	5,182	7,193	5,975
32,900	32,950	6,808	5,196	7,207	5,989
32,950	33,000	6,822	5,210	7,221	6,003
33,000					
33,000	33,050	6,836	5,224	7,235	6,017
33,050	33,100	6,850	5,238	7,249	6,031
33,100	33,150	6,864	5,252	7,263	6,045
33,150	33,200	6,878	5,266	7,277	6,059
33,200	33,250	6,892	5,280	7,291	6,073
33,250	33,300	6,906	5,294	7,305	6,087
33,300	33,350	6,920	5,308	7,319	6,101
33,350	33,400	6,934	5,322	7,333	6,115
33,400	33,450	6,948	5,336	7,347	6,129
33,450	33,500	6,962	5,350	7,361	6,143
33,500	33,550	6,976	5,364	7,375	6,157
33,550	33,600	6,990	5,378	7,389	6,171
33,600	33,650	7,004	5,392	7,403	6,185
33,650	33,700	7,018	5,406	7,417	6,199
33,700	33,750	7,032	5,420	7,431	6,213
33,750	33,800	7,046	5,434	7,445	6,227
33,800	33,850	7,060	5,448	7,459	6,241
33,850	33,900	7,074	5,462	7,473	6,255
33,900	33,950	7,088	5,476	7,487	6,269
33,950	34,000	7,102	5,490	7,501	6,283
34,000					
34,000	34,050	7,116	5,504	7,515	6,297
34,050	34,100	7,130	5,518	7,529	6,311
34,100	34,150	7,144	5,532	7,543	6,325
34,150	34,200	7,158	5,546	7,557	6,339
34,200	34,250	7,172	5,560	7,571	6,353
34,250	34,300	7,186	5,574	7,585	6,367
34,300	34,350	7,200	5,588	7,599	6,381
34,350	34,400	7,214	5,602	7,613	6,395
34,400	34,450	7,228	5,616	7,627	6,409
34,450	34,500	7,242	5,630	7,641	6,423
34,500	34,550	7,256	5,644	7,655	6,437
34,550	34,600	7,270	5,658	7,669	6,451
34,600	34,650	7,284	5,672	7,683	6,465
34,650	34,700	7,298	5,686	7,697	6,479
34,700	34,750	7,312	5,700	7,711	6,493
34,750	34,800	7,326	5,714	7,725	6,507
34,800	34,850	7,340	5,728	7,739	6,521
34,850	34,900	7,354	5,742	7,753	6,535
34,900	34,950	7,368	5,756	7,767	6,549
34,950	35,000	7,382	5,770	7,781	6,563

If taxable income is— At least	But less than	Single	Married filing jointly *	Married filing separately	Head of a household
35,000					
35,000	35,050	7,396	5,784	7,795	6,577
35,050	35,100	7,410	5,798	7,809	6,591
35,100	35,150	7,424	5,812	7,823	6,605
35,150	35,200	7,438	5,826	7,837	6,619
35,200	35,250	7,452	5,840	7,851	6,633
35,250	35,300	7,466	5,854	7,865	6,647
35,300	35,350	7,480	5,868	7,879	6,661
35,350	35,400	7,494	5,882	7,893	6,675
35,400	35,450	7,508	5,896	7,907	6,689
35,450	35,500	7,522	5,910	7,921	6,703
35,500	35,550	7,536	5,924	7,935	6,717
35,550	35,600	7,550	5,938	7,949	6,731
35,600	35,650	7,564	5,952	7,963	6,745
35,650	35,700	7,578	5,966	7,977	6,759
35,700	35,750	7,592	5,980	7,991	6,773
35,750	35,800	7,606	5,994	8,005	6,787
35,800	35,850	7,620	6,008	8,019	6,801
35,850	35,900	7,634	6,022	8,033	6,815
35,900	35,950	7,648	6,036	8,047	6,829
35,950	36,000	7,662	6,050	8,061	6,843
36,000					
36,000	36,050	7,676	6,064	8,075	6,857
36,050	36,100	7,690	6,078	8,089	6,871
36,100	36,150	7,704	6,092	8,103	6,885
36,150	36,200	7,718	6,106	8,117	6,899
36,200	36,250	7,732	6,120	8,131	6,913
36,250	36,300	7,746	6,134	8,145	6,927
36,300	36,350	7,760	6,148	8,159	6,941
36,350	36,400	7,774	6,162	8,173	6,955
36,400	36,450	7,788	6,176	8,187	6,969
36,450	36,500	7,802	6,190	8,201	6,983
36,500	36,550	7,816	6,204	8,215	6,997
36,550	36,600	7,830	6,218	8,229	7,011
36,600	36,650	7,844	6,232	8,243	7,025
36,650	36,700	7,858	6,246	8,257	7,039
36,700	36,750	7,872	6,260	8,271	7,053
36,750	36,800	7,886	6,274	8,285	7,067
36,800	36,850	7,900	6,288	8,299	7,081
36,850	36,900	7,914	6,302	8,313	7,095
36,900	36,950	7,928	6,316	8,327	7,109
36,950	37,000	7,942	6,330	8,341	7,123
37,000					
37,000	37,050	7,956	6,344	8,355	7,137
37,050	37,100	7,970	6,358	8,369	7,151
37,100	37,150	7,984	6,372	8,383	7,165
37,150	37,200	7,998	6,386	8,397	7,179
37,200	37,250	8,012	6,400	8,411	7,193
37,250	37,300	8,026	6,414	8,425	7,207
37,300	37,350	8,040	6,428	8,439	7,221
37,350	37,400	8,054	6,442	8,453	7,235
37,400	37,450	8,068	6,456	8,467	7,249
37,450	37,500	8,082	6,470	8,484	7,263
37,500	37,550	8,096	6,484	8,500	7,277
37,550	37,600	8,110	6,498	8,517	7,291
37,600	37,650	8,124	6,512	8,533	7,305
37,650	37,700	8,138	6,526	8,550	7,319
37,700	37,750	8,152	6,540	8,566	7,333
37,750	37,800	8,166	6,554	8,583	7,347
37,800	37,850	8,180	6,568	8,599	7,361
37,850	37,900	8,194	6,582	8,616	7,375
37,900	37,950	8,208	6,596	8,632	7,389
37,950	38,000	8,222	6,610	8,649	7,403

If taxable income is— At least	But less than	Single	Married filing jointly *	Married filing separately	Head of a household
38,000					
38,000	38,050	8,236	6,624	8,665	7,417
38,050	38,100	8,250	6,638	8,682	7,431
38,100	38,150	8,264	6,652	8,698	7,445
38,150	38,200	8,278	6,666	8,715	7,459
38,200	38,250	8,292	6,680	8,731	7,473
38,250	38,300	8,306	6,694	8,748	7,487
38,300	38,350	8,320	6,708	8,764	7,501
38,350	38,400	8,334	6,722	8,781	7,515
38,400	38,450	8,348	6,736	8,797	7,529
38,450	38,500	8,362	6,750	8,814	7,543
38,500	38,550	8,376	6,764	8,830	7,557
38,550	38,600	8,390	6,778	8,847	7,571
38,600	38,650	8,404	6,792	8,863	7,585
38,650	38,700	8,418	6,806	8,880	7,599
38,700	38,750	8,432	6,820	8,896	7,613
38,750	38,800	8,446	6,834	8,913	7,627
38,800	38,850	8,460	6,848	8,929	7,641
38,850	38,900	8,474	6,862	8,946	7,655
38,900	38,950	8,488	6,876	8,962	7,669
38,950	39,000	8,502	6,890	8,979	7,683
39,000					
39,000	39,050	8,516	6,904	8,995	7,697
39,050	39,100	8,530	6,918	9,012	7,711
39,100	39,150	8,544	6,932	9,028	7,725
39,150	39,200	8,558	6,946	9,045	7,739
39,200	39,250	8,572	6,960	9,061	7,753
39,250	39,300	8,586	6,974	9,078	7,767
39,300	39,350	8,600	6,988	9,094	7,781
39,350	39,400	8,614	7,002	9,111	7,795
39,400	39,450	8,628	7,016	9,127	7,809
39,450	39,500	8,642	7,030	9,144	7,823
39,500	39,550	8,656	7,044	9,160	7,837
39,550	39,600	8,670	7,058	9,177	7,851
39,600	39,650	8,684	7,072	9,193	7,865
39,650	39,700	8,698	7,086	9,210	7,879
39,700	39,750	8,712	7,100	9,226	7,893
39,750	39,800	8,726	7,114	9,243	7,907
39,800	39,850	8,740	7,128	9,259	7,921
39,850	39,900	8,754	7,142	9,276	7,935
39,900	39,950	8,768	7,156	9,292	7,949
39,950	40,000	8,782	7,170	9,309	7,963
40,000					
40,000	40,050	8,796	7,184	9,325	7,977
40,050	40,100	8,810	7,198	9,342	7,991
40,100	40,150	8,824	7,212	9,358	8,005
40,150	40,200	8,838	7,226	9,375	8,019
40,200	40,250	8,852	7,240	9,391	8,033
40,250	40,300	8,866	7,254	9,408	8,047
40,300	40,350	8,880	7,268	9,424	8,061
40,350	40,400	8,894	7,282	9,441	8,075
40,400	40,450	8,908	7,296	9,457	8,089
40,450	40,500	8,922	7,310	9,474	8,103
40,500	40,550	8,936	7,324	9,490	8,117
40,550	40,600	8,950	7,338	9,507	8,131
40,600	40,650	8,964	7,352	9,523	8,145
40,650	40,700	8,978	7,366	9,540	8,159
40,700	40,750	8,992	7,380	9,556	8,173
40,750	40,800	9,006	7,394	9,573	8,187
40,800	40,850	9,020	7,408	9,589	8,201
40,850	40,900	9,034	7,422	9,606	8,215
40,900	40,950	9,048	7,436	9,622	8,229
40,950	41,000	9,062	7,450	9,639	8,243

* This column must also be used by a qualifying widow(er).

Continued on next page

1989 Tax Table—Continued

If taxable income is— At least	But less than	Single	Married filing jointly *	Married filing separately	Head of a household
41,000					
41,000	41,050	9,076	7,464	9,655	8,257
41,050	41,100	9,090	7,478	9,672	8,271
41,100	41,150	9,104	7,492	9,688	8,285
41,150	41,200	9,118	7,506	9,705	8,299
41,200	41,250	9,132	7,520	9,721	8,313
41,250	41,300	9,146	7,534	9,738	8,327
41,300	41,350	9,160	7,548	9,754	8,341
41,350	41,400	9,174	7,562	9,771	8,355
41,400	41,450	9,188	7,576	9,787	8,369
41,450	41,500	9,202	7,590	9,804	8,383
41,500	41,550	9,216	7,604	9,820	8,397
41,550	41,600	9,230	7,618	9,837	8,411
41,600	41,650	9,244	7,632	9,853	8,425
41,650	41,700	9,258	7,646	9,870	8,439
41,700	41,750	9,272	7,660	9,886	8,453
41,750	41,800	9,286	7,674	9,903	8,467
41,800	41,850	9,300	7,688	9,919	8,481
41,850	41,900	9,314	7,702	9,936	8,495
41,900	41,950	9,328	7,716	9,952	8,509
41,950	42,000	9,342	7,730	9,969	8,523
42,000					
42,000	42,050	9,356	7,744	9,985	8,537
42,050	42,100	9,370	7,758	10,002	8,551
42,100	42,150	9,384	7,772	10,018	8,565
42,150	42,200	9,398	7,786	10,035	8,579
42,200	42,250	9,412	7,800	10,051	8,593
42,250	42,300	9,426	7,814	10,068	8,607
42,300	42,350	9,440	7,828	10,084	8,621
42,350	42,400	9,454	7,842	10,101	8,635
42,400	42,450	9,468	7,856	10,117	8,649
42,450	42,500	9,482	7,870	10,134	8,663
42,500	42,550	9,496	7,884	10,150	8,677
42,550	42,600	9,510	7,898	10,167	8,691
42,600	42,650	9,524	7,912	10,183	8,705
42,650	42,700	9,538	7,926	10,200	8,719
42,700	42,750	9,552	7,940	10,216	8,733
42,750	42,800	9,566	7,954	10,233	8,747
42,800	42,850	9,580	7,968	10,249	8,761
42,850	42,900	9,594	7,982	10,266	8,775
42,900	42,950	9,608	7,996	10,282	8,789
42,950	43,000	9,622	8,010	10,299	8,803
43,000					
43,000	43,050	9,636	8,024	10,315	8,817
43,050	43,100	9,650	8,038	10,332	8,831
43,100	43,150	9,664	8,052	10,348	8,845
43,150	43,200	9,678	8,066	10,365	8,859
43,200	43,250	9,692	8,080	10,381	8,873
43,250	43,300	9,706	8,094	10,398	8,887
43,300	43,350	9,720	8,108	10,414	8,901
43,350	43,400	9,734	8,122	10,431	8,915
43,400	43,450	9,748	8,136	10,447	8,929
43,450	43,500	9,762	8,150	10,464	8,943
43,500	43,550	9,776	8,164	10,480	8,957
43,550	43,600	9,790	8,178	10,497	8,971
43,600	43,650	9,804	8,192	10,513	8,985
43,650	43,700	9,818	8,206	10,530	8,999
43,700	43,750	9,832	8,220	10,546	9,013
43,750	43,800	9,846	8,234	10,563	9,027
43,800	43,850	9,860	8,248	10,579	9,041
43,850	43,900	9,874	8,262	10,596	9,055
43,900	43,950	9,888	8,276	10,612	9,069
43,950	44,000	9,902	8,290	10,629	9,083

If taxable income is— At least	But less than	Single	Married filing jointly *	Married filing separately	Head of a household
44,000					
44,000	44,050	9,916	8,304	10,645	9,097
44,050	44,100	9,930	8,318	10,662	9,111
44,100	44,150	9,944	8,332	10,678	9,125
44,150	44,200	9,958	8,346	10,695	9,139
44,200	44,250	9,972	8,360	10,711	9,153
44,250	44,300	9,986	8,374	10,728	9,167
44,300	44,350	10,000	8,388	10,744	9,181
44,350	44,400	10,014	8,402	10,761	9,195
44,400	44,450	10,028	8,416	10,777	9,209
44,450	44,500	10,042	8,430	10,794	9,223
44,500	44,550	10,056	8,444	10,810	9,237
44,550	44,600	10,070	8,458	10,827	9,251
44,600	44,650	10,084	8,472	10,843	9,265
44,650	44,700	10,098	8,486	10,860	9,279
44,700	44,750	10,112	8,500	10,876	9,293
44,750	44,800	10,126	8,514	10,893	9,307
44,800	44,850	10,140	8,528	10,909	9,321
44,850	44,900	10,154	8,542	10,926	9,335
44,900	44,950	10,169	8,556	10,942	9,349
44,950	45,000	10,185	8,570	10,959	9,363
45,000					
45,000	45,050	10,202	8,584	10,975	9,377
45,050	45,100	10,218	8,598	10,992	9,391
45,100	45,150	10,235	8,612	11,008	9,405
45,150	45,200	10,251	8,626	11,025	9,419
45,200	45,250	10,268	8,640	11,041	9,433
45,250	45,300	10,284	8,654	11,058	9,447
45,300	45,350	10,301	8,668	11,074	9,461
45,350	45,400	10,317	8,682	11,091	9,475
45,400	45,450	10,334	8,696	11,107	9,489
45,450	45,500	10,350	8,710	11,124	9,503
45,500	45,550	10,367	8,724	11,140	9,517
45,550	45,600	10,383	8,738	11,157	9,531
45,600	45,650	10,400	8,752	11,173	9,545
45,650	45,700	10,416	8,766	11,190	9,559
45,700	45,750	10,433	8,780	11,206	9,573
45,750	45,800	10,449	8,794	11,223	9,587
45,800	45,850	10,466	8,808	11,239	9,601
45,850	45,900	10,482	8,822	11,256	9,615
45,900	45,950	10,499	8,836	11,272	9,629
45,950	46,000	10,515	8,850	11,289	9,643
46,000					
46,000	46,050	10,532	8,864	11,305	9,657
46,050	46,100	10,548	8,878	11,322	9,671
46,100	46,150	10,565	8,892	11,338	9,685
46,150	46,200	10,581	8,906	11,355	9,699
46,200	46,250	10,598	8,920	11,371	9,713
46,250	46,300	10,614	8,934	11,388	9,727
46,300	46,350	10,631	8,948	11,404	9,741
46,350	46,400	10,647	8,962	11,421	9,755
46,400	46,450	10,664	8,976	11,437	9,769
46,450	46,500	10,680	8,990	11,454	9,783
46,500	46,550	10,697	9,004	11,470	9,797
46,550	46,600	10,713	9,018	11,487	9,811
46,600	46,650	10,730	9,032	11,503	9,825
46,650	46,700	10,746	9,046	11,520	9,839
46,700	46,750	10,763	9,060	11,536	9,853
46,750	46,800	10,779	9,074	11,553	9,867
46,800	46,850	10,796	9,088	11,569	9,881
46,850	46,900	10,812	9,102	11,586	9,895
46,900	46,950	10,829	9,116	11,602	9,909
46,950	47,000	10,845	9,130	11,619	9,923

If taxable income is— At least	But less than	Single	Married filing jointly *	Married filing separately	Head of a household
47,000					
47,000	47,050	10,862	9,144	11,635	9,937
47,050	47,100	10,878	9,158	11,652	9,951
47,100	47,150	10,895	9,172	11,668	9,965
47,150	47,200	10,911	9,186	11,685	9,979
47,200	47,250	10,928	9,200	11,701	9,993
47,250	47,300	10,944	9,214	11,718	10,007
47,300	47,350	10,961	9,228	11,734	10,021
47,350	47,400	10,977	9,242	11,751	10,035
47,400	47,450	10,994	9,256	11,767	10,049
47,450	47,500	11,010	9,270	11,784	10,063
47,500	47,550	11,027	9,284	11,800	10,077
47,550	47,600	11,043	9,298	11,817	10,091
47,600	47,650	11,060	9,312	11,833	10,105
47,650	47,700	11,076	9,326	11,850	10,119
47,700	47,750	11,093	9,340	11,866	10,133
47,750	47,800	11,109	9,354	11,883	10,147
47,800	47,850	11,126	9,368	11,899	10,161
47,850	47,900	11,142	9,382	11,916	10,175
47,900	47,950	11,159	9,396	11,932	10,189
47,950	48,000	11,175	9,410	11,949	10,203
48,000					
48,000	48,050	11,192	9,424	11,965	10,217
48,050	48,100	11,208	9,438	11,982	10,231
48,100	48,150	11,225	9,452	11,998	10,245
48,150	48,200	11,241	9,466	12,015	10,259
48,200	48,250	11,258	9,480	12,031	10,273
48,250	48,300	11,274	9,494	12,048	10,287
48,300	48,350	11,291	9,508	12,064	10,301
48,350	48,400	11,307	9,522	12,081	10,315
48,400	48,450	11,324	9,536	12,097	10,329
48,450	48,500	11,340	9,550	12,114	10,343
48,500	48,550	11,357	9,564	12,130	10,357
48,550	48,600	11,373	9,578	12,147	10,371
48,600	48,650	11,390	9,592	12,163	10,385
48,650	48,700	11,406	9,606	12,180	10,399
48,700	48,750	11,423	9,620	12,196	10,413
48,750	48,800	11,439	9,634	12,213	10,427
48,800	48,850	11,456	9,648	12,229	10,441
48,850	48,900	11,472	9,662	12,246	10,455
48,900	48,950	11,489	9,676	12,262	10,469
48,950	49,000	11,505	9,690	12,279	10,483
49,000					
49,000	49,050	11,522	9,704	12,295	10,497
49,050	49,100	11,538	9,718	12,312	10,511
49,100	49,150	11,555	9,732	12,328	10,525
49,150	49,200	11,571	9,746	12,345	10,539
49,200	49,250	11,588	9,760	12,361	10,553
49,250	49,300	11,604	9,774	12,378	10,567
49,300	49,350	11,621	9,788	12,394	10,581
49,350	49,400	11,637	9,802	12,411	10,595
49,400	49,450	11,654	9,816	12,427	10,609
49,450	49,500	11,670	9,830	12,444	10,623
49,500	49,550	11,687	9,844	12,460	10,637
49,550	49,600	11,703	9,858	12,477	10,651
49,600	49,650	11,720	9,872	12,493	10,665
49,650	49,700	11,736	9,886	12,510	10,679
49,700	49,750	11,753	9,900	12,526	10,693
49,750	49,800	11,769	9,914	12,543	10,707
49,800	49,850	11,786	9,928	12,559	10,721
49,850	49,900	11,802	9,942	12,576	10,735
49,900	49,950	11,819	9,956	12,592	10,749
49,950	50,000	11,835	9,970	12,609	10,763

* This column must also be used by a qualifying widow(er).

50,000 or over—use tax rate schedules

14

How to Get the Most from Your Professional or Personal Service Corporation

This chapter covers what I call the "perilous professions," which the IRS has forced to choose between electing Subchapter S status or having a C corporation which is taxed at a flat 34 percent: corporations whose principal function is "services in the field of law, health, engineering, architecture, accounting, actuarial science, performing arts, or consulting."

Every profession has its own opportunities for maximizing both income and deductible expenses. Naturally, professional and personal service corporations can minimize their taxes at the same time. This is especially important for the corporate owners who have chosen the C corporation, despite its flat 34 percent tax rate. First, let's look at the opportunities and strategies that are common to all professional and personal service corporations; then, we'll look at the opportunities and strategies that benefit specific professional and personal service corporations.

YOUR EMPLOYEES

One of the advantages of being a professional, compared to running a small business, is the ability to get things done with a much smaller staff. Often you can manage very well with only one or two employees.

Your professional corporation can save a great deal of money by arranging matters so that your employees wind up being covered by your pension plan in a different way from your coverage. There are several ways of accomplishing this, according to Harold Glassberg, senior partner of the Westchester, New York, CPA firm, Glassberg, Holden & Mermer.

First, and probably easiest, your pension and profit-sharing plan can be set up with a long vesting period. Three years is the current maximum. Using this strategy, your professional corporation doesn't have to contribute to your employee's pension fund until his or her second-year anniversary. Of course, if your employee leaves before then, your corporation is spared the expense and paperwork of setting up the plan and making the contribution.

If your employee leaves between the second and third anniversary, his or her pension account reverts to your corporation's pension fund. Bear in mind, though, that if your fund acquires the employee's forfeited contribution, your contribution is reduced by the amount of the forfeiture. Thus, if your professional corporation were going to contribute $20,000 to your pension fund this year and it were entitled to acquire an employee's forfeited $5,000 pension-fund contribution, it would pick up that $5,000 and use it for your account, and would be able to contribute only $15,000 on your behalf. You'd still have the $20,000 as your own contribution, even though your corporation could contribute only $15,000 in new money for your account.

There's one danger: You cannot make a habit of firing employees after two and one-half years, shortly before their pension is due to be vested. *Court case:* A doctor who fired his secretaries consistently after they had worked a little over two years was found to have established a pattern over 12 years. His last secretary took him to court, claiming that she had been fired only because her pension was about to become vested, and won. The court ruled in her favor and awarded her back pay, her pension contribution, compensation, and punitive damages.

There are several ways of sidestepping this pitfall. One easy method is hiring office help through an employment agency. Even if they are full-time and work for you for many years, they are not considered your employees—they're the agency's employees. You'll probably be paying a higher hourly rate, but it may well work out cheaper in the end because you don't have to pay the employees' Social Security contribution, their pension contribution, insurance, sick and vacation pay, and other fringe benefits.

Yet another strategy is hiring for just short of six months—a term generally considered permanent. Many major companies hire support staff in this manner: "Your job will be from January 2 through June 15. We're going to lay you off for two weeks, and then we'll rehire you from July 1 through December 15."

Harold Glassberg compares this strategy to rolling over a note: "You just want to get it off your books for a little while. However," he cautions, "make sure that you call this period a layoff, and not a vacation. As long as you call it a layoff, you don't even have to provide medical, pension, or other fringe benefits—even if this employee works for you forty hours a week for years and years."

Still another method, which works especially well in the suburbs, is finding two people to share one full-time job. As long as each of them works less than 1,000 hours a year (less than 20 hours a week, overall), you do not have to include them in your pension and profit-sharing plans. You can also hire college students or young people full-time, because there is a minimum-age requirement for pension and profit-sharing plans. Your corporation does not have to cover anyone under the age of 24½.

For more sophisticated strategies of limiting the pension coverage for your employees, please see pp. 102–04.

PRO-FAMILY DISCRIMINATION

For professionals who need only part-time help, hiring family members may make a great deal of sense. Chapter 18, "How to Profit from Putting Your Relatives on the Payroll," discusses the pros and cons thoroughly. Here, it's important only to know that all employees must be treated equally. The IRS insists that if other employees fill out time cards, your spouse and children must fill out time cards, too. If your corporation pays a certain salary for specific work, it can't pay family members more for performing the same work.

BORROWING FROM YOUR PENSION PLAN

C corporations offer their owner-employees a significant and profitable benefit: the ability to borrow from their pension plans, which S corporation pension funds and Keogh plans do not have. In effect, you have the use of the money twice: You're using it for your pension, and then you're using it again for your own purposes. For details, see Chapter 11, "How to Profit from Your Pension Fund *Before* You Retire."

And now on to more specific benefits, profession by profession.

Kenneth R. Greenhut, senior partner in the New York City accounting firm of Kaufman, Greenhut, Lebowitz & Forman, specializes in working with entertainers, authors, doctors, lawyers, accountants, and architects who have one-person general business or professional corporations. He offers some general rules for dealing happily and profitably with your accountant:

"Make sure that your accountant and tax adviser know your business/profession/industry. Sometimes your accountant will send a form questionnaire to elicit information for the tax season. Very often the questionnaire is overly general, so that it can apply to all clients. Unfortunately, because of this generality, the client may not provide the accountant with enough right answers. Therefore, truly valid deductions may be forgone for no good reason. The solution is to employ a tax professional who knows your profession's legitimate deductions. One way to distinguish true professionals is their more personalized service and their willingness to educate their clients."

Of course, says Greenhut, it's not a one-way street. "There are good ways and bad ways for you to deal with your accountant. It's in your best interest to be considered a 'good' client: one for whom your accountant will try a little harder, work a little extra. One good way for you to deal with your accountant is to stay in touch throughout the year—a five-minute call once a month generally suffices—rather than ignoring him or her until March 10 for the March 15 corporate filing deadline.

"Keep neat records and present your accountant with orderly papers. Respect your accountant's profession. Accountants are only human, and may be put off by shoeboxes of sloppy papers and crumpled-up receipts. Furthermore, it's just not economical for you to give your accountant an extra 20 hours of work just to straighten out your records. Use your accountant's brain, not just his or her clerical or bookkeeping skills."

Here are some of Kenneth Greenhut's specific deductions for accountants and attorneys, architects, doctors and dentists, entertainers, and veterinarians:

ACCOUNTANTS AND ATTORNEYS

Greenhut lumps accountants and attorneys together because they so often refer clients to each other. They also frequently get business from bankers and from insurance people. Accordingly, it's expected—and it makes sense—to entertain professionals in these areas.

Some accountants and attorneys find that belonging to health clubs as well as country clubs helps them meet many potential clients. In order to write off club expenses, you must keep good records. Entertainment logs are necessary; they should include a brief write-up of whom you entertained, the reason for the entertaining, and a follow-up or outcome. *Remember that your corporation has to absorb 20 percent of all meal expenditures: your guests' and yours. This is true of all corporations and unincorporated businesses or professions.*

If your family belongs to the clubs as well, you'll have to prorate dues as well as segregate business from personal expenses.

Trial lawyers have other professional expenses. If an attorney takes on a lawsuit, he or she may need to travel, to entertain and interview witnesses, to subscribe to industry publications to learn more about the area under litigation, and similar details.

ARCHITECTS

Architects can write off enormous travel expenses, says Greenhut. All they have to do is keep a detailed travel log showing why they traveled where, and what they saw. Sketches and photographs are also valuable documentation. Architects and designers have a pretty free hand with travel—as long as their expenses don't eat up half their corporations' earnings—because even the hardest-nosed IRS agent would have a tough time arguing that it was not important to see classic buildings in Paris or Rome, or the Gaudi architecture in Barcelona, or, closer to home, Frank Lloyd Wright's houses or the Beaux Arts buildings of McKim, Mead & White.

Entertainment is also important because wealthy individuals and builders are such a great source of direct business and of referrals. Accordingly, country clubs make sense here, too. Just make sure that you keep your business and personal expenses separate. If your entire family uses the country club, with your spouse playing nonbusiness golf and your kids taking tennis lessons and going to the junior dances, you'll have to prorate your club dues, too, between business and personal use, according to the percentage allocated to business and to personal use. Make sure that you use the club enough and that you keep careful, contemporaneous records. It will be hard for you to justify club membership if you use the club for business only 10 percent of the total time and money you and your family spend there. *Try for at least 50 percent.*

DOCTORS AND DENTISTS

Greenhut's advice and information is applicable primarily to specialists because, he says, "Specialists rely on referrals from internists, family physicians, and general dentists, and not vice versa. Accordingly, specialists need to entertain other physicians and dentists; internists and general dentists do not." The same general advice about country clubs, health clubs, and entertainment given to accountants, architects, and attorneys pertains to medical and dental specialists.

ENTERTAINERS

Greenhut places both active performers and the people responsible for the performances—producers, directors, playwrights, screenwriters, choreographers, et al.—in this category. Technically (and fortunately), however, playwrights and screenwriters are not forced into electing Subchapter S status or paying a flat 34 percent tax if they choose a C corporation. They can follow the advice here and in the following chapter, under "Authors," knowing that they have escaped being members of the "perilous professions."

For the performers themselves, lessons and classes of all kinds are heavy and legitimate expenses. These include, but are not limited to, coaching for voice, breath control, dialect, dance and exercise classes, expenses for special wardrobe, hair styling, makeup, and photographs. If performers have to lose 10 or 20 pounds in a hurry for a specific part, they may have to go to a "fat farm" to drop all that weight in a week or two. Greenhut's advice: "Get a letter from the producer or director saying that your getting the part is dependent on your weight loss."

Other reasonable expenses for performers: If you are filming 12 hours a day or doing 8 shows a week, you may well need a gym and individual instructor for endurance training. You may need fencing lessons for performing Shakespeare or fighting lessons for action scenes. Best of all, if your part requires a dialect, you may need not only language lessons, but also a trip to that foreign country to pick up the character and absorb the national culture and gestures that would give credibility to your part.

Producers, directors, choreographers, and other theatrical professionals have many legitimate travel and entertainment expenses. Think of all the theatrical, film, music, and dance festivals around the world; all the museums and archives. Greenhut also recommends "independent third-party verification that the trip is necessary. Get a proper letter on a letterhead, from a fellow professional. For example, a producer (or director) could write a letter to a writer, composer, choreographer, or performer, saying 'See this director (or producer) in New York/California/Europe.' This type of documentation carries a great deal of weight, should your return ever be audited."

VETERINARIANS

When it comes to professional write-offs, veterinarians have one great advantage over internists and dentists: Even general veterinarians can write off their expenses from breeding and showing their dogs, cats, and horses because their activities in these areas create visibility and generate many patient referrals. In addition, veterinary specialists—and there are as many veterinary specialties now as there are human ones, from dermatologists to ophthalmological surgeons—can write off expenses from entertaining general veterinarians, from whom they receive referrals, just as medical and dental specialists derive referrals from their generalist colleagues.

LAYING YOUR PAPER TRAIL

No matter what your profession, Greenhut urges that you leave a paper trail. In fact, think of it as overkill: The more paper documentation you can generate, the happier your accountant and the IRS will be because there will be fewer questions about gray areas and items for you to prove.

Here are some important areas to remember:

- *Trade show or convention*—keep some exhibitors' materials, preferably with your own comments noted on them, and a record of why you were there, whom you entertained, where, why, and any business that resulted.
- *Country-club entertainment*—keep a log of how often you use the club for business and, if applicable, how often you and your family use the club for personal reasons. Remember to use the club often enough for business to convince the IRS that it is a legitimate deduction.
- *Other entertainment*—keep records of whom you entertain, where, why, and any business that results from it.
- *Travel*—keep a detailed record of where and why you went, whom you saw, why, and any outcome. Newspaper and magazine articles relating to the trip are a great help, as are sketches and detailed notes, depending on their relevance to your profession. So are letters of assignment of work and letters that show, by independent third-party verification, that the trip was necessary.

15

"Nonprofessional"
Career Corporate
Strategies

This chapter is for those owner-employees who are not members of the "perilous professions," as defined by the IRS, and who can take advantage of graduated corporate income-tax rates starting as low as 15 percent. Most of these people are no less professional than those in the preceding chapter; but the IRS divides service corporations into the "perilous" and "safe," and this division is a handy one to adopt for these two chapters.

If you've skipped over Chapter 14 because you know that you aren't a professional, as it is usually defined, stop and read pp. 235–36 for some useful information on how to avoid covering your employees for costly fringe benefits, how to get the best out of your accountant, and the all-important laying of your paper trail. Now turn back to this page. The rest of this chapter deals with strategies to optimize your business deductions—and thus slash your corporate taxes—in a number of different careers.

AUTHORS

No one at the IRS ever asked James Michener to account for the thousands of dollars he spent while living in Hawaii, researching his blockbuster novel of the same name.

You don't have to be a James Michener or a Stephen King. So long as you are a professional, published author, or can prove that you're serious,

241

through professional memberships, representation by a literary agent or contacts with publishers and editors, you can justify enormous expenses. Novels, histories, and biographies may require extensive travel not only for local color and interviews, but also for visiting specific museums and libraries.

Many authors know about writing off foreign travel but are unaware that they can and should visit special libraries and museums to do research, and that these trips are deductible as well. Savvy writers usually combine out-of-town research trips with visits to friends and relatives who live in those cities. It's all perfectly legal, as long as there's a legitimate business reason for the trip. One art and antiques writer I know brags that every trip to Europe he's made in the last ten years has been completely tax-deductible: He's visited museums, attended auctions, comparison-shopped foreign dealers, perhaps interviewed experts for future articles. It's of no tax consequence that he's also had a hell of a good time.

Entertainment is another important and justifiable expense. Authors can and should entertain their sources and their colleagues. Cliché or not, writing is a solitary profession, so networking with other authors and with editors is crucial. Many authors make it a point to have lunch or drinks with colleagues at least twice a week. *This is a reasonable industry standard and has been upheld by the IRS, as long as your entertainment expense isn't 50 percent of your income.* When I was senior editor at a publishing house, I was expected to take authors and agents to lunch at least four times a week; that's the way the publishing industry does business. As an author, entertaining your fellow authors or editors is important (yes, you do take editors to lunch at times—especially after they've entertained you several times, or to thank them after a few article assignments). You trade information about which editors are looking for what types of books or articles, how much they're paying, what they're like to work with, who has moved where, and so on. *Clearly all of this is useful, a source of potential income for you. That's why it's deductible.*

CATERERS/CHEFS/RESTAURANT OWNERS

If you are an upmarket caterer or chef, or expect to be, you'll probably have to spend a fair amount of money sampling other chefs' wares in your own city and other cities. All of these expenses are deductible.

Of course you'll remember to write off the cost of the ingredients you use in catering, or in your restaurant, but *don't forget to write off the ingredients you use in experimenting to create new dishes.*

Other reasonable expenses are cookbooks—including the old, rare, and expensive; utensils (ditto); and the cost of taking workshops abroad with such superstars as Paul Bocuse or Fredy Girardet.

Here's a business expense you may not have thought of that is certain to bring you more clients: Offer to cater a charity function, like a PBS pledge drive or religious or school function, and make sure that your name is mentioned frequently in return for your goodies. Or, offer your services or dinner at your restaurant as a prize for a charity auction. It's a very inexpensive way to get publicity and new clients, and it costs less and has much greater credibility than advertising.

COMMISSION SALESPERSON

Client entertainment and travel are the two largest sources of your business expense. The most useful advice I can give is to keep nitpickingly precise records of these expenses—even when you're exhausted. Fill in your expense account while the details are still fresh in your mind, and *show how your entertainment connects with getting the order or thanking the client for an order.* Take advantage of preprinted forms made by Filofax and its clones.

Seminars to make you a better salesperson? Of course they're deductible. So are health-club expenses for your chronic bad back, a consequence of constant travel. Get a doctor's note.

And don't forget your phone and fax bills!

COMPUTER DESIGNER/PROGRAMMER

Let's start with your largest expenses: computer, software, instruction manuals. You can write off as much as $10,000 a year for this equipment. (Printout paper is in a separate category and doesn't count as part of the $10,000.)

Educational expense may be another large source of potential write-offs. All you have to do to satisfy the IRS is *show that the courses or seminars were taken to improve your skills in your present job*—not to prepare you for a different career. And, of course, if these courses are taught out of town, all your travel expenses and 80 percent of your meal expenses are also deductible.

I don't want to sound as though I'm fixated on bad backs, but they're certainly an occupational hazard of owner-employee computer designers and programmers, who have been known to stay at their desks for 12 to 15 hours at a stretch, leaving only for a quick sandwich from the fridge or a pit stop. If you have back problems, health clubs and professional masseurs or masseuses are a legitimate write-off, as long as you have a doctor's note saying that these treatments are medically advisable. And, while you're at it, get a good, tax-deductible ergonomic chair for your workstation.

CORPORATE TRAINER

Corporate trainers go around the country, giving seminars at large and small corporations, usually on such topics as productivity and better communication. In general, they are reimbursed for their travel expenses, so they aren't a source of write-offs. Their greatest write-offs come from client entertainment, in order to get clients or increase work from existing clients, and long-distance phone and fax expense.

Corporate trainers can also write off the cost of lessons with a voice coach.

FASHION DESIGNERS

Perhaps more than any other career, fashion designers are expected to travel. Viewing the collections in New York, Paris, and Milan is a semiannual must. In addition, fashion designers can and do travel around the world to buy their fabrics and to work with their suppliers and contractors.

Many new fashion designers hire publicists—a wise move to achieve visibility and gain customers quickly. Designers may also entertain media people in order to get wide coverage for their designs; a photo or mention in *Vogue* or *The New York Times* can be worth thousands of dollars in sales.

Fashion designers should also consider donating a piece or an outfit from their collections to a PBS or charity auction. It will give them tremendous publicity and visibility for very little money. Imagine seeing your outfit televised several times a day, or displayed and written up in a catalog for a charity auction!

FINANCIAL ADVISERS

Financial advisers can and should attend many investment seminars and conferences every year to keep on top of what's happening in today's increasingly volatile financial sectors. If they are on the road a great deal, they'll surely need a cellular phone and a portable investment-quote machine like Quo-Trek. Closer to home, they'll probably need investment-portfolio software programs and possibly a number of stock-picking programs out of the dozens available. And, of course, there are many investment newspapers and magazines to subscribe to, and hundreds of investment newsletters.

The proliferation of investment hotline numbers is another rich source of write-offs, and here I speak from personal experience. My husband, a senior options strategist and adviser, calls five hotline numbers every weekday morning to hear the gurus' latest opinions. The cost? Nearly $20 a day, $5,000 a year.

Financial advisers will find many clients through the country-club circuit, and their membership and entertainment expenses here can generate substantial write-offs. See p. 240 for details.

FLORISTS

Successful florists who want to be even more successful should plan to travel to see some of the world's great gardens in the United States and Europe. Often horticultural organizations sponsor such tours, in conjunction with flower-arranging classes. Photographs, notebooks, and sketchbooks are important records to keep, in the statistically unlikely event that the IRS audits your return. If you clearly state the purpose of your business trip and attach a tour brochure, you'll probably answer any IRS questions before they get asked.

Florists, too, can gain lots of inexpensive publicity by donating floral arrangements to houses of worship or charity auctions.

HEADHUNTERS

Headhunters can exist only by being attached—almost umbilically—to the phone, fax, and computer. Their bills for these tools can be astronomical. Andrea, a San Francisco headhunter, whose day often starts at 3:00 A.M. local time in order to talk with clients in Europe, and ends at 9 P.M. talking with clients in Asia, complains of the occupational diseases of constant neck, shoulder, and back pains from being attached to the phone 18 hours a day.

Andrea has two other major sources of write-offs. Her neck, shoulders, and back can get their kinks worked out by a professional masseuse, as long as she has a doctor's note advising such treatment. And she can wine and dine clients and prospects in San Francisco's finest restaurants. How else does one woo clients, or ascertain that prospects have the right social skills for employment by Fortune 500 companies?

RETAIL STORE OWNER

Naturally, the type of retail store will determine what kind of write-offs are reasonable. In general, however, retail store owners will be able to deduct the costs of overseas and domestic buying trips, and of trips to industry shows and to merchandise centers like New York, Chicago, Dallas, and Los Angeles during market week once or twice a year.

TRAVEL AGENTS

For travel agents, all travel is a legitimate business expense. In fact, lust for travel is the basic reason that people become travel agents. The travel industry recognizes that it's important for travel agents to visit sites in order to sell them well and therefore often offers agents free or discounted trips, known as "fam" (familiarization) trips to better acquaint them with what they're selling.

Client entertainment usually takes the form of a travel agent's sending champagne, wine, or flowers to a retail customer's hotel or cruise-ship cabin. And it's deductible, of course. Corporate travel agents will spend more on wining and dining and signing large companies' accounts.

In this exciting entrepreneurial environment of the 1990s, in which over 1 million Americans per year start their own new businesses, the professions and businesses I have written about in these two chapters have barely scratched the surface. They are here simply to give you an idea of how to increase your deductions sensibly and safely while increasing your business, without fear of an IRS audit.

16

Tax Traps and How to Avoid Them

As your corporation grows and flourishes, you must become aware of IRS tax traps, created to ensnare unwary owner-employees. Fortunately, for every trap, there's at least one strategy to disarm and neutralize it and protect you and your corporation from further attacks.

Let's start with a basic overall concept designed to protect you from any IRS "fishing expeditions" and general waste of your and your accountant's valuable time. While most IRS employees are professional and courteous, there are always one or two out of hundreds who are petty bureaucrats, and these are the ones whom fate inevitably chooses to assign to your case. It's basically another corollary of Murphy's Law—like always getting in the wrong line at the bank or supermarket.

Still, just to protect you from such petty bureaucrats, I think it's useful for you to know about the official IRS Statement of Principles and to be ready to cite it—if necessary—to protect yourself from overzealous bureaucrats.

STATEMENT OF PRINCIPLES OF INTERNAL REVENUE TAX ADMINISTRATION

The function of the Internal Revenue Service is to administer the Internal Revenue Code. Tax policy for raising revenue is determined by Congress.

With this in mind, it is the duty of the Service to carry out that policy by correctly applying the laws enacted by Congress: to determine the reasonable meaning of various Code provisions in light of the Congressional purpose in enacting them; and to perform this work in a fair and impartial manner, with neither a government nor a taxpayer point of view.

At the heart of administration is interpretation of the Code. It is the responsibility of each person in the Service, charged with the duty of interpreting the law, to try to find the true meaning of the statutory provision and *not to adopt a strained construction in the belief that he is "protecting the revenue."* [italics mine] The revenue is protected only when we ascertain and apply the true meaning of the statute.

The Service also has the responsibility of applying and administering the law in a reasonable, practical manner. *Issues should only be raised by examining officers when they have merit, never arbitrarily or for trading purposes.* [italics mine] At the same time, the examining officer should never hesitate to raise a meritorious issue. It is also important that care be exercised not to raise an issue or to ask a court to adopt a position inconsistent with an established Service position.

Administration should be both reasonable and vigorous. *It should be conducted with as little delay as possible and with great courtesy and considerateness. It should never try to overreach, and should be reasonable within the bounds of law and sound administration* [italics mine] It should, however, be vigorous in requiring compliance with law and it should be relentless in its attack on unreal tax devices and fraud.

And now on to specific tax traps and how to avoid them and defend yourself against such nasty allegations.

ACCUMULATED EARNINGS TAX TRAP

Under the Economic Recovery Tax Act, your corporation is permitted to accumulate earnings of $150,000 if its principal function, according to the IRS, is "services in the field of law, health, engineering, architecture, accounting, actuarial science, performing arts, or consulting". It is permitted to accumulate earnings of $250,000 if it escapes that narrow "service corporation" classification. If your corporation exceeds those $150,000/$250,000 limits, the IRS may take the position that your company possesses cash and equivalents, like your corporate stock portfolio, that are "greatly in excess of its reasonable business needs" (IRS regulations quoted) and may impose an additional punitive tax on your corporation. It's extremely heavy: a flat 28 percent. This corporate tax is an *additional* tax on top of the normal corporate tax rates, so the *total* tax could go as high as 74 percent (46 percent corporate income tax + 28 percent accumulated earnings tax). Bad as this sounds, six years ago the situation was even grimmer; the total maximum tax was 84½ percent!

Given the potential horror and cost of being caught in the accumulated earnings trap, why would you want to expose your corporation to this kind of risk? Why not avoid any chance of this trap by paying out every dollar of corporate earnings every year as salary and bonus, pension and profit sharing?

The answer is simple. If you have no retained corporate earnings, you'll never be able to invest them to generate dividends that are 70 percent tax-free. That's too valuable a corporate benefit to lose. It makes much more sense to retain $100,000 or so in your corporation to invest for those tax-free dividends. Suppose that $100,000 was invested in a portfolio of preferred and common stocks yielding 9 percent—certainly achievable at current rates. Of the $9,000 in dividends, $6,300 would be completely tax-free; the remaining $2,700 might be taxed as low as 15 or 18 percent (only $405 or $486), for an overall net effective tax rate of only 4.5 or 5.4 percent on the total $9,000. Your corporation keeps around $8,550 out of the $9,000 in annual dividends.

Compare this with your investing $100,000 in those high-yield preferred and common stocks as an individual. The same $9,000 in dividends might be taxed as high as 33 percent. You might wind up giving the IRS $3,000 and keeping only $6,000—only around 70 percent of the $8,550 your corporation would keep.

And that's the tax savings for only one year. Obviously, then, it makes good sense not only to retain earnings in your corporation for investments that generate 70 percent tax-free dividends, but also to concentrate the highest-yielding portion of your stock portfolio (generally preferred and utility stocks) under your "corporate hat" in order to obtain the greatest tax-free dividends. Your individual holdings should *not* consist of high-yield stocks, whose dividends would be taxed unfavorably to you, the high-bracket stockholder. Instead, you, as an individual, should own low-yielding growth stocks,, which generate capital gains that may be taxed more favorably in the future, as they once were several years ago. In this way, your total overall portfolio is balanced between income and growth, with the corporate section of the portfolio deriving its major benefit from its emphasis on dividend income, rather than capital gains.

So that's why you want to retain as much money as possible within your corporation, without skating close to the edge of the $150,000/$250,000 accumulated earnings limit.

Now that you know all about the accumulated earnings trap, here are four strategies to sidestep it. First and generally easiest, you can justify the accumulation of any amount of retained earnings by showing "specific, definite, and feasible plans" (IRS regulations quoted) for the use of that accumulated money. You want to show the IRS that you have a *real plan for expansion*. In this context, it's useful to know what the IRS accepts as reasonable and what it considers unreasonable:

IRS REGULATIONS

§1.537–2. **Grounds for accumulation of earnings and profits**—(a) *In general.* Whether a particular ground or grounds for the accumulation of earnings and profits indicate that the earnings and profits have been accumulated for the reasonable needs of the business or beyond such needs if dependent upon the particular circumstances of the case. Listed below in paragraphs (b) and (c) of this section are some of the grounds which may be used as guides under ordinary circumstances.

(b) *Reasonable accumulation of earnings and profits.* Although the following grounds are not exclusive, one or more of such grounds, if supported by sufficient facts, may indicate that the earnings and profits of a corporation are being accumulated for the reasonable needs of the business provided the general requirements . . . are satisfied:

(1) To provide for bona fide expansion of business or replacement of plant;

(2) To acquire a business enterprise through purchasing stock or assets;

(3) To provide for the retirement of bona fide indebtedness created in connection with the trade or business, such as the establishment of a sinking fund for the purpose of retiring bonds issued by the corporation in accordance with contract obligations incurred on issue;

(4) To provide necessary working capital for the business, such as for the procurement of inventories; or

(5) To provide for investments or loans to suppliers or customers if necessary in order to maintain the business of the corporation.

(c) *Unreasonable accumulations of earnings and profits.* Although the following purposes are not exclusive, accumulations of earnings and profits to meet any one of such objectives may indicate that the earnings and profits of a corporation are being accumulated beyond the reasonable needs of the business:

(1) Loans to shareholders, or the expenditure of funds of the corporation for the personal benefit of the shareholders;

(2) Loans having no reasonable relation to the conduct of the business made to relatives or friends of shareholders, or to other persons;

(3) Loans made to another corporation, the business of which is not that of the taxpayer corporation, if the capital stock of such other corporation is owned, directly or indirectly, by the shareholder or shareholders of the taxpayer corporation and such shareholder or shareholders are in control of both corporations;

(4) Investments in properties, or securities which are unrelated to the activities of the business of the taxpayer corporation; or

(5) Retention of earnings and profits to provide against unrealistic hazards.

It's also important that, according to Regulation §1.537–3(a), the business of your corporation is construed very loosely:

§1.537–3. **Business of the corporation.**—(a) The business of a corporation is *not merely that which it has previously carried on but includes, in general, any line of business which it may undertake.* [italics mine]

Also in your favor, the Tax Court has ruled that the IRS must *prove* that any corporation's tax avoidance was an unreasonable accumulation of earnings and profits. *The burden of proof is on the IRS.*

As a second strategy to avoid the accumulated earnings trap, you can have your corporation declare a dividend, which would be paid out of, and which would therefore reduce, your corporation's accumulated earnings. Granted, it's Hobson's choice for you. Either you pay yourself a dividend, or you pay the accumulated earnings tax. Obviously, you're penalized less by paying the dividend.

However, a third strategy—raising your salary and/or paying yourself a bonus—can be even more advantageous because a corporation does not receive a deduction for paying out dividends, but it does for paying salary or bonus. The advantage of paying a bonus is its flexibility (one year yes, one year no, and in varying amounts); a bonus is much less concrete and attackable by the IRS than a wildly swinging salary would be.

Do not choose a bonus over a salary increase *unless* your pension and profit-sharing plans use total compensation (salary + bonus) as a base, rather than straight salary. Otherwise, you won't be able to increase your pension and profit-sharing contributions and thus lower your taxable corporate income, income taxes, and reduce retained earnings.

In fact, since there are only advantages to one-person and husband-and-wife corporations using total

compensation—rather than salary—as a base for
determining pension and profit-sharing contributions,
make sure that *your* pension and profit-sharing plans
are structured this way.

As a fourth alternative to the accumulated earnings trap, you can have
your corporation elect Subchapter S status. The mechanics and advantages of this strategy are covered completely in Chapter 2.

REASONABLE COMPENSATION TRAP

As tax traps go, the reasonable compensation trap is a fairly simple
one for entrepreneurs and professionals to finesse. You want to call that
money your corporation pays you a salary or a bonus so that your pension
and profit-sharing plans can increase their contributions and lower their
corporate income taxes. The IRS, on the other hand, would like to argue
that the money your corporation pays you in excess of some vague
number is really a dividend. That way, the IRS can tax it twice: once at the
corporate level and once as personal income to you.

In general, if you pay yourself less than $120,000 a year in salary, the
IRS won't come after you, claiming that you're receiving unreasonable
compensation; it has bigger fish to fry. Taking less than $120,000 in salary
is actually the best strategy on several counts because there are other IRS-approved methods of increasing the disposable-income value of that salary:

- Medical, life, and disability insurance paid by your
  corporation
- Substantial pension and profit-sharing programs,
  which alleviate the burden of your own funding of
  your retirement
- Putting family members on the corporate payroll to
  shift income from high-bracket to low-bracket
  taxpayers—a strategy that also permits extending
  the benefits of pension, profit sharing, and IRAs to
  them (see Chapter 18 for details).
- Renting part of your home or apartment to your
  corporation, which can give you generous income
  without your paying heavy taxes because the rent
  you receive is offset by depreciation and other
  write-offs
- Allowances for corporate entertainment and travel,
  as long as you play by the rules

In fact, as any accountant or financial planner will tell you, savvy planning in this area can let you live quite well on a salary of $30,000—$40,000 a year. And, as I've indicated often before, my favorite strategy split between salary and retained corporate earnings leans toward a low-but-comfortable salary, and as much money as practicable (up to $40,000 or so per year *net income*) retained by the corporation. The reason is twofold: On the first $50,000 of taxable income, corporate income-tax rates are lower than personal income-tax rates on the federal level and in many states, and your corporation receives dividends that are 70 percent tax-free. *The more money you can set aside, accumulate in your corporation, and invest, within the limits mentioned above, the greater tax shelter your corporation can provide you. And it's virtually the only tax shelter left that is acceptable to the IRS.*

Whatever salary you choose to pay yourself, a time log is the simplest and easiest way to justify the reasonableness of your salary against any IRS claim that the amount is unreasonable. A time log can prove clearly not only that you spend many, many hours a week devoted to practicing your profession, craft, or business, and therefore have more than earned your chosen salary, but also can be used to document business-related expenses. For example, if your time log can show that you spent considerable time developing new clients or customers, the IRS couldn't possibly object to your taking those valuable customers or clients to lunch or dinner now and then.

SAMPLE TIME LOG FOR A BUSINESS/FINANCIAL ADVISER

This time log is just what the "accounting doctor" ordered. Exhaustive detail? Certainly! But IRS-proof? Absolutely!

Since this adviser works around 70 hours a week, virtually any salary chosen can be justified as reasonable.

You can also prove that your salary is not unreasonably high by collecting a little data on comparable salaries in your field. Clip some help-wanted ads in your city's newspaper, the *Wall Street Journal,* and professional magazines every six months or so. Use these ads in conjunction with your time log to demonstrate that if someone practicing your profession or business around 40–50 hours a week is worth $X, you, who work 60–70 hours a week, are certainly not paying yourself unreasonably at $1.5X–$2X. (It's only when you get greedy and try to get away with paying yourself $5X–$10X that the IRS will make an example of you.)

You'd keep running totals of mileage and expenses for the week, month, and year, of course.

Sunday
2/10/91

9:00–11:30	Review last week's contacts and plan follow-up presentations to made in next two weeks	
11:30–12:00	Drive to Le Chic Country Club; brunch with John Banker	20 mi.
12:00– 2:00	Brunch—John Banker—local bank manager—re his supplying leads to new business executives & professionals in area	$60.00
2:00– 2:30	Drive back from Le Chic Country Club	20 mi.
		40 mi. $60.00

Monday
2/11/91

7:30– 8:30	Read & clip relevant articles from *Wall Street Journal, NY Times, Barron's* & other financial magazines	
8:30–10:00	Write presentation to Client B & take to secretarial service	
10:00–10:30	Drive to secretarial service & park car Parking lot	10 mi. $ 6.75
10:30–11:30	Instruct secretary on typing format, etc., & return to office	10 mi.
11:30–12:00	Return all phone calls	
12:00– 2:00	Review presentation to Client A; lunch at desk	
2:00– 2:30	Return & make phone calls	
2:30– 3:00	Drive to Client A Parking lot	15 mi. $ 8.50
3:00– 5:00	Make presentation to Client A	
5:00– 5:30	Drive to secretarial service Parking lot	15 mi. 7.50
5:30– 6:30	Pick up presentation to Client B and get Xeroxed and put in binders Xeroxing and binders	13.50
6:30– 7:00	Return to office	10 mi.
7:00– 8:00	Pick up phone messages from answering service; go through mail & answer, prepare for secretarial service	
		60 mi. $36.25

Let's say that Tuesday–Friday are essentially the same.

Saturday
2/16/91

9:00–10:00	Prepare bills and checks for P/T bookkeeper	
10:00–10:30	Drive to Le Chic Country Club	20 mi.
10:30– 2:30	Racquetball date with Client A, followed by brunch & signing one-year contract	$68.00
2:30– 3:00	Drive back to office	20 mi.
3:00– 3:30	Review bookkeeper's work	
		40 mi. $68.00

Another strategy for proving that your salary is not unreasonable lies in the timing of its payment. This is not practicable for everyone, but if you can accept its discipline, you can delay paying withholding and Social Security taxes until the end of your calendar or fiscal year and can keep that money in your corporate money-market account, earning interest until the last minute.

If you can manage to live on other money and pay yourself only once a year, you benefit by cutting about 90 percent from your bookkeeping time. No more weekly or monthly salary checks and calculating all the withholding and Social Security taxes. No more monthly or more frequent remittances to federal and state tax collectors on those complicated depositary forms. Your simplified tax reporting will now consist of filling out three out of four IRS and state quarterly reports with the words "NONE PAID" for salary and $0 on all the appropriate lines. Time expended: five minutes—max.

Now let's say you're on a calendar year. By December 10 you have a pretty accurate idea of how much more income your corporation will receive by year-end, how much more it will pay out by then, and what its projected bottom line will be. Say it's estimated at $40,000. You run through a few quick pencil-and-paper calculations like the ones shown below:

Corporate income	$40,000	$40,000	$40,000	$40,000
– Salary	– 20,000	– 24,000	– 28,000	– 32,000
	20,000	16,000	12,000	8,000
– 25 percent pension and profit-sharing contributions	– 5,000	– 6,000	– 7,000	– 8,000
Net corporate income	$15,000	$10,000	$ 5,000	$ 0

Then evaluate them on their comparative advantages and disadvantages. You might rank the fourth choice as worst because it leaves your corporation no net income and puts you, as an individual taxpayer, in a higher tax bracket than do the other alternatives. Or, you might see it as the most desirable choice because you need all the income you can get for your child's college tuition and because your corporation, which is approaching the $150,000/$250,000 accumulated earnings limit, would benefit from not receiving any additional corporate income this year. You might prefer the first alternative because your corporation is just starting to grow and needs to retain as much net corporate income as possible to ensure continuing growth without the need for external financing at a time when interest rates might be 18–20 percent.

Because you have waited to pay yourself until the end of the year, when you could determine accurately how much money your corporation actually earned, you clearly have tied your salary to corporate earnings. Therefore, as far as the IRS is concerned, your salary is not unreasonable.

Interestingly enough, the IRS doesn't seem to care as much whether the salary you pay yourself is unreasonably *low,* as long as you don't try to pay yourself $5,000 a year, year after year. It *does* want to make sure that you're not shirking payment of Social Security taxes, but it won't hunt you down for paying yourself $15,000 or $20,000 a year in salary—especially in the early years—rather than $30,000 or $40,000. Therefore, your only worry is about socking too much money away in your corporation and having it grow too quickly, which might risk triggering the accumulated earnings tax.

CORPORATE LENDER TRAP

People who set up one-person corporations can fall into a big but understandable trap. It's very easy for them to regard their corporation as an extension of themselves, rather than as a separate legal entity, so they often unthinkingly dip into the corporation's funds whenever they run short of cash. This tapping of the "corporate wallet," as it's called, is extremely dangerous because it can lay you open to an IRS charge that your corporation is a sham: Your casual behavior in taking money from your corporation whenever you like has demonstrated that there is no true legal wall between you and your corporation.

Of course, you can still borrow money from your corporation. Just observe these precautions and formalities. Prepare a written note stating the amount you are borrowing, the repayment date, and a repayment schedule if you plan to pay off the loan in installments. It's best to have the loan mature in a year or less—you can always roll it over. The IRS doesn't like to see five-year loans to officer-stockholders on your corporation's books.

Changes in the deductibility of interest—outside of mortgage interest, it's not deductible anymore—and the imputed-income rules call for a little strategy with your calculator. The imputed-income rules state that if you receive an interest-free loan from your corporation, you are receiving a taxable fringe benefit on which you owe income tax. For example, if you borrowed $10,000 from your corporation interest-free, and interest rates were 12 percent, you would have imputed income of $1,200 (the interest that you ordinarily would have paid on the loan). If you are in the 33 percent federal tax bracket, you would have to pay $396 in federal income taxes because you received that $10,000 tax-free loan from your corporation.

Obviously, you are still better off paying the IRS $396 in additional taxes than paying a lender $1,200 in nondeductible interest.

If you choose to pay your corporation $1,200 in interest, instead of accepting a tax-free loan, you won't be socked $396 as tax on imputed income. But your corporation will have to pay tax on the $1,200 interest it has earned.

Is this a better strategy than the interest-free loan? Possibly, if your corporation is in the 15 percent bracket and will pay only $180 in federal income taxes on the interest it has received. (Remember that you're really transferring that $1,200 from your personal pocket to your corporate pocket; but on a near-term basis, you'll still be paying out $1,200—even if it's to your own corporation.)

If your corporation is in the 25 percent bracket, it will be paying $300 in federal income taxes, and it's much less of a good deal. If your corporation is in the maximum 34 percent bracket, it's a bad deal. You'll pay your corporation $1,200 in loan interest, and it will pay the IRS $408 in taxes on the interest. *You're much better off taking the interest-free loan and paying $396 to the IRS yourself.*

Last but not least, make sure that your certificate of incorporation stipulates that your corporation can lend you money. If it doesn't, a brief statement of the plan—with as general wording as possible—and a corporate resolution, approved at a special meeting of your corporation, will serve the purpose. Here's the format to use:

[NAME OF YOUR CORPORATION] LOANS TO STOCKHOLDERS PLAN

ARTICLE I—Benefits
The Corporation is empowered to lend money to all eligible stockholders.

ARTICLE II—Eligibility
All corporate officers employed on a full-time basis at the date of inception of this Plan who own 50 percent or more of the outstanding shares of this Corporation are eligible stockholders under this Plan.

ARTICLE III—Limitations
The Corporation shall not lend any eligible stockholder more than $_____ in any fiscal year.

All loans must be repaid within _____.

Interest charged will be based upon [some rate tied to the prime rate is always a good choice.]

MINUTES OF SPECIAL MEETING OF BOARD OF DIRECTORS
OF
[NAME OF YOUR CORPORATION]

A special meeting of the board of directors of [name of your corporation] was held on [date] at [time] at [address where meeting was held].

All of the directors being present, the meeting was called to order by the chairman. The chairman advised that the meeting was called to approve and adopt a loans to stockholders plan. A copy of the plan was presented to those present and upon motion duly made, seconded, and unanimously carried, it was

> RESOLVED, that the "Loans to Stockholders Plan" presented to the meeting is hereby approved and adopted, that a copy of the Plan shall be appended to these minutes, and that the proper officers of the corporation are hereby authorized to take whatever action is necessary to implement that Plan, and it is further
> RESOLVED, that the signing of these minutes by the directors shall constitute full ratification thereof and waiver of notice of the meeting by the signatories.

There being no further business to come before the meeting, upon motion duly made, seconded, and unanimously carried, the meeting was adjourned.

_____
Secretary

_____   _____
Director   Director

BAD-DEBT TRAP

Bad debts are actually more of a problem than a trap. The key is determining when a debt becomes bad.

Your corporation's treatment of a bad debt depends on whether it's on a cash basis or an accrual basis. If your corporation is on a cash basis, you can write off only the amount it actually has lost—not the amount of money it is owed. John is a dentist who has made a bridge for which he charges $1,000. His cost in materials and lab charges is $200. The patient absconds with his bridge. John's real loss is only $200—the amount he's actually spent—so that's all his professional corporation is permitted to write off.

Now let's look at the same case, only this time John's professional corporation is on an accrual basis. Since he had to count the $1,000 as income as soon as his corporation was entitled to receive it, his corporation is entitled to deduct the entire $1,000. Again, the equation is in equilibrium and nets out to $0.

Since the Tax Reform Act of 1986, the IRS no longer permits the use of the reserve method of writing off bad debts. Only those receivables which actually become worthless during the tax year and are specifically written off the books are deductible.

Bad business loans are treated similarly to bad debts. With loans, it's even more crucial to keep meticulous records than it is with merchandise or services, for which you'd be able to show a file of bills and correspondence. Bad loans, like bad debts, are deductible in the year in which they become worthless. You'll need proof of the loan itself, proof that you tried to collect, and proof that the loan indeed has become worthless.

AT-RISK TRAP

The at-risk rules are applied generally to prevent tax-shelter abuses. They limit the amount of money you may write off to the amount for which you are actually liable and will have to pay at some point in the future— hence the term "at risk." However, because of their loose wording, the at-risk rules sometimes entrap people who might not think they fall within the scope of tax-shelter statutes—like the shareholders of a closely held corporation.

In order to determine whether your corporation has a loss under at-risk rules and its limitations, if any, use IRS Form 6198, "At-Risk Limitations," shown on the next page. For most one-person corporations, this is a very simple calculation. As you can see from lines 7 and 9 (or 12 and 14), you determine the at-risk amount at the end of the year. Therefore, the easiest way to get around an at-risk limitation, if it appears to be developing, is to put up some more cash or recourse debt at the end of the year.

These are some of the most common tax traps. With a little judicious planning, you should be able to avoid them all.

Form **6198**

At-Risk Limitations

► Attach to your tax return.
► See separate instructions.

Department of the Treasury
Internal Revenue Service

OMB No. 1545-0712

1989

Attachment
Sequence No. **31**

Name(s) as shown on return: WONDERFUL COMPANY, INC.

Identifying Number: 00-0000000

Description of activity: GRAPHIC DESIGN

Part I Current Year Profit (Loss) From the Activity, Including Prior Year Nondeductible Amounts. See Instructions. (Enter losses in parentheses.)

1 Ordinary income (loss) from the activity. See Instructions	1	(3,000 -)
2 Gain (loss) from the sale or other disposition of assets used in the activity (or your interests in the activity) that you will be initially reporting on:		
a Schedule D	2a	—
b Form 4797	2b	—
c Other form or schedule	2c	—
3 Other income or gains from the activity from Schedule K-1 of Form 1065 or Form 1120S, whichever applies, that were not included above on lines 1 through 2c	3	—
4 Other deductions or losses from the activity, including investment interest expense, that were not used in figuring amounts on lines 1 through 3	4 (	—)
5 Current year profit (loss) from the activity. Combine lines 1 through 4. See Instructions before completing the rest of this form	5	(3,000 -)

Part II Simplified Computation of Amount At Risk (See Instructions for who may use this part.)

6 Adjusted basis (as defined in section 1011) in the activity (or adjusted basis of interest in the activity) on the first day of the tax year. Do not enter less than zero	6	3,000 —
7 Increases for the tax year	7	1,500 —
8 Add lines 6 and 7	8	4,500 —
9 Decreases for the tax year	9	500 —
10 Amount at risk. Subtract line 9 from line 8 and enter result here ► .... Also enter the result in the entry space for line 10. However, if the result is less than zero, enter zero in the entry space for line 10 and see **Pub. 925** for information on the recapture rules. **Note:** You may want to use Part III to see which computation (Part II or III) gives you the larger amount at risk. Enter the larger amount (but not less than zero) on line 20, Part IV	10	4,000 —

Part III Detailed Computation of Amount At Risk (If you completed Part III of Form 6198 for 1988, see Instructions for Part III before completing this part for 1989.)

11 Investment in the activity (or investment in interest in the activity) at effective date. Do not enter less than zero	11	
12 Increases at effective date	12	
13 Add lines 11 and 12	13	
14 Decreases at effective date	14	
15 Amount at risk (check box that applies):		
a ☐ At effective date. Subtract line 14 from line 13. Do not enter less than zero.		
b ☐ From 1988 Form 6198, line 19. (Do not enter the amount from line 10 of the 1988 form.)	15	
16 Increases since (check box that applies):		
a ☐ Effective date		
b ☐ The end of your 1988 tax year	16	
17 Add lines 15 and 16	17	
18 Decreases since (check box that applies):		
a ☐ Effective date		
b ☐ The end of your 1988 tax year	18	
19 Amount at risk. Subtract line 18 from line 17 and enter result here ► .... Also enter the result in the entry space for line 19. However, if the result is less than zero, enter zero in the entry space for line 19 and see **Pub. 925** for information on the recapture rules. Also enter on line 20 if you are not using the amount from Part II	19	

Part IV Deductible Loss

20 Amount at risk from line 10 or 19, whichever is larger. Do not enter less than zero	20	4,000 —
Note: If line 20 is zero, enter zero on line 21. You do not have a deductible loss this year.		
21 **Deductible loss.** Enter the smaller of the loss on line 5 or the amount on line 20. See the Instructions for where to report any deductible loss and any carryover	21 (	3,000 —)

Note: If this loss is from a passive activity, get **Form 8582,** Passive Activity Loss Limitations, or **Form 8810,** Corporate Passive Activity Loss and Credit Limitations, to see if the loss is allowed under the passive activity rules. If part of the loss is subject to the passive activity loss rules and part of it is not, allocate the loss and take the ratable portion attributable to the passive activity loss rules to Form 8582 or Form 8810, whichever applies.

For Paperwork Reduction Act Notice, see page 1 of Instructions for Form 6198

Form **6198** (1989)

17

How to Avoid the Personal Service Corporation and Personal Holding Company Traps

Two tax traps are so important that they deserve their own chapter: the personal service corporation trap and the personal holding company trap. Since most one- or two-person corporations deal in services, let's defuse that trap first.

THE PERSONAL SERVICE CORPORATION TRAP

According to the Internal Revenue Code, a *personal service corporation* is a corporation whose principal activity is the performance of personal services that are performed substantially by *employee-owners,* defined as any employee who owns more than 10 percent of the outstanding stock of the corporation. Clearly, all professional corporations, all "perilous profession" corporations—which overlap, but are not identical to professional corporations—and, in fact, virtually all one- or two-person corporations are considered to be personal service corporations.

Under Treasury Regulation §1.269A-1, the IRS is permitted to "reallocate income and tax benefits between personal service corporations and their employee-owners, if:

261

(1) Substantially all of the services of the personal service corporation are performed for or on behalf of one other entity, and
(2) The principal purpose for which the corporation was formed or availed of is the evasion or avoidance of Federal income tax. Such purpose is evidenced when use of the corporation either reduces the income of any employee-owner, or secures for any employee-owner one or more tax benefits which would not otherwise be available."

It's easy to see that these rules were created because many professionals were incorporating and having their corporations work exclusively for one employer or enter into a professional partnership. In effect, they were substituting their professional corporations for themselves as employees, such as a pathologist who incorporates but works exclusively for one hospital.

There are two major strategies for skirting the professional service corporation trap successfully. Since, in order for the IRS to win its reallocation bid, it has to prove *both* the above points, all you need to is counter *either* claim. The first is usually easier: diversify your client list. There's an excellent business reason for this strategy, too. You're more secure with a broader client base than with only one client. If that one client should leave, your corporate income for the year could drop precipitously.

Liability protection is your answer to the second IRS claim. Owner-employees of general corporations have it easier here because incorporation, virtually by definition, insulates them from personal liability. For professional-corporation owner-employees, using this tack is a bit more difficult because professional-corporation shareholders may still retain unlimited personal liability for their own negligence.

Accordingly, professional-corporation owner-employees should use the multiple-client strategy as a defense against an IRS attempt to reallocate their corporate income. General-corporation owner-employees can use either the multiple-client strategy or the limited-liability strategy.

Actually, the possibility of reallocation of income from your corporation to yourself, as an individual, is no longer the threat it was several years ago, when the maximum individual federal income-tax rate was 50 percent. Then the IRS could really profit from reallocating virtually all your income from a corporate 15, 25, or 34 percent bracket to your individual 50 percent bracket. Now that your maximum effective individual tax bracket has dropped to 33 percent, the IRS would have to reallocate corporate income only under $75,000 to profit from the differential in tax brackets. Above $75,000, the corporate rate is 1 percent higher than the individual rate, so reallocation is counterproductive.

Furthermore, most tax professionals feel that the one- or two-person corporation is generally unlikely to be audited by the IRS—much less likely, in fact, than a sole proprietorship. The only exception is flagrant abuse of the corporate structure—e.g., gross income of $100,000, salary of $20,000, and "creative fringe benefits" of $60,000. As long as you stay on the conservative side of creativity, the probability of your corporation's facing an IRS audit is quite low.

THE PERSONAL HOLDING COMPANY TRAP

Somewhat similar to the personal service corporation trap is the personal holding company trap. The concept of the personal holding company—the "incorporated pocketbook"—has been in existence for half a century, so there are many well-honed strategies for avoiding this common and expensive trap.

Before the personal holding company was targeted by the IRS, wealthy people could turn their stock portfolios over to their newly formed corporations, which benefited from the dividend exclusion which was then 85 percent. Dividend income of $100,000, fully taxable to those individuals, could be transformed into taxable corporate income of only $15,000. Obviously, these corporations performed no real work; they were a tax sham, and accordingly were taxed punitively.

Since the Internal Revenue Code defines a personal holding company as any corporation where at least 60 percent of adjusted ordinary gross income is considered "personal holding company income" and where, in the last half of the year, "more than 50 percent of its outstanding stock is owned, directly or indirectly, by or for not more than five individuals," the key is understanding the ins and outs of that personal holding company income.

PERSONAL HOLDING COMPANY INCOME

At first glance, the five categories of personal holding company income can make you think that all income, unless earned for performing a specific service, falls into that highly taxed category. *Fortunately, that's not true.* Each category is encrusted with exceptions whose net effect is to protect you if that income is *actually earned.* For example, rents are personal holding company income, *unless* they constitute 50 percent or more of your corporation's adjusted ordinary gross income—in which case your corporation is probably in the real estate business. Copyright royalties are personal holding company income, *unless* the owner-employee is the creator of the copyrighted work, as I am in my own corporation. Then the royalties are considered ordinary earned income.

Here are the categories, with their exceptions in abbreviated form. If you think that any are especially applicable to you, consult a tax professional to learn all the ramifications. This is one area where you can't afford to make a mistake.

(1) DIVIDENDS, ETC.—Dividends, interest, royalties (other than mineral, oil, or gas royalties or copyright royalties), and annuities . . .

(2) RENTS—The adjusted income from rents; except that such adjusted income shall not be included if—

(A) such adjusted income constitutes 50 percent or more of the adjusted ordinary gross income . . .

(3) MINERAL, OIL, AND GAS ROYALTIES—The adjusted income from mineral, oil, and gas royalties; except that such adjusted income shall not be included if—

(A) such adjusted income constitutes 50 percent or more of the adjusted ordinary gross income . . .

(4) COPYRIGHT ROYALTIES—Copyright royalties; except that copyright royalties shall not be included if—

(A) such royalties . . . constitute 50 percent or more of the ordinary gross income . . .

(5) PRODUCED FILM RENTS—

(A) Produced film rents; except that such rents shall not be included if such rents constitute 50 percent or more of the ordinary gross income . . .

LIKELY VICTIMS: HOW TO AVOID THE TRAP

Most owner-employees don't have to worry much because the 60 percent passive-income rule is pretty generous. It means that your corporation can receive over half its income from interest and dividends—59 percent, in fact. Still, there are two broad classes of owner-employees who might be vulnerable to the personal holding company trap, plus a third Jack-of-all-trades group.

Authors and artists who create and sell one major work every two or three years typify one group. An author or artist with an established $150,000 stock portfolio yielding 10 percent might have a three-year stream of corporate income like this:

	Earned Income	Dividend Income	Total Income	Dividends as Percent of Total (PHC = 60%)
Year 1	$ 0	$15,000	$ 15,000	100%
Year 2	5,000	15,000	20,000	75
Year 3	100,000	15,000	115,000	13

Years 1 and 2 are problems because the dividend income is 100 percent of the total income the first year and 75 percent the second year. Unless something is done, that author or artist will be caught in a personal holding company trap.

Women corporate owners who take a fairly long maternity leave are the second group of potential victims. It's easy to see how that same $15,000 annual dividend income, which was never a problem when a woman worked full-time for her successful one-person corporation, suddenly rises to a significant percentage of her annual corporate income because she's taken six or eight months off and corporate earned income has dropped to only $2,000 or $3,000 a month. Unless that woman moves decisively before the third or fourth quarter of any problem year, she will be caught in a personal holding company trap.

Actually, avoiding the personal holding company trap is fairly simple for these creative artists and executive mothers, although it requires a little advance planning. Since dividend income is relatively predictable and is generally paid to shareholders every quarter, you can assume that 25 percent of the dividend income is paid every three months. (Bond income is paid semiannually.) In the case of Year 2, above, the shareholder's corporation receives $3,750 every quarter. In order to reduce the personal holding company percentage to an acceptable and safe 59 percent or less, either the dividend and interest income must be decreased, the earned income must be increased, or both. If the owner-shareholder sells the stock or bond that produces that $3,750 income after the second quarterly payment and buys municipal bonds, whose income does not count in personal holding company calculations, he or she will have $7,500 passive (unearned) income, a personal holding company figure of 60 percent. Additional *earned* income of *only $200* in sales or fees will reduce that percentage further to a safe and acceptable 59 percent.

Structuring your corporation's investment portfolio so that some interest and dividends are received every month, rather than all received in the March-June-September-December cycle, increases your flexibility. In many cases, a shift as great as from high-dividend stocks to municipal bonds is not necessary. It may suffice (and make more sense) to sell only one or two of those high-yield stocks and buy low- or no-dividend aggressive growth stocks to tilt the personal holding company percentage downward.

At the beginning of the next year, when high corporate interest and dividend income no longer poses a personal holding company threat, the owner-shareholder sells the municipal bonds or growth stocks and repurchases the high-yield securities. Ideally, forecasting earned income and balancing it with high-yielding stocks whose dividends are 70 percent tax-free should permit sophisticated owner-shareholders to receive around 55 percent in dividend income every year—a very profitable percentage that is still too low to trigger the personal holding company trap.

The jack-of-all-trades problem is slightly more difficult to solve, for all that it is self-induced. In this case, owner-shareholders get into hot water by doing "a little of this and a little of that," all under a single corporate umbrella. Thus, their corporation may dabble in real estate, but the rental operation produces, say, only 35 percent of their corporation's income, rather than the 50 percent that would exclude it from personal holding company income. Their corporation has some oil and gas interests that produce 20 percent of their corporate income, rather than the 50 percent that would exclude it from personal holding company income. Their corporation owns stocks and bonds that produce 10 percent of their corporate income. You guessed it: Their corporation is a personal holding company.

There are two basic solutions for this self-created problem. Owner-shareholders should either concentrate their efforts within one corporate structure so that their income from one area, like real estate, is high enough to exclude it from personal holding calculations; or, if they are determined to empire-build in many areas, they should form a corporation for each activity so that their personal holding company income from each area is *calculated and excluded separately*. This is one example where the whole's being greater than the sum of its parts works against you. However, by electing to file as a "consolidated group," affiliated corporations can offset losses against gains.

Like other tax traps, the personal service corporation and personal holding company traps are avoidable. Once you know that the traps are there and what actions trigger them, you'll know how to maneuver around them and often how to manipulate them to your own corporate advantage.

18

How to Profit from Putting Your Relatives on the Payroll

In this chapter, I'll discuss how men and women can put their wives, husbands, children, and parents on the corporate payroll—all very profitably.

There are two major reasons to put your relatives on the corporate payroll: business reasons and tax reasons. Of these, business reasons are by far the more important for hiring your spouse and your children. Even if you have a professional corporation that your spouse may not be permitted to continue after your death, his or her knowledge of its workings and value may still be critical in the future. Of course, if you have a general business corporation, which you want your spouse to be able to step in and run should you become ill, his or her knowledge of its functioning is even more important.

From another standpoint, your children's learning your business or knowing about your profession is important, too. Going to daddy's or mommy's office is great fun; but behind that, at some point, should come the knowledge that this is what daddy or mommy does to earn a living. Without meaning to sound like a drudge or a judge, I believe that children should learn the value of work and the value of money at an early age. These are key lessons for their future.

WHAT YOUR SPOUSE CAN DO

Businesses, professions, marriages, and working styles all differ. Therefore, this section discusses the most extensive and ideal job description. Use as much of it as you can and are comfortable with.

One major group of tasks can be classified as "support system": receptionist, clerical, secretarial. There are some basic advantages to using your spouse rather than outside help:

> • You can arrange more flexible hours.
> • You won't have to pay for help you don't need, as with some temporaries or part-timers, whom you may have to pay on a standby basis.

Far more important, your spouse becomes familiar—almost by osmosis—with the workings of your business and profession. And he or she is nearly always more motivated than an outside employee.

The second classification can be called "management trainee" or "partner." If your spouse is willing to work with you, it can be an ideal setup. Both of you are inspired to work extra hard to build something together. The success of some "mom-and-pop" ventures is legendary. This job description is vague, of necessity, but would include tasks like dealing with clients, research, preparation of reports, purchasing, scheduling, sales, and other relevant work.

WHAT YOUR CHILDREN CAN DO

Children love to work, to accomplish something successfully. And children are more persistent and capable—at younger ages—than you might think. Just watch a five-year-old take all afternoon to build a castle out of Lego blocks.

My oldest friend put his three children—now in their twenties—to work when they were very young. "When they were little—around four years old—they separated invoices into file copies by color, stuffed bills into window envelopes, and stamped and sealed them. When they were six or seven, they could do some simple filing. When they were nine or ten, they wrapped packages, answered the phone, and entered orders in the books. By the time my kids were twelve or thirteen, they were making out checks to vendors for $20,000. Of course, I still signed them. Did they understand what they were doing, and were they learning the business? You bet!" He smiles. "I have no worries about one or all of them taking over when the time comes."

One little girl, the daughter of a lawyer, started taking telephone messages at home for her father when she was seven. This little job taught her business telephone manners, accuracy, and something about her father's work. She also loved helping her father and earning her own pocket money, rather than having to ask her parents. She felt very important and capable.

Robert, an art dealer, has been taking his son, Jesse, to auctions and museums since he was four years old. At the age of eight, Jesse had advanced to bidding at auctions, under his father's instructions. Now Jesse is 14, and all the dealers and auction houses know Jesse and accept his bids. Jesse is learning his father's business at an extremely early age, is starting to build up his own inventory, and is possibly one of the youngest "management trainees" on record. He spends his salary "buying more pictures—or toys."

Please don't feel that putting your kids to work is slave labor. Experts like Montessori and Piaget have found that children love to work—often at the same tasks as their parents—and that it gives them very strong feelings of self-worth.

Working for money is even more valuable. It teaches children many important lessons about how to use money, saving versus spending (delayed versus immediate gratification), buying wisely, and budgeting.

WHAT YOUR PARENTS CAN DO

Unlike hiring your wife and children, where business advantages overshadow tax advantages, juicy as they are, the primary reason to hire your parents is the tax benefits you will derive.

Let's assume that your parents are retired and are over the age of 72, so that their Social Security income is not reduced by earned income. Let's also assume that you are contributing $12,000 a year to their support. That $12,000 is not tax deductible, although you might be able to claim your parents as dependents if you provided more than half their support. If you are in the 33 percent bracket, the $4,000 for your parents' exemptions would be worth $1,333 in cash; you'd be out-of-pocket $10,667. In fact, you would have to earn $18,000 in pretax dollars to give your parents that $12,000; or $16,000 to give them the $10,667.

Therefore, if at all feasible, consider having your parents work for you. Perhaps your father could work as a consultant to your corporation—after all, you might have inherited or developed the business from him. (It's okay for your corporation to hire a consultant; just don't call yourself one.)

Here's another idea: He could simply be a nonspecific "elder statesman" type of adviser, based on the fact that he has experienced more business and economic cycles than you have and that you can benefit from that experience. If you pay your father $1,000 a month as an independent contractor, that's $12,000—the amount of your contribution to your parents' support. *The difference is that your corporation is paying the $12,000 out of pretax income; you are not paying it with your hard-earned after-tax dollars.*

Paying a parent as an independent contractor has yet other advantages. Your corporation won't have to pay Social Security, or make pension contributions.

To satisfy the IRS that a parent really and truly is acting as a consultant and independent contractor, keep detailed records in your parent's time file and in your diary. What you should aim for are diary entries that read something like this:

1/4/91	10:00–12:00	Meeting with F. Entrepreneur re: cash-forecasting plans for first quarter
1/8/91	3:00– 4:30	Conference with F. Entrepreneur re: impact of interest-rate hikes on plans for first quarter

Your mother might do some research, secretarial, or clerical work. Or, if she's knowledgeable and experienced, she, too, might function as a consultant. The key here is plausibility: for the nature of the work your parents are doing, for its actual performance, and for the reasonableness of their pay.

WHAT TO PAY YOUR SPOUSE

Obviously, how much your corporation pays your spouse depends on many factors—primarily:

- How much and what kind of work he or she is doing
- How much money your corporation has available to pay your spouse
- The impact of state and local income taxes— sometimes these systems favor two-paycheck families, sometimes they penalize them

In a sense, comparable salaries that would be paid to outside employees are really irrelevant because, if you want to pay your spouse substantially more than the going rate, you can do it easily by making him or her a vice president of your corporation. Even if you have a professional corporation, in which your spouse can't take over directly, you can argue that, in addition to your spouse's being paid, say, as office manager, he is also being paid to familiarize himself with your practice so that he can hire licensed professionals to substitute for you in your practice should you become ill or incapacitated. In the worst case, he has to be able to value your practice so that he can sell it in an emergency without being taken advantage of. No general office manager has those responsibilities, so you are entitled to pay your spouse substantially extra.

There are two basic strategies—both, essentially, the same ones you might choose between in determining what salary to pay yourself:

Low Salary/High Retained Corporate Earnings

Advantages	*Disadvantages*
(1) Low Social Security contributions from your spouse and from your corporation.	(1) Low pension contributions because of low salary. Remember that your corporation takes pretax deductions for them.
(2) Low income taxes payable.	(2) If retained corporate earnings grow too quickly, your corporation may be letting itself in for a tax on its accumulated earnings.
(3) High retained corporate earnings can be invested in stocks whose dividends are 70 percent tax-free.	

High Salary/Low Retained Corporate Earnings

Advantages	*Disadvantages*
(1) High pension contributions resulting from high salary paid. Remember that your corporation takes deductions for them.	(1) High Social Security contributions from your spouse and from your corporation.
(2) By paying out corporate profits as high salary, retained corporate earnings grow more slowly and thus are less likely to trigger the accumulated earnings trap.	(2) High income taxes for your spouse.
	(3) Lower retained corporate earnings available for investment in stocks whose dividends are 70 percent tax-free.

IT MAKES SENSE TO HIRE MY FATHER AS _____.

IN ORDER TO IMPLEMENT THIS STRATEGY, I WILL HAVE TO DO THE FOLLOWING:

1. _____

2. _____

3. _____

IF MY CORPORATION PAYS HIM $_____ AS AN INDEPENDENT CONTRACTOR, INSTEAD OF MY CONTRIBUTING $_____ TO HIS SUPPORT, IT WILL SAVE ME $_____ A YEAR IN FEDERAL INCOME TAXES.

IT MAKES SENSE TO HIRE MY MOTHER AS _____.

IN ORDER TO IMPLEMENT THIS STRATEGY, I WILL HAVE TO DO THE FOLLOWING:

1. _____

2. _____

3. _____

IF MY CORPORATION PAYS HER $_____ AS AN INDEPENDENT CONTRACTOR, INSTEAD OF MY CONTRIBUTING $_____ TO HER SUPPORT, IT WILL SAVE ME $_____ A YEAR IN FEDERAL INCOME TAXES.

IT MAKES SENSE TO HIRE MY SPOUSE AS _____.

IN ORDER TO IMPLEMENT THIS STRATEGY, I WILL HAVE TO DO THE FOLLOWING:

1. _____

2. _____

3. _____

I WANT MY CORPORATION TO PAY HIM/HER A HIGH/ LOW SALARY BECAUSE _____

_____

WHAT TO PAY YOUR CHILDREN

Reasonableness of salary and comparable salary are serious issues here; there's no way you can argue successfully that a six-year-old is worth $10,000 a year to your corporation, no matter how it may enhance your tax picture if you get your way.

Is a ten-year-old or a twelve-year-old worth a $5,000 salary? Probably yes, if he or she works for you 10–15 hours a week. Think of it as Saturday or part of Saturday plus being your home answering service one or two weeknights after 5:00. Obviously, an older child who puts in longer hours and does more work could be paid substantially more.

You can pay your child up to $7,100 a year without his or her paying a penny in federal income tax if you don't claim your child as a dependent. You may want to work out the tax benefits of keeping your child as a dependent vs. his or her keeping the $3,100 standard deduction and $2,000 individual exemption.

Here's how your child can earn $7,100 tax-free:

$7,100	salary
−2,000	IRA contribution
$5,100	
−2,000	individual exemption
$3,100	
−3,100	standard deduction (single)
$ 0	

Unfortunately, your corporation and your child will have to make Social Security contributions on his or her salary, but at least your corporation can write off its share.

If your corporation is able to hire two of your children at $7,100 a year, your tax savings can really add up. Look at this example, which assumes that your corporation hires your children for two years, and compare it with your corporation's paying you that $14,200 in additional salary or bonus:

FEDERAL INCOME TAX ON $14,200 IN YOUR BRACKET

28% (Net Taxable Income = $30,950 − $74,850)	33% (Net Taxable Income = $74,850 − $155,320)
$3,976	$4,686
× 2 years	× 2 years
$7,952	$9,372

Don't feel that you have to limit your child's salary to $7,100. If your situation warrants it, your corporation might hire your child as its computer programmer at $12,500. After deducting the first $7,100, his or her net taxable income is only $5,400, on which the federal income tax is only $814. Compare that to your having to pay $3,500–$4,125 in federal income taxes if you were to pay yourself that additional $12,500 as salary or bonus.

CHILD #1   NAME _____

              AGE   _____

IT MAKES SENSE TO HIRE _____AS _____.

IN ORDER TO IMPLEMENT THIS STRATEGY, I WILL HAVE TO DO THE FOLLOWING:

1. _____

2. _____

3. _____

IF MY CORPORATION PAYS HIM/HER $_____ A YEAR, INSTEAD OF MY TAKING THAT AMOUNT IN ADDITIONAL COMPENSATION, IT WILL SAVE ME $_____ A YEAR IN FEDERAL INCOME TAXES.

CHILD #2   NAME _____

              AGE   _____

IT MAKES SENSE TO HIRE _____AS _____.

IN ORDER TO IMPLEMENT THIS STRATEGY, I WILL HAVE TO DO THE FOLLOWING:

1. _____

2. _____

3. _____

IF MY CORPORATION PAYS HIM/HER $_____ A YEAR, INSTEAD OF MY TAKING THAT AMOUNT IN ADDITIONAL COMPENSATION, IT WILL SAVE ME $_____ A YEAR IN FEDERAL INCOME TAXES.

WHAT ABOUT IRAs?

Even if you're hiring ten-year-olds, IRAs make sense because they offer tax-free compounding of dividends, interest, and capital gains. The $2,000 annual contribution is the only tax shelter available to most taxpayers and should certainly be utilized to maximum advantage. If your seven kids can all work for your corporation, set up seven IRAs!

AND PENSION PLANS?

It may sound silly to think of a pension plan for a fifth-grader, and, in fact, your corporation does not have to make pension contributions for any employee under the age of 24½. However, since it's all in the family, it pays for your corporation to set up defined-contribution plans for your children. They're probably making so little money that they will be eligible to have both IRAs and pension plans! As you know by now, defined-contribution plans let your corporation contribute—and deduct—25 percent of employee salaries. By hiring family members, your corporation saves taxes, too.

And here's another advantage. Unlike outside employees, who might take their vested pension contributions when they leave your corporation, family members are more likely to stay with you and keep your corporate pension fund growing.

Not every small general or professional corporation can put some or all of its owner-shareholder's relatives on the payroll. But for those that can, a small corporation can really flourish as a "money machine" and save both itself and you thousands of tax dollars a year.

19

How to Borrow from Your Corporation

Like a pension fund, but with far fewer restrictions, a small corporation can be treated like a private bank by its owner-employees, as long as it's done legally. You can borrow from your corporate piggybank for any reason or no reason, and very little paperwork is necessary to mollify the IRS.

Start by reviewing the section titled "Corporate Lender Trap" in Chapter 16 (pp. 256–58), which explains how to avoid the pitfalls.

If your certificate of incorporation has not already stipulated that your corporation can lend you money, enact a corporate resolution, approved at a special meeting of the board of directors of your corporation. (Yes, that can be you alone!) You can use the format on pp. 257–58.

Then prepare a written note stating the amount that you are borrowing, the repayment date, and a repayment schedule if you plan to pay in installments. Try to have the loan mature in one year or less; you can always renew it. The IRS doesn't like to see five-year loans to officer-stockholders on your corporate books.

If you are borrowing for a mortgage, the interest on your loan is deductible on your personal income-tax return. Therefore, you may wish to choose an interest rate that is high but not outrageous, so that you can deduct high mortgage-interest payments while putting money into your corporation. This strategy is especially successful if you are in the 33 percent bracket and your corporation is in the 15 percent bracket. *Just make sure that the mortgage-interest payments and other investment income don't exceed 59 percent of all corporate income, so that you don't trigger the personal holding company trap.*

If you are borrowing for any purpose other than a mortgage, the interest on your loan is no longer deductible on your personal income-tax return. Therefore, you will probably be better off taking a tax-free loan from your corporation even though you will have to pay income tax on what the IRS views as a taxable fringe benefit. (For a more complete discussion of the imputed-income rules, see pp. 256–57.)

Here's how to work out the numbers to decide whether you are better off paying interest to your corporation, or accepting a tax-free loan and paying personal income tax on the imputed income:

My personal tax bracket is _____%

My corporation's tax bracket is _____%

I plan to borrow $_____
at an interest rate of _____%

Annual interest payment $_____

If I take a tax-free loan, I will have to pay an imputed-income tax
  of $_____

If I pay interest to my corporation, it will have to pay income tax
  of $_____

> In all cases, you will be paying less if you take the interest-free loan and pay the tax on imputed income than if you pay interest to your corporation. However, in some cases, you may wish to transfer funds from your high-bracket personal pocket to your low-bracket corporate pocket, and an interest-bearing loan is one way to do it.

20

How to Take Money Out of Your Corporation

There are many ways you can siphon money out of your corporation legally—often without paying income taxes on it. And isn't that one of the reasons you incorporated?

The money you pull out of your corporation falls into two major categories: taxable and nontaxable. Obviously, some of it must get taxed; but even the taxable categories have their uses.

Taxable	*Nontaxable*
Salary	Expense accounts
Bonuses	Employee benefit plans
Commissions	Sale of your assets to the
Fees for special services	corporation (if structured
Dividends	correctly)
Rent (only partially taxable)	Lease of your assets to the
	corporation (if structured
	correctly

SALARY

As long as your compensation is reasonable, there are no problems about your corporation's paying you what you—as president—think your job is worth. In general, questions of unreasonable compensation arise only when

- Your corporation's creditors fear that your "excessive" salary will leave your company insolvent or bankrupt and will leave them holding the bag; or
- The IRS takes the position that your company should be paying non-deductible dividends rather than deductible salary; or
- Other stockholders feel that your salary is eroding profits that they should be receiving as dividends. (Of course, in a one-person or small family corporation, this is not a problem.)

Let's assume that you are not in trouble with any creditors. That leaves the IRS. As I mentioned earlier, the best way to justify your salary as reasonable is to keep a small file of competitive salaries shown in help-wanted ads from newspapers and professional journals. Jot down the source and date on the ad. Feel free to pay yourself more than the going rate because your hours are longer and your duties are broader; in addition to running your business or practicing your profession, you're probably managing your corporation's investments and pension and profit-sharing funds.

To a great extent, what you choose to pay yourself may depend not only on how profitable your corporation is and how much money you need to live on, but also on the tax structure where you live. (See Chapter 13, "How to Use Your C Corporation to Beat the Taxmen," for detailed strategies.) For example, if you live in Alaska, Connecticut, Florida, Nevada, New Hampshire, South Dakota, Tennessee, Texas, Washington, or Wyoming, it's a smart move to pay yourself a high salary because these states do not tax personal earned income, although some do tax interest and dividends. But, if you live in Hawaii, where personal income-tax rates for most people can run as high as double the corporation income-tax rate, you'll want to pay yourself a low salary and keep correspondingly more income in your corporation.

RAISING YOUR SALARY

As your corporation prospers, you will probably want to raise your salary. Moderate raises are easy to justify: you've logged in another year with your corporation, or competitive salaries have risen proportionately. Hefty raises (generally over 35 percent) require more specific and substantive justification; your client base has increased, your duties have expanded. *Avoid the trap of claiming that your previous salary was too low and that this generous raise is merely "playing catch-up"; paying yourself what you deserved all along.* Similarly, don't give yourself back pay for all the years that your corporation was struggling to establish itself and couldn't afford to pay you a fair salary.

Although they are quite logical, these reasons won't stand up with the IRS because business law presumes that you have performed your job voluntarily for the pay that you received and therefore are not entitled to collect more money for that past work unless you made an agreement with your company that it would pay you additional salary when it could afford to. Without that agreement, you can still compensate for that lost salary by declaring a one-time bonus in recognition of your past work. *Then,* bearing your myriad duties in mind, raise your salary to a competitive level.

BONUSES

Apart from the one-time bonus just discussed, there are other strategic reasons to pay yourself bonuses, rather than set a fixed salary. Bonuses are much more flexible; you can determine them at the very end of your corporate year and can pay out as high or low a percentage of your corporate profits as you wish. You can adjust them every year according to your needs and according to any changes in the tax laws. Further, if your corporation is on an accrual accounting system, it can declare and deduct your bonus 2½ months before it pays the bonus to you and you have to pay taxes on it.

You may run a small risk that the IRS will try to declare your bonus a dividend in disguise. *You can demolish such a claim by demonstrating the legitimacy of variable or incentive compensation in your business or profession.*

Two key areas are the connection of your bonus to the services you have performed and the reasonableness of your bonus in terms of your total compensation package. Common sense and moderate greed apply: a $15,000 bonus on a $20,000 salary looks suspect; on a $50,000 salary, it's quite reasonable and would most probably go unquestioned.

COMMISSIONS

Commissions are another sensible and flexible way to take cash out of your corporation, especially if *you* make all or most of the key, lucrative sales. Basing pay on commissions is a time-honored method of compensation and, as such, should go unquestioned by the IRS. Just make sure that you have a set formula for calculating commissions and that it is in line with commissions paid to competing salespeople. You can still reasonably pay yourself at a somewhat higher rate than other salespeople, if it's to your advantage to do so, because you have additional responsibilities: sales manager, supervision, managing the pension and profit-sharing fund, etc.

FEES FOR SPECIAL SERVICES

Admittedly, this is a minor area, but it may have a substantially greater impact on owner-employees with nonworking spouses. Even a tiny general business corporation can have outside directors, and outside directors are entitled to fees for attending board meetings. These fees are classified as earned income. For your spouse, annual director's fees of $2,000 (or whatever the IRA contribution limit is) permit the creation of a $2,000 deduction and simultaneously may increase your joint potential deductible IRA contribution from $2,250 (one working spouse, one nonworking spouse) to $4,000 (two working spouses).

Your annual director's fee won't provide as much of a tax advantage because it will be taxed at your highest income-tax rate. Nonetheless, it offers real tax advantages because it lets you pull $2,000 a year out of your corporation every single year. Over the life of your corporation, the total $4,000 annual directors' fees can add up to over $100,000—a figure that surely moves the $150,000/$250,000 limitation on retained corporate profits in your corporation farther into the distance.

DIVIDENDS

First, a word of caution: Don't pay dividends unless and until you have to. Remember that your corporation can deduct salaries, bonuses, commissions, fees of all kinds; *it can't deduct dividends.* Accordingly, your corporation should consider paying dividends only as part of corporate restructuring in connection with more serious and substantive estate planning (see Chapter 23) or when it is approaching the $150,000/$250,000 accumulated earnings limit.

Instead of paying dividends, consider increasing your salary or paying yourself a bonus. Under most conditions, you can take cash out of your corporation this way and forestall the dividends that are really a tax liability.

RENT

If your corporation can rent property that you own personally, your playing landlord to your corporation can provide many tax advantages because rental income can generate so many write-offs that a good part of the rent comes to you tax-free.

Schedule E on the next page shows a simple example of a corporation's renting one room of a four-room condominium or cooperative apartment from its president as office space. The corporation pays rent of $500 a month—$6,000 a year. Based on the owner's pro rata cost of 25 percent of the apartment's basis of $300,000 over 31½-year straight-line depreciation, the annual depreciation is $2,381. After the owner deducts $1,000 for cleaning and maintenance and $500 for insurance, he or she winds up with net taxable income of only $2,119. This rental provides a cash flow of $4,500 ($6,000–$5,000 actual expenses), of which the $2,381 of depreciation is fully sheltered from income taxes—federal, state, and local.

Entrepreneurs fortunate enough to begin renting space to their corporations in the early 1980s can take advantage of more generous depreciation because they can depreciate their rental property over 10 years. (Similar rental property placed into service now must be depreciated over 31½ years.) In the margin of Schedule E on the next page, I have shown what the depreciation and cash flow would look like if this property had been rented to the corporation beginning in the 1980s. The big difference is the amount of annual depreciation: $7,500 versus $2,381. And, because of this $5,000-plus difference in depreciation, the lucky entrepreneur can pay himself or herself an extra $3,600 in rent while enjoying a much lower net taxable income of $600. This rental provides a cash flow of $8,100 ($9,600–$1,500 actual expenses), of which the $7,500 of depreciation is fully sheltered from federal, state, and local income taxes.

> Always show a small profit on your office rental. It makes your Schedule E—and the rest of your return—both easier and more plausible.

In most situations, you're better off having your corporation pay you high (but fair-market) rent than high salary or bonus. You're still sucking money out of the corporation, but rent possesses the double advantage of providing tax-sheltered income and not being subject to Social Security contributions from you or your corporation.

> Spend some time on a little tax planning every year, with updates and revisions every quarter. A little judicious juggling will help you select the right combination of salary, bonus, commissions, fees, and rents, with the minimum of taxes.

SCHEDULE E (Form 1040)	**Supplemental Income and Loss**	OMB No. 1545-0074
Department of the Treasury Internal Revenue Service	(From rents, royalties, partnerships, estates, trusts, REMICs, etc.) ▶ Attach to Form 1040 or Form 1041. ▶ See Instructions for Schedule E (Form 1040).	**1989** Attachment Sequence No. **13**

Name(s) shown on return: ENTREPRENEUR

Your social security number: 000 00 0000

Part I — Income or Loss From Rentals and Royalties   Caution: *Your rental loss may be limited. See Instructions.*

1 Show the kind and location of **rental property**:
123 EASY STREET, New York, NY 10021
OFFICE SPACE

		Yes	No
2 For each rental property listed on line 1, did you or your family use it for personal purposes for more than the greater of 14 days or 10% of the total days rented at fair rental value during the tax year?	A		✓
	B		
	C		
3 For each **rental real estate property** listed on line 1, did you actively participate in its operation during the tax year? (See Instructions.)	A	✓	
	B		
	C		

Rental and Royalty Income:		Properties A	B	C	D Totals (Add columns A, B, and C)	
Rents received	4	6,000 —			4	6,000 — 9,600
Royalties received	5				5	
Rental and Royalty Expenses:						
Advertising	6					
Auto and travel	7					
Cleaning and maintenance	8	1,000 —				
Commissions	9					
Insurance	10	500 —				
Legal and other professional fees	11					
Mortgage interest paid to banks, etc. (see Instructions)	12				12	
Other interest	13					
Repairs	14					
Supplies	15					
Taxes	16					
Utilities (see Instructions)	17					
Wages and salaries	18					
Other (list) ▶	19					
Add lines 6 through 19	20	1,500 —			20	1,500
Depreciation expense or depletion (see Instructions) $300,000÷4÷31½	21	2,381 —			21	7,500
Total expenses. Add lines 20 and 21	22	3,881 —				9,000
Income or (loss) from rental or royalty properties. Subtract line 22 from line 4 (rents) or line 5 (royalties). If the result is a (loss), see Instructions to find out if you must file **Form 6198**	23	2,119 —				600-
Deductible rental loss. **Caution:** Your rental loss on line 23 may be limited. See Instructions to find out if you must file **Form 8582**	24	(0)( )( )				

25	**Income.** Add rental and royalty income from line 23. Enter the total income here	25	2,119 —	600 -
26	**Losses.** Add royalty losses from line 23 and rental losses from line 24. Enter the total losses here	26	(0)	
27	Combine amounts on lines 25 and 26. Enter the net income or (loss) here	27	2,119 —	600 -
28	Net farm rental income or (loss) from Form 4835. (Also complete line 43 on page 2.)	28	0	
29	Total rental and royalty income or (loss). Combine amounts on lines 27 and 28. Enter the result here. If Parts II, III, and IV on page 2 do not apply to you, enter the amount from line 29 on Form 1040, line 18. Otherwise, include the amount from line 29 in the total on line 42 on page 2	29	2,119 —	600 -

For Paperwork Reduction Act Notice, see Form 1040 Instructions.   Schedule E (Form 1040) 1989

Now we come to the juicy part: the tax-deductible goodies and perks that are actually even better than cash because they are deductible by your corporation but are not treated as income to you. Here, as in other corporate and individual tax areas, subtle creative accounting can pay off; gross outright greed will get you in trouble.

EXPENSE ACCOUNTS

Here's the bad news. Expenses must not only be accurate—no more extrapolating from weekly or monthly estimates—but "contemporaneous." For practical purposes and mollifying the IRS, that means logging them in within a week, if not sooner. Needless to say, office-supply companies, tax advisory services, and organization/planning experts are having a field day. Most of them feel that you need

- A diary or log in your car's glove compartment
- A pocket diary for your attaché case
- A desk diary for your office, into which expenses from your car and pocket diaries can be transferred.

Now here's the good news. As long as you document your expenses and they seem reasonable, you can enjoy a very generous expense account. Taking clients to lunch or dinner at elegant restaurants is quite all right—as long as you note the client's name, company, and purpose of the entertainment on your copy of the bill or charge slip and in your diary. If you are a gourmet, having your corporation underwrite your *canard au vinaigre myrtille* is a lovely fringe benefit. Just make sure that you're entertaining a legitimate client and discussing business; and don't submit a bill for $300 for lunch unless that client's business is worth thousands of dollars to your corporation.

It's also perfectly legal for your company to pay for your theater, opera, concert, dance, and sports tickets—if you take a customer or client along. One supersaleswoman I know takes her customers to the theater or opera three times a week—five or six times a week when the out-of-town buyers come in for trade shows. Her problem is overkill, not the IRS. "I've had to see *Phantom of the Opera* eight times so far!" she half-complains.

Remember that your corporation can write off only 80 percent of its expenditures for business meals and entertainment.

Travel is another area where owner-employees can benefit. That's why professional seminars are held on Cape Cod or the Pacific Northwest in the summer and in Florida or the Caribbean in the winter. You can attend and even take your spouse along tax-deductibly, as long as you can demonstrate a valid business or professional reason for your attending and your spouse's presence. Documentation is critical: Keep the program, your notes, a diary or log, a collection of other attendees' business cards with useful notations on the back, any follow-up steps you took when you returned—anything that will validate your need to have attended that most useful seminar, trade show, or convention.

Even day trips can be written off profitably. One writer I know flew up to Boston to present a proposal to a new magazine. The fact that she chose that specific day in order to attend a jewelry auction on Newbury Street certainly did not invalidate the deductibility of her trip. It was simply shrewd planning.

Health club, town, and country club memberships and expenses make wonderful expense-account deductions, too. As discussed more fully in Chapter 14, "How to Get the Most from Your Professional or Personal Service Corporation," be sure that the bulk of your expenses are for client entertainment and not for personal or family use, or you run the risk of prorating and possibly losing these deductions.

True, there are many owner-employees who brag, "I never eat out, go out, or travel unless I can make it a deductible business expense." This strategy works best when you can tie the expenses to specific, actual work and clients that are producing income for your corporation, and when the amounts of the expenses bear a reasonable relationship to the income those clients generate or that your corporation earns. You take a $10,000 client to lunch at the Four Seasons or Spago, not a $500 client. You take the $500 client to lunch at a good local Chinese or Italian restaurant or a French bistro. And, of course, the IRS will take a very dim view of your entertainment expense's eating up all but $4.98 of your corporate profits year after year.

EMPLOYEE BENEFIT PLANS

By now you should be familiar with medical, dental, and insurance plans that are available to you tax-free even if you are the sole employee of your corporation. *Educational plans are possibly even more profitable.* Under present law, your corporation can send you (back) to school for any relevant advanced or refresher course or program—tax-free, as long as it will maintain your skills, rather than prepare you for another career. Of course, as the CEO of your own company, that gives you very wide scope.

As always, the "rule of reason" applies. A crafts course might be deductible for an antiques dealer—to learn how furniture or silver is made and, incidentally, to learn firsthand how to recognize forgeries. Or for a surgeon—to develop hand and finger strength and maintain manual dexterity. Deductions for foreign-language courses depend on their relevance to your work. MBA programs are never questioned.

There are even ways to arrange for your corporation to legitimately deduct your children's educational expenses. You need professional help to structure such a plan, but obviously it's worth it. In general, you will have to set up the plan years in advance to establish its credibility. The plan has to be nondiscriminatory, open to children of all employees. Of course, if you're the only employee or the only employee with children, that's no problem.

If your corporation has other employees with children, here's a strategy to make this plan apply only to your children without seeming to. Make the eligibility apply to employees who have worked for a certain period of time, rather than to the children of those employees—e.g., employees who have worked at least ten hours per week for the last three years, or at least eight weeks in each of the last three summers. Of course, since you'll make sure that only your children work for your corporation during summer vacations, only they will qualify for your corporation's college scholarships.

It's most important to have a children's scholarship plan set up by tax professionals. The stakes are too high for you to lose this valuable benefit by making a tiny error that you don't even recognize.

SALE OF YOUR ASSETS TO YOUR CORPORATION

Selling your assets to your corporation provides two very profitable and useful services:

- It gives you cash.
- By taking cash out of the corporation, it postpones the day of reckoning when your corporation reaches the $150,000/$250,000 accumulated earnings limitation.

It may pay for you, rather than for your corporation, to buy an asset and then turn around immediately and sell it to the corporation. What do you get for this extra work? Instant cash—use of the money for years.

Now that interest payments other than on mortgages are no longer deductible, this strategy works best during a slow automotive year when dealers are offering "zero financing." (I put the term in quotation marks because the dealers will try to make up this part of their profit in other areas. Be warned!)

Assuming that you are able to buy a new car for $15,000 and arrange three-year, true zero-percent financing, you immediately sell the car to your corporation as a business car for $15,000 and pocket the cash. Then you pay off the car loan over three years. Result: you have three years' use of the $15,000, on which you might be earning 8–9 percent, or $3,600–$4,000 + .

If you are selling your corporation an asset that is not new, you will have to establish a fair-market value for it. Suppose it's antique furniture for your office or art for your waiting room. You can obtain records from *Art at Auction* indexes, found in most large libraries. Remember that this must be a valid arm's-length transaction, at a fair-market price, and with a real bill of sale. The *objets d'art* must remain in your office; they can't float around your home.

Remember, too, that at some point when you liquidate your corporation, the art and antiques you sold to it will have to be valued. Any great loss in value may come back to haunt you then by creating tax problems.

LEASING OF YOUR ASSETS TO YOUR CORPORATION

One form of leasing to your corporation has already been discussed in this chapter: renting office space to your corporation. You can also lease art, antiques, and furniture to your corporation and obtain most of the tax benefits of selling them. In addition, the advantages of leasing over selling are

- You are able to pull a steady stream of income out of your corporation (rather than a lump sum) without paying Social Security taxes on it
- You are able to negotiate the lease for more or less money, depending on the art market and your financial needs
- You retain ownership of the assets
- Your corporation is able to lease many assets, rather than to purchase only one

Leasing your art and antiques to your corporation is a little-known way of taking cash out of your corporation—while adding status and elegance to your office. Done correctly—by using terms comparable to those obtained from an art-rental company, in order to prove that your lease is an arm's-length transaction—it will provide you and your corporation with substantial tax deductions, and with physical beauty.

Of course, most small corporations will not be able to use all ten major strategies in this chapter to pull cash out of their corporations. But it's a sure bet that most owner-employees will find at least half a dozen profitable strategies here that can give them thousands of dollars in cash and tax-free benefits every year.

21

How to Take Assets Out of Your Corporation

This chapter deals with taking assets out of your corporation while it's still a going venture. Taking assets out of your corporation as part of the liquidation process when you retire is covered in the last chapter, "How to Use Your Corporation in Estate Planning."

Taking assets out of your corporation is like being the only customer in a bargain basement. In one corner is a beautiful, well-maintained, five-year-old car. Original cost: $15,000. Sale price: $4,999. In another corner is a five-year-old computer. Original cost: $10,000. Sale price: $495. It's obsolescent for your business purposes, but just perfect for the kids. Also on sale are office or waiting-room furniture you'd like to replace, a type-writer, a stereo system.

These assets are so cheap because they have short useful lives (usu-ally five years) and are now completely depreciated. Remember that "useful life" is an accounting concept and may bear little relation to actual functioning reality. While a typewriter may have a nominal useful life of five years, most hardworking authors keep their favorite machines for 20, 30, and even over 40 years.

Start thinking of your corporation as a marvelous source of "pre-owned" but wonderful merchandise. Now that the company car has been completely depreciated, it makes business and tax sense to buy a new one and start the depreciation cycle all over again. Through buying, writing off, and then selling the company car and buying a new one, your corporation can write off around $15,000 every five years from this asset alone, and provide you and your family with excellent, gently used cars.

Since your corporation's sale of the car to you must be handled as an arm's-length transaction, you must arrive at a fair price. The easiest way to do this is to collect ads from newspapers and specialized magazines like *Trading Post* and prices from the *Blue Book*. The best time to find low prices is September–October, when the new models come out. All used cars become a year older then, and prices drop a notch. It's perfectly reasonable for you to choose the lowest of the three or four prices you've collected. To be on the safe side, use that price—don't go even $100 below it.

Of course, you can finance the car by giving your corporation a note, rather than paying a lump sum. Here, too, do some comparison shopping. A "sweetheart" interest-free or even 5 percent loan is bound to raise questions, especially now that imputed interest is a key issue. As discussed earlier, you are usually better off taking the interest-free loan and paying tax on the imputed interest. However, if you are in a higher tax bracket than your corporation, this is an opportunity to shift money from your pocket into your corporation by charging a high rate of interest. Comparison-shop the banks and car dealers on a used-car loan, and choose the middle or highest interest rate.

It's more difficult to price used office equipment or furniture, so you really have more maneuverability in negotiating a price that is favorable to you. "Sweetheart" deals are harder to prove. Remember that your basic strategy consists of your corporation's sucking all the benefits out of an asset through depreciation, and then selling it to you at a low but fair (and therefore unquestionable) price.

Use this strategy of taking assets out of your corporation in conjunction with that of taking cash out of your corporation judiciously, and you'll enjoy many years of tax-free and tax-advantaged benefits.

22

How to Use Your Corporation as a Deferred-Compensation Tool

This chapter is tricky because time constraints force me to write it on the basis of critical assumptions, rather than enacted tax law. As I write this in early September 1990, it seems probable that we will have a tax increase, but no one knows what kind, how large, or when it will become effective.

Whatever form the tax increase takes, it's a reasonable assumption that it will be in effect in 1991 and thereafter. Now here's where our decision tree bifurcates. If personal federal income-tax rates are higher in 1992 and subsequent years than in 1991, it's foolish to have a deferred-compensation arrangement with your corporation because if you use it, your taxes will be higher. If, however, personal federal income-tax rates are the same or lower than in 1991, setting up a deferred-compensation agreement may be a smart move. For purposes of this chapter, let's assume that tax rates will be the same or lower in 1992 and subsequent years than in 1991.

A deferred-compensation agreement is pretty simple. It's a contract that you and your corporation enter into that permits you to defer up to

100 percent of your compensation (salary and/or bonus, depending on how the agreement is drawn) every year. The rationale behind deferred-compensation plans used to be the assumption—true in the past, problematic in the future—that when you received all this money at some point in the future, you would be in a lower tax bracket and consequently would pay less income tax on it. Now the critical assumption is that any time you can defer income and the tax on it for at least a year, it's worth doing some number crunching. If you can defer at least $1,000 in taxes every year, you will probably profit by having a deferred-compensation agreement.

Deferred compensation benefits owner-employees who may not need very high current income and can afford to defer $5,000–$10,000 a year or more. A lawyer must draw up a valid deferred-compensation agreement, setting forth the amount or percentage of salary or bonus to be deferred, the number of years the funds will be deferred, and how the funds will be paid out. The agreement can be drawn flexibly enough so that you agree to defer only your bonus, which, in your one-person corporation, you control completely. The cost of drawing up a deferred-compensation agreement varies; a lawyer who specializes in them should charge no more than two or three hours of time.

The deferred-compensation must be a valid written plan. It must impose reasonable obligations on your corporation to pay the deferred compensation, and it must arrange its finances so that it will be able to pay you the money at the end of the deferral period. The deferred-compensation agreement must not be a sham, where, at the end of the time, your corporation cannot pay you. It must be both willing and able to pay you the money that you have merely deferred, not relinquished.

What's in It for Your Corporation

A deferred-compensation plan benefits your corporation, too. First, a deferred-compensation agreement permits your corporation to accumulate money in a special fund—without running afoul of the $150,000/$250,000 accumulated-earnings limitation and potential tax—because it's for a valid business purpose. In addition, because deferred-compensation plans are not qualified under §401 of the Internal Revenue Code, your corporation can make use of the assets in your deferred-compensation fund: borrow against them, use them as collateral, and so on.

Your corporation can fund (but not physically protect) your deferred-compensation plan any way it wants to. If it puts $50,000 of your deferred-compensation fund into the stock market and the $50,000 grows to $100,000, depending on the terms of your deferred-compensation agreement, your corporation can either pay you the $100,000 and write off an expense of $100,000 rather than the $50,000; or pay out the original

$50,000, write off $50,000, and keep the $50,000 itself, in the corporate kitty. Your corporation can put the deferred-compensation money into a money-market fund, bonds, or real estate. In fact, your corporation doesn't even have to fund your deferred-compensation plan; it can just pay you your deferred compensation at the end of the contracted time period.

RISKS OF DEFERRED-COMPENSATION AGREEMENTS

In setting up a deferred-compensation plan, you are accepting two forms of risk. First, you become an unsecured creditor of your corporation. All you have is your corporation's promise to pay you at some future date—it's just an IOU by any other name. *The plan must remain only a promise:* Once your corporation funds or insulates this money in any way, the IRS holds that you have constructive receipt of the money, and you lose the deferral tax benefit. So your first risk is that your corporation won't have the money for you when your deferred-compensation agreement falls due.

The second risk is that your corporation does have the money for you, but that its other creditors want to attach it. (They are legally entitled to.) About the only very minor step you can take is to have your corporation set up a trust which segregates your deferred-compensation money in a trust account, but does not protect it from other creditors.

ALTERNATIVES TO DEFERRED-COMPENSATION AGREEMENTS

In light of these potential risks, why bother with deferred-compensation agreements at all? say many estate planners. Instead, take your money out now as salary, bonus, or with some of the strategies described in Chapter 20, "How to Take Money Out of Your Corporation."

If you are over 40 or, better yet, over 50, another excellent way of putting money aside tax-free is to set up a defined-benefit pension plan, rather than a defined-contribution plan. The older you are, the more a defined-benefit plan works to your advantage, because you have to fund all your retirement benefits in only 10–20 years, rather than the 30–40 years a younger employee has to fund them.

Defined-benefit plans are more costly to set up and recalculate every year because these tasks must be done by a licensed actuary, and they call for enormous contributions every year, which can cripple your cash flow. Nevertheless, they can be advantageous, and you *can* protect yourself and your company. Make certain that you structure your company's defined-benefit plan so that you don't have to fund each year's contribution all at once. There are ways to set up the plan so that if your corporation gets caught short one year, it can make up the shortfall without penalty over the next three years.

If deferred compensation sounds attractive to you, talk with your attorney and accountant to find out how much you should defer, according to your cash-flow requirements. Start by using the worksheet below to estimate your tax savings for each year that you defer your compensation.

You need to set up the plan, through which you may defer up to 100 percent of your total compensation year by year, only once. Unfortunately, however, in order to avoid any appearance or taint of constructive receipt of the funds, you must make the decision on how much to defer at the beginning of the year—e.g., January 15, 1991, for the year 1991. If you would like more flexibility in planning, choose a *percentage* to defer, rather than a dollar amount, or simply set up the deferred-compensation agreement, as mentioned earlier, to defer only your bonus—a most flexible arrangement.

Amount to be deferred $_____

Tax bracket this year   _____%

Tax bracket in deferral year   _____%

Difference between tax brackets _____%

Amount saved through deferral $_____

23

How to Use Your Corporation in Estate Planning

This chapter, too, is problematical, and for the same reason as the preceding chapter. It, too, is based on critical assumptions, rather than on enacted legislation. The key to estate planning is the creation of capital gains—or, even more favorably, the transformation of ordinary income into capital gains. The Tax Reform Act of 1986 killed the favorable tax treatment of capital gains which, as I write in September 1990, are now taxed the same as ordinary income. However, given the fact that restoration of a favorable capital-gains tax is a priority for both President Bush and Congressman Rostenkowski, chairman of the House Ways and Means Committee, it is highly probable that a capital-gains tax—or at least indexing of capital gains—will be legislated before the end of 1990. Accordingly, this chapter has been written using the critical assumption that some kind of favorable capital-gains treatment will be enacted before this book is published.

There is another reason that this chapter is problematic. In the 15 years since I started writing about the one-person corporation, liquidation and estate-planning rules have changed many times. Furthermore, it is certain that they will change many times more between the time that you read this book and the time that you're ready to do some serious estate planning, or thinking of liquidating your corporation.

Therefore, think of this chapter as a menu. When you are ready to do your actual planning, check the most recent legislation that affects one-person and small corporations, and get some help from tax professionals who specialize in this area.

As you know by now, a small corporation is an excellent vehicle for estate planning. In large part, the profits created by and accumulated through the "tax shelter" feature of your corporation can be sheltered further from income taxes, gift taxes, and estate taxes through various estate-planning strategies.

This chapter explores several methods of using your corporation as an estate-planning tool—including

- Liquidation of your corporation
- Tax-free transfer of your corporation to your heirs
- Dividend policies

LIQUIDATION OF YOUR CORPORATION

Liquidating your corporation can play a major role in your estate planning. When you liquidate your corporation—generally, when you retire—you'll distribute the assets and liabilities to all the shareholders in exchange for their stock on a pro rata basis. The excess of the value of the assets over the liabilities and investment in the stock is treated as a capital gain, which may be taxed favorably. If you have left money in your corporation, rather than paying it out as dividends, this may be your chance to turn those unpaid dividends into capital gains by waiting until you liquidate your corporation.

You don't have to sell the stock in your corporate portfolio either. You are permitted to distribute in cash or in kind: You give your stock back to your corporation, and your corporation gives you its assets—its stock portfolio and anything else it owns. You send your corporation's IBM and AT&T to the transfer agents, who will reissue the stock in your name alone.

You will have to notify the IRS 30 days after adopting your plan of liquidation, but in a one-person corporation, a meeting of your board of directors can take all of five minutes.

The IRS treats liquidation of your corporation as a sale because it is really a sale of your company stock. If a capital-gains law is enacted, the liquidation of your corporation may have beneficial tax consequences.

As of mid-1990, there are two methods of liquidating your corporation: the lump-sum method (§331) or the installment method. To understand how these work and how they differ from each other, let's take the same corporation through the two liquidation options.

Example: Wonderful Corporation liquidates on June 30, 1991. It has fixed assets valued at $30,000, receivables of $90,000, and inventory of $30,000. Your basis in your company's stock is $30,000.

§331—LUMP-SUM METHOD

The lump-sum method is a complete liquidation. When you use this method, each asset takes a basis to its value at the date of liquidation:

Total assets	$150,000
Less basis in stock	− 30,000
Capital gain	$120,000

Your capital gain may be taxed at the same rate as ordinary income, it may be taxed at a more favorable rate, or it may be indexed. If it should be indexed and you have owned your corporation for ten or twenty years or more, indexing will reduce your gain sharply, and you will probably pay very little tax.

To elect the lump-sum method of liquidation, your corporation will file IRS Form 966.

INSTALLMENT METHOD

The installment method is really a subcategory of §331. This method is suitable only for sales of real estate, plant and equipment, or other major tangible assets worth at least $50,000.

Under the installment method, the corporation makes the sale at the corporate level at liquidation and passes the mortgage notes on to the shareholder, who is taxed as payment is received, as though he or she had made the installment sale.

When Wonderful Corporation is sold using the installment method, first the owner (or his or her accountant) must calculate the gross profit percentage by dividing the gross profit (total assets less the stockholder's basis) by the contract price (total assets):

$150,000 − $30,000 = $120,000
$120,000 ÷ $150,000 = 80%

Since the gross profit percentage is 80 percent, only 80 percent of each annual installment will be taxed at capital-gains rates, which may (or may not) be lower than ordinary-income rates. The remaining 20 percent is treated as a return of capital and therefore is not taxed.

If Wonderful's sole owner-employee takes 30 percent in 1991—the year of the sale—as her first installment, the calculations look like this:

$45,000	installment payment
-9,000	return of capital
$36,000	gain—possibly taxed at favorable
	capital-gains rates

In the next seven years—from 1992 through 1998—if 10 percent is paid out each year, the calculations for each year look like this:

$15,000	installment payment
-3,000	return of capital
$12,000	gain—possibly taxed at favorable
	capital-gains rates

The installment method of liquidation is very complicated. It requires professional tax advice. *If you choose this method, you must make certain that your corporation is in liquidation status throughout this entire ten-year period.*

> *Strategy:* Close down your corporation, but still work in semiretirement as a sole proprietor. Many entrepreneurs do, quite successfully.

To elect the installment method of liquidation, your corporation files IRS Form 966.

HOW TO RAISE THE BASIS OF YOUR STOCK

This is a good place to talk about the basis of your stock: what it is and how to raise it. In the preceding calculations, you may have noticed that the basis of your stock was subtracted from your corporate assets to arrive at your capital gain. Therefore, the higher the basis of your stock, the lower will be your taxable capital gain.

The basis of your stock is a dollar amount consisting of the assets that you contribute to your corporation at its beginning and throughout its life. Even a service corporation can use contributions: office furniture, a computer, a business library. All these assets are valued at their cost, not their current replacement value.

Assets you contribute to your corporation increase the value of the outstanding shares of your stock pro rata. If you issued shares of your corporation at different times, you may wind up with shares at differing bases, just as if you had purchased stock at varying prices.

By increasing the basis of your stock as much as possible, when you liquidate your corporation, as much money as possible is treated as a return of capital and is therefore exempt from income taxes. If your stock had a basis of $30,000 and you liquidated your corporation, which had assets of $150,000, the $30,000 would be treated as a return of capital. You would subtract the $30,000 from $150,000 and start your calculations with $120,000.

How can you contribute to your service corporation during its life? Choose the area in which corporations receive preferential treatment over individuals—stocks—and give your corporation either cash, with which it can buy stocks, or the stocks themselves. As soon as the stocks are transferred to your corporation, the dividends become 70 percent tax-free.

> Remember: once you give the cash or stock to your corporation, you cannot take the money back or use those dividends yourself without having your corporation declare a distribution and being taxed on it.

You might also buy paintings, works of art, and antiques and contribute them to your corporation in order to raise the basis of your stock, but you will have to use your personal funds to buy them. You are increasing the basis of your stock, but you are also increasing the assets of your corporation. Because you are adding the same amount of money to both sides of the equation, there is actually no change. It makes much more sense to give your corporation money to purchase stocks or to give your company the stocks themselves, because corporations can shelter 70 percent of dividends from taxes, whereas individuals cannot.

> If you transfer stocks to your corporation, remember to use your cost—and not their current market value—as the basis.

Obviously, it's a very shrewd move for a 55- or 60-year-old entrepreneur or professional to incorporate, turn over her stock portfolio to her corporation, and enjoy receiving dividends which are 70 percent exempt from federal income taxes. As long as her earned corporate income comprised 40 percent or more of her total annual corporate income, she would avoid the personal holding company trap. She could then retire at 65 or 70, having accumulated lots of tax-free dividends. The basis of the stock she had donated to her corporation would be fairly high. As a result, when her corporation was liquidated, a substantial portion of the assets would be treated as a return of capital and would therefore be free of tax.

COLLECTING YOUR PENSION

Collecting your pension is part of liquidating your corporation and planning your estate. However, tax laws have changed so much in this area and are bound to change even more by the time you're ready to contemplate retirement, that it's mandatory to get up-to-the-minute professional advice before you make what might turn out to be an irrevocable decision.

RECAPITALIZING YOUR CORPORATION

Rather than liquidating your corporation when you retire, you may wish to transfer it to your heirs tax-free, especially if they already work for the company. Recapitalization is a form of corporate reorganization in which your common stock is converted into preferred stock, which is limited in par value.

Note: Although, as of September 1990, the "freezeout" plan of recapitalization discussed below is no longer in effect, I am writing about it because Congressman Rostenkowski, chairman of the House Ways and Means Committee, has introduced a similar new freezeout plan. Some form of recapitalization is likely to become law by early 1991, when this book is published, simply because some favorable tax treatment is needed to preserve the small family-owned company.

Under the freezeout form of recapitalization, after your common stock is converted to preferred stock, your new preferred stock can accumulate dividends and can either retain or cede voting control to the new generation. You have transferred the value of your old common stock to your new preferred stock. You then give the low-value common stock to your children or heirs, who are now running the company.

In transferring the value of your old common stock to your new preferred stock by effecting a freezeout, you have frozen the value of the preferred stock and thus frozen the cost of any future estate taxes your heirs might have to pay. Your preferred stock is similar to a bond: its value is fixed.

What *does* appreciate is the new common stock—if your heirs are running the company profitably. But any appreciation of their stock is safe from taxation until they actually dispose of it.

HOW TO USE PREFERRED STOCK IN YOUR ESTATE PLANNING

Let's look at some numbers to see how the preferred stock, with its frozen value, actually transfers appreciation in a company's value to the new generation.

In this case, let's assume that a 60-year-old father recapitalizes his corporation. He wants to retain control of his corporation, so he issues voting preferred stock that gives him over 50 percent of the votes. One simple way to do this: give each share of preferred stock ten votes and give each share of common stock only one vote.

Year 1: Father recapitalizes $100,000 corporation. Preferred stock now worth $100,000; common stock, given to children, worth some minimal amount.

Year 10: Father dies, still running the company, which is now worth $1 million, thanks to his children's talents. As his preferred stock is frozen at $100,000, the children's common stock is worth $900,000—an amount that has been removed neatly and quite legally from their father's estate. Only the $100,000 of preferred stock winds up in his estate.

It's perfectly legal to roll over the assets of the corporation to future generations. These children—the new owners—can recapitalize the company at some future time to benefit *their* children. They use the same technique: recapitalizing and transferring all the value of their common stock into preferred stock, whose value is frozen. Then their children's common stock profits from any appreciation in value.

> This strategy really works only for general business corporations. For professional corporations to be permitted to utilize this strategy, parent and children must all be licensed in the same profession.

FINESSING THE FREEZEOUT

Even without the freezeout—or with a less profitable version of it—here's a sophisticated strategy to transfer your company's business to your children. *And it works right now.*

Let's assume that you and your spouse own all the stock of Wonderful Corporation, which is valued presently at $2 million, and that your total estate is $2.5 million. As your business continues to prosper and as inflation continues, the final cash outlay for death taxes will surely be prohibitive.

Your problem is exacerbated because your assets are so illiquid; 80

percent is stock in your closely held corporation. You and your spouse have been understandably reluctant to make substantial transfers to Jimmy, your 28-year-old son who is a company vice president, because such transfers would trigger heavy gift taxes. In addition, Wonderful, which already provides maximum salaries and perks to the three of you, is increasing its profitability rapidly. If Wonderful doesn't start paying dividends soon, the IRS may impose a penalty tax on its unreasonably accumulated earnings.

Tricky problems inspire creative solutions, and this one can benefit your favorite charity. You and your spouse can set up a 15-year *nonreversionary charitable lead trust* (a trust in which a charity is the beneficiary). When the trust terminates, its assets go to Jimmy. You give all your stock in your company to the trust, and Wonderful starts paying dividends to the trust.

> The charity's share must be fixed at a percentage designed to provide a gift-tax charitable contribution deduction of just less than 60 percent. (Otherwise the stock has to be sold within five years or the trust has to pay annual penalties.)

The trust should have five trustees: you, your spouse, Jimmy—also named as the trust's sole remainderman—and two reliable friends. Having just you and your spouse as trustees could trigger estate-tax problems.

If this trust is designed correctly—get it set up by an expert—Wonderful will be passed on to Jimmy in 15 years, free of estate and gift taxes, no matter how much the company may be worth at that time. You and your spouse will continue to have *de facto* (but not *de jure*) control of Wonderful, and your company's paying dividends to the charitable trust will give it relief from any accumulated-earnings-tax problems.

This estate-planning chapter has outlined many juicy strategies for saving thousands of tax dollars. But don't jump in just yet. Remember to look at the whole picture. You can't do estate planning in a vacuum: estate planning has income-tax, gift-tax, and corporate-tax implications and consequences. That's why you must have professional help.

Here are some helpful ground rules:

Under federal law and many state laws, there are no estate or gift-tax implications between spouses. (Check your local statutes, which may vary.) You can leave other heirs up to $600,000, as of September 1990, without triggering federal estate taxes.

"Plan for today as though you had died last night" is a common slogan among estate planners. To prevent your assets from being taxed away, you must keep current. You may not have to rewrite your will more than once every five years, but you should certainly review it every year.

Don't do fancy tax planning if it's not necessary—and it usually isn't if your company is worth less than $150,000.

If your corporation is worth less than $500,000—e.g., the parent in a parent/child corporation—the new owner may be able to sell or transfer the corporation and use a stepped-up basis as its cost. For example, if the corporation was worth $250,000 at the date of the owner's death, the new owner takes $250,000 as the new cost basis. If the new owner then sells the company for $300,000, his or her profit is merely $50,000. Any appreciation during the old owner's life is not counted; it is tax-free.

> Let your plans make business and economic sense.
> Don't make any elaborate moves just to save taxes.

Above all, explore the potential your corporation gives you. Enjoy it!

INDEX